COMPUTER GRAPHICS AND
REPORTING FINANCIAL DATA

COMPUTER GRAPHICS AND REPORTING FINANCIAL DATA

IRWIN M. JARETT
Fingraph Corporation
Springfield, Illinois

A Ronald Press Publication

JOHN WILEY & SONS

New York   Chichester   Brisbane   Toronto   Singapore

Library of Congress Cataloging in Publication Data:

Jarett, Irwin M.
    Computer graphics and reporting financial data.

    "A Ronald Press publication."
    Includes index.
    1. Computer graphics.   2. Industrial management—
Graphic methods.   3. Management information systems.
I. Title.
HD30.2.J37   1983   658′.05443   82-23765
ISBN 0-471-86761-6

Printed in the United States of America

10 9 8 7 6 5 4 3

To Ronnie
because she is always
there.

PREFACE

This book was written to be a handbook, a continuing source of ideas for the design of a Graphic Management Information System (GMIS). To that end there are a lot of samples and examples to help you use the concepts described in the book. It is not a book about the technology of computer-generated graphics; it is a book about how to apply that technology to improve the productive use of information by all levels of management as they make critical operating and strategic decisions.

Chapters 1 through 4 are structured to lead you from the definition of a Graphic Management Information System (GMIS) to "how to design one."

Chapter 1 defines business graphics and describes how they are now being used in business and can be used in the future. The perspective in this chapter should provide a working view of the tremendous potential promised by this new computer graphic information transfer tool.

Chapter 2 sets the GMIS within the context of the management functions. Key factors and key indicators are described as they assist in the management decision making process. The three key differences between a Management Information System (MIS) and a GMIS are established. For those of you who are familiar with management theory, this chapter is worth reviewing because of the thrust toward "graphic decision making."

Chapter 3 describes the basic graphic symbols used to communicate business data. The symbols are used to build the foundation for a graphic language that will communicate data through imagery as simply, correctly, and quickly as we learn to distinguish among the shapes of trees, people, and letters in the alphabet. The chapter concludes with a graphic description of the financial statements required by the American Institute of Certified Public Accountants (AICPA) to report the results and status of a business. Table 3.1 is worth copying as a working tool during the design and installation of a GMIS.

Chapter 4 describes how to use the graphic language to describe any database. The concept of data disaggregation is used to show how a review of key graphic indicators can lead quickly to a description of business problems and opportunities. A GMIS design sheet is presented and examples of how to use it are given.

I highly recommend that the first four chapters be read before you attempt to use the rest of the book. You must have a clear idea of what the graphic symbols show and how they are combined to describe data before the rest of the chapters will be fully useful. Chapters 3 and 4 are absolutely essential to understanding this book.

Finally, Chapters 5 through 15 describe the foundation for a complete GMIS based on the financial and operating data normally used in business. Each chapter describes a complete subsystem that links together through the key indicators shown in Chapter 16. The specific chapters should be reviewed depending on the system you are considering. For example, if you are considering a top level financial graphic system, see Chapter 5; if you want to design a graphic inventory control system, see Chapter 8, and so on. Each of the systems chapters (5 through 15) presents a complete graphic description of that subsystem. The linkage to other systems is described if you wish to pursue it.

Chapter 16 is the key indicator/key ratio chapter that ties all of the more commonly used critical business ratios to the GMIS described in the systems chapters (Chapters 5 through 15). Chapter 16 contains an index to the key indicators, a description of a management instrument panel, and a visual summary of the power of graphic communication. This chapter could be briefly reviewed to see the basic structure of the key indicators described throughout the book, and then referred to as you study any of the systems chapters.

Chapter 17 shows the five critical concerns for media presentation of information. Examples are provided showing the effect on the transfer of information of size, quality of reproduction, type font, sequence, the use of color, and other media. Chapter 17 could be reviewed by itself except that the change in information transfer will not be apparent unless you are familiar with the ratio chart formats. The ratio chart is the only format used to describe the effect of the appropriate use of media. Chapter 17 deals only with basic media concerns. This chapter is the cornerstone for output media design. As noted in Chapter 2, the proper use of media offers, perhaps, the single most important benefit of a GMIS, a benefit worth taking the time to understand. (A book should be published showing the full potential of information transfer using media.)

HOW TO USE THIS BOOK

This book should be of immense value for anyone involved in *Graphic Management Information Systems*. The professional accountant, the CEO, the line manager, the MIS or DP director, and the college faculty member will all benefit. The book provides a comprehensive introduction in Chapters 1 to 4. Chapters 5 through 15 provide details about the structure of disaggregation as well as specific functional information. Note that the shaded areas of the design sheets indicate those charts that are used as examples for each chapter. Chapters 16 and 17 summarize by providing a basic foundation for using and presenting the information. There are numerous ways to use Chapters 5 through 15. However, they should always be closely tied to the first four and the last two chapters.

IRWIN M. JARETT

Springfield, Illinois
April 1983

ACKNOWLEDGMENTS

It would take a separate book to acknowledge all of the friends and supporters who made this book possible. To all of you whose names I must omit, forgive me, but please know that you have contributed, and it is appreciated. However, there are a few special people and firms who, in fairness, must share the credit given to this work:

I thank first of all, Alex S. Jarett, M.P.A., C.P.A., whose absolute dedication to this project for the past two years gave me the strength to continue. You will see his hand in almost every page where he suggested, outlined, edited, criticized, and finally, in frustration, rewrote certain sections. He absolutely refused to let anything but our best go to the publisher. The clearness of the presentations is due to his professionalism.

Fingraph Corporation, Springfield, Illinois, provided talent and support. I thank the following people for their own special contributions: Eric Parsloe for his willingness to schedule the time; John Schmidt and his crew for a program that works; Laurie Putnam, Gordon Suggs and Charles Baumgardner for their countless hours preparing and checking the charts used in this manuscript; the typing staff for their patience in correcting the many mistakes we made.

Digital Equipment Corporation, Merrimack, New Hampshire, provided equipment and some of their vast pool of talented people. Bill Kiesewetter and Mark Roberts shared in the risk and seldom wavered—simply put, the project from which the ideas in this book were crystallized would not have existed without their direct and continued support. Howard Johnson of Digital Equipment Corporation shared this vision. His probing, questioning, understanding, and patience helped form the practicality of these ideas. To all the rest of you at DEC—thanks!

Southern Illinois University School of Medicine, Springfield, Illinois and Dean Richard H. Moy, M.D., for his understanding and support.

Ann Buttvick for being there when I needed her this past decade. Her patience and professional skills helped prepare this manuscript. The people in the typing pool made the first complete draft a reality.

Marcie Johnson for her critiques and guiding direction toward educational theory.

Alan Schmidt at the Harvard Computer Graphics Laboratory for his continued support and critiques of my ideas.

Stan Klein, for writing about my ideas when I first introduced them.

Marjorie Maws, Ira Altman, and the whole crew at Professional Education Center whose continued faith gave me the forum to present and refine these ideas, first with the Harvard Computer Graphics Executive Management Seminars and later with the Datamation Seminars.

Carl Machover, President of Machover and Associates, for his critical analysis of the market.

Randy Stickrod, Publisher of Computer Graphic World, San Francisco, California, for providing me a public forum where I could express my ideas.

Allan Paller for the excellent start he provided.

Dick Lynch at John Wiley & Sons for his faith and patience.

Few people have been so blessed with so many supportive friends. I love you all!
To you dear readers, please share any credit with these fine people, and assign to me alone the faults.
Finally, a special acknowledgment to Debbie and Andy for understanding their father's concepts. To Ronnie, who through the years has patiently given up her time with me because she has faith and believes in what we are doing. What a wonderful lady I love and happen to be married to.

I.M.J.

CONTENTS

All of the graphs in this book (except some of those in Chapter 17) were produced by FINGRAPH™ Graphic Management Information System on a Digital Equipment Corporation PDP 1134™ computer with a VT 125™ Graphic Terminal and LA 34™ graphic printer.

FINGRAPH is a structured graphics system that converts any financial, accounting, or any other structured database into easy-to-understand standard graphic formats. The systems designed in this text can easily be set up using the FINGRAPH system.

FINGRAPH is the registered trademark of Fingraph Corporation. PDP 1134, VT 125, and LA 34 are registered trademarks of Digital Equipment Corporation, 111 Powdermill Road, Maynard, MA 01754.

COMPUTER GRAPHICS AND REPORTING FINANCIAL DATA

CHAPTER 1

BUSINESS COMPUTER GRAPHICS

The purpose of this chapter is to describe a basic problem in the use of information for making business decisions as currently supplied by Management Information Systems (MIS) and to describe a potential solution to the information problem. This book shows how to design and install a Graphic Management Information System (GMIS) concentrating on the financial planning and control aspects of the business. These same graphic design concepts can be transferred to any organized database.

There is a growing problem in the design, installation, and management of large management information systems. The principal problem in data management is the sheer volume of internally generated data presented to management in traditional tabular form. The average manager is not physically capable of reading (now considered a left brain function) all of the data printed by even the slowest computer printer. As a result it is not possible for the valuable information in the printouts to be transferred into the manager's brain where it can be merged with other information, interpreted, analyzed, and finally acted on based on the cumulative experience of the manager. The frustration of having so much information presented to busy managers has resulted in certain fundamental attitudes about data presentation that need to be re-examined in light of the new technology discussed in this book. The attitudes are: (1) tabular reports are poorly designed and contain information that is not required to operate efficiently and effectively, and (2) all of the relevant information required to evaluate organizational performance can and should be condensed onto one (or very few) page(s).

Attitude 1. Tabular reports are poorly designed and contain information that is not required to operate effectively.

Although it is probably correct that some of the information in those stacks of tabular reports is redundant, it is a crucial error to conclude that the information is not useful or necessary. In most instances those reports were designed by competent financial, operations, and systems people with the full support of management. I would propose a counterproposition that the information presented in those mounds of tabular reports is the minimum

1

amount required to fully understand all of the organizational interrelationships. As noted earlier, the manager is physically unable to read and absorb all of the information. Thus it can be stated that the problem is not that the information contained in the tabular reports is inappropriate or that the reports themselves are poorly designed; more likely the problem is the physical inability of the manager to read the reports. Displaying the same information in the same formats on CRTs has certainly not resolved the problem. In some cases it has actually made the information less mobile. The human visual system simply cannot *read* fast enough. Thus the negative attitude about the current information system is based on the human inability to input the current presentation formats into our brains using the current reading skills.

Attitude 2. All of the relevant information required to evaluate organizational performance should be condensed onto one page.

This "one-page" attitude is the direct result of Attitude 1; if the information is no good, just condense it onto one page. (One page may be two or three pages but certainly few.) In many cases this attitude has resulted in a one-page report so crammed with numbers in rows and columns that the information is indecipherable. In other instances there is so little information that the report is useless.

The one-page attitude also results from the ever increasing time crunch of most managers. They certainly do not have the time to read all of the available tabular reports but they still have a basic intellectual need for information so they are seduced into reading only a few pages to save time. The attitude is understandable but again it is based on the physical handicap of our current reading skills that limits the amount of information that can be input to our brains by "reading" tabular reports.

1. A POTENTIAL SOLUTION

A potential solution to the problem described above is a financial graphic language that utilizes the full pattern recognition ability of the human system, such ability generally described as a function of the right brain. The human system has an enormous and so far untapped ability to input large amounts of information rapidly and accurately based on our ability to recognize patterns. The more highly trained systems will instinctively take action based on either the recognition of a certain pattern or a change in a pattern. For example, airline pilots are trained to "see" the instrument panel. The only time the pilots "read" an instrument (a left brain function) is when the pattern changes—and a problem has been noticed. The human system helps us drive a car and it puts our feet on the brakes when a child runs in front of the car—an abnormal pattern. There is a constant interaction required between the right brain and the left brain functions to create the human system. A proper combination of the right and left brain functions are necessary for flying and driving, and humans can be trained to achieve that balance.

This same pattern recognition ability can be utilized to permit a considerable amount of information to be input into the brain by "seeing" the expected graphic patterns that describe the performance of the business—a graphic management instrument panel. A standardized financial graphic language will permit the human system to input a considerable amount of data as rapidly as the chart or graph can be seen, a rate of input so fast and accurate that it is hard to imagine. Appropriately designed patterns will also input the relative size and importance of activities, and unusual relationships or patterns will be recognized and matched to experience. Action (decisions) will be based on a more informed basis and a more balanced functioning of the left and right side of the brain.

Because of the new computer technology, it is now technologically and economically feasible to create and use a financial graphic language and to present business information graphically in a fair and consistent way. This new opportunity is found within the confines of what is now called *computer business graphics.*

2. DEFINITIONS OF COMPUTER BUSINESS GRAPHICS

Computer business graphics is *the science and art of transferring information through the sense of sight.* The approach of defining a field or profession as the combination of art and science has been used over and over again but continues to be a useful device for highlighting specific points around which a debate may flow. The same definition could have been used for the word graphics or the phrase business graphics. Thus each word and phrase must be examined to see how the meaning of the definition changes, if at all, by combining the three words—Computer Business Graphics.

3. A SCIENCE

The concept of graphics as a science comes from the fact that the components of good graphics are based on a number of the hard and social sciences. The hard science includes most prominently the sciences of color, mathematics, sight, neurology (i.e., right brain/left brain functions), statistics, physics, and cartography. The social science includes psychology, sociology, education, and a number of business disciplines. The contributions each of the sciences makes to quality graphics is the subject of a number of books and research papers. Though a broad range of science need be considered, they are all used to understand how information is consistently transferred from a graphic representation into the human brain and how the brain receives the input, organizes it, and uses it in performing specific tasks.

4. AN ART

As complicated as the supporting sciences might be, the art of graphics is even more complex. The artist must blend a knowledge of the related science with a specific knowledge of the information source, how useful that information is to the performance of the specific task, how the human brain can best receive the information to perform the task, and the graphic format(s) that best meet those requirements. The search for quality in graphics is one that pays high dividends because the human seeing the graphics can receive the message and quickly put it to proper use. Translated into business words, quality graphics is a most efficient way to increase the productivity of humans through the consistent and dependable transfer of information.

As with all art forms, one person's art is another person's wasteland, and so it is today with computer business graphics:

Except for one not so small difference —the message to be transferred by computer business graphics is purposeful and measurable and the use of the message is predictable.

Thus there can be no compromise in quality, for the result of poor quality graphics is predictable—no message is transferred—or even worse, the wrong message is transferred.

5. GRAPHICS

But what is graphics? Do business graphics differ? And what dimension does computer business graphics add? The results of a small unscientific survey I took during a number of my recent Executive Briefing seminars indicate that of those who attended and responded, over 90 percent considered graphic arts to be concerned with the presentation of data in a chart or graph format, a most narrow view. The graphic arts, in fact, include the entire range of data presentation and publication, including the written word, chart, graphs, drawings and paintings, photography, and films, plus the complete range of crafts including pottery, weaving, woodworking, and so on. Such a wide view of graphics is obviously different than the narrow views brought to the Briefings, and, perhaps, about as useful. All of the graphic arts are not practically useful for the consistent and dependable transfer of business information in our modern society. However, during the Dark Ages when the printed word was, for all intents, banned, the Sufis found the arts and crafts an effective way to record the history of the time and to display their consistent layers of meaning.

The concept of graphics used in this book includes the wide range of data presentation and publication available in the ever-changing business world. Such a view of graphics permits us to examine the potential use of quality graphics at every information transfer point in the organization. Such a broad view obviously permits a wide latitude in using graphics in business and also carries with it the responsibility to fairly present alternative solutions to an information transfer problem and to critically examine the effects of proposed graphics solutions.

6. BUSINESS GRAPHICS

But this book is concerned with business graphics (and, mostly, the financial control graphics associated with a GMIS) rather than generalized graphics and, as such, one could justify the concept that the broad potential range of graphics must thus be narrowed. No so—if anything, the addition of the adjective *business* to the noun *graphics* expands the view of graphics, for business, in its broadest sense, encompasses our entire economic system, a system of such magnitude that we would surely not find any severe limitations in where to look for business graphic applications. As small to international-sized businesses become more complex and the time to receive information and make decisions becomes more compressed, the need for appropriate business graphic communication will expand experientially. Thus the limitations of the scope of this book are due to time, space, and understanding, not definition.

7.   COMPUTER BUSINESS GRAPHICS

Finally, the word *computer* is attached to the phrase *business graphics*. It was not uncommon during the early days of computers in business, when older models were being replaced at an ever-accelerating speed, to find an installation where the latest system was an emulation of an earlier computer, that was in itself a simulation of an even earlier computer, that was an exact copy of a punched card system, that was an exact replica of a bookkeeping machine system, that was an automation of a hand-operated bookkeeping system designed in the late 1800s. The criticism of those systems was that such an approach did not make full use of the powers of the computer; it only made the old out-of-date system run faster. Since the 1870 census, the truly new chart and graphic formats designed to present data to the public can be counted on one finger of one hand. But now we can do them all on a computer, and faster. Somehow the story sounds familiar.

When computers were first introduced, one of the great hopes was to use them to produce quality charts and graphs. The available equipment was simply not sufficient. Finally, the equipment became sufficient and we experienced another rise in expectations. This time the software was not available. Now the technology and the software have merged together with microtechnology to put computer graphics in even the smallest computers; ironically, having both equipment and software so widely available at so affordable prices may cause computer business graphics to fail for the third time. Until now there has been no definition of quality computer business graphics and we are repeating (faster) the graphic errors of the 1870s.

But what potential does the addition of computers offer to business graphics? First, the computer offers the same potential benefits (and problems) for business graphics that it does for MIS—for they are the same system. Business graphics cannot present data points if they are not collected and organized by the MIS.

Second, and equally important, is the media potential. A properly designed GMIS includes a full range of media presentations from which an information appropriate selection of media can be made. For example, daily "flash" reports and key graphic indicators might be presented to operating management on a color graphic CRT as a management instrument panel. Weekly senior staff meetings might be suported by the instrument panel and a set of predefined visuals (slides, overheads) and an interactive "what if" session with the system. A monthly or quarterly board meeting could be supported with large updated wall hangings, a fully automated slide show controlled by the computer on a large screen, a four-color book quality printed take-along report, an interactive "what if" session, and a take-along videodisc for home viewing, all prepared automatically each month by the predefined GMIS. Animation is also possible if the imagination and budget are in harmony. The power of the computer has opened the entire range of the graphic art and presentation media to the business community. Thus the addition of the computer to business graphics enlarges even more the range and complexity of the art.

In the three meeting examples given above, it is assumed that data will be presented, analyzed, and interpreted using charts, graphs, pictures, words, and tabular presentations of numbers. The graphic art skill will be used to assure that the information so presented is easily assimilated by the viewer and that the message is correctly received. Type fonts, page design, graphic formats, shadings, sentence and word spacing, underlines, headings, color, all must be blended to achieve the optimum information transfer, and once the appropriate presentation is established, it will be repeated consistently by the GMIS. As Marshall McLuhan* said, "The medium is the message." The concept of media is explored in Chapter 17.

8. A BIGGER FIELD

Until now, the case of computers for Computer-Aided Design (CAD) and Computer-Aided Manufacturing (CAM) were not considered specifically to be part of business computer graphics. How interesting since business is where CAD/CAM is useful. With only a little extra effort CAD/CAM can be tied directly to the financial reporting system through the GMIS. The use of mapping techniques in marketing have not been closely tied to the MIS, rather they have been designed as a freestanding system independent of the business system. How interesting since marketing is integral to business and the product pricing, motivation, and costing strategies must be fully integrated to affect market share. The analysis of sales mix variance shown in the sales system, Chapter 13 would be useful to any sales manager. Once again a GMIS application.

By now it should be apparent that business computer graphics is a vast field encompassing the full range of information transfer required to run a complex business organization. Artificial boundaries will not hold up under even cursory examination. The skills necessary to design and manage such a vast enterprise are, at this point in time, sorely lacking. Few if any have had the opportunity to design and install a complete graphic management system using the full potential of the computer graphic medium, observe it in use over time, correct deficiencies, and test the results. Some of us are working on it. But the systems are complex. It takes a long time to design and install them, even longer to see how they work, and most important, to discover how well management can use them.

*Marshal McLuhan, *The Medium Is the Message*, Random House, New York, 1967.

CHAPTER 2

MIS VS. GMIS

The primary role of the Chief Financial Officer (CFO) is to assist the Board of Directors and the corporate management in optimizing the return on the invested capital of the owners, the shareholders. This responsibility includes, among others, the duties of protecting the assets, and recording and reporting the performance of all of the corporate activities. The CFO is also held accountable for preparing and communicating the budget, and in most instances is required to summarize and communicate the long range plan. The reporting and communication function depends most heavily on the formality of the accounting system and the data accumulated through the normal activities of the firm. In the past decade the CFO has become a critical member of the management team charged with the design and installation of the management information system.

This book concentrates on the communication aspect of the CFO. The introduction of a computer-generated graphic management system changes all of the communication ground rules.

1. THE LANGUAGE OF BUSINESS

Accounting is sometimes referred to in an almost offhanded manner as the language of business. However, the reference deserves serious attention and can shed considerable light on the motivations for using computer graphics in financial reporting. Improperly used, computer graphics can distort the picture of performance by presenting a language that business people simply do not understand. Linguistics, the systematic study of language, offers a useful insight into the appropriate way to use the power of computer graphics to enhance, rather than damage, the information conveyed in accounting reports. Accounting has as its primary purpose the systematic collection and communication of information of a specific type to be used for analysis and decision making. It is the communications aspect of accounting that poses some of the most critical problems and important opportunities in the current business environment.

Spoken language comprises a universal and primary human behavior that is both complex and sophisticated. The study of spoken language reveals system and structure at levels so deep that we are unable to explain the underlying mechanisms. The purpose of language is to achieve language efficiency while communicating across a large group of people in diverse situations. Such efficiency is achieved by using consistent speech patterns. The human brain demonstrates an incredible facility for pattern recognition across all the senses, to the degree that the facility is used at an unconscious level much of the time. Dr. R.W. Sperry recently received the Nobel Prize for his pioneering work in establishing the roles of the right and left brain in human communication. In spoken language, a relatively small number of sound elements are used from among those humans are capable of producing. To be understood, the sounds must form a discernible pattern or there is no language. Once established, the standard patterns are hardly noticed (except when an unfamiliar accent is heard) and they serve as a more or less transparent vehicle for content. However, the slightest change in the expected pattern can convey a message different from the actual words spoken (i.e., when someone is angry, it is usually easy to tell by the change in inflection). The written language depends exclusively on a set of graphic symbols defined by humans to represent the spoken language. The Compact Edition of the Oxford English Dictionary (Oxford University Press, 1971, p. xii) makes the following observations:

> The pronunciation is the actual living form or forms of a word, that is, the word itself, of which the current spelling is only a symbolization—generally, indeed, only the traditionally preserved symbolization of an earlier form, sometimes imperfect to begin with, still oftener corrupted in its passage to our time...But the living word is sound cognizable by the ear, and must therefore be itself symbolized in order to reach the understanding through the eye.

The full range of graphic symbols are called the *alphabet* and consist of vowels and consonants. A highly structured set of rules, most often strictly adhered to but sometimes broken, determine the usage and sequence of the alphabet to create a useful living symbol of the word. Additional rules, called grammar, are used to link the words into a defineable and understandable pattern representing language.

Accounting, in its theory and practice, gives a clear reflection of the purpose and structure of a language. Anthony (in *Financial Accounting*) explicitly identifies accounting as a communication process, a "language [that] encompasses precisely written phrases and symbols used to convey information about the resource flows measured for specific organizations." Accounting as a profession recognizes unique responsibilities well beyond those of other professions (including the legal questions of a public license) to provide to users adequate, understandable and dependable financial information. This uniqueness has the following major implications for the use of computer graphics. First, to the extent that the use of computer-generated graphics can make a substantial contribution to the more effective and understandable communication of accounting information, it must considered by the profession. Computers were originally used by accountants because they offered a solution to the problems of collecting, processing, storing, and reporting the ever-growing volume of accounting data. Today, however,the solution has become part of the problem. The computer churns out more and more tabular reports that do not communicate because they cannot be read. A properly structured financial graphic language offers the potential of communicating the financial information hidden in the rows and columns of the tabular reports.

Then if the technology is to be applied to the presentation of financial information, the second major implication is the absolute need for standards, for structure and system in the use of computer graphics. Expressed in linguistic terms, attention must be given to the alphabet—the graphic symbols of numbers, grammar—the elements of expression and the rules for their combination, and semantics—the actual meanings conveyed. Computer graphics offer almost limitless possibilities in terms of the shapes, colors, and other attributes that can be employed to portray data. Language, as noted above, implies the use of a limited set of elements selected from the total available, and their use in systematic and structured ways to produce discernible patterns. Decisions about the new graphic language must be made on the basis of adequate knowledge of accounting and graphic presentation requirements. The degree to which the proper, intended meaning is accurately conveyed by the entire financial graphic system cannot be left to chance. This book is designed to show how graphic symbols are used to represent living "symbols" of "data", to give a set of grammatical rules that express the data and combine it into meaningful information, and to demonstrate an approach to the semantics of graphic symbols to enhance the meaning of the information.

The next section of this chapter presents a brief discussion of management, managers, and management information systems. The final section presents the critical distinctions between an MIS and a GMIS.

2. MANAGEMENT, MANAGERS, AND MANAGEMENT INFORMATION SYSTEMS

The following discussion about management and managers is used to set a context for the building of a GMIS.

Management is the art of planning, organizing, staffing, directing, and controlling an organization to best meet its stated purpose and goals. The management functions include the following activities:

PLANNING. The art of recording vision and foresight in a systematic way, or deciding in advance as a basis for doing. (Vision is defined as what should be; foresight as what will most likely be. A good manager blends the two and creates reality.)

ORGANIZING. The configuring of available resources in anticipation of action.

STAFFING. Placing people in the best possible position to facilitate carrying out the organization's plan.

DIRECTING. The action part of management; seeing that people use the resources to meet the plan.

CONTROLLING. The appropriate use of information about the results of using the firm's resources (money, material, and people) to alter the operation of the organization so as to better achieve its purpose, goals, and objectives.

The chief executive of an organization can share (delegate) the authority and responsibility to plan, organize, staff, direct, and control, but the final accountability cannot be delegated. Therefore, the MIS must be designed to clearly communicate how managers have performed their assigned roles.

Supervision and management are, in reality, synonymous terms. By convention, the term supervision is used to describe the process of exercising management over an individual or group of individuals. The term management is used to describe the exercising of management over many organizational resources, including people, on a broader organizational and functional basis.

The degree of responsibility, knowledge, expertise, specialization, technological skill, and sophistication required of an individual should govern both the kind and the degree of management exercised over the individual. Such an approach does not imply complete absence of management over highly specialized or highly competent individuals. Rather, it means that they require different management than individuals of other types or levels.

As managers move to successively higher levels of management, the constraints and trappings of each former role (i.e., the role of profession, discipline, occupation, or former position) must be discarded and the role of the new responsibility must be assumed. The higher the individual moves in the organizational hierarchy, the more the constraints can interfere if they are not redirected toward corporate benefit.

For an individual to operate according to plan, the plan must be communicated and understood. Further, the manager must accept the plan and be formally committed to it. Such knowledge and commitment usually requires participation in the development of the plan. We can successfully plan for others only so long as they have no viable alternative.

For a high level manager, implementation should mean seeing that things get done. It should not mean making all decisions or doing all the work.

Management control is most effectively exerted through planning and evaluation. The higher a manager operates in the organizational hierarchy, the more important it is to know and to utilize control points of the organization.

A. Distribution of the Management Time

The lowest levels of management spend most of their time in directing. The information base is mostly internal and is usually concerned with short timeframes—days, weeks, or a month. The middle levels are more concerned with staffing, directing, and controlling, and the timeframes become quarters and annual periods. The information base remains primarily internal. The top levels of management are concerned mostly with planning, organizing, and controlling, and their time span ranges from quarterly through five-year plans and longer. The information base is primarily external as the top management group is interested in how the resources can be directed toward the future in the external business world. Thus internal information must be communicated in such a way as to enable management to quickly relate internal information about the business to external information about the business commmunity.

B. Management Systems

To a manager, the primary significance of viewing an organization as a system should be the recognition of the inevitable interrelatedness of the organization's parts and functions.

To be effective, every organization (system) must have direction (purpose) and must be consciously seeking certain defined outcomes (goals and objectives). Insuring that these requirements are met is a primary management responsibility. Communicating the fiscal implications of those requirements and comparing the results to plan to assist management is a primary responsibility of the CFO.

All management functions should occur as simultaneous processes rather than discrete functions to be performed at different times or by different persons. No part of an organization (a system) can be significantly altered without affecting other parts of the organization. Further, the organization's relationships to society (its suprasystem) and to its programs (subsystems) will be changed as well. Reducing or otherwise altering the availability or utilization of an organization's resources (cost reduction or cost containment, for example), without redefining the desired or expected outcomes, can result in an increase in waste and a reduction in both effectiveness and efficiency.

C. Decision Making

There is risk involved in every decision. Some managers exhibit a decision habit pattern that makes their decisions predictable, almost without regard to the individual circumstances and the information supplied.

Each individual approaches decision making differently. The difference in style is a reflection of the decision maker's experience, value system, self-perception, willingness to take risks, and various other factors.

Many managers are unrealistically optimistic about the "batting average" they or their subordinate should maintain in decision making. Decision making regarding implementation should occur at that level of the organizational hierarchy where the responsibility for implementation of the decision is delegated.

It is just as important a managerial responsibility to see that decisions are not made precipitously as it is to make them and to see that they are made when needed and appropriate. Managers must have and use information in order to make rational decisions and to take rational action. Too much information or the wrong information, however, is equally detrimental. Examination of both the results of decisions and the decision-making process itself should be an effective learning experience for any manager. Decision makers must be accountable for their decisions and for the decisions of their subordinates. Once decisions are made, they should be transmitted to the affected persons as quickly as possible.

Not to act or not to decide is in itself, a decision.

D. Key Factors—Key Indicators

Managers at levels tend to use information in a highly predictable way. First, they logically divide into a limited number of key performance areas those organizational activities for which they are held responsible. Each key performance area is seen to contribute to the overall success of meeting the organizational goals and objectives. At the top level of the organization, these key areas are usually defined as the key functions of the organization (such as Financial, Sales, Marketing, Manufacturing, Research and Development. etc.). Second, within each function, the responsible managers tend to further subdivide the functions into *key factors* that define the specific performance of that function in meeting its goals. Key factors are qualitative descriptors used to judge how well that level or area of the organization is meeting its defined goals and objectives. The descriptors are directly related to the specific type of activities required at that level. For example, a line foreperson might be interested in the key factors of production, quality, and personnel. The CFO might also be interested in production, quality, and personnel for the whole firm, not just for one line. The opinion of how well or badly that level or area is doing is based on a human interpretation of a set of *key indicators* defined by the organization.

Key indicators are measures of movement within a key factor selected by management as accurate indicators of movement. Key indicators are those quantifiable items of information that collectively provide a database for evaluating key factors. They always describe change, and may depict a trend. They are always in the form of numbers, rates, ratios, proportions, or percentages. The information required is deduced by first determining what indicators are appropriate. The information needed to develop the indicators is then gathered. All the data are not necessary to provide the information required to produce the key indicators.

Key factors provide a basis for organizing the perceived success or failure of an organization in meeting its purpose. They may relate to one or more goals and/or objectives, describe the success or failure of many programs, provide the basis for describing the relative performance in terms of perceived objective attainment, or provide the basis for describing the perceived effectiveness of the organization.

Each key factor represents the qualitative interpretation of a number of key indicators selected in advance as indicating movement within that key factor. Only humans can make the judgment on what the indicators indicate and determine the information required for such judgments. The knowledge and experience of the individual(s) in making the judgment(s) will affect the value and appropriateness of the judgment. An inexperienced person cannot properly understand the meaning of a change in a key indicator as related to a key factor and the overall corporate performance.

3. LEARNING

Learning is the linkage between management, experience, and information. Without learning, there is no requirement for information, and learning cannot occur without requiring more and different information.

Humans tend to learn more quickly and effectively when they experience the need to know. It is difficult to "teach" humans. If we can provide information and try to stimulate the need to know, the individual must learn. Learning is an internal, personal process. It can be imposed only under the most stressful conditions. Although there are common learning patterns, individuals have their own learning patterns and their cultures, climates, family lives, and so on, all influence their learning processes.

Learning is cumulative. Each new "piece" of learning is acquired within the context and the framework of all prior learning and is integrated into our total storehouse of knowledge. Learning occurs both intentionally and unintentionally, for the sake of learning and for utility, with ease and with difficulty, and with experience.

What we often call *insight* is the conscious realization that something we have learned applies in a different, often unexpected way. Insight may occur in the direction of induction or deduction.

Learning is not always helpful. The wrong things can be learned, and can detract from our ability to perform or to continue learning.

A. Learning and Information

In order to learn, information must be available when the need to know occurs. The form of information and how it is presented are as critical as the information itself if learning is to occur. We are highly conditioned. Overcoming our conditioned behavior and responses is a prerequisite to creativity and an expanded capability. When we have repeated experiences without appropriate information, or with only the same inadequate information, we stop learning. We develop conditioned responses reacting on the basis of habit, impulse, or other inappropriate criteria.

Information must be used for it to have value. Unused information is unneeded information. It is not only costly to accumulate and store—it confuses. Further, unused information reduces our ability to secure, organize, and retrieve the information we do need.

Data are generic. Data become information when they are identified or used for a particular purpose.

B. Information

Needed information may not be available. Under such conditions, we have the alternative of proceeding without the required information or, in some cases, postponing action until the necessary information is secured or developed. Information may exist but not be available or accessible. To be of value information must be both available and accessible. It must be organized, or organizable, and must be capable of reorganization to be of value. Organization of information is what makes access possible.

Information should be kept current according to a plan decided on beforehand. Information should be subjected to periodic checks for reliability and validity, as well as accuracy and completeness.

Information may be separated into four basic information categories:

Category	Major Use
Historical	Reference and perspective
Operational	Implementation or action
Standard	Planning and evaluation
Forecast	Long range planning

C. Management Information Systems (MIS)

An MIS is the organized body of information available to management. An MIS should provide all managers and, in fact, all employees within the organization with the information they need, at the time they need it, and in the most useful form. An MIS should integrate planning, organizing, staffing, directing, and controlling information. It should reflect the process nature of organizations, rather than reflect the misconception that information exists in unrelated categories. Data should be available for evaluation of the activities being monitored and designed as an inherent part of the MIS design. An MIS should be capable of responding to the need to know rapidly enough to permit use of the information in decision making and in the conducting of routine operations. As noted earlier, information should be used as a tool for learning, as well as monitoring.

An MIS should be designed in such a way as to allow change in programs and policy without concomitant change in the design of the information system. Proper structuring of key factors, key indicators, and the information needed will allow the user to address the system and obtain a direct response to the question being asked. Proper structuring will enable the MIS to respond at the same level of complexity as the question being asked. The proliferation of information and data, the increasing complexity of our social system, swiftly advancing technology, and the increasing rate of change make the design of an MIS more crucial. The combination of these conditions and the price/ performance capability of the newest generation of microcomputers has made a hand-operated MIS a viable and adequate alternative only for small organizations. An MIS should be designed in such a way as to facilitate the manager's job of running the organization rather than the MIS running the manager.

4.   THE NEW LANGUAGE OF BUSINESS

This book is written on the assumption that computer graphics will revolutionize the transfer of business and financial information by utilizing the pattern recognition ability of the human system to see and recognize the underlying data patterns communicated by the graphic language. As noted earlier, this pattern recognition ability is one of the most powerful responses of the human system. When properly understood and utilized, massive amounts of data will be transferred simply by the presentation of the data in a predetermined and expected set of graphic formats. The human system will be trained to recognize the expected pattern of the information being presented. If there are no unexpected changes—inflections—the data will be input. Only when the graphic pattern is distorted will the input be refused and the left brain activated to review the data and input the appropriate data. Thus graphics will eventually be used as an input/output (I/O) device to the human decision-making system. When the proper balance occurs between the data presented, the format of the data presentation, the presentation media, and a trained human system, the data will be input to the brain as rapidly as the chart, the financial icon, can be flashed through the human visual system.

The CFO must now be concerned with the design and implementation of the new GMIS. There are a number of similarities between the concepts of the old MIS and the new GMIS. But, even more important to the CFO are the differences, differences so critical that unless properly planned, the resulting information will most likey be ineffective and useless and could be totally misleading.

These critical differences are categorized in the following areas:

1.   Data to be presented.
2.   Data presentation formats.
3.   Presentation media.

A.   Data To Be Presented

Almost every manager has a set of special key indicators stored at his or her work station. Whenever a higher ranking manager calls to ask "How are things?", the manager uses those special key indicators to answer. Those key indicators are seldom if ever formalized in an MIS. In most instances the key indicators are ratios or relationships seen and understood by the one manager for they require data from a number of data sources. Most system designers would ignore these indicators because they already have too much information that is required to be shown by the formal accounting control systems. However, with computer-generated graphics those ratios could easily be shown and they may very well be the missing part of the performance picture. Such potential does not mean that all data relationships can or should be shown; what it does mean is that data rejected out of hand previously must now be reconsidered. Nonfinancial data will become more and more important as it is used to describe volume, velocity and costs per unit. More detailed data may have to be recorded, moving the recording function closer and closer to the point of the transaction in order to link the nonfinancial data to the financial data. Once the linkage is made, the presentation of the data in graphic form will more closely represent an accurate picture of corporate activity.

However, moving the recording function closer to the transaction highlights a basic design difference between the MIS and the GMIS. The MIS design is severely limited by the presentation format, as discussed later. As a result, the basic concept of information gathering and representation is based on an aggregate view of data. Data is collected at the lowest level and summarized to the top. Responsibility reporting provides details at the appropriate levels and exceptions to the higher levels. If the exceptions are to be reviewed, the design assumes a disaggregation of the information as a reverse pattern of the way it was accumulated. Such a view of data aggregation and disaggregation has resulted in important data banks designed so they do not relate to each other. The requirement for a GMIS design cuts across all data banks and will most likely require that information be disaggregated by showing relations across the corporate system. For example, key indicators will require that data from a personnel, human accounting, or payroll system be tied directly to production data to show productivity information. The importance of this difference is described in Chapter 4.

B.   Data Presentation Formats

The MIS design has been severely restricted because the output was limited to a tabular presentation. Even CRT reports were limited to tabular designs. Tabular designs cause data to enter the brain primarily through the reading process of the brain. Such restrictions on presentations limit the type and amount of information that can be properly summarized and input to the human brain.

As noted earlier, the potential number of graphic formats is almost endless. A limited number of graphic formats must be defined to perform a specific data transfer task if a living financial graphic language is to be developed. If the information to be transferred is complex, then it may take all of the formats to properly communicate the information contained in the data. One of the misconceptions in the newly emerging graphic information field is that showing it all on one page is a good presentation goal. In graphics, where a great deal of data can be absorbed quickly, it may be more efficient to show the data in a number of graphs, each one designed to most appropriately display a particular aspect of the information. The concept of format can be closely linked to the linguistic concept of semantics, the meaning conveyed by the graphic sequence. It will take the whole sequence of graphic "words" for communication to occur. Leaving out one format is similar to eliminating one word from a sentence. The graphic language is described in Chapter 3.

C. Presentation Media

The MIS is limited to the printed media or the CRT as normal output. But the GMIS is limited only by imagination, training, and costs.

The CFO must be aware of the most appropriate graphic alphabet for presenting financial information. Internal usage standards based on public knowledge will determine the formats and the sequence of formats will deliver the message. The full power of transferring information by means of computer graphics will be realized when the full media potential is understood. Just as there is an almost unlimited array of computer graphic formats, there is an almost unlimited media potential. I used the phrase "Media Emersion" in the January, 1982 issue of *Computer Graphic World*. The phrase is defined as:

> providing information to the business executive utilizing all of the most appropriate data formats and media to transfer specific types of information.

Each presentation should be reinforced with supporting media that affects all of the human senses. Such a concept of media could eventually place the executive in a holographic representation of "Space Ship Corporation" as it moves through time reflecting the complex assumptions of a competitive economy. Such media potential demands even more concern for developing a media communication language that permits properly structured formats and media that are data driven rather than random unstructured formatting that is defined by the individual designing the presentation. Accounting exists as an effective communication discipline because of the formal rules governing the data accumulation and the presentation formats.

For now, the major media concerns surround color, motion, type of printed output, and interaction. CFOs must learn about computer graphic media, establish corporate presentation standards based on those now being developed (just as accounting systems are based on generally accepted accounting procedures), and involve media experts who can assist them in using media to communicate information. As of now, few, if any CFOs have media experience or competency. This critical design difference is discussed in detail in Chapter 17.

CHAPTER 3

FINANCIAL GRAPHIC STANDARDS—AN ORGANIZED APPROACH

This chapter presents the structure for a financial graphic language. All financial and mathematical statements require that numbers add, subtract, multiply, and divide. M. Georges Cuisenaire, a Belgian mathematician, discovered that young children three to five years of age could learn to add, subtract, multiply, and divide quickly if given a set of small wooden rods, cut into various lengths from 1 mm to 10 mm with each length color-coded. When given the rods and left alone for several hours, the children knew, for example, that two red rods equalled one blue rod, two blue rods equalled one yellow rod, four red rods equalled one yellow, and so on. Within a year, using these rods as a learning device, the children learned how to use advanced matrix algebra.* This same concept of using rods to add, subtract, multiply, and divide are used as the basis for all of the mathematics in the following explanations. Multiplication is not yet defined as a graphic standard.

The chapter is divided into the following sections: (1) suggested graphic standards, (2) the suggested financial graphic standard formats, and (3) suggested graphic standards to present the financial statements recommended by the American Institute of Certified Public Accountants.

1. SUGGESTED GRAPHIC STANDARDS

The suggested graphic standards are designed for printed graphic reports. Current surveys in the business graphic field indicate that the majority of computer graphic usage will, in the near term, result from hard copy printed graphics. Other presentation media such as slides and overheads will be the next highest use, and the graphic CRT will have the least use. Until graphic CRTs are in common use, the printed report will still be the primary presentation media and should dictate presentation design. Because the

*For more information on Cuisenaire Rods, direct inquiries to: Cuisenaire Company of America, Inc., 12 Church Street, New Rochelle, N.Y. 10805.

impact of the graphic CRT on human behavior is still so unclear, it would be difficult to develop presentation standards just for the CRT ignoring the printed material. Therefore, the presentation standards described throughout this book assume that the CRT presentation will be a direct reflection of the printed material rather than the printed material being a direct reflection of the CRT. In fact, some of the presentations possible on the CRT could not be adequately shown on paper. This assumption about the medium that controls design is critical to the rapid development of pattern recognition. If the patterns change because the presentation format or modality changes, then the persons utilizing it will be forced to consciously and continuously make the adjustment and they may refuse. If, however, the patterns are the same regardless of the medium, then no adjustment is necessary and the pattern recognition can be strengthened by using a proper mix of media.

For example, if the printed report shows three charts on a page, it would be appropriate to show the same three charts on a CRT screen. It would be acceptable to show one of the printed charts the size of the full screen or to show six charts (from two pages) to make a different point and to take advantage of the sizing capabilities of the CRT. It would *not be acceptable* to change the headings or the graphic design. The following general standards were taken from Schmid's Handbook of Graphic Presentations, 1979, The American Standard ASA Y15.1-1959, *Illustrations for Publications and Projections** and our own experience.

1. *Borders.*   Clearly defined borders should be used for each chart or graph. The borders or shape of the chart or graph should not detract from the content.

2. *Background.*   The background should be unobtrusive (i.e., an off-white).

3. *Color.*   If color is used, it should be used to identify or highlight. A maximum of six colors should be used with a legend to identify. Only one color should be selected to highlight areas for further review; for example, red is an excellent color to draw attention to a particular point. (For more on color, see Chapter 17.)

4. *Dimensions.*   In general, three-dimensional forms should not be used where the reader is asked to infer volume of the three-dimensional form.

5. *Data.*   All financial data should be depicted as elements on the graphic statements and the numbers shown so that they can be footed to the absolute totals. The numbers should be located at the end of the horizontal bars and relatively small in size and separated from the bar. Data should not be placed inside the bar.

6. *Time Series.*   A time series shown with bar charts should be shown with vertical rather than horizontal bars.

7. *Width of Bars and Spacing.*   Bars should be of uniform width and evenly spaced. The bars should not be either disproportionately long and narrow or short and wide. For financial graphics, special relationships between the elements are described later.

8. *Scale.*   A carefully planned scale should be included in every chart. In addition:

*Calvin F. Schmid, *Handbook of Graphic Presentations*, 2nd. edition, Wiley, New York, 1979.

   a. Scales should begin at zero,

   b. Scales should never be broken,

   c. Intervals should be in round numbers.

9. *Legends and Identifications.* The legend and chart identification should always be in the same place. Throughout this book the legend is shown in the top left-hand corner (insert) and the chart identification, date, and scale in the top right-hand corner insert. Other locations and identifiers are acceptable but should not clutter the picture.

The following standards are more clearly related to financial graphics.

A. Amount of Data

There is no agreement in the literature regarding how much data can be input to the human brain using graphic presentations. For example, a number of writers suggest that the information that goes into the brain using a map is significantly higher than the amount of information that can be put into the brain using the graphic representation of operating data. However, there are no controlled studies to support such an observation. The material that is available indicates, however, that at some point there is an absolute limit to the amount of information that can be seen by the human visual system in any given moment. A graph that is cluttered with too much information and too much data will simply not be seen by the untrained human who has to put out too much effort. The criteria for the appropriate amount of data should be established somewhere along the following lines—if the information presented on the chart can be seen and assimilated without having to be read, then the chart contains an appropriate amount of information. Behind that statement, however, is a series of important assumptions:

1. The individuals who see the data are familiar with the operations of the firm and have some experience in reading data about the firm in tabular form.

2. The viewer has been trained in graphic pattern recognition and is a graphic literate. This statement indicates that the viewer knows what is being shown, understands the graphic formats and graphic statements, and can see the graphic words. Such users can relate the information to their experience by *seeing* without having to *think* about it.

3. The data or information being presented is of concern to the viewer and that performance can be improved as a result of viewing the data. This assumption is based on the fact that if the information is not perceived to be of value to the viewer, then you can put as little or as much on a chart as you want and it will not be used.

To understand the material presented in this text, you must fully understand and agree that the results of operations reflect a system, that such results have a consistency, and that such consistency can be repesented by the patterns of a well organized and well thought out graphic representation. Therefore, the charts must be constructed so the data drive the format to create a pattern of operations that is more important than the data themselves. This requirement is built into all of the charts presented in this text. Thus the trained viewer should learn to see the patterns, not read the data.

Finally, if the design requirements presented in this book are met, viewers can see the patterns much more quickly than they could from tabular statements. Therefore, the concept that all information should be on one page is no longer valid. The main reason for the "putting it all on one page" concept was that management did not have time to read all of the prepared reports.

Now, however, if the information is shown correctly on a graph, all the information can be seen rapidly and input to the mind. Ten charts can be seen much more quickly and the information input much more effectively than could be read from the "all on one page." It is the difference in the time that it takes to get the information into the brain that is the critical distinction. Every attempt should be made to put the appropriate amount of information on each chart so only those charts actually necessary to describe the data will be presented, keeping in mind that too much information put on one chart destroys the entire purpose of charting.

Rules for Amount of Data

1. Show only one *type* of pattern per chart—do not mix type of patterns or type of information.
2. Clearly separate data with different scales—use different charts for different scales.
3. Compare items that have clear relationships, and the same basic data structure (i.e., show the relationship between *number* of units sold by product type and revenue by product type; don't show numbers by product type and revenue by customer type within the same borders).
4. Use only the number of elements that fit gracefully within the standard presentation size and permit properly proportioned bars to be shown for the primary and comparative presentations.

B.   Headings

All titles in the graphic financial statements should be centered and identical to the headings used in tabular financial reporting. For public statements no abbreviations should be used and no coding other than that which would normally be used in a tabular statement. For internal reporting, common abbreviations are appropriate and, eventually, when the users are so familiar with the patterns that they know the elements by position and shading, certain graphic comparisons may be made without names or numbers.

It is important to distinguish between the title of the chart and the name of the elements shown. There should be a clear separation from the headings and the body of the chart. If color is used as an indexing device, then the borders and the titles can be enough color to provide that indexing. The elements of the chart should be a single color with shading and should not be disturbed or distorted by the use of color for indexing.

C.   The Suggested Graphic Alphabet

Here are four letters of the alphabet: *A, B, C,* and *D.* The A is a graphic representation of the sound "ah," the B is a graphic representation of the sound "bah," the C is a graphic representation of the sound "cah," the D is a graphic representation of the sound of "dah," and so on. In this manner, the lexicographers have built the entire alphabet. Using the alphabet with consonants and vowels, we put together a series of letters to form words that, when put together, form sentences and those sentences form paragraphs.

Shown in Exhibit 3.1 is a blank representation of data. If we add a scale to that blank representation of data, we now have a graphic representation of the number 50, Exhibit 3.2. That representation of 50 is to numbers what the alphabet is to sounds. Considering graphics in this manner permits the development of structured and organized ways to build certain relationships between the bars as graphic representations of data. Such relationships will, over a period of time, give the same form of meaning and understanding to number relationships that the alphabet helps us give to the human thought process using the written word. This section of the chapter describes the graphic alphabet and how it is put into graphic words and then into structures that build sentences. The remainder of the book shows how these sentences are built to describe certain kinds of data relationships.

2. THE FINANCIAL GRAPHIC STANDARD FORMATS

All of the financial charts shown in this book are built from a set of standard components and presented in one of a range of standard formats. This section demonstrates how to see and understand a chart with the standard components. Other sections demonstrate how to use the key financial formats.

The standards use a mixture of horizontal and vertical bars to present information. Up to three bars can be combined to show three pieces of information about one element. A chart is made up of 10 or less elements.

Exhibit 3.3 is made up of one element that shows the Net Sales (A) for a company called TESTCO (B).

Look at the legend in the top left-hand corner, marked C. This legend describes what type of data is shown in the chart. In this chart the following types of data are being shown:

1. The dark black bar in the middle shows the primary data. The primary data is that which is most important. In most cases, it will be data for the current year.

2. The darkest shaded bar below and behind the primary bar shows the data that should be compared first to the primary bar. This bar is called the first comparative bar and will always be below and behind the primary bars. In many cases this data will be either budget data or prior year data. This bar will always be the same size as but half covered by the primary bar.

3. The lightest shaded bar above and behind the primary bar shows the data that should be compared second to the primary bar. This bar is called the second comparative bar and will always be above and behind the primary bars. This data may be budget, prior years, or forecast data. This bar will always be the same size as, but two-thirds covered by, the primary bar.

Thus when all three bars are shown, the image is that the primary bar is closest, the first comparative is behind the primary bar, and the second comparative bar is behind the other two.

Now look at the chart identification on the top right-hand corner, marked D. This shows the chart number (10-998), the period shown (December), and the scale size (millions).

The numbers at the end of each bar (E) show the total net sales. The primary sales were $2,927 million or $2,927,000,000. The first comparative sales were

EXHIBIT 3.1

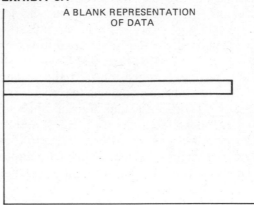

A BLANK REPRESENTATION
OF DATA

EXHIBIT 3.2

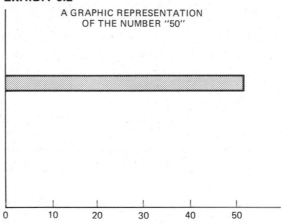

A GRAPHIC REPRESENTATION
OF THE NUMBER "50"

$2,466 million or $2,466,000,000. The second comparative sales were $2,100 million or $2,100,000,000.

The scale (F) is on the bottom of the chart. All chart scales in this book start at zero. To avoid confusion no scales will be broken.

Exhibit 3.4 shows four elements of sales by division: North, South, East, and West. The legend on the upper left shows that each element is made up of the primary bar, the actual sales for 1981, and the first comparative, the prior years' sales.

The legend on the upper right shows that this chart is for December and the scale size is in thousands.

This simple format compares sales between divisions and between sales in 1981 and the year before. As shown in Exhibit 3.3, a third bar could be added to compare this data with the budget.

A. Time Series

Exhibit 3.5, Chart #10-008, is a time series chart. This chart shows sales by month for TESTCO. The legend on the upper left-hand corner indicates that the primary data is for 1981 and the first comparative is for the prior year. The

EXHIBIT 3.3

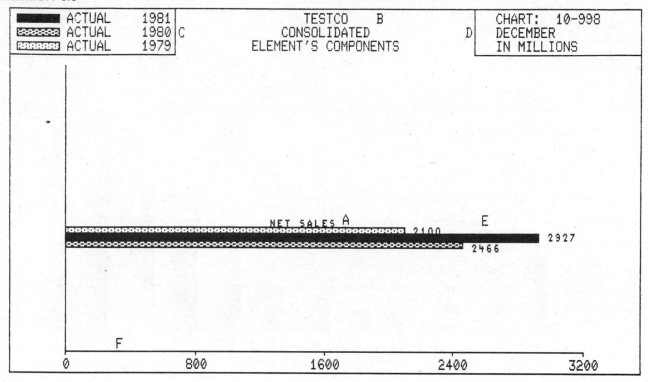

	ACTUAL	1981		TESTCO B		CHART: 10-998
	ACTUAL	1980	C	CONSOLIDATED	D	DECEMBER
	ACTUAL	1979		ELEMENT'S COMPONENTS		IN MILLIONS

NET SALES A   2100   E
2466
2927

F

0   800   1600   2400   3200

EXHIBIT 3.4

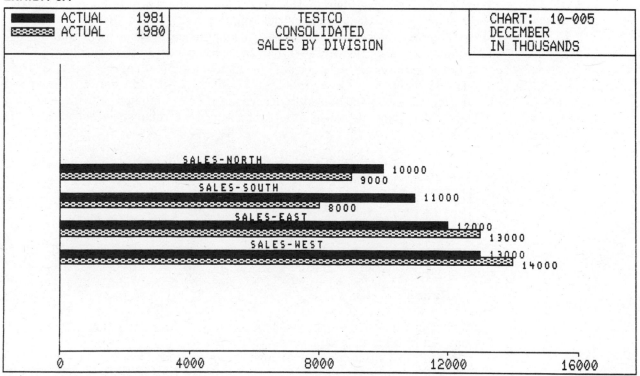

	ACTUAL	1981	TESTCO	CHART: 10-005
	ACTUAL	1980	CONSOLIDATED	DECEMBER
			SALES BY DIVISION	IN THOUSANDS

SALES-NORTH   10000
9000
SALES-SOUTH   11000
8000
SALES-EAST   12000
13000
SALES-WEST   13000
14000

0   4000   8000   12000   16000

23

EXHIBIT 3.5

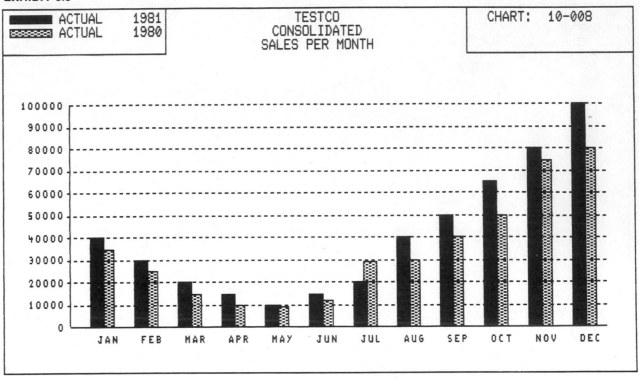

first element from the left shows January sales. The second element from the left shows February sales, and so on. The entire chart shows the earnings cycle for TESTCO. The scale is on the left and no numbers are shown in the body of the chart. The pattern is the critical picture.

By comparing actual to prior year performance it is easy to see that in July, net sales was significantly less than the same period in the prior year.

Later in the book it is desirable to refer to a symbol representing the time series chart format. This symbol is used in much the same way that standard flow chart symbols are used to describe a flow of management information. Exhibit 3.6 illustrates the symbol for the time series chart used throughout the book.

EXHIBIT 3.6

B.   Ratios

Ratios can be critical in explaining key relationships in any organization. The financial graphic language shows ratios two ways.

In Exhibit 3.7 two charts are shown as one picture. The two charts show two different pictures of the return on sales ratio for 1981 as compared to budget.

The chart on the right, marked A, shows the absolute value of the ratio. You can see that Return on Sales was 24.2% in 1981. The chart on the left, marked B, shows the numerator and denominator of Return on Sales, Net Income divided by Sales.

EXHIBIT 3.7

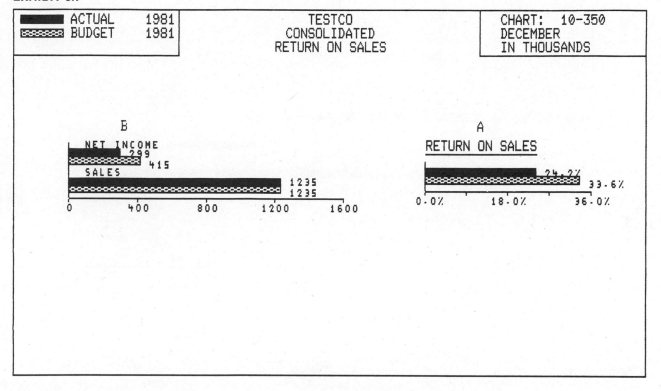

By comparing the budgeted data to the actual sales you can see why both pictures of the ratio help you. The chart on the right shows that Return on Sales was less than budget. The chart on the left shows these additional pieces of information:

1. How the ratio is calculated: net income divided by total sales.
2. Why the ratio changed: the ratio was off from budget because net income was less than budget.
3. The significance of the change: net income decreased about $116 thousand

Exhibit 3.8 illustrates the graphic symbol for the ratio format to be used throughout the book.

EXHIBIT 3.8

EXHIBIT 3.9

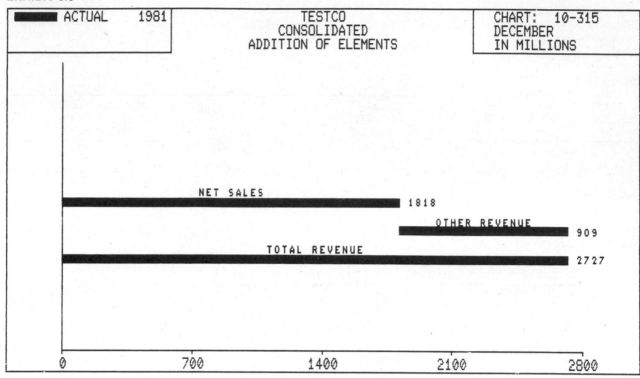

| ACTUAL | 1981 | TESTCO
CONSOLIDATED
ADDITION OF ELEMENTS | CHART: 10-315
DECEMBER
IN MILLIONS |

NET SALES — 1818
OTHER REVENUE — 909
TOTAL REVENUE — 2727

0   700   1400   2100   2800

EXHIBIT 3.10

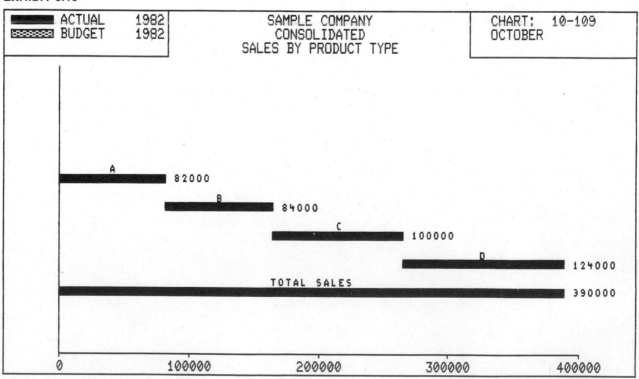

| ACTUAL | 1982 | SAMPLE COMPANY
CONSOLIDATED
SALES BY PRODUCT TYPE | CHART: 10-109
OCTOBER |
| BUDGET | 1982 | | |

A — 82000
B — 84000
C — 100000
D — 124000
TOTAL SALES — 390000

0   100000   200000   300000   400000

EXHIBIT 3.11

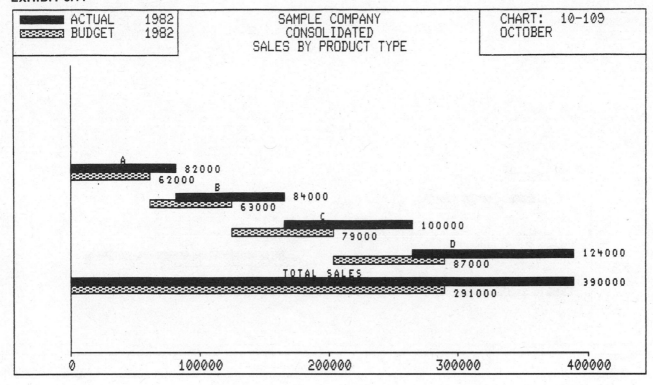

C. The Component Chart

In many cases you will want to show the details that make up a significant element. For example, you may want to see how the sales by division or by product add to equal the total sales element. Any time you want to see what parts are added to make up the whole of a significant item, and to show their relationship to the whole, a *component chart* is used. As noted earlier, the Quissinard approach is used throughout this book to display addition, subtraction, and division.

Exhibit 3.9 is a simple example of the addition of components. The first component, Net Sales, starts to the left, at the axis; the second component, Other Revenue, starts where the first component, Net Sales, stops but lower on the chart. The Total Revenue bar starts back at the axis indicating a total and extends out as far as the end of the Other Revenue bar. To view the chart, note that Net Sales plus Other Revenue equals Total Revenue.

Sales by Product Type, Exhibit 3.10, shows the make-up of sales by product type for Sample Company. To see the makeup of Total Sales, add sales of products A, B, C, and D to equal Total Sales.

When the budget data is added in Exhibit 3.11, the chart shows that although sales are larger than budget, the overall *pattern* of sales has remained the same as a percent of *Total Sales*. The important picture here is the pattern of product type sales as they relate to Total Sales.

In the final example, Exhibit 3.12, the overall pattern of sales has changed from budget. In 1982 Product A did not sell as well as budgeted and Product D sold very well!

EXHIBIT 3.12

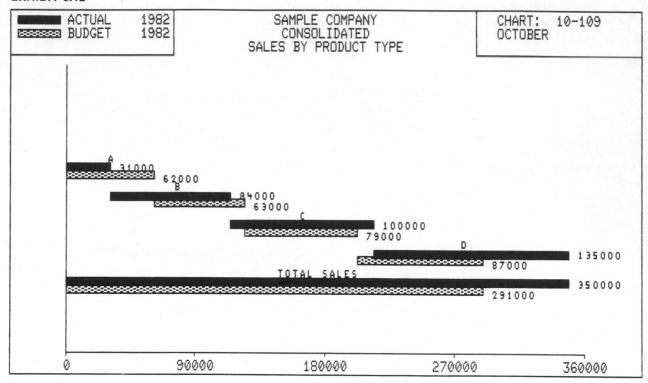

EXHIBIT 3.13

Exhibit 3.13 illustrates the graphic symbol used to describe the component format.

D. Item Chart

There are many cases when you need to compare significant items *to each other*. To do this use an item chart.

Exhibit 3.14 compares sales by product type to each other and budget. It is easy to see that product A had the least amount of sales in 1982 and much less than budgeted and Product D had the most sales in 1982 and much more than budgeted.

In an item chart all of the elements start at the axis. To compare items to each other they should start at the axis to avoid confusion.

In Exhibit 3.15 accounts receivable is categorized by age. You can see that

EXHIBIT 3.14

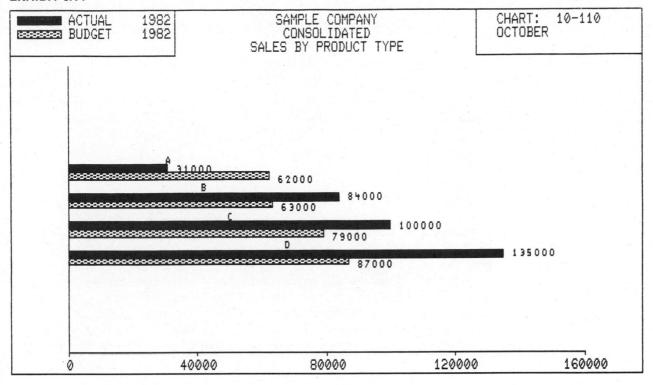

| ACTUAL 1982 | SAMPLE COMPANY | CHART: 10-110 |
| BUDGET 1982 | CONSOLIDATED SALES BY PRODUCT TYPE | OCTOBER |

A 31000
62000
B 84000
63000
C 100000
79000
D 135000
87000

0   40000   80000   120000   160000

EXHIBIT 3.15

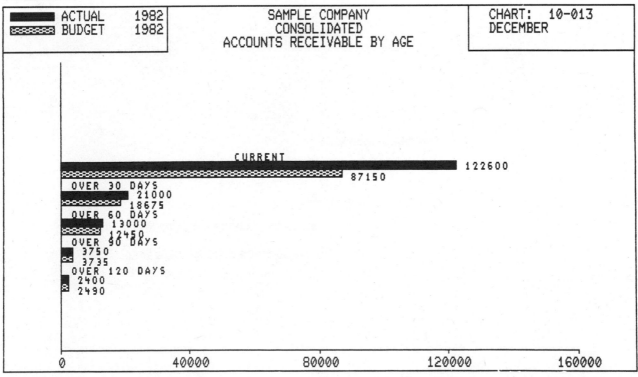

| ACTUAL 1982 | SAMPLE COMPANY | CHART: 10-013 |
| BUDGET 1982 | CONSOLIDATED ACCOUNTS RECEIVABLE BY AGE | DECEMBER |

CURRENT 122600
87150
OVER 30 DAYS
21000
18675
OVER 60 DAYS
13000
12450
OVER 90 DAYS
3750
3735
OVER 120 DAYS
2400
2490

0   40000   80000   120000   160000

29

current accounts receivable is the most significant type of accounts receivable. The use of the item chart this way shows a frequency distribution.

Exhibit 3.16 illustrates the graphic symbol used for the item chart.

EXHIBIT 3.16

E.   Variance Chart

In many cases you will want to see the variance from a standard, a budget, or the previous year. The variance can be shown in actual amounts or as a percentage of change.

Exhibit 3.17 shows the dollar variance of sales from budget for each product type. A negative variance is shown to the left of the axis and a positive variance is shown to the right of the axis. In this example, Product A's sales were less than budgeted and Product D's sales were greater than budgeted.

Exhibit 3.18 illustrates the graphic symbol used for the variance chart.

EXHIBIT 3.17

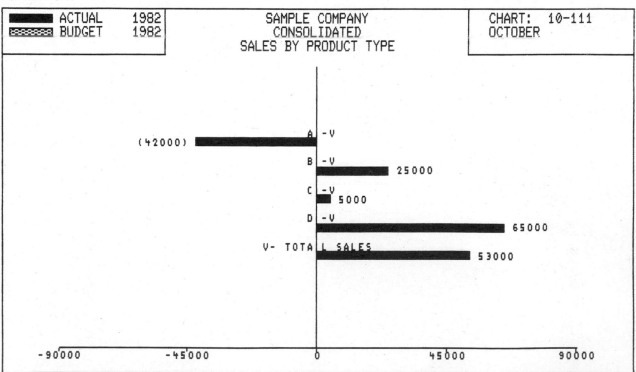

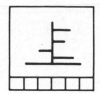

EXHIBIT 3.18

3. COMBINATIONS OF THE BASIC CHART FORMATS

The five basic charts already presented can be combined to present additional data relationships. The next set of six standard financial graphic chart formats are a combination of the first set of basic chart formats.

A. Multiple Ratios

The multiple ratio chart is used to compare two or more ratios to each other. The chart is simply a combination of two or more ratio chart formats on one page. No more than four ratios to a chart is recommended to avoid confusion.

Exhibit 3.19 illustrates an example of a multiple ratio chart. This chart shows the four DuPont ratios for a sample company, Testco. The DuPont ratios are a common set of four ratios used for management analysis because of their critical relationships. Return on Sales × Asset Turns × Leverage equals the Return on Investment.

EXHIBIT 3.19

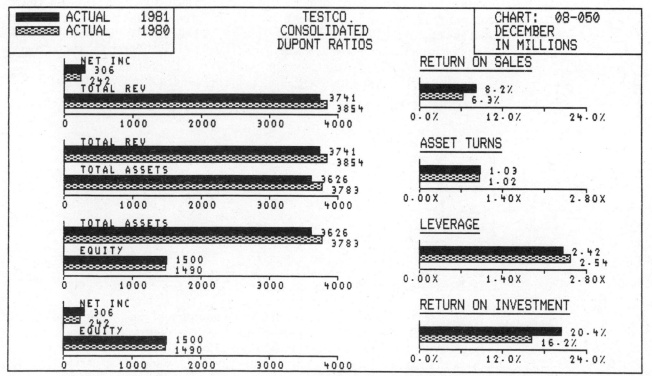

EXHIBIT 3.20

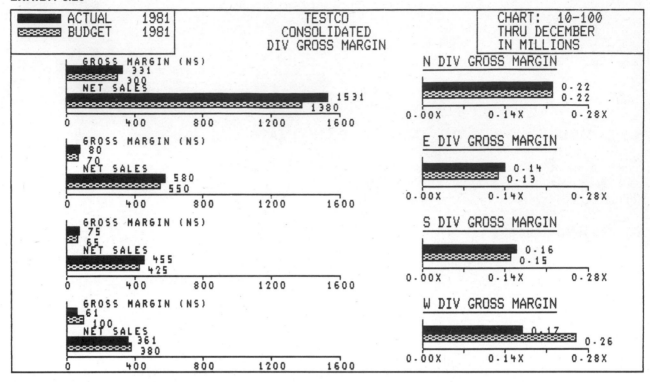

Exhibit 3.20 shows another example of the multiple ratio format. This example shows the same ratio gross margin for four divisions of the sample company, Testco. By looking down the right-hand column of charts it is easy to spot that the West Division is off from budget. A look to the divisions' make-up of the ratio on the left gives a clue as to why the ratio was off and also shows that the West is not an important division compared to the North.

Exhibit 3.21 illustrates the graphic symbol for the Multiple Ratio Chart Format.

EXHIBIT 3.21

B. Co-Relationship Component

The co-relationship component chart is two component charts shown side by side. This chart format is used to compare the components of one whole to the components of another closely related whole. For example, Exhibit 3.22 shows a co-relationship component chart illustrating Sales versus Cost of Goods Sold for Testco Company. The left-hand chart shows the components of sales by

EXHIBIT 3.22

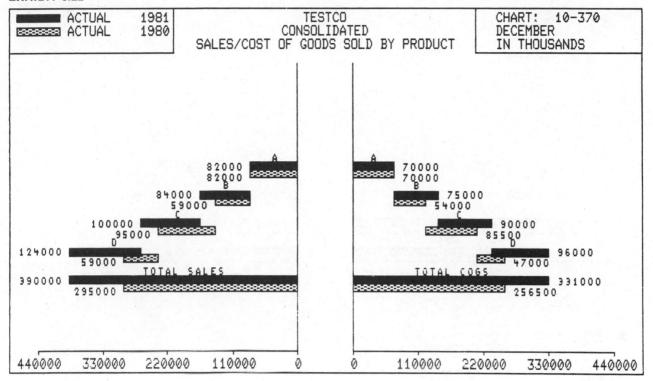

product type. The right-hand chart shows the components of cost of goods sold by the same product types.

Exhibit 3.23 illustrates the graphic symbol used for the co-relationship component chart.

EXHIBIT 3.23

C.   Co-Relationship Item

The co-relationship item chart is two item charts shown side by side. This chart format is used to compare how individual items of one set of data relate to the individual items of another closely related set of data.

Exhibit 3.24 shows a co-relationship item chart illustrating Sales versus Cost of Goods Sold for Testco Company. The left-hand chart shows the items of sales by division. The right-hand chart shows the components of cost of goods sold by the same divisions.

Exhibit 3.25 illustrates the graphic symbol used for the co-relationship item chart

EXHIBIT 3.24

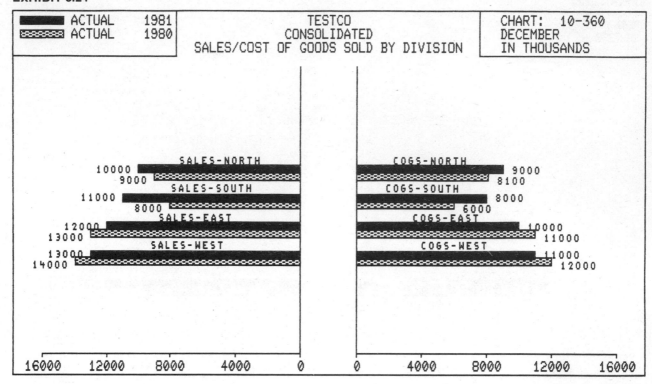

EXHIBIT 3.25

D. Twin Component Chart

The twin component chart shows two component charts placed side by side. The twin component chart differs from the co-relationship component chart in both its appearance and in the type of data shown. The vertical axes of the co-relationship component chart are shown close together whereas the vertical axes of the twin component chart are not shown together. The twin component chart is used to compare the components of one whole to the components of another whole. The data need not be as closely related as that shown in the co-relationship component chart.

Exhibit 3.26 shows an example of the twin component chart format. The components of administrative expenses for two divisions are shown. The difference in patterns describes the picture. Division A is shown on the left and division B is on the right.

EXHIBIT 3.26

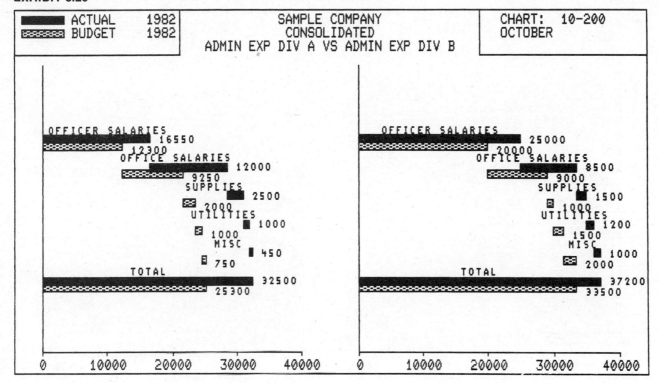

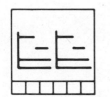

EXHIBIT 3.27

Exhibit 3.27 shows the graphic symbol used for the twin component chart.

E.   The Twin Item Chart

The twin item chart is two item charts placed side by side. The twin item chart differs from the co-relationship item chart both in its appearance and in the type of data shown. The twin item chart axes are not placed together as in the co-relationship item chart. The twin item chart is used to compare individual items of two sets of data. The data need not be as closely related as that shown with the co-relationship item chart formats.

Exhibit 3.28 shows an example use of the twin item chart format. The individual components of administrative expenses for two divisions are compared. Division A is shown on the left and division B on the right.

Exhibit 3.29 shows the graphic symbol for the twin item chart format.

EXHIBIT 3.28

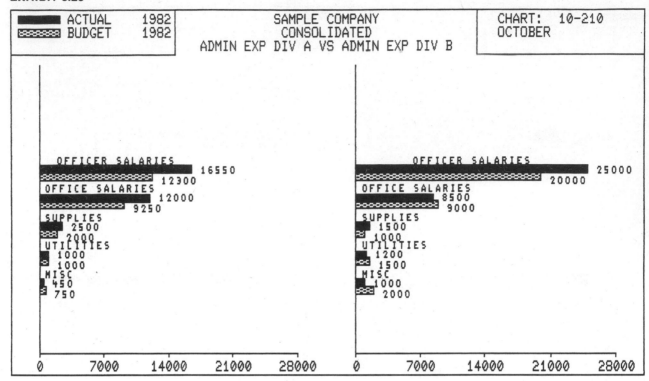

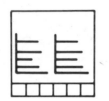

EXHIBIT 3.29

F.   Twin Variance Chart

The twin variance chart is two variance charts shown side by side. It is used to compare the variance of one set of data to the variance of another set of data.

Exhibit 3.30 shows an example of the twin variance chart format. The variance chart on the left shows the variance from budget for the administrative expenses for the A division. The variance chart on the right shows the variance for the same expenses for the B division.

Exhibit 3.31 illustrates the graphic symbol used for the twin variance chart format.

EXHIBIT 3.30

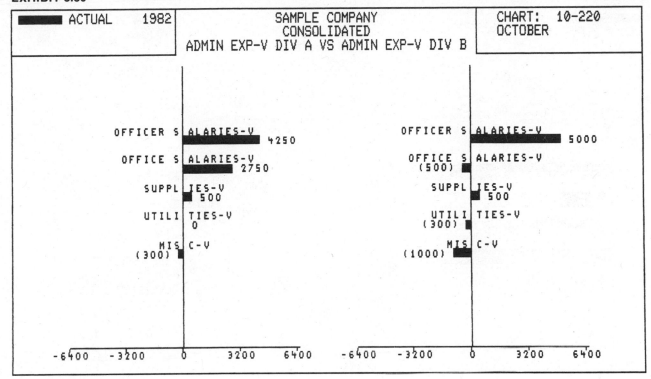

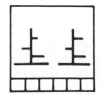

EXHIBIT 3.31

G. Component/Item Plus Variance

This chart format is a subformat for the twin component and item charts. It combines a component or item chart on the left with a variance (percentage or actual difference) chart on the right. This gives the viewer a chance to see how each element adds up to the whole or compares to each other on the left, and how those same elements vary from a standard, previous year, or budget. This format follows closely that used in many tabular MIS Systems. Exhibit 3.32 shows an item chart on the left with a percentage variance chart on the right. The percentage variance chart shows the percentage change in data for an element relative to the original data. Although the actual difference between actual 1981 and 1980 for the File category is larger than that for the Accessories category, the original data is smaller for the Accessories category than for the File category, thus the relative (percentage) change is the same. Exhibit 3.33 shows a component chart on the left with an actual difference

EXHIBIT 3.32

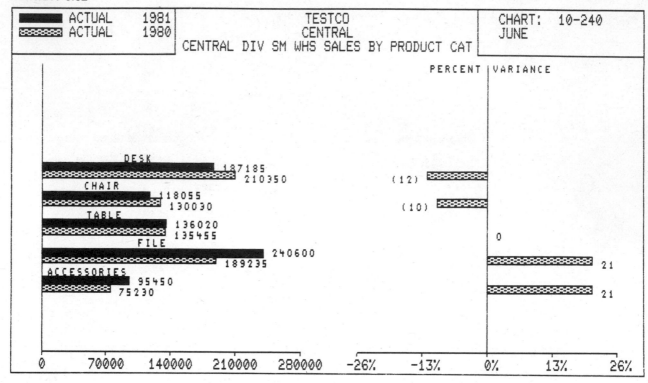

EXHIBIT 3.33

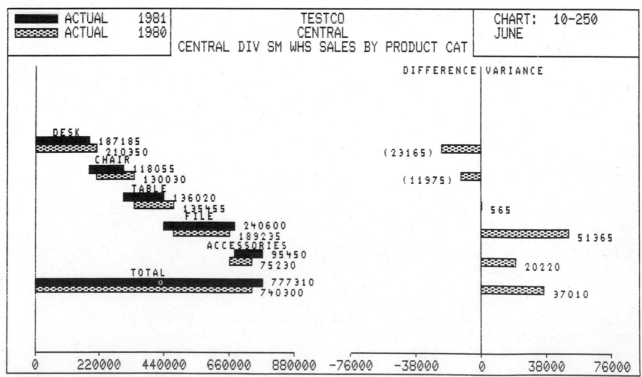

variance chart on the right. The difference variance shows the actual change between two data bars for the same element.

The left-hand chart shows that the overall make-up is similar to that budgeted, although there have been individual differences. The right-hand chart shows exactly where these differences occurred.

4. SUGGESTED SPECIFIC FINANCIAL GRAPHIC STANDARDS

A. The Income Statement

Using the component format, the statement of income is easy to show graphically. Remember that elements add by moving *away* from the axis.

Subtraction is shown by moving the operand *towards* the axis. Thus in Exhibit 3.34 Total Revenue (A) minus Cost of Goods Sold (B) equals the Gross Margin (C).

Exhibit 3.35 shows a simple graphic income statement. To see the relationships shown by this chart, note that Sales plus Other Revenue equals Total Revenue. Total Revenue minus Cost of Goods Sold equals the Gross Margin. The Subtotal Gross Margin goes back to the axis to indicate a subtotal. Gross Margin minus Operating Expenses, Administrative Expenses and Other Expenses equals Net Income.

By adding the budget data, you can see if the pattern of earnings has changed from expected. In Exhibit 3.36 the overall pattern of revenue and expenses has remained the same, although earnings have increased. Note the change in Other Revenue that was required to almost double the Net Income.

EXHIBIT 3.34

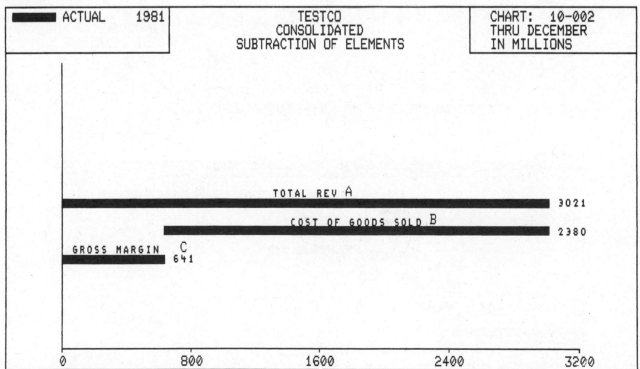

EXHIBIT 3.35

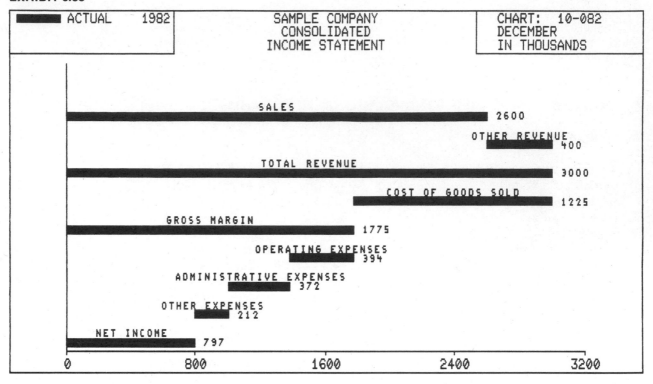

EXHIBIT 3.36

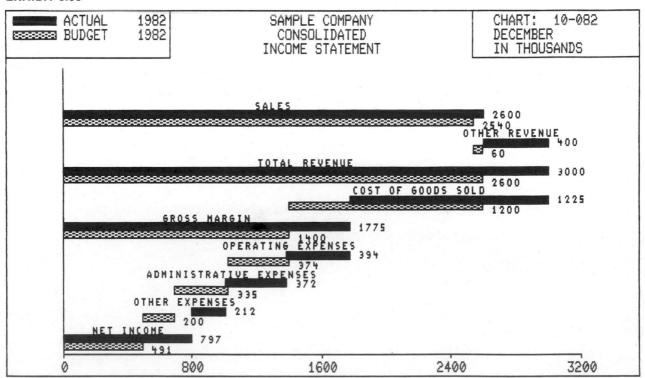

EXHIBIT 3.37

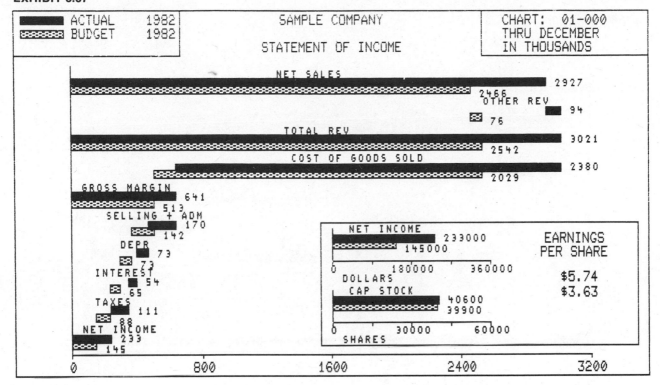

Finally, it is often desired to show earnings per share with the income statement. Exhibit 3.37 shows how this is done.

Exhibit 3.38 illustrates the graphic symbol used for the income statement.

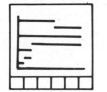

EXHIBIT 3.38

B. The Balance Sheet

The balance sheet shows the financial position at a point in time. The financial standards make it easy to show the information in a balance sheet by using the co-relationship component format shown earlier.

Chart 10-255 shows the make-up of assets for a Sample Company. To read the chart, Exhibit 3.39, note that Cash plus Accounts Receivable plus Inventory equals Current Assets. Property, Plants, and Equipment less Accumulated Depreciation equals Net Property, Plant, and Equipment. Current assets plus Net Property, Plant, and Equipment plus the other listed Assets equals Total Assets. This chart gives a complete picture of the components of assets, a reflection of investment strategy.

EXHIBIT 3.39

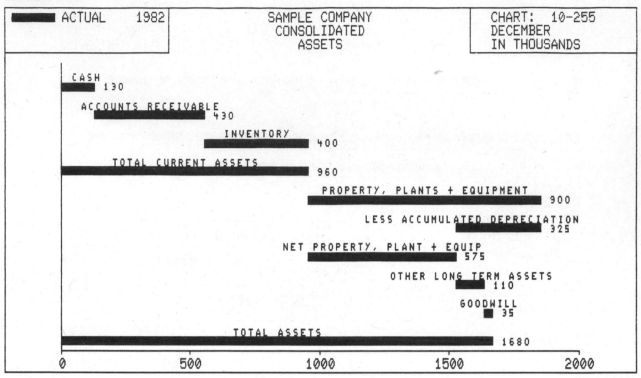

| ACTUAL 1982 | SAMPLE COMPANY CONSOLIDATED ASSETS | CHART: 10-255 DECEMBER IN THOUSANDS |

```
CASH
  130
      ACCOUNTS RECEIVABLE
        430
              INVENTORY
                400
    TOTAL CURRENT ASSETS
                960
                    PROPERTY, PLANTS + EQUIPMENT
                                              900
                       LESS ACCUMULATED DEPRECIATION
                                          325
            NET PROPERTY, PLANT + EQUIP
                575
                       OTHER LONG TERM ASSETS
                          110
                              GOODWILL
                                35
            TOTAL ASSETS
                                  1680

  0         500       1000      1500      2000
```

EXHIBIT 3.40

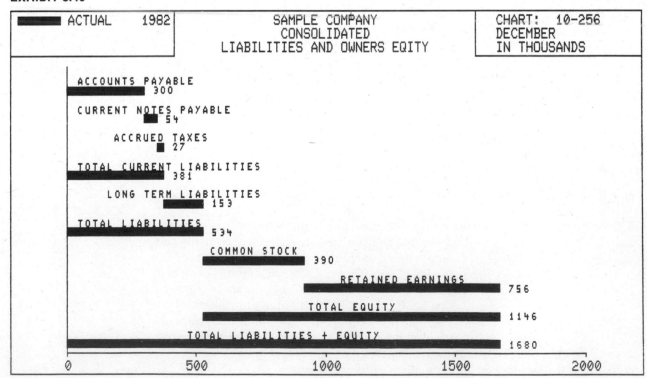

| ACTUAL 1982 | SAMPLE COMPANY CONSOLIDATED LIABILITIES AND OWNERS EQITY | CHART: 10-256 DECEMBER IN THOUSANDS |

```
  ACCOUNTS PAYABLE
          300
  CURRENT NOTES PAYABLE
          54
      ACCRUED TAXES
          27
 TOTAL CURRENT LIABILITIES
          381
      LONG TERM LIABILITIES
          153
 TOTAL LIABILITIES
          534
          COMMON STOCK
                390
                RETAINED EARNINGS
                                    756
          TOTAL EQUITY
                                    1146
    TOTAL LIABILITIES + EQUITY
                                    1680

  0         500       1000      1500      2000
```

42

EXHIBIT 3.41

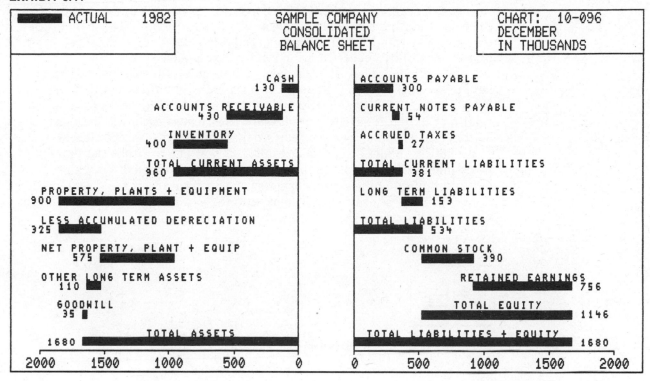

| ACTUAL 1982 | SAMPLE COMPANY CONSOLIDATED BALANCE SHEET | CHART: 10-096 DECEMBER IN THOUSANDS |

CASH 130
ACCOUNTS RECEIVABLE 430
INVENTORY 400
TOTAL CURRENT ASSETS 960
PROPERTY, PLANTS + EQUIPMENT 900
LESS ACCUMULATED DEPRECIATION 325
NET PROPERTY, PLANT + EQUIP 575
OTHER LONG TERM ASSETS 110
GOODWILL 35
TOTAL ASSETS 1680

ACCOUNTS PAYABLE 300
CURRENT NOTES PAYABLE 54
ACCRUED TAXES 27
TOTAL CURRENT LIABILITIES 381
LONG TERM LIABILITIES 153
TOTAL LIABILITIES 534
COMMON STOCK 390
RETAINED EARNINGS 756
TOTAL EQUITY 1146
TOTAL LIABILITIES + EQUITY 1680

2000 1500 1000 500 0   0 500 1000 1500 2000

EXHIBIT 3.42

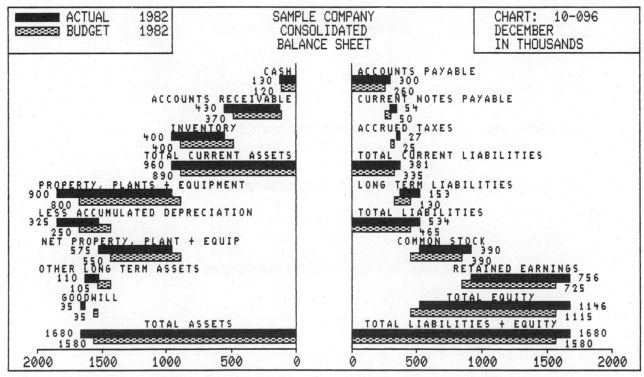

| ACTUAL 1982 / BUDGET 1982 | SAMPLE COMPANY CONSOLIDATED BALANCE SHEET | CHART: 10-096 DECEMBER IN THOUSANDS |

CASH 130 / 120
ACCOUNTS RECEIVABLE 430 / 370
INVENTORY 400 / 400
TOTAL CURRENT ASSETS 960 / 890
PROPERTY, PLANTS + EQUIPMENT 900 / 800
LESS ACCUMULATED DEPRECIATION 325 / 250
NET PROPERTY, PLANT + EQUIP 575 / 550
OTHER LONG TERM ASSETS 110 / 105
GOODWILL 35 / 35
TOTAL ASSETS 1680 / 1580

ACCOUNTS PAYABLE 300 / 260
CURRENT NOTES PAYABLE 54 / 50
ACCRUED TAXES 27 / 25
TOTAL CURRENT LIABILITIES 381 / 335
LONG TERM LIABILITIES 153 / 130
TOTAL LIABILITIES 534 / 465
COMMON STOCK 390 / 390
RETAINED EARNINGS 756 / 725
TOTAL EQUITY 1146 / 1115
TOTAL LIABILITIES + EQUITY 1680 / 1580

2000 1500 1000 500 0   0 500 1000 1500 2000

43

Exhibit 3.40 shows the make-up of liabilities and stockholders equity. Accounts Payable plus other short-term liabilities equals Current Liabilities. Current Liabilities plus Long-Term Liabilities equals Total Liabilities. Common Stock and Retained Earnings equals Total Equity. Total Liabilities plus Total Equity equals Total Liabilities and Equity.

To show the complete balance sheet, Exhibit 3.41, the two charts are placed next to each other. Assets are shown on the left, Liabilities and Stockholders Equity are shown on the right. Note that the current Ratio is easily seen by relating Current Assets to Current Liabilities; leverage can also be seen in the bottom right-hand corner. You can *see* that the balance sheet balances!

By adding budget data in Exhibit 3.42 you can see that the pattern of investment and source of funding has remained as budgeted. You can see also that by combining the simple formats you can create words and sentences to show a great deal of financial information—"graphic paragraphs." Exhibit 3.43 illustrates the graphic symbol for the Balance Sheet.

EXHIBIT 3.43

EXHIBIT 3.44

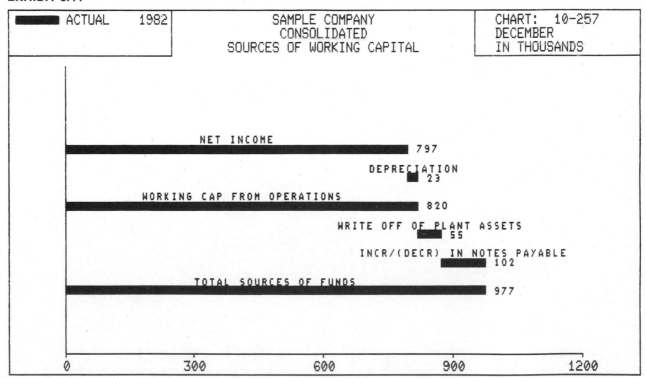

C.   Statement of Changes in Financial Position

Exhibit 3.44 shows the sources of working capital for Sample Company. Net Income plus noncash Depreciation equals Working Capital from Operations. Working Capital from Operations plus the noncash loss on the write off of Plant Assets plus the increase in Notes Payable equals the Total Sources of Funds.

Exhibit 3.45 shows where the funds were used in 1982. It is easy to spot that a major use of funds was an increase in working capital.

By combining the sources and uses charts, you can show Exhibit 3.46, the Statement of Changes in Financial Position. The sources of funds are shown on the left and the uses of funds are shown on the right.

Now by adding budget data in Exhibit 3.47, you can see that some changes occurred that were not budgeted.

For example, by looking at the left a major source of funds in 1982 was net income over budget. By looking at the right, a major use of funds was an increase in Working Capital and other assets did not increase as much as planned.

Exhibit 3.48 illustrates the graphic symbol used for the statement of changes in financial position.

The statement of changes in financial position is often accompanied with a schedule of the changes in working capital. This schedule can also be presented graphically, as shown in the next section.

EXHIBIT 3.45

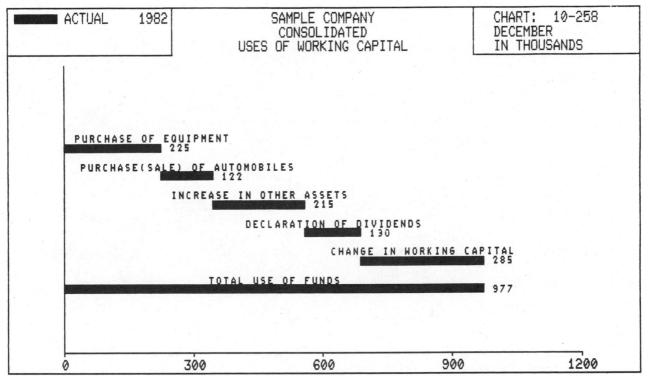

EXHIBIT 3.46

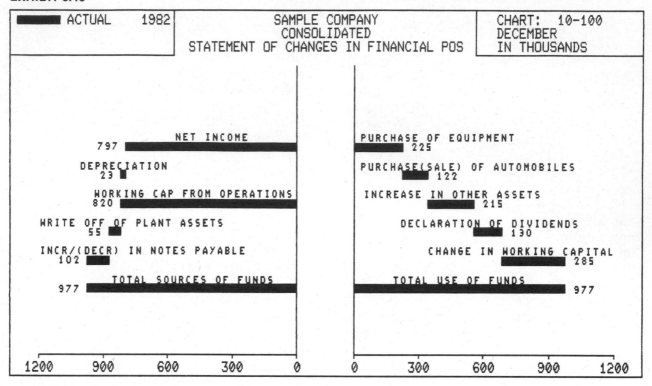

EXHIBIT 3.47

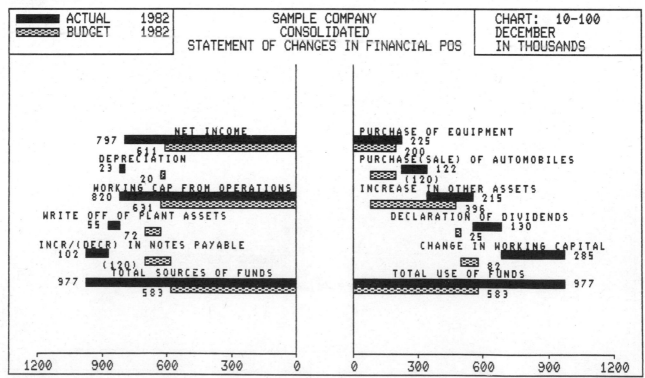

46

EXHIBIT 3.48

D. Changes in Working Capital

The changes in working capital shows the changes in current assets and current liabilities. By combining a few simple variance charts, the graphic words are able to graphically present this statement.

Exhibit 3.49 shows the total changes in current assets, current liabilities and working capital. The chart on the upper left shows the changes in current assets. The chart on the upper right shows the changes in current liabilities. The chart in the center and on the bottom summarizes the changes in working capital. Exhibit 3.50 shows the graphic symbol.

EXHIBIT 3.49

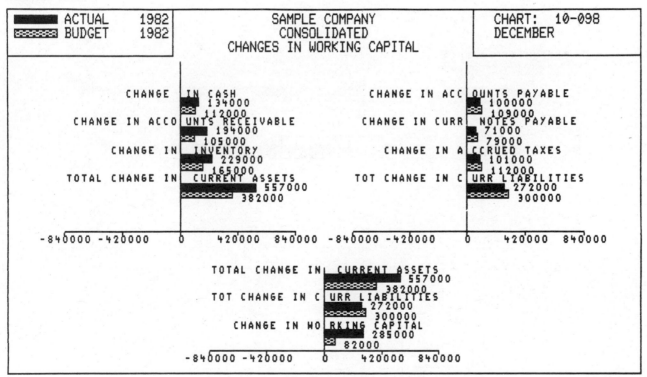

EXHIBIT 3.50

E. Statement of Retained Earnings

The final specific financial graphic standard format is the statement of retained earnings. Exhibit 3.51 illustrates the statement of retained earnings and its graphic symbol is shown in Exhibit 3.52. To read the chart note simply that the beginning balance of retained earnings plus any additions to retained earnings, minus any subtraction to retained earnings equals the Ending Balance of Retained Earnings for the period.

EXHIBIT 3.51

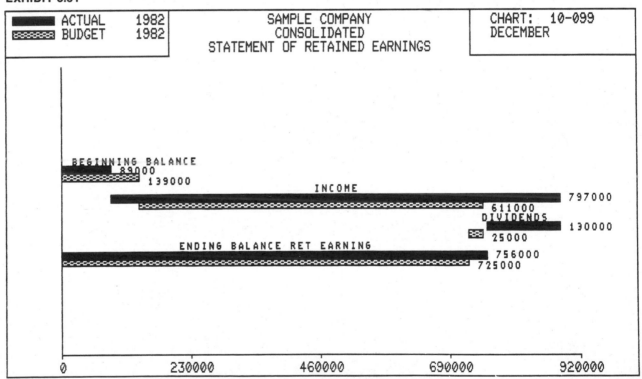

EXHIBIT 3.52

5. SUMMARY

Table 3.1 summarizes the standard chart formats presented in this chapter. The left-hand column lists the title of the chart format. The middle column states the use of the chart or the data relationship shown by the chart format. The right-hand column shows the graphic symbol used to describe each chart format.

Study this table and mark its place in your handbook, for it will become a common tool as you design your GMIS.

Chapter Four describes how to design your GMIS using the concepts developed in Chapters 1, 2, and 3.

TABLE 3.1.   Table of Standard Charts

Standard Chart Format	Data Relationship Described	Graphic Symbol
	Basic Chart Formats	
Time Series	Pattern of data over time.	
Ratio	a. Absolute value of the ratio. b. Changes in the numerator related to changes in the denominator. c. Absolute value of those changes.	
Component	How the parts, or components, add to make the whole and how each component relates to the whole.	
Item	How the individual items relate to each other.	
Variance	Net change from a basic comparison such as a standard, budget, or historic data—actual or percentage.	

TABLE 3.1. Table of Standard Charts (continued)

Standard Chart Format	Data Relationship Described	Graphic Symbol
Combinations of The Basic Chart Formats		
Multiple Ratios	Comparison of two or more ratios to each other.	
Co-Relationship Component	Comparison of the components of one set of data to the components of another set of data. Often describes a direct relationship between the information in each chart.	
Twin Component	Comparison of the components of one whole to the components of the other. The data need not be as closely related as those shown in co-relationship chart.	
Twin Item	Comparison of the items of one set of data to the items of another set of data.	
Twin Variance	Comparison of the variances among one set of data to the variances of another set of data.	
Specific Financial Graphic Formats		
Income Statement	Results of business activity; the pattern of earnings.	

Balance Sheet	Position of a company at a point in time; the relationships of the components of assets and equities.	
Statement of Changes in Financial Position	Source and uses of funds during the operating period.	
Changes in Working Capital	Net change in the mix of working capital items over the operating period.	
Retained Earnings Statement	Total activity in the retained earnings during the operating period.	

CHAPTER 4

HOW TO DESIGN A GRAPHIC MANAGEMENT INFORMATION SYSTEM

1. HOW TO SHOW THE IMPORTANT DATA RELATIONSHIPS

A. Introduction

In Chapter 3 the standard graphic formats were described. The analogy between the standard formats and a graphic language was presented where graphic format was considered to be a graphic word. The analogy is extended further in this chapter. Here the graphic words are used to show the underlying changes in a business as described by the changing graphic patterns. Methods for building the standard graphic formats into a Graphic Management Information System (GMIS) are demonstrated.

Table 3.1 is a working summary of the standard chart formats divided into the following sections:

1. Basic chart formats.
2. Primary combinations of the basic chart formats.
3. Specific financial graphic formats.

As noted in Chapter 3, each chart format is designed to show a specific data relationship. It is important to know exactly what you want to see as the data change, and use the specific set of charts that accurately describe the data relationship they are designed to show. If you want to compare individual items to each other, use an item chart. If, however, you want to show how the components relate and add to make the whole, the component chart will present a different picture and pattern of the same data than will the item chart, especially when comparing to prior years' data.

The graphic symbols are shown in the right-hand column of Table 3.1. These symbols are used in Chapter 4 to show how to design a GMIS and in the rest of the book to show examples of a GMIS design.

B. Examples of How Each Chart Format Shows a Particular Data Relationship

This section gives an example of how each chart shows a particular data relationship. It is important that this point be understood and practiced. A common misuse of graphics is to try to show all of the data relationships with one chart. Even the simplest graphics are complex; trying to show too much information on one chart will result in a chart that is easily misinterpreted and, in many cases, never understood. Showing each data relationship in specific chart formats, you can describe all the key data relationships for a given set of data that can be quickly seen and understood. The critical point is that a well designed GMIS using specific formats to describe specific points can be *seen* and *understood* in less time than complex charts or tabular statements. For example, Exhibit 4.1 shows how the Sample Company's sales components add to equal the Total Sales.

Looking at the chart you can see the make-up of sales—product type A's sales, plus product type B's sales, plus product type C's sales, plus product type D's sales add up to make Total Sales. By comparing this year to budget you can see that the *pattern* of current sales is not the same as budgeted.

Exhibit 4.2 shows the same data on an item chart. An item chart shows how the individual items relate to each other; use it to compare product A's sales to product B's sales and so on. Do not use a component chart to compare how the individual items relate to each other, nor the item chart to show how the items equal the total.

EXHIBIT 4.1

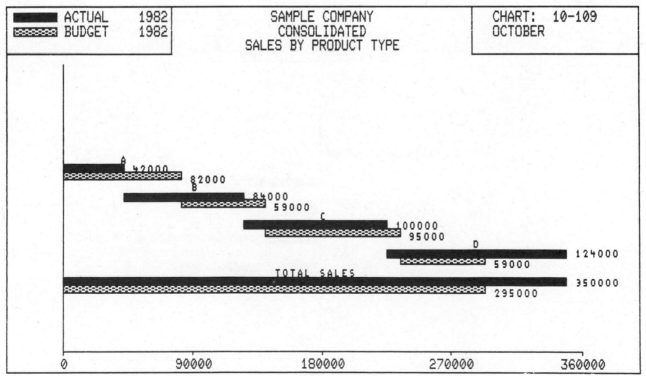

EXHIBIT 4.2

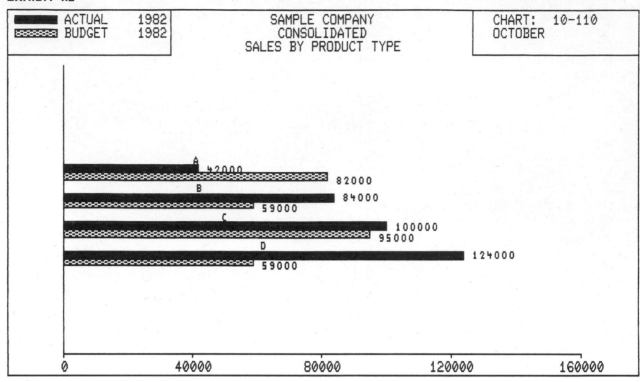

▬▬▬ ACTUAL	1982	SAMPLE COMPANY
▨▨▨ BUDGET	1982	CONSOLIDATED

SALES BY PRODUCT TYPE

CHART: 10-110
OCTOBER

A 42000
82000
B 84000
59000
C 100000
95000
D 124000
59000

0   40000   80000   120000   160000

EXHIBIT 4.3

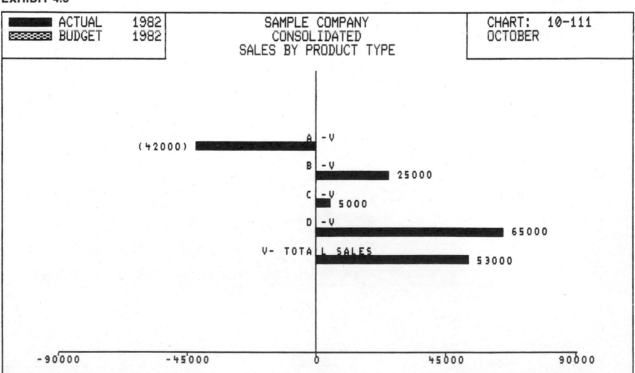

▬▬▬ ACTUAL	1982	SAMPLE COMPANY
▨▨▨ BUDGET	1982	CONSOLIDATED

SALES BY PRODUCT TYPE

CHART: 10-111
OCTOBER

A - V (42000)
B - V 25000
C - V 5000
D - V 65000
V- TOTAL SALES 53000

-90000   -45000   0   45000   90000

54

Exhibit 4.3 shows the variances between actual and budgeted data for sales for this company. If you want to look at the variances between this year and budget, use a variance chart. The variance chart will show you quickly and correctly where the variances occurred from budget and their importance. It is easier and more accurate to get this information from the variance chart than from the item chart or the component chart. You can show either the actual dollar variance, the percentage variance, or both depending on your information needs. You can also show a component or an item chart together with a variance chart for a more complete picture.

C.   Why Multiple Charts Are Used To Show the Complete Picture

As described in the preceding sections, each standard chart format describes a particular data relationship. By showing the standard data relationships in specific chart formats, you can describe all of the key data relationships for a given set of data in a sequence that is easy to get to and understand.

This concept of using multiple charts, where each chart shows predefined relationships, is a more effective and efficient use of graphics than trying to put all of the information on one graph or redesigning the charts each time. It is more effective because each chart can be understood and more efficient because it takes less time to get to specific data relationships.

2.   ADDING ANOTHER DIMENSION: LEVEL OF DATA

A.   Concept of Aggregation

The level of data can best be explained in terms of aggregation and disaggregation. Aggregation decribes how data is actually collected. For example, if you have one salesperson making sales, his or her activity is the lowest level of data. If you have several salespeople making sales, all of their sales must be added to create a second level. The sum of all the business revenue from all sources might finally go to the income statement, an even higher level. The data that an executive looks at to make a decision are almost always data that have been aggregated through a series of data levels.

B.   Concept of Disaggregation

Disaggregation describes how the executive uses information to make decisions. For each level of corporate activity, the executive is concerned with key indicators that provide an overall picture of how the areas are performing. At the highest level the CEO might review a weekly report showing the key indicators for his or her company. If any of the ratios or indicators are significantly different than budget or industry, the CEO would ask an analyst to investigate the discrepancy. The key indicators are presented in aggregate form. Once an overall trend is spotted, more detailed information must be reviewed. Graphing key indicators is nothing new; CEOs of major corporations have long had their management reports summarized with graphic summaries. The difference is that a fully linked GMIS will permit the CEO to search for the cause of the change in the indicators by peeling off successive layers of related charts. Sometimes the ratios mix data that are not collected in an aggregate way. Ratios such as sales per employee require data collected from a human factors system and a sales system. The GMIS offers the potential to link the information supporting the key indicators in a *logical graphic sequence* that will cut across several data banks to show several levels of data—thus the concept of disaggregation.

C. Example Sequence of Disaggregation

Here is a simple example of a disaggregation sequence to show the concept. Exhibit 4.4 shows a 12-month time series of sales for a Sample Company.

EXHIBIT 4.4

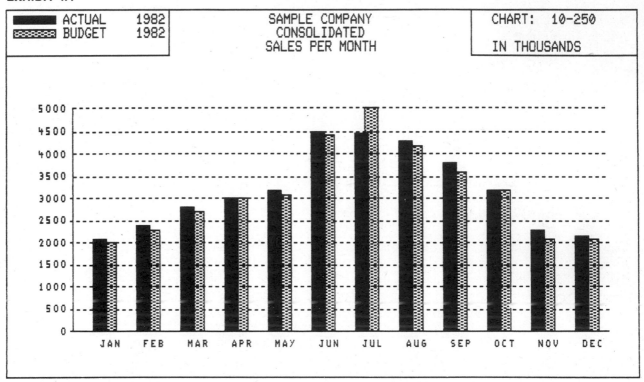

The sales for the month of July are lower than budgeted. A sales variance chart showing the variance from budget by region for July shows which divisions were off from budget. It is easy to spot from Exhibit 4.5 that the northern region is off from budget. A third chart, Exhibit 4.6, shows the sales variance for July for the northern region by sales manager. This chart shows that Jacob is the sales manager responsible for the significant variance in the northern region for July. Finally, a component chart (Exhibit 4.7) for Jacob's division shows that Jacob was budgeted to sell to four customer types. Customer type A did not buy anything from Jacob in July, and this is the apparent reason for variance from budget. This sequence of disaggregation moved from an overall indicator of sales compared to budget to the key reason for the variance in four easy to see charts. The same disaggregation concept can lead you quickly through a massive data base.

EXHIBIT 4.5

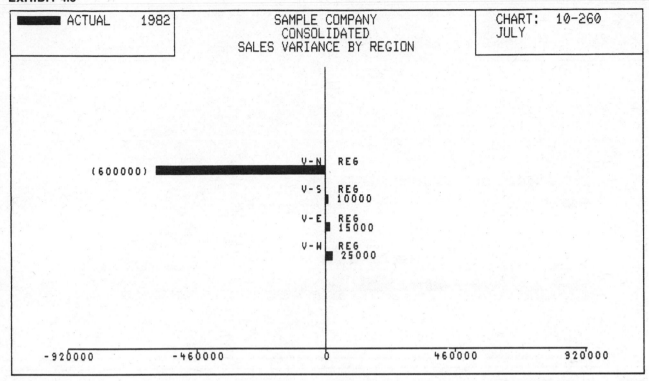

| ACTUAL 1982 | SAMPLE COMPANY CONSOLIDATED SALES VARIANCE BY REGION | CHART: 10-260 JULY |

```
                                            V-N  REG
            (600000) ████████████████████
                                            V-S  REG
                                              █ 10000
                                            V-E  REG
                                              █ 15000
                                            V-W  REG
                                              █ 25000


    -920000        -460000          0           460000         920000
```

EXHIBIT 4.6

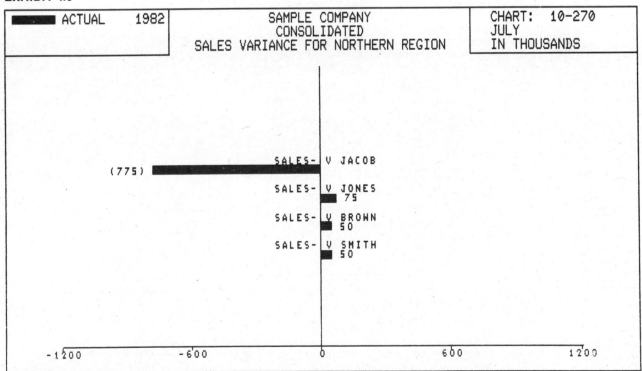

| ACTUAL 1982 | SAMPLE COMPANY CONSOLIDATED SALES VARIANCE FOR NORTHERN REGION | CHART: 10-270 JULY IN THOUSANDS |

```
                                      SALES- V JACOB
              (775) ██████████████████
                                      SALES- V JONES
                                         █ 75
                                      SALES- V BROWN
                                         █ 50
                                      SALES- V SMITH
                                         █ 50


    -1200           -600            0            600           1200
```

57

EXHIBIT 4.7

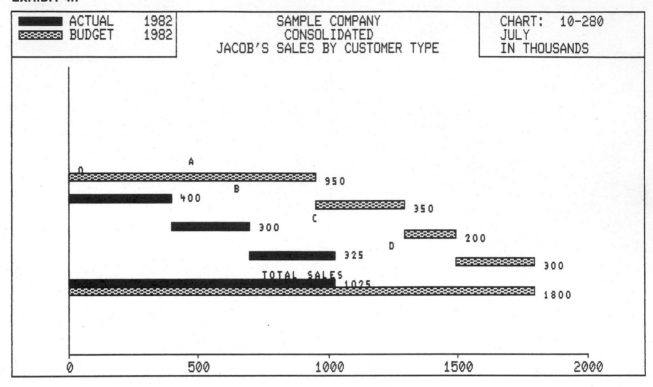

D.　Summary of Disaggregation Concept

The preceding example shows how executives can use the GMIS to analyze trends and relationships. They start with the key indicators, the top level of aggregated data (the first sales chart), and disaggregate through successive layers of the database searching for the reasons the key indicators changed. The power of the GMIS is that it permits the executive to *see* successive layers of data quickly.

3.　DISAGGREGATION OF MULTIPLE DATA LEVELS PLUS MULTIPLE CHARTS

A GMIS will combine the two concepts described to form a consistent description of the relationships inherent in all databases:

1.　The concept that *each* level of data can be described by a series of related charts that show specific data relationships.
2.　The concept that the various levels of data can be linked together and disaggregated using the same types of charts to show the levels of related data.

To control one of the key factors in business—sales, there may be four or five key indicators the sales executive needs to see to review sales for the entire company. By carefully defining the key indicators in the sales sequence and linking the different levels to the key indicators, the executive can disaggregate the sales data to control corporate sales.

Each corporate key factor (as described in Chapter 2) works the same way. There is a series of key indicators shown by a series of high level charts. *Each* of the key indicators is supported by a series of sequences that supports those key indicators showing specific data relationships for different levels of the data. If all the graphic sequences for each key factor are fully linked, the result is a GMIS. The rest of the book shows exactly how to design such a linkage. For each key factor in business we have designed the fundamental key indicators and the graphic sequences necessary to support the key indicators. Following are some examples to make it easier to follow the rest of the text.

4. MAKING IT EASY TO DESIGN APPLICATION SYSTEMS: USING STANDARD GMIS FORMS

A. Sales Application Sequence: An Example

Exhibit 4.8 shows a hierarchical diagram of how the sales sequence is disaggregated through different data levels. For example, key indicators for sales are Sales, Gross Margin and Return on Sales. If these indicators show that further investigation is necessary, then sales can be broken down by customer type, by product type, or by division. These three views of sales describe a most complex set of relationships. The bottom of the diagram shows where the transactions actually occur. The arrow on the left-hand side of the diagram describes the data aggregation flow, summarizing sales.

The disaggregation flow is shown on the right side of the diagram by the arrow going down and titled Disaggregation. The manager will start with the total sales figure. The sales figure can be disaggregated by customer type, by product type, or by division at the first level of data. The division on the right side of the diagram describes part of the second level of data. The division sales are further disaggregated to show (1) the division sales by customer type, (2) the division sales by product type, or (3) a territory within the division. Going

EXHIBIT 4.8

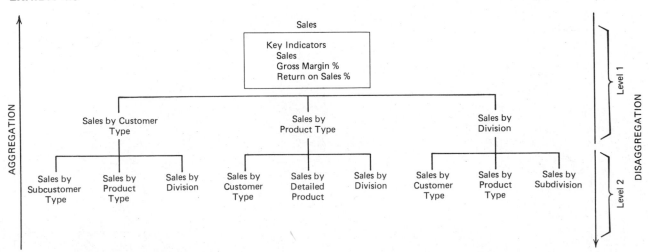

even further to the right within the territories you could disaggregate to the lowest level of customer transactions. This chart shows how the data levels aggregate and disaggregate among the sales sequences.

As described in Section 3, the design of a GMIS requires designing those charts that will display the key relationships for each level of data similar to that shown in Exhibit 4.8.

Exhibit 4.9 shows the first level design of the sales disaggregation system using the graphic symbols developed and summarized in Table 3.1. At the top level is a time series of sales. Sales are disaggregated by customer type in the following ways.

EXHIBIT 4.9.   Sales disaggregation system using graphic symbols

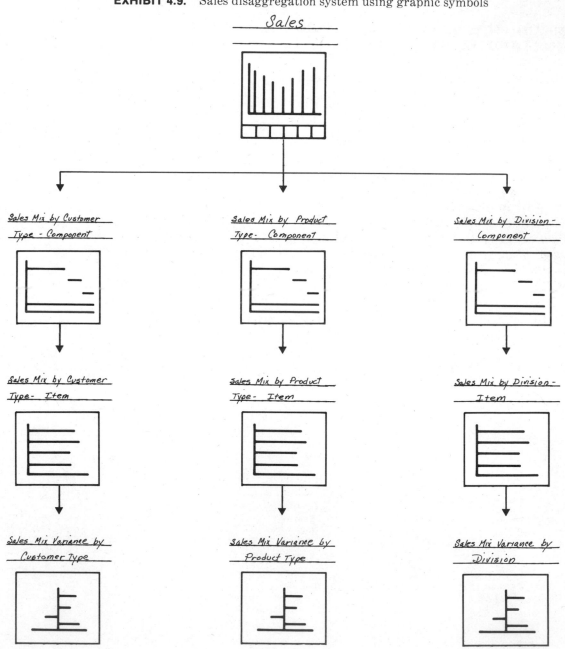

1. A Component chart is used to show how the sales to the customer type add up to the whole.
2. An item chart is used to compare the sales to the customer types to each other.
3. A variance chart is used to show which customer type is off budget.

The sales are further disaggregated the same way to show sales by product type and sales by division.

Exhibit 4.9 is a good example of a simple disaggregation. It is easy to understand and it shows a most common pattern of disaggregation. We have found that most disaggregation patterns start in a similar fashion.

The key indicators are often shown with a time series chart and disaggregated in to a component, item, and variance picture to show all of the basic data relationships.

Table 1 lists the common disaggregation patterns for each level of data. We have found that the level of disaggregation will always work with one of these three types of disaggregation patterns. By looking at the three columns you can see that there are simple indicators of actual numbers, indicators that are ratios, and combinations of indicators. The left-hand column lists the standard chart format used in the disaggregation. An example of the simple indicator is the monthly figure, such as sales, compared to budget or last year. For simple indicators the common disaggregation pattern is: (1) a time series chart, (2) a component chart, (3) an item chart, and (4) a variance chart for each level of data.

A number of key indicators are ratios. In fact, we highly recommend that at least two indicators be used for each key factor—one showing the actual data over time, and the other showing a ratio to provide a leveling effect of content for the data. The common disaggregation pattern would be:

1. A time series showing the ratio over time.
2. A ratio chart showing the two components of return on sales as net income divided by sales. Sales can be disaggregated as follows.
   a. A component chart.
   b. An item chart.
   c. A variance chart.

TABLE 4.1. Disaggregation Pattern For Each Level by Type of Indicator

Standard Chart Format	Type of Disaggregation Pattern		
	Simple	Ratio	Combination
Time Series	1	1	1
Ratio		2	2
Component	2	3	
Item	3	4	
Variance	4	5	
Co-Relationship Component			3
Co-Relationship Item			4
Twin Component			3
Twin Item			4
Twin Variance			5

If net income needs to be disaggregated further, the user would then need a whole new sequence. The net income sequence disaggregates net income into its basic relationships.

Finally, there are combinations of the two common disaggregation sequences. For example, if the key indicator is a time series of the monthly overall gross margin percent, the subsequent component, item, and variance charts might be shown as a co-relationship chart or a twin chart comparing sales on the left side to the cost of goods sold on the right side. An example of this type of sequence is shown in Chapter 11. These variations are often useful when the items portrayed in the ratio chart are very closely related. Following are samples of three simple forms we use to design a sequence. Each form describes the three basic types of disaggregate patterns. Exhibit 4.10 is an example of the first form to be described (Number 102).

5. BASIC GMIS DESIGN FORM

A. Part A

Look at the top of the form marked A. The information presented under this heading is the same in this and the other forms presented in this chapter. In the top left-hand corner is the area to be filled in with the organization name, who prepared the form and when, and who reviewed the form and when. To the right is an area that describes the six small boxes underneath each of the symbols in the main portion of the form. We explain these boxes after we look at the form itself. Finally, on the far right-hand corner of the heading is an area to be labeled with the name of the system described by this form. In this example the system described is Sales. The form itself is describing data level 1 of 2, and we can also see that it is page 1 of 4 pages. This means that there are four pages that describe the entire sales sequence and there are two data levels that describe the entire sales sequence.

B. Part B

The section of the form part B is used to design the sequence of disaggregations for the application being designed. By looking at the intersections, A1, A2, A3, and so on, we can see that each symbol represents the time series chart. The second row, labeled B1, B2, and so on, consists of the symbol for the ratio charts. The third row, labeled C1, C2, and so on, consists of the symbol representing the component charts. The fourth row, labeled D1, D2, and so on, consists of the symbols representing the item charts. And finally, the fifth row, labeled E1, E2, and so on, consists of those graphic symbols representing the variance chart.

As you can see, this form is used to disaggregate both the *simple* and the *ratio* key indicator sequence, as described in Table 4.1. This example describes sales, level 1 of 2, page 1 of 4. Refer back to Exhibit 4.8 which shows the disaggregation pattern for a total sales sequence. Thus Exhibit 4.10 shows the key chart formats for level 1, as described in Exhibit 4.8. In the form we have the key indicators: sales, gross margin percentage, and return on sales percentage represented with a time series chart. Gross margin percentage and return on sales are further disaggregated into a ratio chart. And finally, sales is disaggregated into sales by customer type, sales by product type, and

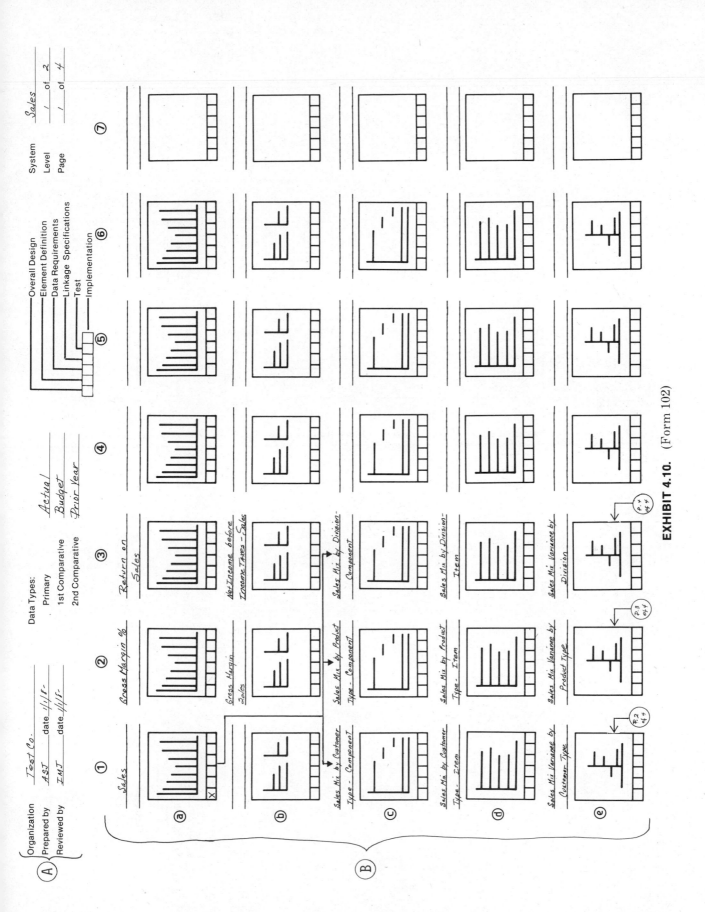

EXHIBIT 4.10. (Form 102)

63

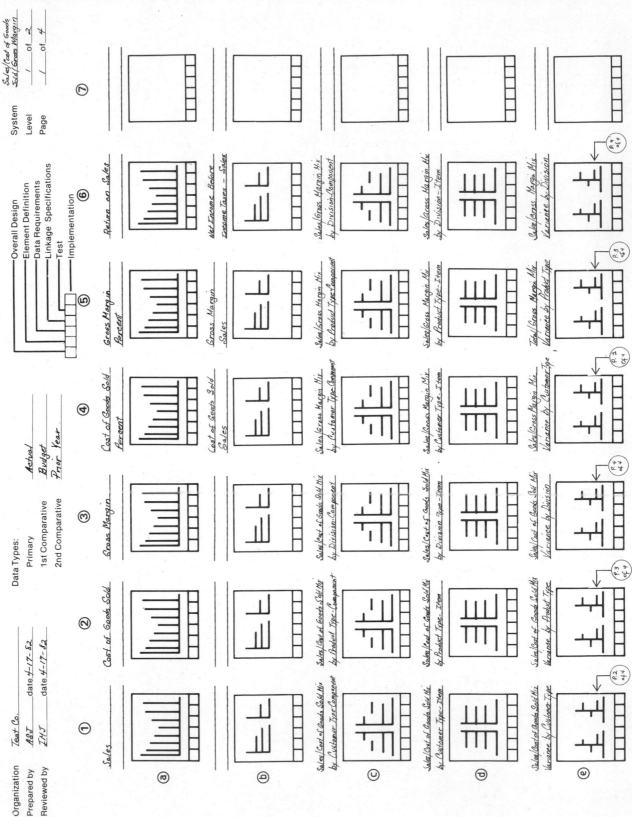

EXHIBIT 4.11. (Form 103)

64

sales by division. For each disaggregate pattern of customer type, product type, and division we've chosen to show a component chart, an item chart, and a variance chart. Refer again back to Exhibit 4.8. As shown in the disaggregation pattern, level 2 shows the breakdown of the sales by customer type, the sales by product type, and the sales by division. We would fill out this form, 102, for each one of these data levels. For example, the breakdown of sales by customer type into sales by subcustomer type, sales by product type, and sales by division would each be shown on a separate form. This sequence explains why there are four pages to a total sales sequence: One page shows level 1, another page shows the breakdown of sales by customer type, another page shows the breakdown by product type, and the last page shows a breakdown by division (see Chapter 13).

As you can see, this form can be used to both design and control the installation of the GMIS. As noted in the description of the heading above, labeled A, there were six boxes underneath each symbol. As shown in the heading, each one of these boxes stands for a specific function in the installation of the GMIS. The box to the far left represents the stage of overall design. The next five boxes represent the steps of detailed design and implementation of a GMIS once the overall design is completed. The material in this text represents the overall design of an entire GMIS. This form can be used as a control form in the job of actually installing the system. As each step is completed, the box underneath each symbol can be checked off. For example, looking at Chart A1, Sales, once the overall design has been made, the box to the far left can be checked off. Once the elements that are going to be represented in the chart have been defined, the second box from the left can be checked off, and so on. These steps are further defined at the end of this chapter.

6. GMIS FORM FOR DESIGNING DISAGGREGATION OF COMBINATION INDICATORS

Exhibit 4.11 shows GMIS Form 103. Form 103 is a variation of Form 102. Form 103 is used when the disaggregate pattern is being designed for those indicators that are combination indicators as described in Table 4.1.

The first row of Form 103 is still a time series chart; the second row is still a ratio chart. The changes between this form and the previous form, 102, occur in the third, fourth, and fifth rows—C, D, and E, respectively. The component, item, and variance charts are in co-relational format. Notice also on the right-hand column there are blank boxes to be filled in with any particular type of chart format not shown on the form you are using. The form shown here is filled out for level 1, page 1, of the Sales/Cost of Goods Sold/Gross Margin application (see Chapter 13).

7. GMIS DESIGNED FOR THE SPECIFIC FINANCIAL GRAPHIC FORMATS

Exhibit 4.12 illustrates GMIS Form 101. This is often the first form used in the design of the GMIS; you can see this is very different from the other two forms. The heading of the form marked A is similar to Forms 102 and 103. The difference between Form 101 and the other two forms lies in the body of the

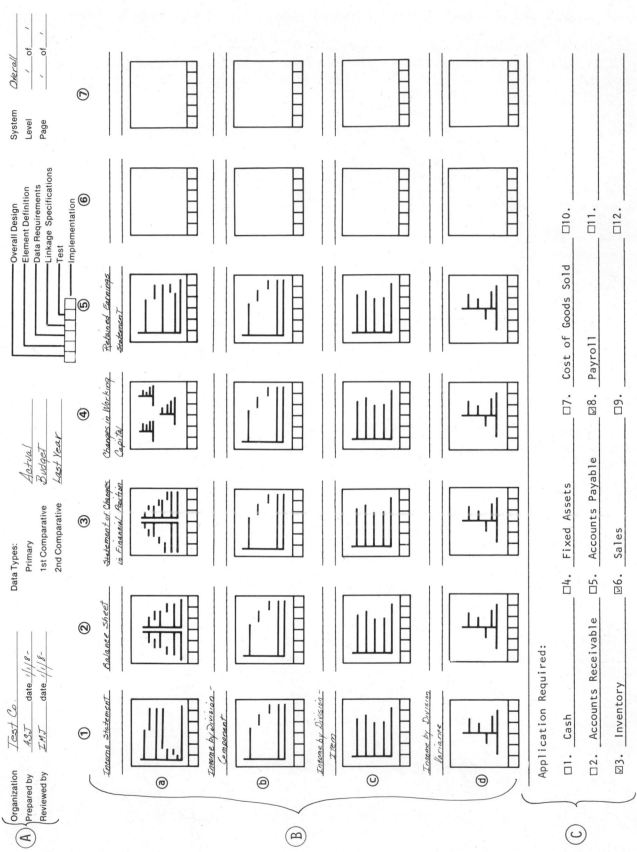

EXHIBIT 4.12 (Form 101)

A
Organization _Test Co._
Prepared by _ASJ_ date _1/1/8-_
Reviewed by _IMJ_ date _1/1/8-_

Data Types:
Primary _Actual_
1st Comparative _Budget_
2nd Comparative _Last Year_

Overall Design
Element Definition
Data Requirements
Linkage Specifications
Test
Implementation

① Income Statement
② Balance Sheet
③ Statement of Changes in Financial Position
④ Changes in Working Capital
⑤ Retained Earnings Statement
⑥
⑦

ⓐ Income Statement
ⓑ Income by Division - Component
ⓒ Income by Division - Item
ⓓ Income by Division Variance

B

System _Overall_
Level _/ of /_
Page _/ of /_

C
Application Required:

☐ 1. Cash
☐ 2. Accounts Receivable
☑ 3. Inventory
☐ 4. Fixed Assets
☐ 5. Accounts Receivable
☑ 6. Sales
☐ 7. Cost of Goods Sold
☐ 8. Payroll (☑)
☐ 9. _____
☐ 10. _____
☐ 11. _____
☐ 12. _____

00

form itself, marked B, and in the bottom section, marked C. Looking at each symbol on the top row, we can see that each symbol is representing those specific financial graphic formats. On the top left-hand corner, box A1, is the symbol for the income statement; box A2 is the symbol for the balance sheet; box A3 is the symbol for the statement of changes in financial position; box A4 is the symbol for the changes in the working capital; box A5 is the symbol for retained earnings statement. This is the form that would be used in many cases to design the beginning of the GMIS if the financial statements were to be shown. In this example, an income statement, a balance sheet, a statement of change in financial position, a changes in working capital statement, and a retained earnings statement are shown. Also note in rows B, C, and D, net income is broken up by division. B1 shows net income by division with a component chart, C1 shows net income by division with an item chart, and D1 shows net income by division with a variance chart. In many situations this form may be all that is necessary for the design of the GMIS. For example, with smaller companies it may only be necessary to break up one or two items from the income statement and the balance sheet using a component, item, and variance chart.

In most cases, however, it is desirable to have an entire set of sequences for applications that derive from the major financial statements. In these cases when designing the GMIS you would check the application required in the lower section of the form marked C. For example, in this particular case, inventory, sales, and payroll applications are checked. These check marks mean that inventory, sales, and payroll have their own set of graphic sequences. If there are other sequences not listed on this chart where a design is warranted, the designer can fill in lines 9, 10, 11, and 12.

8. STEPS TO DESIGNING YOUR GMIS

There are three steps to the design and implementation of the GMIS.

Overall design
Detail design
Implementation

A. Overall Design

The following are the key steps to the overall design of a GMIS.

1. Determine those key factors that are most important to a decision making process; start with an area where the database is solid and can be accessed
2. For each key factor, determine those key indicators that best help your management control the business.
3. Design the GMIS by disaggregating the key indicators as described previously.

B. Detailed Design

The following are the steps to the detailed design of a GMIS.

1. Once the overall designs of the charts have been completed, the elements of each chart must be defined.

2. Once the elements of each chart have been defined, it should be determined what data are required for the charts themselves (for example, actual, budget, or last year's data).

3. Once the data requirements and the element definitions have been made, linkage specifications must be accomplished—this means that the procedures for linking the graphics to the database or the data files must be outlined and written.

4. A small section of the overall design should be coded and tested to ensure that the linkage can be carried out efficiently.

C. Implementation

Once the overall design and the detail design have been done, the actual implementation of the GMIS must be performed. This includes actually getting the graphic system installed and set up on your computer system.*

The rest of the book is concerned with the overall design of the GMIS. For each major application (key factor) in financial control we have suggested those key indicators and supporting graphic sequences that could be used to control those applications. Each chart is described to help you understand what to look for. A sample set of charts has been prepared for each application to show you how the results might look.

CHAPTER 5

GRAPHIC FINANCIAL STATEMENT SEQUENCES

At each level of the organization, managers have key indicators shown in their reporting systems that give information concerning their level of responsibility. At many levels of the organization, the basic financial statements are used both to show overall structure of the organization and to provide information to extract many key indicators, such as in ratio analysis. These graphic financial statements and their supporting graphic sequences are an essential ingredient in the GMIS. This chapter describes the graphic financial statements and their supporting graphic sequences. Chapter 16 provides a summary of the key indicators as presented in the entire handbook.

Exhibit 5.1 lists the basic financial statements and the sequence in which they are to be shown. For example, the income statement is shown in the income sequence, the balance sheet is shown in the corporate control sequence, and so on. Each of the sequences is described in this chapter.

EXHIBIT 5.1

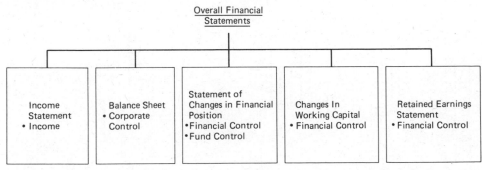

Author's Note: Throughout Chapters 5–15, the shaded areas indicate those charts that are used as examples for each chapter.

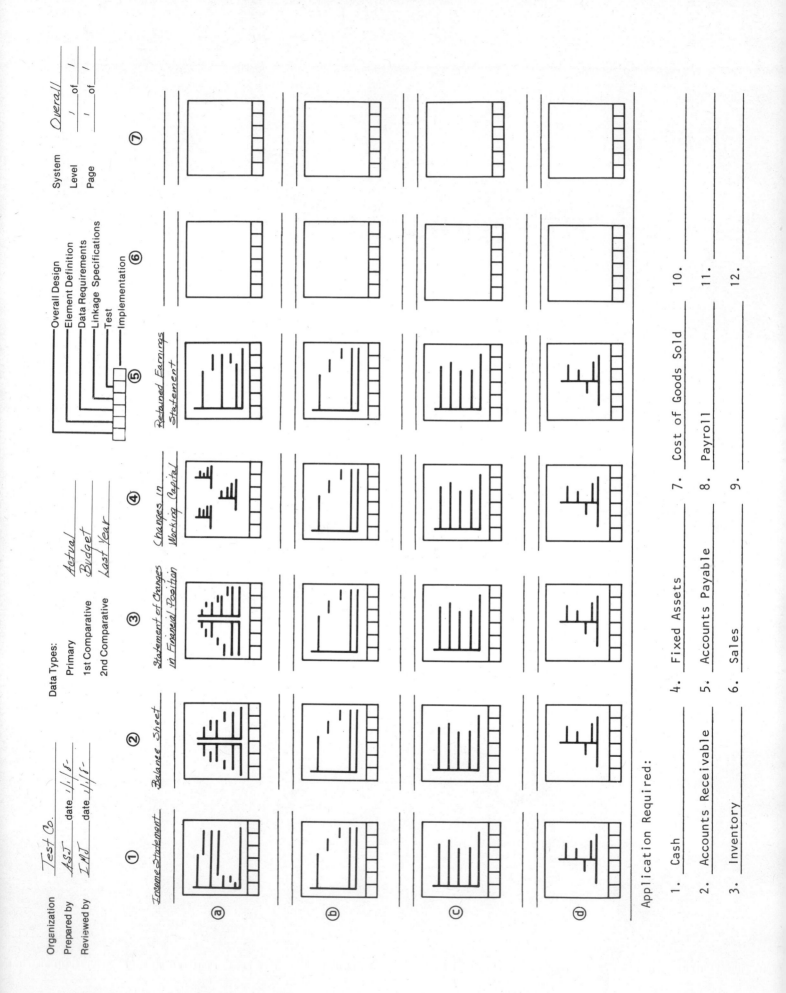

Row Col	Name of Chart	From	To	Descriptions
A1	Income Statement	Original	System: Income, Page 1 of 3, Chart A1	The Income Statement is the first key indicator of the overall corporate performance. The templates shown by this particular symbol will be similar for all corporations. However, each industry and each corporation within an industry will have its own unique pattern, like fingerprints. The analysts who become familiar with the templates of good performance will be able to match that template to their own company and to the companies they are analyzing to determine where and why the variances occur. The more often the patterns are observed and used for performance evaluation, the more useful they become. Disaggregation of the income statement is shown in the income system, describing both a corporate and responsibility sequence (see income system, page 1 of 3, Chart A1).
A2	Balance Sheet	Original	System: Corporate Control, Page 1 of 1, Chart A2	The Balance Sheet is a picture of the overall corporate investment and fund-raising strategy. The assets show the result of the corporate strategies of investment, and the liabilities and equity funding mix describe the relationships between those two strategies and the results of operations. The income statement is merged in the next three statements.
A3	Statement of Changes in Financial Position	Original	System: Financial Control, Level 1 of 1, Page 1 of 1, Chart A3	How the funds were obtained and how they were used during a stated period of time. The linkage between operations and capital expenditures are shown in the presentation of this statement.
A4	Changes in Working Capital	Original	System: Financial Control, Level 1 of 1, Page 1 of 1, Chart A4	Effect on funds of the use of current assets and current liabilities and the various cycles that affect them. The changes in working capital are mostly affected by operational decisions, whereas the fixed assets, long-term debt, and equity clearly reflect the long-term strategy of the corporation.
A5	Retained Earnings Statement	Original	System: Financial Control, Level 1 of 1, Page 1 of 1, Chart A5	Net changes in retained earnings as affected by operations, corporate investment, dividend decisions, and other equity transactions. It shows the net effect of all corporate activity.

EXHIBIT 5.2

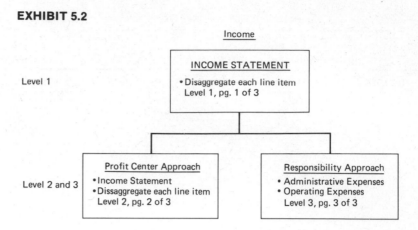

1.   THE INCOME SEQUENCE

The income statement is disaggregated into three distinct sequences as shown in Exhibit 5.2. Level 1 is the overall corporate control sequence. The line item components of the income statement are disaggregated and described by the detailed line items that support the total. The level 2 sequence describes a profit center approach. Level 3 shows a responsibility accounting sequence and assigns the operating and administrative expenses directly to the manager responsible for spending the money. Thus level 3 could be used as a further disaggregation of level 2 to control operating and adminstrative expenses. Where profit center accounting is not appropriate, the system could disaggregate directly from the income statement to the responsibility sequence.

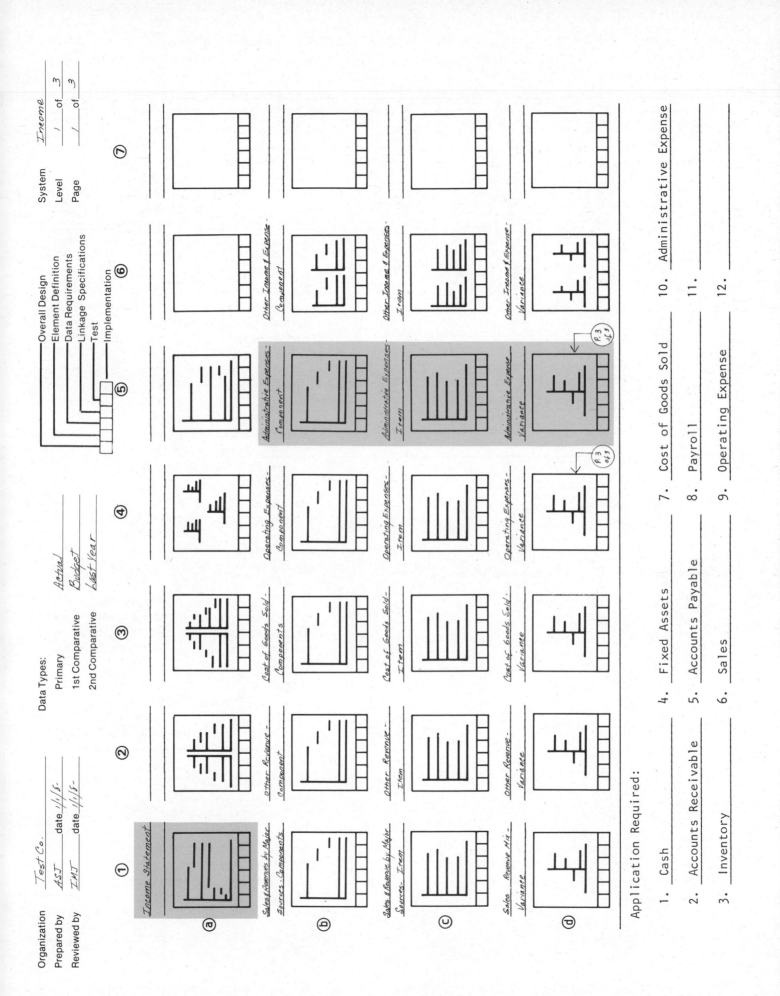

Organization _Test Co._
Prepared by _ASJ_ date _1/15-_
Reviewed by _IMJ_ date _1/15-_

System _Income_
Level _1_ of _3_
Page _1_ of _3_

Data Types:
Primary _Actual_
1st Comparative _Budget_
2nd Comparative _Last Year_

Overall Design
Element Definition
Data Requirements
Linkage Specifications
Test
Implementation

① ② ③ ④ ⑤ ⑥ ⑦

ⓐ Income Statement
ⓑ Sales & Revenues by Major Sources - Components
ⓒ Sales & Revenue by Major Sources - Item
ⓓ Sales Revenue Mix - Variance

Other Revenue - Component
Other Revenue - Item
Other Revenue - Variance

Cost of Goods Sold - Components
Cost of Goods Sold - Item
Cost of Goods Sold - Variance

Operating Expenses - Component
Operating Expenses - Item
Operating Expenses - Variance

Administrative Expenses - Component
Administrative Expenses - Item
Administrative Expense - Variance

Other Income & Expense - Component
Other Income & Expense - Item
Other Income & Expense - Variance

p. 3 of 3

Application Required:

1. Cash
2. Accounts Receivable
3. Inventory
4. Fixed Assets
5. Accounts Payable
6. Sales
7. Cost of Goods Sold
8. Payroll
9. Operating Expense
10. Administrative Expense
11.
12.

Row Col	Name of Chart	From	To	Descriptions
A1	Income Statement	System: Overall, Level <u>1</u> of <u>1</u>, Page <u>1</u> of <u>1</u>, Chart A1	B1–B6	First key indicator of the overall corporate performance. The templates shown by the income statement symbol will be similar for all corporations. However, each industry and each corportion within an industry will have its own unique pattern. Corporate managements will want to become familiar with the templates of good performance, either industry-specific or from their own sets of performance standards, and match the performances of their companies to that "good" template. They will want to determine why there is a difference in the performance pattern and this set of sequences shows how to disaggregate and isolate the differences. The more often the patterns are observed and used for performance evaluation, the more useful they become. Disaggregation of the income statement is shown by the line items below.
B1	Sales and Revenues by Major Sources— Components	A1	C1	Relative importance of each of the major sources of revenues to the overall corporate revenue. Each corporation will determine which way to categorize the major revenue elements. Each element will be further disaggregated at level 2, and in the sales/ gross margin system.
C1	Sales and Revenues by Major Sources— Item	B1	D1	Relative size of the individual income and revenue sources as compared to each other. The relative performance of the most important sources of revenue can be easily compared.
D1	Sales/Revenue Mix— Variance	C1	Sales System, Level <u>1</u> of <u>2</u>, Page <u>1</u> of <u>4</u>, Chart A1	Variance from plan and/or prior year for the various sales and revenue components. If further analysis is required, each component can be further disaggregated into similar sequences for each element starting with Chart B1. If further analysis of sales variance is required, the disaggregation would normally move to the sales system, level 1 of 2, page 1 of 4, Chart A1.
B2	Other Revenue— Component	A1	C2	Relative importance of the various components of other revenues as compared to the total other revenue.
C2	Other Revenue— Item	B2	D2	Relative size of the individual components of other revenues as compared to each

Row Col	Name of Chart	From	To	Descriptions
				other. It would be relatively easy to note any major shift in the relationship of other revenues.
D2	Other Revenue—Variance	C2	—	Variances from plan and/or prior year for the individual components of other revenues. This is the last chart shown in this sequence. If further analysis is required, each component of other revenue can be further disaggregated into similar sequences starting with B2.
B3	Cost of Goods Sold—Component	A1	C3	Relative importance of the various components of cost of goods sold as compared to the total cost of goods sold.
C3	Cost of Goods Sold—Item	B3	D3	Relative size of the individual components of cost of goods sold as compared to each other and which of the components are not performing as expected and might require additional control efforts.
D3	Cost of Goods Sold—Variance	C3	—	Variance from plan and/or prior year for the individual components of cost of goods sold. If further analysis is required, a complete system of cost of goods sold disaggregation can be found at the sales/gross margin and cost of goods sold systems, level 1 of 2, Chart A1 and A4.
B4	Operating Expenses—Component	A1	C4	Relative importance of the individual line items that make up the operating expense as compared to the total operating expenses.
C4	Operating Expenses—Item	B4	D4	Relative size of the individual line items that make up operating expenses as compared to each other. This chart shows the largest expense categories and provides a good picture of where controls or further analysis might be required.
D4	Operating Expenses—Variance	C4	System: Income Level 3 of 3, Chart A1	Variances from plan and/or prior year for the individual components that make up the line items of operating expenses. If further analysis is required, each of the line items can be further disaggregated into a similar sequence starting with B4. Also, a responsibility accounting system could be shown as described in system income, level 3 of 3, page 3 of 3, Charts A1 and subsequent.

Row Col	Name of Chart	From	To	Descriptions
B5	Administrative Expenses— Component	A1	C5	Relative size of the individual line items that make up the administrative expenses as compared to the total administrative expense.
C5	Administrative Expenses—Item	B5	D5	Relative size of the individual line items that make up administrative expense as compared to each other. The chart also shows which line items account for the largest expenses and where additional controls might be required.
D5	Administrative Expense— Variance	C5	System: Income, Level 3 of 3, Page 3 of 3, Chart A3	Variance from plan and/or prior year for the line items that make up administrative expenses. If further analysis is required, each of the line items could be further disaggregated into similar sequences starting with B5. In addition, the responsibility disaggregation is shown in System Income, Level 3 of 3, Page 3 of 3, Chart A3.

NOTE: Cost of goods sold, operating expenses, and administrative expenses all contain payroll expenses. If further disaggregation of payroll is required, they can be found in the payroll system, level 1, page 1 of 4, Charts A1 through A4.

Row Col	Name of Chart	From	To	Descriptions
B6	Other Income and Expenses— Components	A1	C6	Twin component chart used to show other income and other expenses on one chart. If either is unusually significant to the corporation, separate charts might be more desirable. On the left-hand side is the other income and on the right-hand side, the other expenses. The left-hand side shows the relative importance of the line items that make up other income as compared to the total of other income. The right-hand side shows the relative importance of the individual line items that make up the other expenses as compared to the total expenses.
C6	Other Income and Expenses—Item	B6	D6	Left-hand side shows the relative size of the individual line items that make up other income as compared to each other. The right-hand side shows the relative size of the individual expenses as compared to each other.
D6	Other Income and Expenses— Variance	C6	System: Income, Level 2 of 3, Page 2 of 3, Chart B6	Left-hand side shows the variances from plan and/or prior year by the individual line items that make up the other income. The right-hand side shows the variance

76

Row Col	Name of Chart	From	To	Descriptions
				from plan and/or prior year for the line items that make up the other expenses. If further analysis is required, each of the various line items can be further disaggregated into graphic sequences starting at B6. Other income and expenses are also disaggregated by profit center as shown in system income, level 2 of 3, page 2 of 3, Chart B6.

The following is a description of a profit center disaggregation showing responsibility for profits by profit center. Level 1 of 3 is a corporate disaggregation and level 3 is a responsibility accounting disaggregation of expenses.

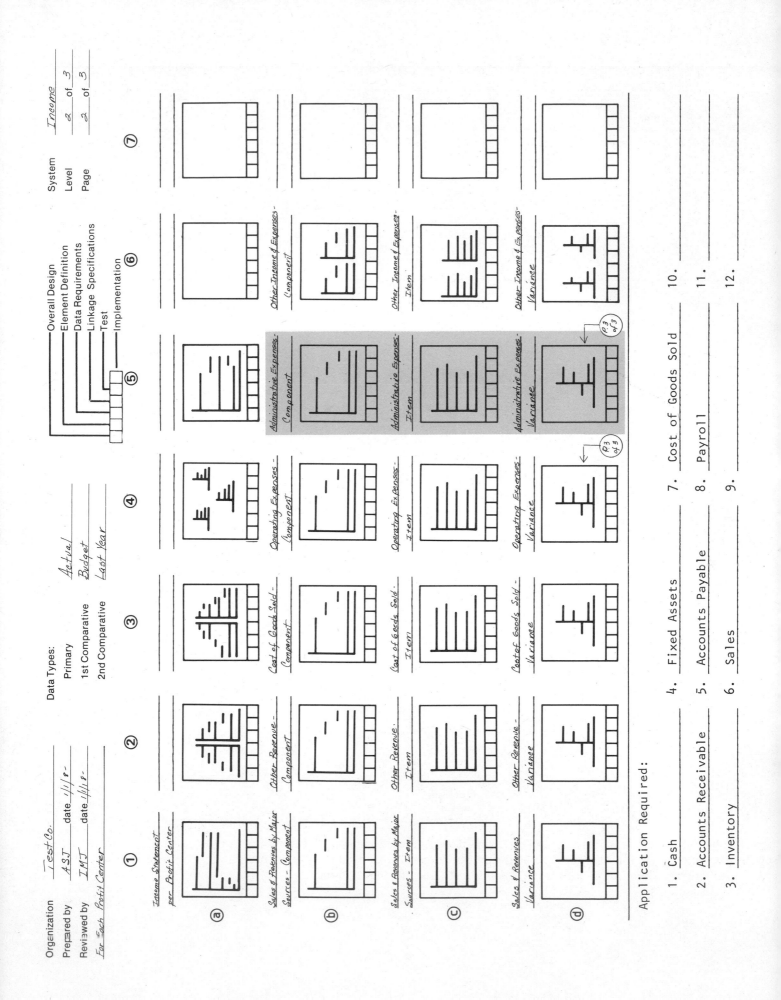

Organization _Test Co._
Prepared by _ASJ_ date _1/1/8-_
Reviewed by _IMJ_ date _1/1/8-_
For Each Profit Center

Data Types:
Primary _Actual_
1st Comparative _Budget_
2nd Comparative _Last Year_

Overall Design
Element Definition
Data Requirements
Linkage Specifications
Test
Implementation

① ② ③ ④ ⑤ ⑥ ⑦

(a) _Income Statement per Profit Center_

(b) _Sales & Revenues by Major Sources - Component_ | _Other Revenue - Component_ | _Cost of Goods Sold - Component_ | _Operating Expenses - Component_ | _Administrative Expenses - Component_ | _Other Income & Expenses - Component_

(c) _Sales & Revenues by Major Sources - Item_ | _Other Revenue - Item_ | _Cost of Goods Sold - Item_ | _Operating Expenses - Item_ | _Administrative Expenses - Item_ | _Other Income & Expenses - Item_

(d) _Sales & Revenues - Variance_ | _Other Revenue - Variance_ | _Cost of Goods Sold - Variance_ | _Operating Expenses - Variance_ | _Administrative Expenses - Variance_ | _Other Income & Expenses - Variance_

_p.3 of 3_

Application Required:

1. Cash
2. Accounts Receivable
3. Inventory
4. Fixed Assets
5. Accounts Payable
6. Sales
7. Cost of Goods Sold
8. Payroll
9.
10.
11.
12.

Row Col	Name of Chart	From	To	Descriptions
A1	Income Statement Per Profit Center	System: Income, Level 1 of 3, Page 1 of 3, Chart A1	B1	Basically shows the same pattern as the overall corporate system. There will be differences, however, that identify the operating pattern of the individual profit centers. The profit center income statement will be disaggregated in the same way as the corporate income statement. The only difference is that line item responsibility can be assigned to the lower levels. The templates of "good" performance described in level 1 can also be used to evaluate profit center performance. Performance variances can be analyzed in the following sequences. The more often the patterns are observed and used for performance evaluation, the more useful they become. Disaggregation of the income statement is shown by the various line items below.
B1	Sales and Revenues by Major Sources—Component	A1	C1	Relative importance of the individual revenue sources as compared to total profit center revenue.
C1	Sales and Revenue by Major Sources—Item	B1	D1	Relative size of the individual income and revenue components as compared to each other and the largest source of revenues for the profit center.
D1	Sales and Revenues—Variance	C1	System: Sales, Level 1 of 2, Page 1 of 4, Chart A1	Variance from plan and/or prior year for the various sales and revenue sources. If further analysis is required, each component can be further disaggregated into similar sequences starting at B1. If further analysis of sales variance is required, the disaggregation would normally move to the sales system, level 1 of 2, page 1 of 4, Chart A1.
B2	Other Revenue—Component	A1	C2	Relative importance of the various sources of other revenues for the profit center as compared to the total other revenue.
C2	Other Revenue—Item	B2	D2	Relative size of the individual sources of other revenue as compared to each other.
D2	Other Revenue—Variance	C2	—	Variances from plan and/or prior year for the individual sources of other revenue. This is the last chart shown in this sequence. If further analysis is required, each source of other revenue can be further disaggregated into similar sequences start-

Row Col	Name of Chart	From	To	Descriptions
				ing with B2. At this point it may be necessary to use the books of record for more detailed analysis.
B3	Cost of Goods Sold— Component	A1	C3	Relative importance of the various components of the cost of goods sold as compared to the total cost of goods sold for the profit center. The cost of goods sold is categorized the same as the sales revenues for comparison.
C3	Cost of Goods Sold— Item	B3	D3	Relative size of the individual components of cost of goods sold as compared to each other. The pattern of charts B3 and C3 should closely approximate the pattern of Charts B1 and C1. The two charts could be combined into a co-relationship chart as shown in the sales/gross margin system.
D3	Cost of Goods Sold— Variance	C3	System: Cost of Goods Sold Level $\underline{1}$ of $\underline{2}$, Page 1 of 4, Charts A1 and A4	Variance from plan and/or prior year for the individual components of cost of goods sold. If further analysis is required, a complete system of cost of goods sold describing the various relationships is found at the cost of goods sold system, level 1 of 2, page 1 of 4, Charts A1 and A4.
B4	Operating Expenses— Component	A1	C4	Relative importance of the individual line items that make up the overall operating expenses as compared to the total operating expenses for the profit center.
C4	Operating Expenses—Item	B4	D4	Relative size of the individual line items that constitute operating expenses as compared to each other.
D4	Operating Expenses—Variance	C4	System: Income, Level $\underline{3}$ of $\underline{3}$, Chart A1	Variances from plan and/or prior year for the individual components that make up the line items for operating expenses. If further analysis is required, line items can be further disaggregated into a similar sequence to that starting at B4. Also, a responsibility accounting system can disaggregate the expenses to the lowest level of management within the profit center as described in income system, level 3 of 3, page 3 of 3.
B5	Administrative Expenses— Component	A1	C5	Relative size of the individual line items that make up the administrative expenses as compared to the total administrative expense.
C5	Administrative Expenses—Item	B5	D5	Relative size of the individual line items that make up the profit center administrative expenses as compared to each other.

Row Col	Name of Chart	From	To	Descriptions
D5	Administrative Expense—Variance	C5	System: Income Level 3 of 3, page 3 of 3, Chart A3	Variance from plan and/or prior year for the line items that make up administrative expenses. If further analysis is required, each of the line items could be further disaggregated into similar sequences starting with B5. In addition, the responsibility disaggregation is shown in income system, level 3 of 3, page 3 of 3, Chart A3.
B6	Other Income and Expenses— Component	A1	C6	Combination chart using two component charts to describe the source of other income and other expenses. On the left-hand side is the other income and on the right-hand side, the other expenses. The left-hand side shows the relative importance of the line items that make up other income as compared to the total of other income. The right-hand side shows the relative importance of the individual line items that make up the other expenses as compared to the total expenses.

NOTE: Cost of goods sold, operating expenses, and administrative expenses all contain payroll expenses. If further disaggregation is required for the profit center, the disaggregation can be found in the payroll system, level 2, Page 1 of 8, Charts A1 through A4.

Row Col	Name of Chart	From	To	Descriptions
C6	Other Income and Expenses—Item	B6	D6	Left-hand side shows the relative size of the individual line items that make up other income as compared to each other. The right-hand side shows the relative size of the individual expenses as compared to each other.
D6	Other Income and Expenses—Variance	C6	—	Left-hand side shows the variances from plan and/or prior year by the individual line items that make up the other income. The right-hand side shows the variance from plan and/or prior year for the line items that make up the other expense. If further analysis is required, each of the various line items can be further disaggregated into graphic sequences starting at B6. No further sequences are shown.

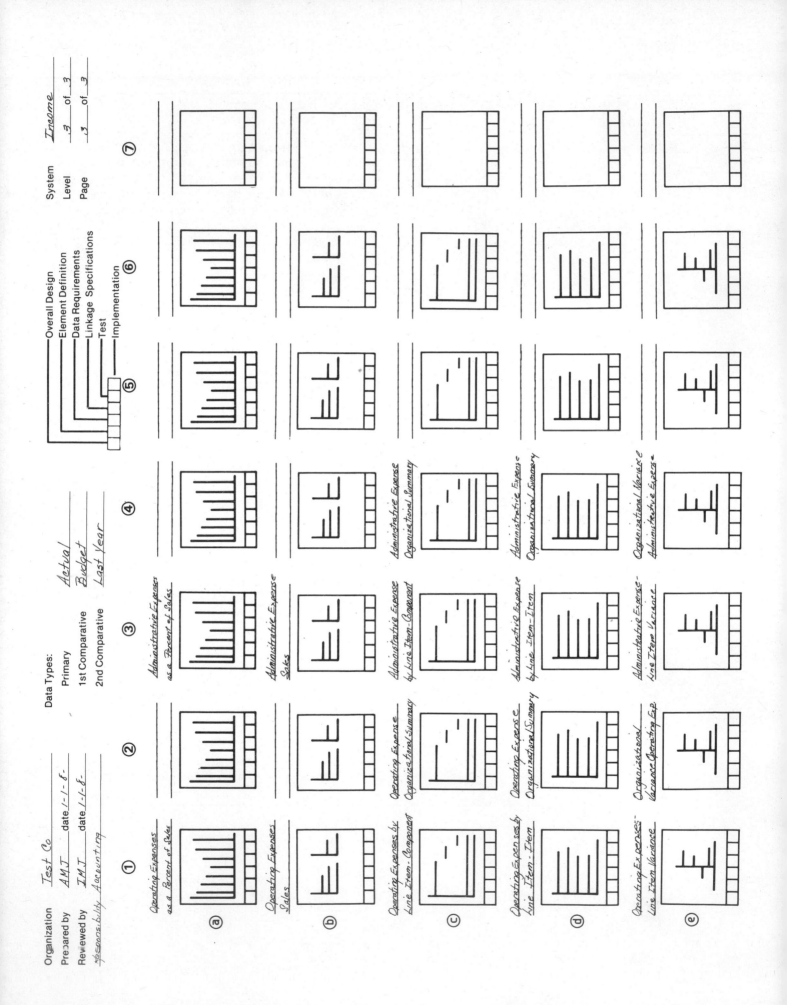

Organization _Test Co_
Prepared by _AMJ_ date _1-1-8-_
Reviewed by _IMJ_ date _1-1-8-_
Responsibility Accounting

Data Types:
Primary _Actual_
1st Comparative _Budget_
2nd Comparative _Last Year_

Overall Design
Element Definition
Data Requirements
Linkage Specifications
Test
Implementation

⑤ ⑥

System _Income_
Level _3_ of _3_
Page _3_ of _3_

① ② ③ ④ ⑤ ⑥ ⑦

ⓐ _Operating Expenses as a Percent of Sales_
Administrative Expenses as a Percent of Sales

ⓑ _Operating Expenses Sales_
Administrative Expense Sales

ⓒ _Operating Expenses by Line Item - Component_
Administrative Expense by Line Item - Component _Administrative Expense Organizational Summary_
Operating Expense Organizational Summary

ⓓ _Operating Expenses by Line Item - Item_
Administrative Expense by Line Item - Item _Administrative Expense Organizational Summary_
Operating Expense Organizational Summary

ⓔ _Operating Expenses - Line Item Variance_
Administrative Expense - Line Item Variance _Organizational Variance Administrative Expense_
Organizational Variance Operating Exp.

NOTE: This is the system that controls expense spending by responsibility area—the responsibility accounting system sequence. This sequence shows how each level of the organization has spent corporate resources they control as compared to their expense budget. At the lowest organizational level, individual managers are held accountable for specific line items and variance from budget for each line item is shown. The total of their actual spending, their budget, and the variances therefrom are carried to the next level of management. The next level of management is responsible for its own line items and the related variances, plus the total spending for each of the managers under it. This level of the chart shows the individual line items for the managers and their total spending, plus a one-element presentation of the total spending for each manager. The same process of summary by responsibility area occurs until all levels of management are shown. This graphic sequence shows the relationship of spending control by responsibility area.

Description of System <u>Income</u>   Level <u>3</u> of <u>3</u>   Page <u>3</u> of <u>3</u>

Row Col	Name of Chart	From	To	Descriptions
A1	Operating Expenses as a Percentage of Sales	System: Income, Level <u>2</u> of <u>3</u>, Page <u>2</u> of <u>3</u>, Chart D4	B1	Trend of total operating expenses as a percentage of sales. Variances from plan and/or prior year are easily discernable. Also, significant trends can be spotted rapidly and additional control exerted if necessary.
B1	N: Operating Expenses D: Sales	A1	C1	Relative size of the operating expenses to sales. If the change in the ratio is due to a change in the relative size of the operating expense, then the disaggregate analysis of that expense would take place starting at C1 below. If the change in the ratio is due to a change in the relative size of sales, then the disaggregate analysis would start with the sales system.
C1	Operating Expenses by Line Item—Component	B1	D1	One for each of the operating managers who have spending responsibility. This chart shows the relative importance of each of the line items as compared to the total operating expenses over which the manager has direct spending control. The total of these expenses will be shown as one element on the responsibility chart sequence starting at C2.
D1	Operating Expenses Line Item—Item	C1	E1	Relative importance of the line items as compared to each other over which the manager has direct spending control. The chart shows which of the items is the largest expense and where additional controls may be required.
E1	Operating Expenses Line Item—Variance	D1	—	Variance from plan and/or prior year for the individual line items of the responsible manager. If further analysis is required at this level, it might be necessary to go directly to the books of record.

Row Col	Name of Chart	From	To	Descriptions
C2	Operating Expense Organizational Summary	B1	D2	Companion chart to all of those shown in the sequence starting at C1. This sequence shows all of the operating expenses spent by each of the cost centers reporting to a manager, including their own. One element in this chart is the total of each of the charts in the previous sequence. It shows the relative importance of the individual cost centers controlled by this manager as compared to the total expenses this manager controls.
D2	Operating Expense and Organizational Summary	C2	E2	Relative importance of the individual cost centers controlled by this manager as compared to each other. This chart shows which of the cost centers is most off budget.
E2	Organizational Variance—Operating Expense	D2	C1 If Required	Variance from plan and/or prior year for the cost centers controlled by this manager. If further analysis is required, each of the cost centers can be disaggregated as described in the sequence starting at C1.
A3	Administrative Expenses as a Percentage of Sales	System: Income, Level 2 of 3, Page 2 of 3, Chart D5	B3	Trend of total administrative expenses as a percentage of sales. Variances from planned and/or prior year are easily discernable. Also, significant trends can be spotted rapidly and additional control exerted, if necessary.
B3	N: Administrative Expense D: Sales	A3	C3 C4	Relative size of the administrative expenses to sales. If the change of the ratio is due to a change of the relative size of the administrative expense, the disaggregation would take place starting at C3 below. If a change in the ratio is due to a change in the relative size of sales, then a disaggregate analysis would start with the sales system.
C3	Administrative Expense by Line Item—Component	B3	D3	One of these charts for each of the administrative managers who have spending responsibility. This chart shows the relative importance of each of the line items as shown to a total administrative expense over which the manager has direct spending control. The total of these expenses will be shown as one element on the responsibility chart sequence starting at C4.
D3	Administrative Expense by Line Item—Item	C3	E3	Relative importance of the line items as compared to each other over which the manager has the direct spending control. The chart shows which of the items is the

Row Col	Name of Chart	From	To	Descriptions
				largest expense and where additional controls may be required.
E3	Administrative Expense by Line Item—Variance	D3	—	Variance from plan and/or prior year for the individual line items of the responsible manager. If further analysis is required at this level, it might be necessary to go directly to the books of record.
C4	Administrative Expense— Organizational Summary	B3	D4	Companion chart to all of those shown in the sequence starting at C3. This sequence shows all of the administrative expenses spent by each of the cost centers reporting to a manager, including their own. One element in this chart is a total of each of the charts in the previous sequence. It shows the relative importance of the individual cost centers controlled by this manager as compared to the total expenses this manager controls.
D4	Administrative Expense— Organizational Summary	C4	E4	Relative importance of the individual cost centers controlled by this manager as compared to each other.
E4	Administrative Expense— Organizational Variance	D4	C3	Variance from plan and/or prior year for the cost centers controlled by this manager. If further analysis is required, each of the cost centers can be aggregated as described in the sequence starting at C3.

2. THE INCOME STATEMENT

Chart 10-082 shows an example of a graphic income statement. The legend on the top left-hand corner illustrates that the dark bars show actual 1982 data and the shaded bars show budgeted 1982 data. The legend on the top right-hand corner shows that the dollars are in thousands. To read the chart, note that sales plus other revenue equals total revenue. Total revenue minus cost of goods sold equals gross margin. The gross margin minus operating expenses minus the administrative and other expenses equals net income. The purpose of this chart is to show the pattern of earnings. Here we can see that the overall pattern of earnings is as budgeted although there are some differences in individual items.

Each of the items listed in the chart can be further analyzed with supporting charts. The supporting charts could range in number from one or two charts to a whole system of supporting charts.

For example, if after looking at the income statement you wanted to see what made up administrative expenses, you might look at Charts 10-083, 10-084, and 10-085 which separate administrative expenses by type. 10-083

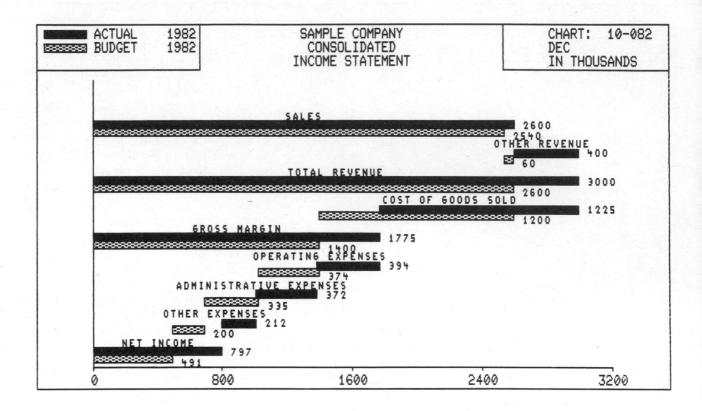

ACTUAL 1982
BUDGET 1982

SAMPLE COMPANY
CONSOLIDATED
INCOME STATEMENT

CHART: 10-082
DEC
IN THOUSANDS

SALES 2600
2540
OTHER REVENUE 400
60
TOTAL REVENUE 3000
2600
COST OF GOODS SOLD 1225
1200
GROSS MARGIN 1775
1400
OPERATING EXPENSES 394
374
ADMINISTRATIVE EXPENSES 372
335
OTHER EXPENSES 212
200
NET INCOME 797
491

0   800   1600   2400   3200

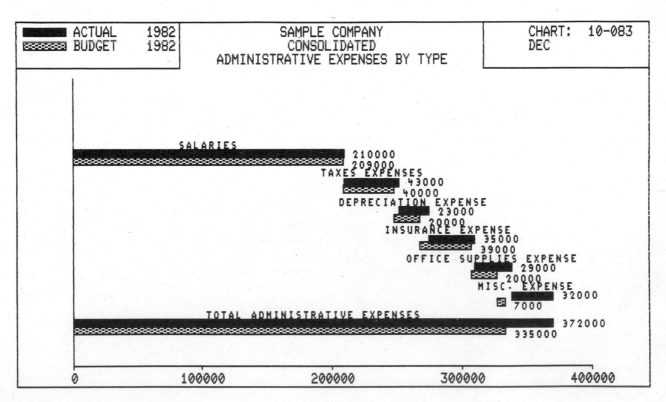

ACTUAL 1982
BUDGET 1982

SAMPLE COMPANY
CONSOLIDATED
ADMINISTRATIVE EXPENSES BY TYPE

CHART: 10-083
DEC

SALARIES 210000
209000
TAXES EXPENSES 43000
40000
DEPRECIATION EXPENSE 23000
20000
INSURANCE EXPENSE 35000
39000
OFFICE SUPPLIES EXPENSE 29000
20000
MISC. EXPENSE 32000
7000
TOTAL ADMINISTRATIVE EXPENSES 372000
335000

0   100000   200000   300000   400000

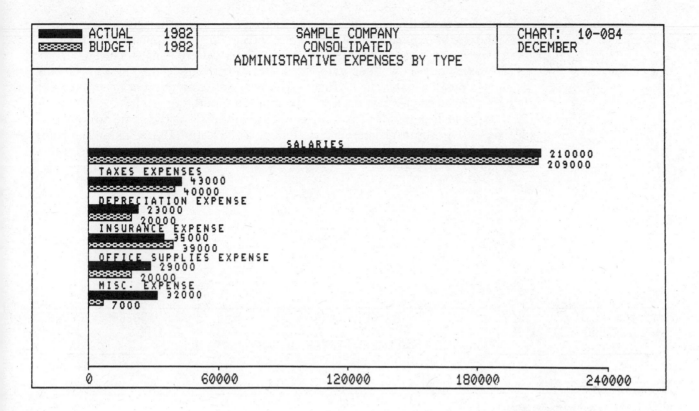

SAMPLE COMPANY
CONSOLIDATED
ADMINISTRATIVE EXPENSES BY TYPE

CHART: 10-084
DECEMBER

ACTUAL 1982
BUDGET 1982

SALARIES 210000 / 209000
TAXES EXPENSES 43000 / 40000
DEPRECIATION EXPENSE 23000 / 20000
INSURANCE EXPENSE 35000 / 39000
OFFICE SUPPLIES EXPENSE 29000 / 20000
MISC. EXPENSE 32000 / 7000

0   60000   120000   180000   240000

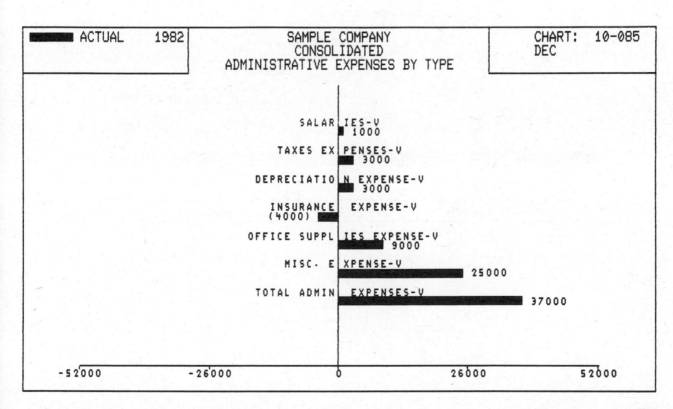

SAMPLE COMPANY
CONSOLIDATED
ADMINISTRATIVE EXPENSES BY TYPE

CHART: 10-085
DEC

ACTUAL 1982

SALARIES-V 1000
TAXES EXPENSES-V 3000
DEPRECIATION EXPENSE-V 3000
INSURANCE EXPENSE-V (4000)
OFFICE SUPPLIES EXPENSE-V 9000
MISC. EXPENSE-V 25000
TOTAL ADMIN EXPENSES-V 37000

-52000   -26000   0   26000   52000

87

shows the overall make-up of administrative expenses. Chart 10-084 compares each type of expense; salaries are clearly the largest expense. Chart 10-085 shows the variances from budget for administrative expenses. The bars to the left of the axis show a negative variance and the bars to the right of the axis show a positive variance. Office supplies expense and miscellaneous expense experienced the largest positive variance from budget.

Another look at administrative expense might show the same administrative expense by division. Charts 10-086, 10-087, and 10-088 show the components, items, and variances from budget, respectively, of administrative expense by division.

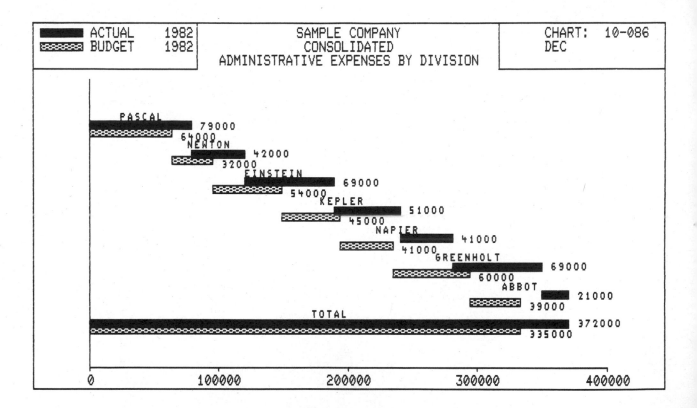

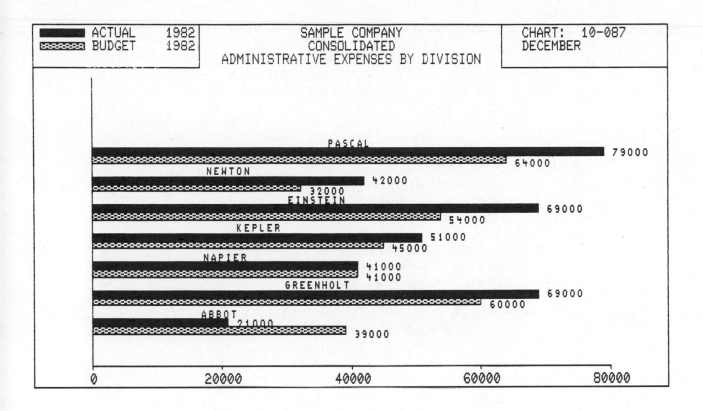

ACTUAL 1982
BUDGET 1982

SAMPLE COMPANY
CONSOLIDATED
ADMINISTRATIVE EXPENSES BY DIVISION

CHART: 10-087
DECEMBER

PASCAL 79000
64000
NEWTON 42000
32000
EINSTEIN 69000
54000
KEPLER 51000
45000
NAPIER 41000
41000
GREENHOLT 69000
60000
ABBOT 21000
39000

0   20000   40000   60000   80000

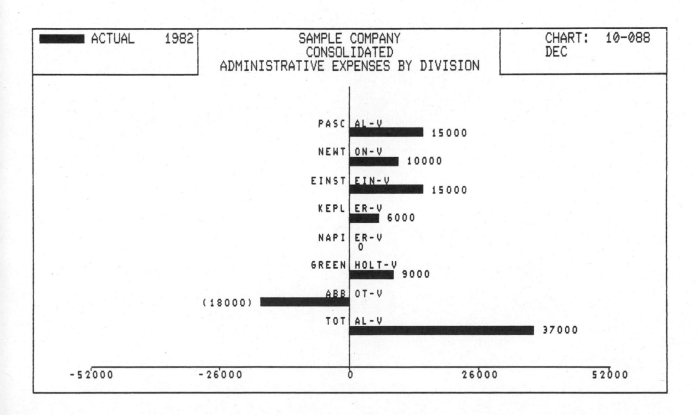

ACTUAL 1982

SAMPLE COMPANY
CONSOLIDATED
ADMINISTRATIVE EXPENSES BY DIVISION

CHART: 10-088
DEC

PASCAL-V 15000
NEWTON-V 10000
EINSTEIN-V 15000
KEPLER-V 6000
NAPIER-V 0
GREENHOLT-V 9000
ABBOT-V (18000)
TOTAL-V 37000

-52000   -26000   0   26000   52000

89

3. CORPORATE CONTROL—THE BALANCE SHEET

The balance sheet outlined in Exhibit 5.3 is a picture of the results of the investment and funding strategy of the corporation. The left-hand graph shows where corporate management has decided to invest the stockholders' money to create a viable business and to provide an acceptable return for the investors. The right-hand graph shows where the corporation obtained the funds necessary to achieve the approved investment mix. Asset control is designed to show the effectiveness of assets utilized to create revenues. Each industry will have an investment pattern that forms an acceptable template of asset mix necessary to earn a profit. Major variances from such a template should be closely analyzed for problems or opportunities. The liability side is controlled by a similar template of industry-set funding patterns so the credit worthiness of the company can be maintained and the best possible leverage within the industry's standards are utilized to ensure an appropriate return on equity. Control concepts are shown in the sequences that disaggregate from the balance sheet.

EXHIBIT 5.3

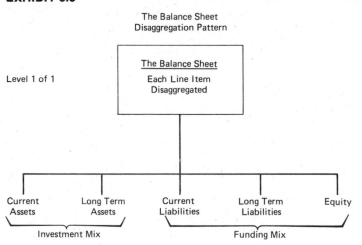

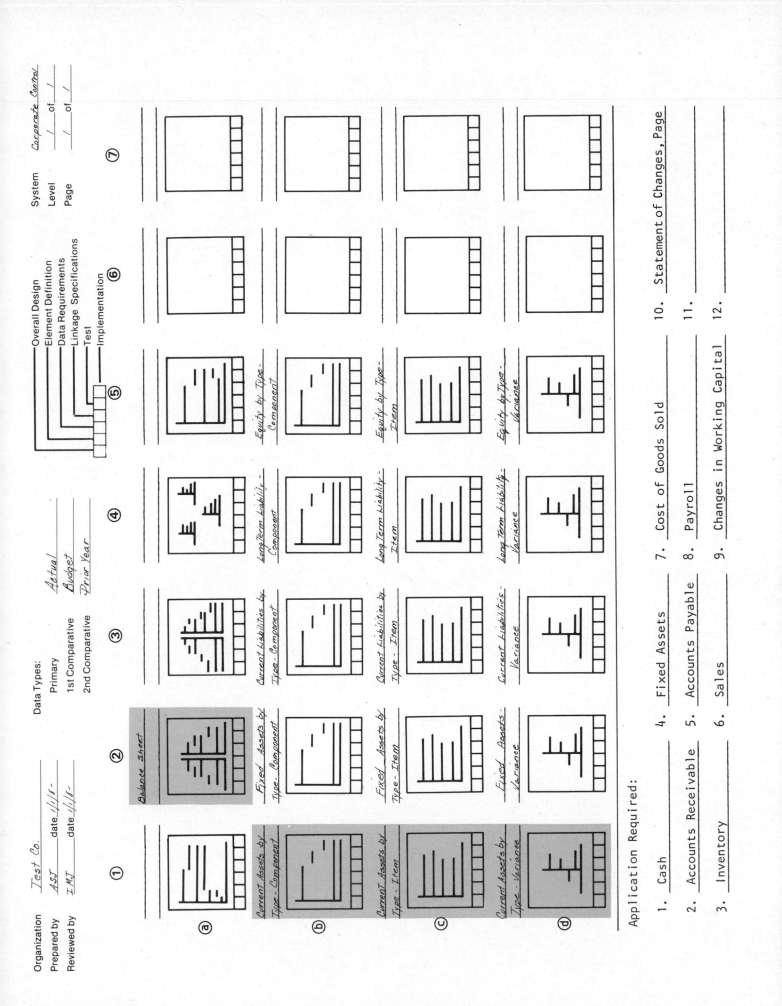

Organization: Test Co.
Prepared by: ASJ date 1/1/5-
Reviewed by: IMJ date 1/1/5-

System: Corporate Control
Level: 1 of 1
Page: 1 of 1

Data Types:
Primary: Actual
1st Comparative: Budget
2nd Comparative: Prior Year

Overall Design
Element Definition
Data Requirements
Linkage Specifications
Test
Implementation

① ② ③ ④ ⑤ ⑥ ⑦

ⓐ
ⓑ Current Assets by Type-Component
ⓒ Current Assets by Type-Item
ⓓ Current Assets by Type-Variance

② Balance Sheet
Fixed Assets by Type-Component
Fixed Assets by Type-Item
Fixed Assets-Variance

③ Current Liabilities by Type-Component
Current Liabilities by Type-Item
Current Liabilities-Variance

④ Long Term Liability-Component
Long Term Liability-Item
Long Term Liability-Variance

⑤ Equity by Type-Component
Equity by Type-Item
Equity by Type-Variance

Application Required:

1. Cash
2. Accounts Receivable
3. Inventory
4. Fixed Assets
5. Accounts Payable
6. Sales
7. Cost of Goods Sold
8. Payroll
9. Changes in Working Capital
10. Statement of Changes, Page
11. _____
12. _____

Description of System Corporate Level 1 of 1 Control Page 1 of 1

Row Col	Name of Chart	From	To	Descriptions
A2	Balance Sheet	System: Overall, Level 1 of 1, Page 1 of 1	B1-B5	Co-relationship chart using two component graphs. The left-hand graph shows the relative importance of the various types of corporate investments as compared to the total corporate assets. An examination of the asset mix shows a template of the corporate investment strategy. The right-hand graph describes the relative importance of the various sources of funds—liabilities and equity as compared to the overall funding of the corporation. Just as the asset side describes the corporate investment strategy, the liability and equity side describes the corporate funding strategy.
B1	Current Assets by Type—Component	A2	C1	Expanded detail of the current assets element shown on the balance sheet. The chart shows the relative importance of the detailed components of current assets as compared to the total current assets.
C1	Current Assets by Type—Item	B1	D1	Relative size of the detailed components of current assets as compared to each other. This chart is also useful for seeing any preliminary problems in current asset control as shown by major changes in plan.
D1	Current Assets by Type—Variance	C1	System: Financial Control, Level 1 of 1, Page 1 of 1, Chart A4	Variance from prior year and/or budget for the detailed components of current assets. It is one of the basic charts used to describe the use of funds in the financial control section, control, level 1 of 1, page 1 of 1, Chart A4. See financial control for a further picture of how the sequences link together.
B2	Long-Term Assets by Type—Component	A2	C2	Relative importance of the detailed components of long-term assets as compared to the total long-term assets. This chart would show any change in the pattern of asset mix.
C2	Long-Term Assets by Type—Item	B2	E2	Relative size of the detailed components of long-term assets as compared to each other. This chart would show any change in the pattern of asset mix as the result of a change in corporate investment strategy.
D2	Long-Term Assets—Variance	C2	System: Financial Control, Level 1 of 1, Page 1 of 1, Chart A3	Variance from prior year and/or plan for the detailed components of long-term assets. Major purchases or sales would be fully apparent at this point. Further analy-

Row Col	Name of Chart	From	To	Descriptions
				sis of this chart is used in the financial control section where these items become part of the statement of changes in the financial position shown in financial control system, level 1 of 1, page 1 of 1, Chart A3.
B3	Current Liabilities by Type—Component	A3	C3	Relative importance of the detailed components of current liabilities as compared to the total liability.
C3	Current Liabilities by Type—Item	B3	D3	Relative importance of the detailed components of current liabilities as compared to each other. Major changes in the credit situations of the firm can be easily spotted by major changes in the current liability pattern. Significant growth in corporate activities could also be reflected as the liability section changes. Any change in the mix of current liabilities would be apparent.
D3	Current Liabilities—Variance	C3	System: Financial Control, Level 1 of 1, Page 1 of 1, Chart A4	Variance from plan and/or prior year of the detailed components of current liabilities. Further analysis of this chart is shown in the financial control system where this chart becomes a part of the description of the change in working capital (see financial control, level 1 of 1, page 1 of 1, Chart A4).
B4	Long-Term Liability—Component	A2	C4	Relative importance of the detailed components of long-term liability as compared to the long-term liabilities.
C4	Long-Term Liability—Item	B4	D4	Relative size of the detailed components of long-term liabilities as compared to each other. Any major funding, refunding, or repayment would be readily apparent in this chart.
D4	Long-Term Liability—Variance	C4	System: Financial Control, Level 1 of 1, Page 1 of 1, Chart A3	Variance from last year and/or plan for the detailed components of long term liabilities. Further analysis of this chart is provided in the financial control system, level 1 of 1, page 1 of 1, Chart A3.
B5	Equity by Type—Component	A2	C5	Relative importance of the detailed components of equity funding, including retained earnings, as compared to the total equity funding.
C5	Equity by Type—Item	B5	D5	Relative importance of the detailed components of equity funding as compared to each other. It shows the major source of equity funding.

Row Col	Name of Chart	From	To	Descriptions
D5	Equity by Type— Variance	C5	System: Financial Control, Level 1 of 1, Page 1 of 1, Chart A3	Variance from prior year and/or budget points to any major changes in equity funding. Further analysis of these vari- ances is provided in the financial control, level 1 of 1, page 1 of 1, Chart A3.

3. THE BALANCE SHEET

Chart 10-096 shows an example of a balance sheet presented in a graphic
format. The legend in the top left-hand corner illustrates that the dark black
bars show actual 1982 data. The shaded bars show Budget 1982 data. The
legend on the top right-hand corner shows that the data are in thousands.

The plot on the left shows assets, and the plot on the right shows liabilities
and owners equity. Look at the left-hand plot (assets). To read the chart note
that cash plus accounts receivable plus inventory equals total current assets.
The next three bars show the make-up of net property, plant, and equipment.
Property, plant, and equipment less accumulated depreciation equals net
property, plant, and equipment. Now add current assets plus net property,
plant, and equipment to other long-term assets and goodwill and you get
total assets.

Looking at the right-hand plot, accounts payable plus the current notes
payable plus accrued taxes equals total current liabilities. Add in long-term
liabilities and we have total liabilities. The next three bars show the make-up
of equity. Common stock plus retained earnings equals total equity. Now add
total liabilities and total equity and we have total liabilities and equity.

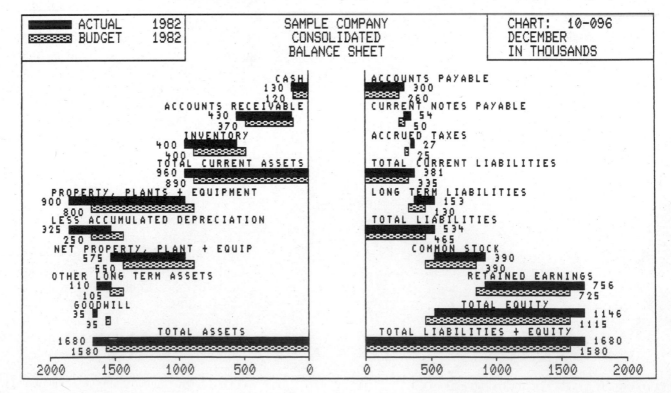

Each of the items on the balance sheet can be further supported by more detailed charts. The supporting charts range from one or two to a whole system of charts, depending upon the significance of the supporting information.

For example, Charts 10-079, 10-080, and 10-081 show a breakdown of inventory by division. Chart 10-079 shows the amounts of inventory in each

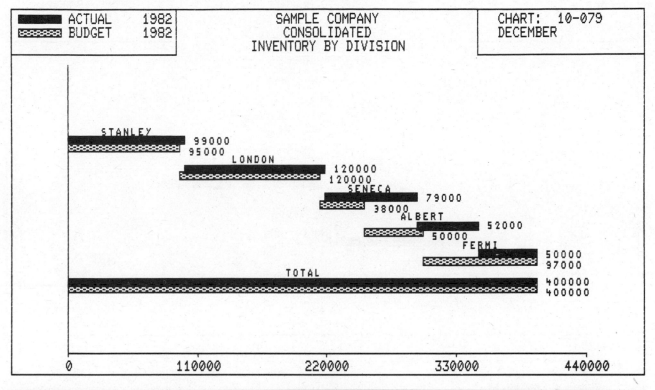

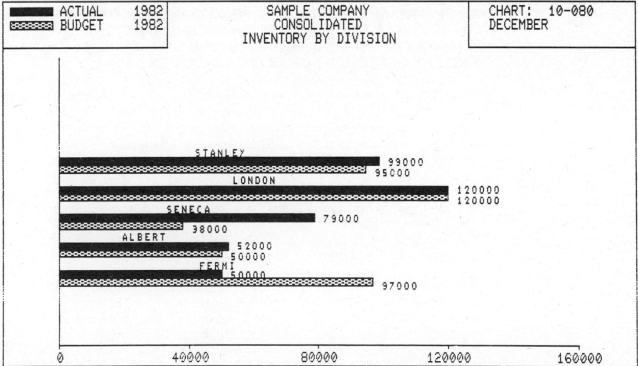

division that add up to total inventory. Chart 10-080 compares the amount of inventory in each division to each other. Chart 10-081 shows the variances from budget in inventory by division.

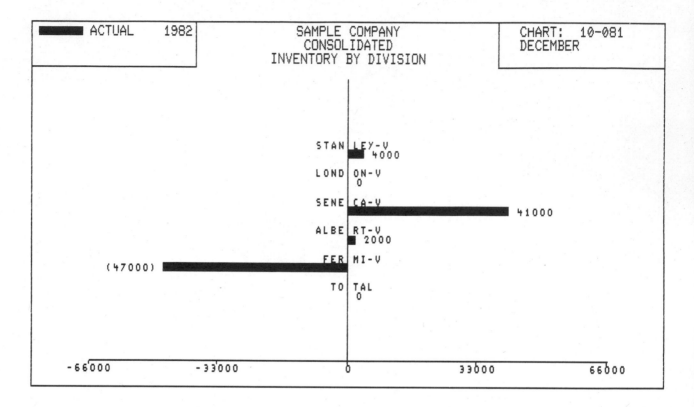

4. FINANCIAL CONTROL AND FUND CONTROL: GRAPHING THE STATEMENT OF CHANGES OF FINANCIAL POSITION, THE STATEMENT OF CHANGES IN WORKING CAPITAL, AND THE STATEMENT OF RETAINED EARNINGS

There are two systems described in this section; the first, financial control, provides a historical perspective of the sources and uses of funds on a working capital basis. The statements graphed in this sequence include the statement of changes in financial position, the statement of changes in working capital, and the statement of retained earnings. The second system described in this section is the financial control sequence. The financial control sequence provides a view into the future by providing a 12-month rolling picture of expected source and use of funds. This particular view is based upon cash rather than working capital.

A. Financial Control

This system of three charts and their subsequent disaggregation is one of the major views of company control used in a corporate system. Exhibit 5.4 describes the flow of this system. Here you see the results of all the activities of a corporation as compared to the plan for controlling corporate funds. The fund cycle shown in this sequence is prepared on a working capital basis to

EXHIBIT 5.4

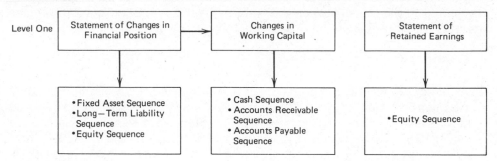

take full cognizance of the effect of the various time cycles inherent in current assets and current liabilities. The working capital approach provides a better picture of the use of cash than a picture shown strictly in terms of cash movement.

If used properly, the financial control system can enable the manager to completely control funds that flow in and out of the corporation. Exhibit 5.4 shows the flow of the financial control system. The statement of changes in financial position disaggregates into the fixed assets, long-term liability, and equity sequences, Chapters 9, 11, and 12, respectively. The statement of changes also disaggregates into the changes in working capital. The working capital items fully disaggregate into major control sequences for cash, accounts receivable, inventory, and accounts payable discussed in Chapters 6, 7, 8, and 10, respectively. Funds, long-term debt, and equity are normally shown only at the corporate level and are controlled at that level. These items are based on corporate strategy and normally cannot be allocated easily at the lower levels. Long-term assets, however, can be disaggregated by location and by uses, and the depreciation can be shown as a part of profit center overhead. Long-term assets can also be used to show a return on assets computation for various profit centers (see Fixed Assets, Chapter 9). The final statement describing the sequence, the statement of retained earnings, shows the final loop in the investment and reinvestment cycle of corporate activities. The power of the financial control system lies in the fact that all of the in-flows and out-flows of working capital are represented in the system. Therefore, the manager or executive can effectively control the in-flows and out-flows of working capital by the use of this system. As described earlier, each major source and use of working capital does flow through these statements, and each major source and use of working capital can be supported by its own major control sequence. For example, working capital items are fully disaggregated into the major control sequences for cash, accounts receivable, inventory, and so on. Because this control sequence is a composite of the result of the three cycles, normal descriptive formats are not used, and the following discussion replaces the normal format.

B. Statement of Changes in Financial Position

The statement of changes in financial position disaggregates in the four basic sequences as shown in the flow chart of financial control, level 1 of 1, page 1 of 1. The first one is the supporting statement of changes in working capital as shown in A4. The other three sequences are the detailed analysis of the changes in long-term assets, long-term liability, and equity as previously described in the corporate control system, level 1 of 1, page 1 of 1, sequence starting at charts B2, B4, and B5, respectively.

Changes in Working Capital

The changes in working capital (Chart A4) supports the statement of change in financial position (Chart A3), and it is further disaggregated into detailed control systems discussed as separate chapters in this text. Changes in working capital disaggregates into cash, accounts receivable, inventory, and accounts payable control sequences shown in Chapters 6, 7, 8, and 10, respectively.

Statement of Retained Earnings

The statement of retained earnings closes the cycle of fund activities. An additional disaggregation may be required for specific corporate activities, but the only one shown for this example is the disaggregation by changes in equity sections as discussed in corporate control system, level 1 of 1, page 1 of 1.

A sequence linking the basic fund control process is shown in the next system. These two approaches were determined to provide both a historical perspective as shown by the statement of changes in financial position and a pathway into the future as shown by the funds control system. By proper use of both systems, a picture of corporate fund control can be developed.

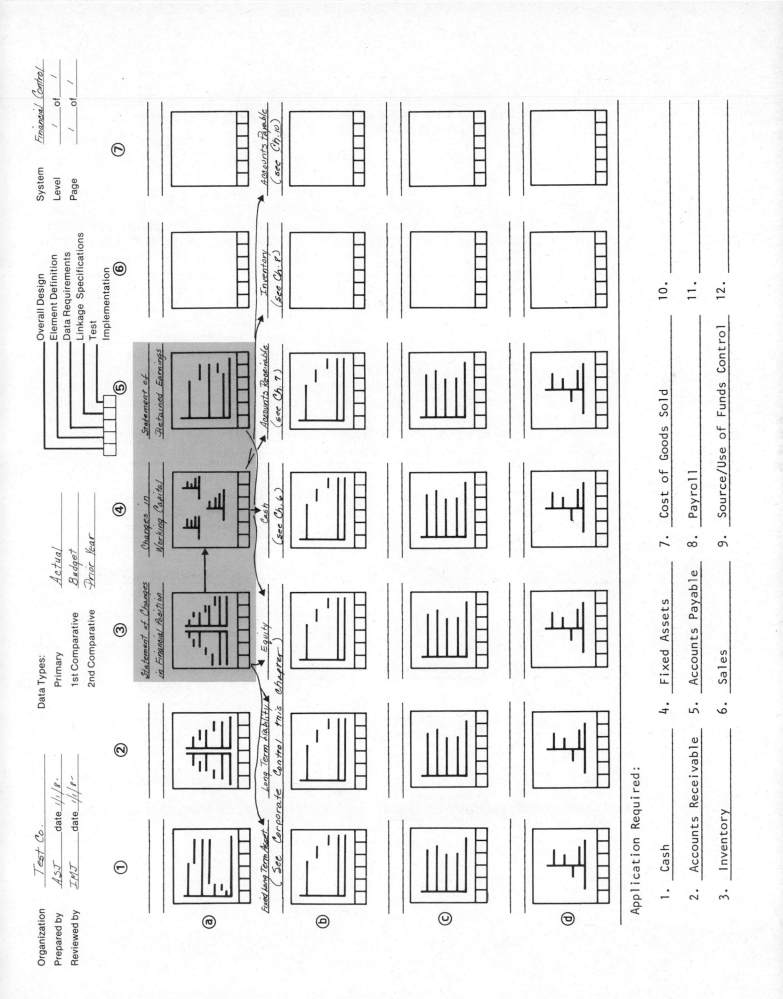

5. THE STATEMENT OF CHANGES IN FINANCIAL POSITION, CHANGES IN WORKING CAPITAL, AND STATEMENT OF RETAINED EARNINGS

Chart 10-100 is an example of a statement of changes in financial position presented in a graphic format. The legend on the top left-hand corner demonstrates that the dark black bars represent actual 1982 data. To read the chart, look at the left-hand plot. This shows the make-up of the sources of funds. Net income plus depreciation equals working capital from operations. Adding in the write-off of plant assets and the increase in notes payable gives the total source of funds. The right-hand plot shows the use of funds. The purchase of equipment plus the other listed uses of funds equals the total use of funds.

As with the other charts shown, each item on the chart can be supported with a more detailed chart; for example, Chart 10-098 shows a breakdown of the changes working capital. This chart is really a combination of three variance charts. The left-hand chart shows the changes in current assets (i.e., cash, accounts receivable, and inventory increased). The right-hand chart shows the changes in current liabilities and the bottom chart summarizes the change in current assets, current liabilities, and current working capital.

Chart 10-099 shows another standard financial statement in graphic format, the statement of retained earnings. To read the chart note that the beginning balance plus income minus dividends equals the ending balance of retained earnings.

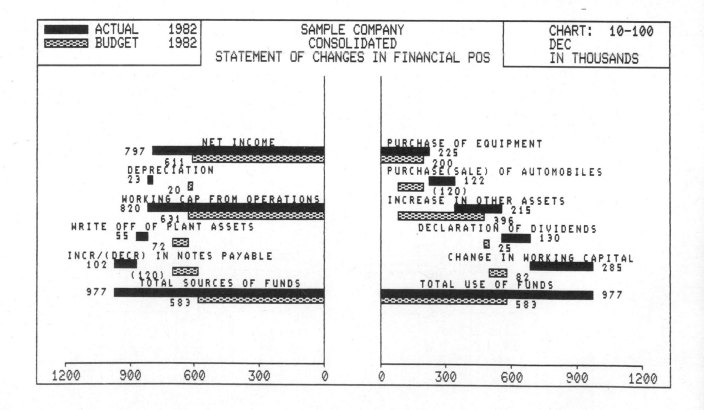

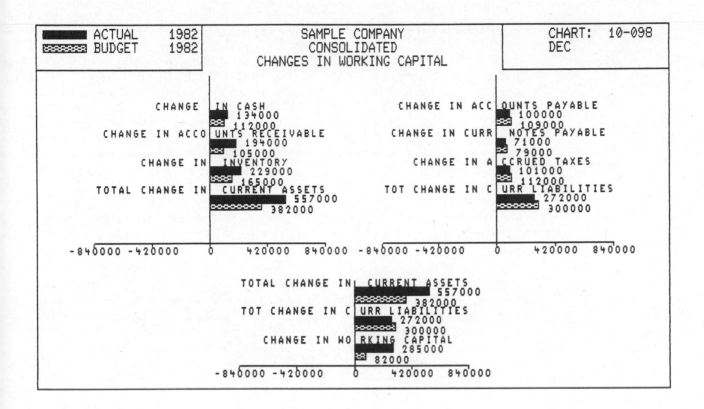

ACTUAL 1982
BUDGET 1982

SAMPLE COMPANY
CONSOLIDATED
CHANGES IN WORKING CAPITAL

CHART: 10-098
DEC

CHANGE IN CASH
134000
112000

CHANGE IN ACCOUNTS RECEIVABLE
194000
105000

CHANGE IN INVENTORY
229000
165000

TOTAL CHANGE IN CURRENT ASSETS
557000
382000

CHANGE IN ACCOUNTS PAYABLE
100000
109000

CHANGE IN CURR NOTES PAYABLE
71000
79000

CHANGE IN ACCRUED TAXES
101000
112000

TOT CHANGE IN CURR LIABILITIES
272000
300000

-840000 -420000   0   420000 840000   -840000 -420000   0   420000 840000

TOTAL CHANGE IN CURRENT ASSETS
557000
382000

TOT CHANGE IN CURR LIABILITIES
272000
300000

CHANGE IN WORKING CAPITAL
285000
82000

-840000 -420000   0   420000 840000

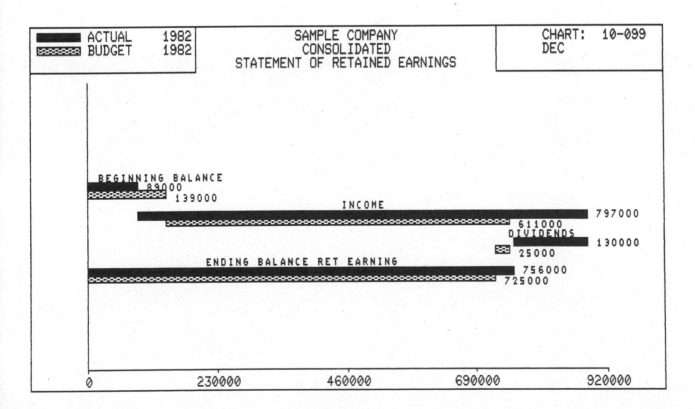

ACTUAL 1982
BUDGET 1982

SAMPLE COMPANY
CONSOLIDATED
STATEMENT OF RETAINED EARNINGS

CHART: 10-099
DEC

BEGINNING BALANCE
89000
139000

INCOME
797000
611000

DIVIDENDS
130000
25000

ENDING BALANCE RET EARNING
756000
725000

0   230000   460000   690000   920000

101

6. FUNDS CONTROL SYSTEM

This is the special system described in the system, financial control. It provides a view into the future by providing a 12-month rolling picture of expected source and use of funds, similar to the statement of changes in financial position. This particular view is based on cash rather than working capital. It requires that specific assumptions be made about the collection cycles in accounts receivable, the payment cycles in accounts payable, the turnover cycles in inventory, and the days to billing control placed in the sales and accounts receivable systems. It is assumed that these cycles are factored into the plan as shown in this system. This system as described uses the following elements for comparisons: The primary bar is the budget bar showing from where the expected funds are coming and how they are to be used in the plan for spending them. The first comparative is the past 12-month actual figure and for this sequence we are suggesting that the second comparative be last year's budget. These three bars give each element a historical and future perspective about where the corporation expected to go last year, where they actually went, and now, where they expect to go.

For this example, we have chosen to show a 30, 60, 90, 120, 270, and 360-day plan. Each corporation will determine the series that would be most suitable for their presentation. Because each of the plans are identical in terms of the charts except for the timing they show, only one description is provided.

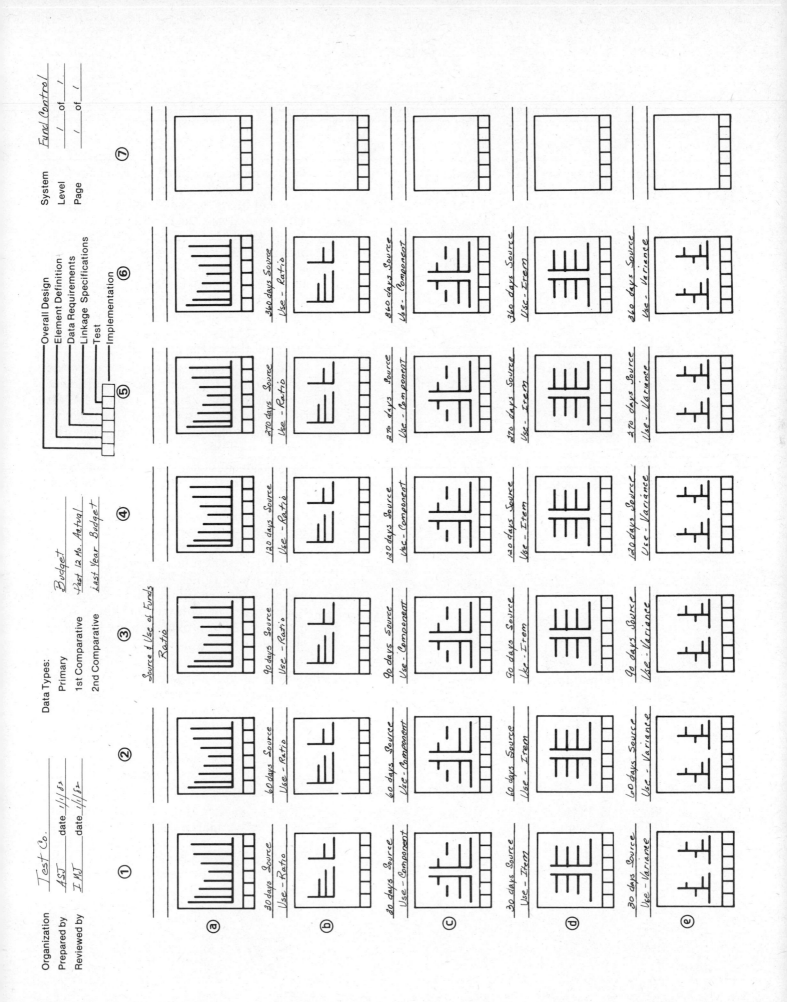

Organization Test Co.
Prepared by ASJ date 1/1/83
Reviewed by IMJ date 1/1/83

Data Types:
Primary Source & Use of Funds
1st Comparative Budget
Past 12 Mo. Actual
2nd Comparative Last Year Budget

Overall Design
Element Definition
Data Requirements
Linkage Specifications
Test
Implementation

System Fund Control
Level 1 of 1
Page 1 of 1

① ② ③ ④ ⑤ ⑥ ⑦

(a) 30 days Source Use - Ratio | 60 days Source Use - Ratio | 90 days Source Ratio | 120 days Source Use - Ratio | | 270 days Source Use - Ratio | 360 days Source Use - Ratio

(b) 30 days Source Use - Component | 60 days Source Use - Component | 90 days Source Use - Component | 120 days Source Use - Component | | 270 days Source Use - Component | 360 days Source Use - Component

(c) 30 days Source Use - Item | 60 days Source Use - Item | 90 days Source Use - Item | 120 days Source Use - Item | | 270 days Source Use - Item | 360 days Source Use - Item

(d) 30 days Source Use - Variance | 60 days Source Use - Variance | 90 days Source Use - Variance | 120 days Source Use - Variance | | 270 days Source Use - Variance | 360 days Source Use - Variance

Description of System Fund Control Level 1 of 1 Page 1 of 1

Row Col	Name of Chart	From	To	Descriptions
A3	Source and use of Funds—Ratio	Original	B1	Twelve-month running picture using 100% as the expected target. For example, if the source of funds for the next 30 days equals the expected use, the ratio as shown in A2 would equal 100%. As shown in the examples, the 100% line is the base line. If there is an excess of funds, they would be shown above the base line; if there is a shortage of funds, they would be shown below the base line. It is possible for a shortage in required funds and bank borrowing or other short-term solutions to be required.
B1	30 Days—N: Source D: Use	A1	C1	Relative size of the source of funds to the use of funds. If the source is not sufficient to cover the use, then there would be less than 100% showing. The relative significance of any shortage or excess is shown by this comparison.
C1	Source and Use of Funds—Component	B1	D1	Co-relationship showing where the funds come from and where they are to be used. The right-hand side shows relative importance of the various sources of funds as compared to the overall source of funds and the left-hand side shows the relative size of the use of funds as compared to the overall use of funds. This chart would be useful in determining where additional funds might be obtained or where some might be cut to provide a more balanced picture.
D1	Source and Use of Funds—Item	C1	E1	Relative size of the individual sources and individual uses of funds as compared to each other. Once again this shows the relative importance of expected sources and uses of funds as compared to prior year budget and the actual results. It provides some idea of the changing mix in both the sources and uses of funds, and could be a primary indicator of future cash problems.
E1	Source and Uses of Funds—Variance	D1	—	Twin variance showing the variance from budget as compared to the last 12 months actual and last year's budget. This picture of change would provide a clear insight into the changing mix of source and use of funds. When seen with the other charts in this sequence, an overall picture of the

Row Col	Name of Chart	From	To	Descriptions
				changing source and use of funds patterns emerges. Each of the sequences described are required to support each of the time periods. As noted, all of the other descriptions of the sequence A2 through A6 are identical to this one. If all these charts were prepared and laid side by side, they would provide a sense of motion showing the past and expected change in the funding activities of the corporation.

CHAPTER 6

CASH CONTROL

The system shown in this section is designed to show cash flow as seen by the behavior of the various components of cash receipts and expenditures during the month. The basic assumption is that cash flow is planned and that the planning considers the accounts payable, inventory turnover, and accounts receivable cycles. This system relates directly to the fund control system because the budget shown in this system is the one created to provide the future perspective. The basic difference in the two systems is that this system is a month-to-month control of the cash and the fund control system is designed to show from where the cash is expected to come and where it is expected to be used. The cash control system is much more operationally oriented even though it is balanced with the capital expenditures. Some companies may choose to use only the cash control system and not the fund control system.

As shown in Exhibit 6.1, the system is first entered by reviewing the net cash position for each month. The summary of cash activity shows how the ending cash position was caused by cash that was on hand at the beginning of the month plus the collections less operating expenditures plus other cash sources less net capital expenditures that equals cash at the end of the month. If cash shows a major variance from plan or negative position, this sequence is designed to show what caused that position. The disaggregation takes place by first showing the elements of collections compared to plan, expenditures compared with plan, and the cash sources and the net capital expenditures compared to plan. That picture is disaggregated into the details of each of the elements. The summary is also repeated for each division in level 2.

When collections vary widely from plan, Chart C1 (page 108), there are two basic reasons: the accounts receivable cash collections are delayed and are not coming in per plan, sales are below plan, or both. If sales are the problem, a review of the sales system would be appropriate to determine where and why sales are below budget, thus causing the cash flow shortage. If accounts receivable cash collections are delayed, they are further disaggregated in the cash system by division and customer type in level 2.

The net cash operating expenses sequence includes the plan for inventory purchase and turnover and all other operating expenditures and considers the average payment cycle for accounts payable. The difference in ending balances in net cash expenditures can be explained by the accounts payable sequence to see if the accounts payable cycle is accurate. A review of the

EXHIBIT 6.1

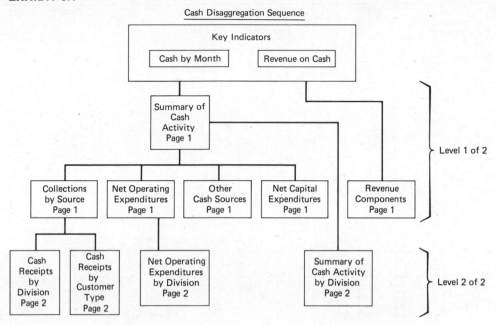

inventory system to make sure that the purchases and the in-flows and out-flows have worked according to plan may be necessary. The expenses are further disaggregated by cash expenditures by division, and can also be reviewed in the disaggregation shown in the income system.

The variances in the other cash sources will be disaggregated into the line items in the income system. The net capital expenditures can be further disaggregated in the capital budgeting system. Seeing the cash position on a monthly basis disaggregated in this way provides an appropriate picture of the cash flow cycle throughout the corporate activities.

The final sequence, revenue on cash, Chart A6 (page 108), is a suggestion of the type of information that can be shown graphically without considerable effort. Once this suggested sequence of charts is shown, it gives an overall view of the effectiveness of the corporate use of excess cash.

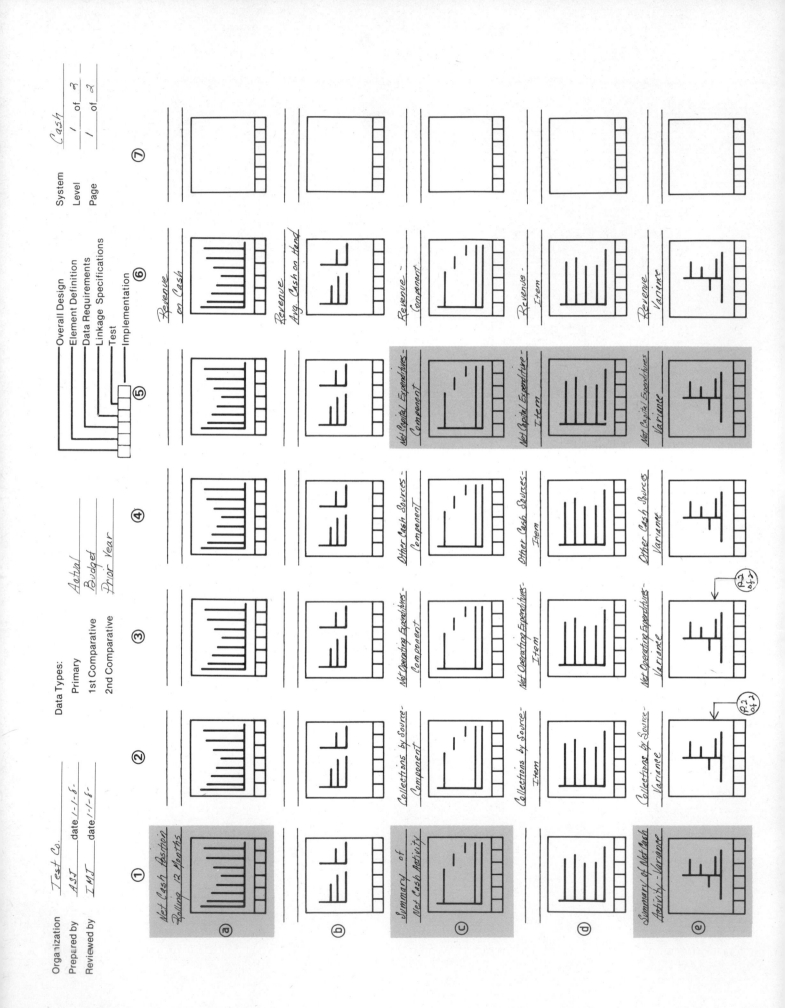

Row Col	Name of Chart	From	To	Descriptions
A1	Net Cash Position Rolling 12 Months	Original	C1	Time series showing the net cash on hand at the close of each monthly period for the past 12 months as compared to the budget and the prior year.
C1	Summary of Net Cash Activity	A1	E1	Beginning cash balance, cash collections for the month, plus other cash sources that equal total cash available for the period, minus the net operating and net capital expenditures for the month that equal the net cash on hand at the end of the month. This chart shows the relative importance of the individual components as they affect the net cash position each month.

The pattern describes the normal and/or expected activity for that particular month. There will be seasonal patterns and they can be planned. |
E1	Summary of Net Cash Activity—Variance	C1	E2–C5	Variance from plan and/or prior years for all cash activities.
C2	Collections by Source —Component	C1	D2	Disaggregates the collections elements shown in Chart C1 by source of collections. Sources would include receivables, perhaps by type, and/or direct cash sales and/or any other source of cash normal to operations. It shows the relative importance of each source of collection as compared to the total collections.
D2	Collections by Source —Item	C2	E2	Relative size of the source of collections as compared to each other. Any change in the mix of collections would become apparent here.
E2	Collections by Source —Variance	D2	System: Cash, Level <u>2</u> of <u>2</u>, Page <u>2</u> of <u>2</u>, Charts A1 and A2	Variance from plan and/or prior year for the various sources of cash collections. If further analysis is required, the collections are broken down further using the sequences in the cash system, level 2 of 2, page 2 of 2, Charts A1 and A2.
C3	Net Operating Expenditures— Component	C1	D3	Line item operating expenditures as disaggregated from the net operating expenditure element in C1. The chart shows the relative importance of each of the line item expenditures to the total net operating expenditures.
D3	Net Operating Expenditures—Item	C3	E3	Relative size of the line item operating expenditures as compared to each other. It also describes various seasonal patterns and changes in mix of expenditures.

109

Row Col	Name of Chart	From	To	Descriptions
E3	Net Operating Expenditures— Variances	D3	System: Cash, Level 2 of 2, Page 2 of 2, Charts A4 and A5	Variances of net operating expenditures from plan and/or prior year. If further analysis is required, this sequence is disaggregated further in the cash system, Level 2 of 2, Page 2 of 2, Charts A4 and A5. It would also be possible to go directly to the expense disaggregation in the income system. The difference, however, is that the income sequence is shown on the accrual basis. This sequence is shown on a cash basis.
C4	Other Cash Sources —Component	C1	D4	Disaggregates the other cash sources into the individual types of sources. It would show the relative importance of the various other cash sources to the total of the cash source.
D4	Other Cash Sources —Item	C4	E4	Relative size of the individual other sources of cash as compared to each other. It shows the largest additional source of cash other than collections by operations.
E4	Other Cash Sources —Variances	D4	—	Variances from plan and/or prior year for the other cash sources. If further analysis is required, each source could be further disaggregated following the same sequence as in C4 or it might be appropriate to go to the original records.
C5	Net Capital Expenditures— Component	C1	D5	Disaggregates the capital expenditure elements shown in C1. It shows the relative importance of capital expenditures by type to overall net capital expenditures.
D5	Net Capital Expenditures—Item	C5	E5	Relative size of the individual net capital expenditures compared to each other.
E5	Net Capital Expenditures— Variance	D5	—	Variance from plan and/or prior year for the individual components of net capital expenditures. If further analysis is required, each element could be further disaggregated in the same sequence starting at C5. It might also be appropriate at this point to go directly to the original books to further analyze any ledger variances.
A6	Revenue on Cash	Original	B6	Example of the types of charts that can be shown describing the relative efectiveness of cash management. The revenue earned on cash balances can become a useful control tool to ensure that the company does not keep too much idle cash on hand. This chart shows the percentage of return

Row Col	Name of Chart	From	To	Descriptions
				by average cash on hand for the past 12 months as compared to budget and prior year.
B6	N: Revenue D: Average Cash on Hand	A6	C6	Relative size of the revenue received from effective use of cash balances as compared to the average cash on hand. The average cash on hand would be the beginning balance plus the ending balance divided by two or could be an average of the weekly balances or an average of the daily cash balances. Each company would have to make its own decision on how that balance would be computed. Different computations will show differing results in this ratio. The revenue for this example is described as interest earned in idle or excess balances in the bank plus discounts earned. The company should determine its own definition of revenue and the same sequencing would occur. If a change in the ratio was due to a significant change in the relative size of the revenue, then a disaggregation would continue in C6. If the change in the ratio is due, however, to a change in the relative size of the average cash on hand, disaggregation might take place by starting with Chart A1.
C6	Revenue— Component	B6	D6	Disaggregation of the revenue bar into the detailed source of revenue shown in this computation. It describes the relative importance of the individual components of the total revenue.
D6	Revenue—Item	C6	E6	Relative size of the individual revenue items as compared to each other. It also shows the largest source of revenue from the use of funds.
E6	Revenue—Variance	D6	—	Variance from plan and/or prior year for the individual revenue components. If further analysis is required, each revenue element could be further disaggregated in a sequence similar to that starting at C6. It is also possible at this point that it would be necessary to go to the original books of record for additional information.

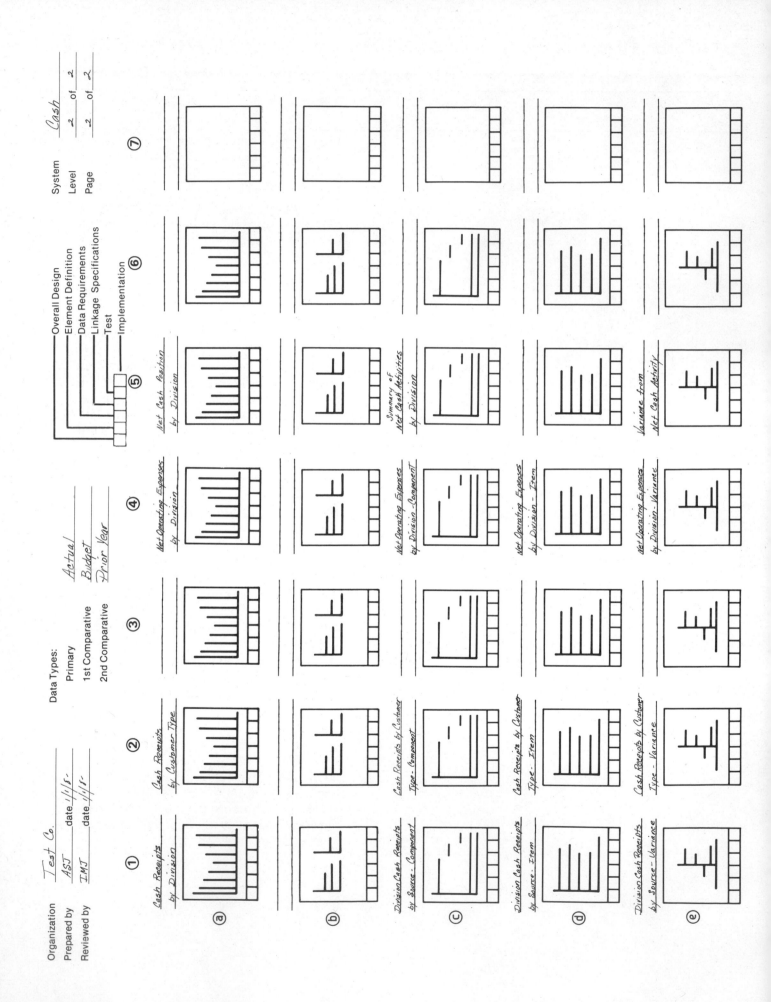

Organization: Test Co.
Prepared by: ASJ   date 1/1/5-
Reviewed by: IMJ   date 1/1/5-

Data Types:
Primary — Actual
1st Comparative — Budget
2nd Comparative — Prior Year

System: Cash
Level: 2 of 2
Page: 2 of 2

Overall Design
Element Definition
Data Requirements
Linkage Specifications
Test
Implementation

Columns: ① ② ③ ④ ⑤ ⑥ ⑦

(a) Cash Receipts by Division | Cash Receipts by Customer Type | Net Operating Expenses by Division | Net Cash Position by Division

(b)

(c) Division Cash Receipts by Source - Component | Cash Receipts by Customer Type - Component | Net Operating Expenses by Division - Component | Summary of Net Cash Activities by Division

(d) Division Cash Receipts by Source - Item | Cash Receipts by Customer Type - Item | Net Operating Expenses by Division - Item

(e) Division Cash Receipts by Source - Variance | Cash Receipts by Customer Type - Variance | Net Operating Expenses by Division - Variance | Variance from Net Cash Activity

Row Col	Name of Chart	From	To	Descriptions
A1	Cash Receipts by Division	System: Cash, Level <u>1</u> of <u>2</u>, Page <u>1</u> of <u>2</u>, Chart E2	C1	Time series showing the total cash receipts for the past 12 months by division compared to budget and last year. Seasonal patterns will emerge.
C1	Division Cash Receipts by Source —Component	A1	D1	Relative importance of the various sources of cash receipts to the total divisional receipts.
D1	Division Cash Receipts by Source —Item	C1	E1	Relative size of the sources of receipts for the division as compared to each other. The most important divisional source will be apparent.
E1	Division Cash Receipts by Source —Variance	D1	—	Variance from plan and/or prior year for the individual sources of cash for the division. If further analysis is required, each source could be further disaggregated into a sequence similar to that starting in C1. However, it may be time at this level to go directly to the original books of record for further analysis.
A2	Cash Receipt by Customer Type	System: Cash, Level <u>1</u> of <u>2</u>, Page <u>1</u> of <u>2</u>, Chart E2	C2	Review of cash receipts by customer type as opposed to showing it by division. This sequence is another way of showing the relative importance of the source of operational funds. This chart shows the total cash receipts by customer type from operating sources for the past 12 months as compared to the budget and prior year.
C2	Cash Receipts by Customer Type— Component	A2	D2	Relative importance of the cash receipts by customer type as compared to total cash receipts.
D2	Cash Receipts by Customer Type —Item	C2	E2	Relative size of the cash receipts by customer type as compared to each other. This chart clearly shows the most important customer type.
E2	Cash Receipts by Customer Type— Variance	D2	—	Variances from plan and/or prior year for the cash receipts by customer type. If further analysis is required, each customer type could be further disaggregated into a more detailed customer type sequence similar to that starting at C2. Also, additional analysis could take place by going directly to the accounts receivable system to see whether the collection time has changed. A change in the collection cycle would cause a change in cash receipts by customer type.

113

Row Col	Name of Chart	From	To	Descriptions
A4	Net Operating Expenses by Division	System: Cash, Level 1 of 2, Page 1 of 2, Chart E3	C4	Disaggregation of the total net operating expenses as shown by division, showing the past 12 months of operating expenses of the division as compared to budget and last year actual. Seasonal patterns will be apparent.
C4	Net Operating Expenses by Division —Component	A4	D4	Relative importance of the individual line items that make up the net operating expenditures for the division.
D4	Net Operating Expenses by Division —Item	C4	E4	Relative size of the individual line items spent by the division as compared to each other. The chart clearly shows the largest expenditure by division.
E4	Net Operating Expenses by Division —Variance	D4	—	Variances from plan and/or prior year for the individual line items of the net operating expenditures for the division. If further analysis of the variances is required, each element could be further disaggregated into a sequence similar to that starting at C4. Additional analysis could be made by going directly to the accounts payable system or to the expense sequence in the income system.
A5	Net Cash Position by Division	System: Cash, Level 1 of 2, Page 1 of 2, Chart C1,	C5	Disaggregates the chart from the cash system level 1 of 2, page 1 of 2, Chart C1, by division. It shows the net cash position for each division for the past 12 months.
C5	Summary of Net Cash Activities by Division	A5	E5	How the net cash changed for the division from the prior month. It starts with cash on hand, adds the cash receipts from operations less net operating expenses by division, less any capital expenditures by division, plus any other income for the division showing the resulting net cash balance. This chart is identical to the overall summary of cash activities as shown in C1, level 1 of 2 of this sequence except that it is by division.
E5	Variances from Net Cash Activity	C5	—	Variances from plan and/or prior year for the net cash activity for the division. If further analysis is required, each element could be further disaggregated as shown by Charts C2 through C5 at level 1 of this cash system. It is also possible that further analysis would take place at the original books of record.

1. CASH

Chart 10-001 shows a time series of net cash by month. We can see that in October, November, and December the cash balance was less than budgeted.

Chart 10-002 shows the net cash activity for October. We can see that the overall pattern of cash activity has remained the same, although there have been changes in a few items. The next chart, Chart 10-006, shows us exactly where those changes occurred. It shows us the variances from budget in the cash activity statement. The most significant variance was in capital expenditures.

The next three charts, 10-003, 10-004, and 10-005, give us a picture of capital expenditures for October. The first chart, 10-003, shows us the overall pattern of capital expenditures. It is easy to spot that there have been some significant changes. By looking at an item chart we can see that Mead's and Harrow's divisions have made the most significant amount of capital expenditures. The last chart in the sequence shows us that capital expenditures were larger than budget because of Mead, Harrow, and Willow, despite the fact that Rosemont, Janner, Aspnor, and Tremont had Capital Expenditures less than budgeted.

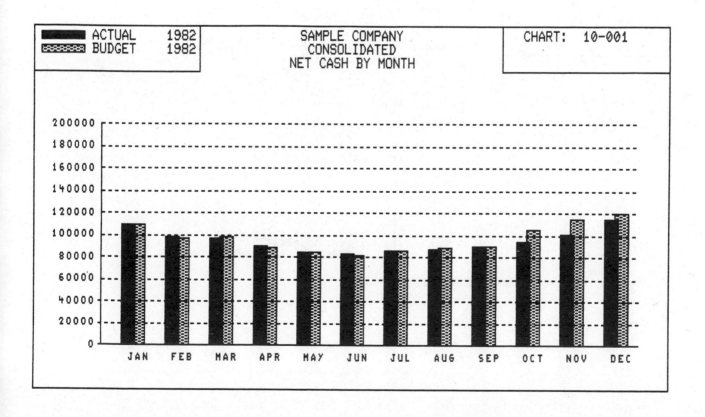

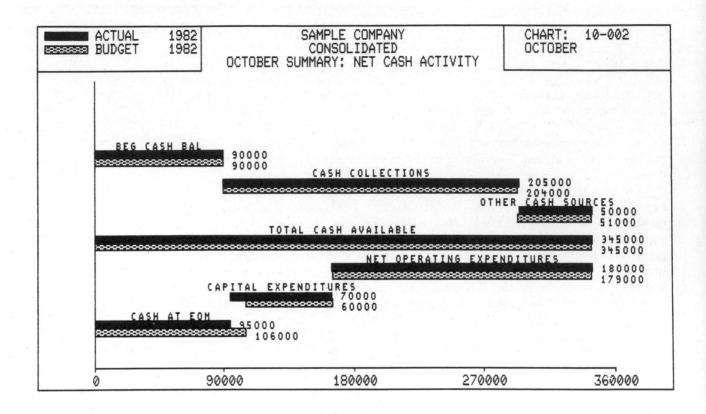

OCTOBER SUMMARY: NET CASH ACTIVITY

BEG CASH BAL — 90000 / 90000

CASH COLLECTIONS — 205000 / 204000

OTHER CASH SOURCES — 50000 / 51000

TOTAL CASH AVAILABLE — 345000 / 345000

NET OPERATING EXPENDITURES — 180000 / 179000

CAPITAL EXPENDITURES — 70000 / 60000

CASH AT EOM — 95000 / 106000

0   90000   180000   270000   360000

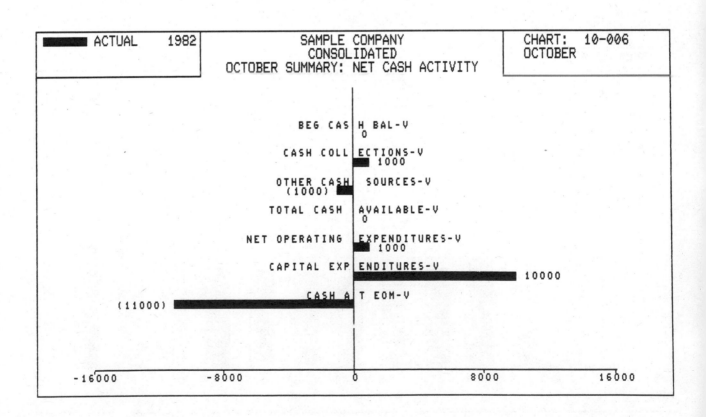

OCTOBER SUMMARY: NET CASH ACTIVITY

BEG CASH BAL-V — 0

CASH COLLECTIONS-V — 1000

OTHER CASH SOURCES-V — (1000)

TOTAL CASH AVAILABLE-V — 0

NET OPERATING EXPENDITURES-V — 1000

CAPITAL EXPENDITURES-V — 10000

CASH AT EOM-V — (11000)

-16000   -8000   0   8000   16000

116

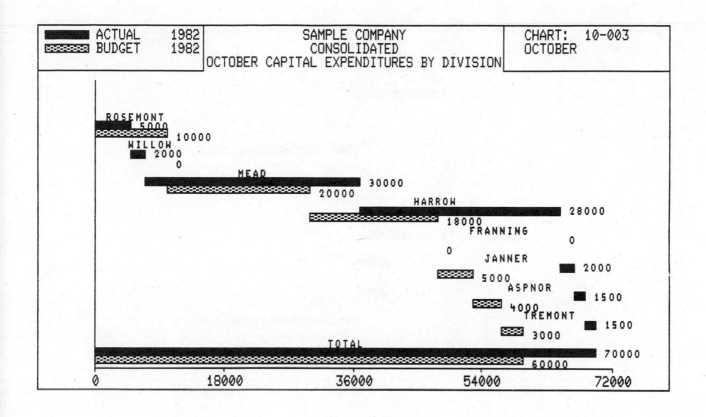

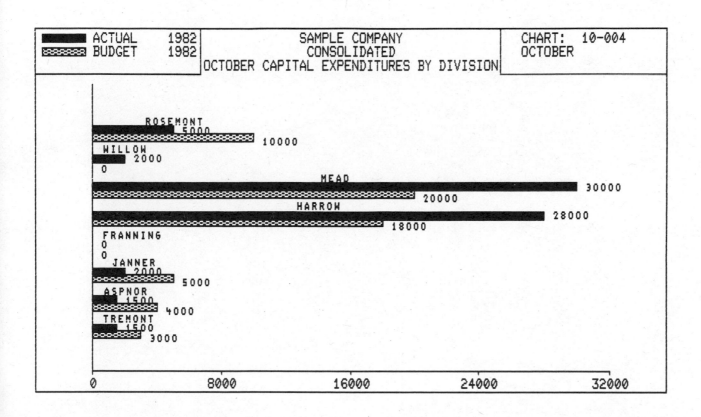

117

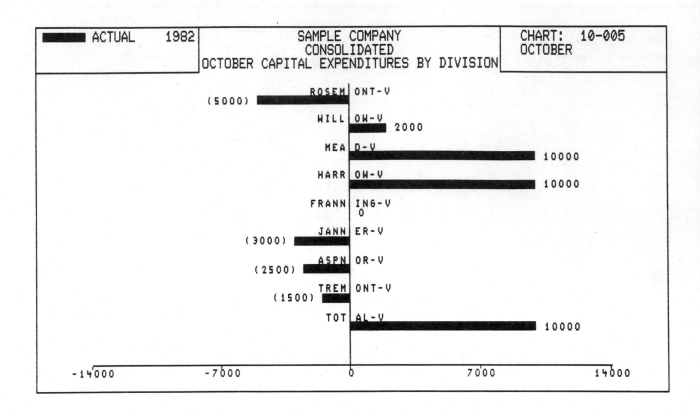

CHAPTER 7

ACCOUNTS RECEIVABLE

The purpose of this chapter is to describe a set of chart sequences that will help control accounts receivable as an investment that should receive a pre-determined rate of return. The return is computed as a part of the overall budgeting process. These charts show how well the company is doing in meeting the specific investment goals in accounts receivable. The financial control sequences, Chapter 5, show how an increase in receivables beyond that planned causes funds to be diverted to cover the increased investment in receivables, and other projects may have to be pushed back until the additional funds can be freed. Therefore, this sequence helps explain why funds may not be available for corporate or divisional investment, and where credit losses can be reduced. Exhibit 7.1 illustrates the pattern of disaggregation shown in this chapter.

EXHIBIT 7.1

Accounts Receivable
Disaggregation Sequence

Key Indicators
• Accounts Receivable Balance EOM
• Accounts Receivable Turnover
• Average Collection Period
• Days to Billing

Level One of Two

Accounts Receivable by Customer Type
Page 1 of 4

Accounts Receivable by Division
Page 1 of 4

Accounts Receivable by Aging
Page 1 of 4

Level Two of Two

Accounts Receivable by Detailed Customer Type

Accounts Receivable by Division

Accounts Receivable by Aging

Accounts Receivable by Customer Type

Accounts Receivable by Sub-Division

Accounts Receivable by Aging

Accounts Receivable by Customer Type

Accounts Receivable by Division

Page 2 of 4

Page 3 of 4

Page 4 of 4

The first basic indicator used in accounts receivable shows the composition of the investment in accounts receivable at the end of the month by customer type, division, and aging. This sequence shows the various pictures of receivables as of the balance sheet date. This sequence starts at level 1 of 2, page 1 of 4. The second type of indicators shows the activities of accounts receivable as described by the accounts receivable turnover, the average collection period, and the number of days to billing. This second type also disaggregates into the accounts receivable balances.

As shown by Exhibit 7.1, the key indicators disaggregate into accounts receivable by customer type, division, and aging. The charts for this level are shown on level 1 of 2, page 1 of 4. As shown in the exhibit, each of these breakdowns are further disaggregated on level 2, pages 2, 3, and 4 of 4.

Seeing the various pictures of accounts receivable provides management with a directed path toward a particular problem area. The customer type and the divisional sequences are a responsibility presentation of the status of the accounts receivable. The aging sequence can be seen as an overall corporate view of the accounts receivable line item. For example, if the company sells by customer type and if a customer type requires an excessive amount of receivables over plan and/or prior year, it is easy to assign responsibility for the added investment. A similar analysis could be shown for each division to see which customer type is requiring excess accounts receivable funding.

It is still necessary to look at the total corporate line item of all accounts receivable. The aging of the total receivables might show some problems not apparent in the individual responsibility accounts. (See level 1 of 2, page 1 of 4, Chart C3.)

The overall investment in accounts receivable could rise if the sales rise and the accounts receivable investment were still in control. For example, if receivables rise, but the turnover, average collection period, and days to billing indicators stay constant, then the investment in receivables has stayed constant in relation to sales. If the indicators change, further disaggregation is required.

The level 2 description shows only one set of disaggregated charts. However, another set of charts would be required for each customer type, each division, and each aging schedule.

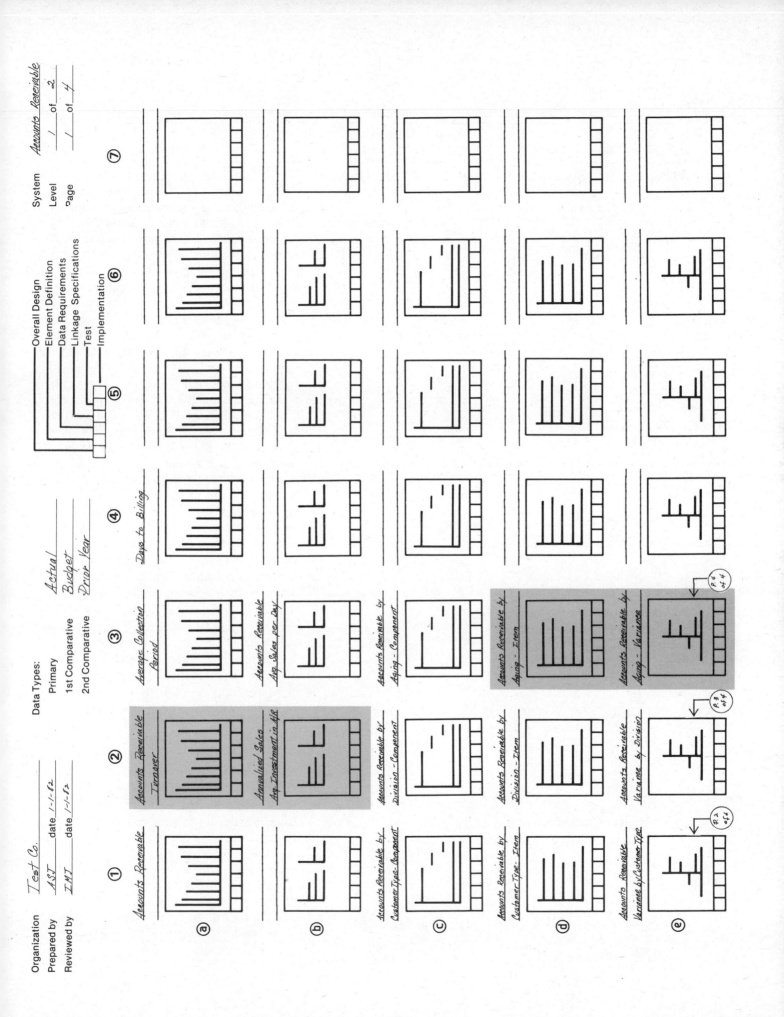

Row Col	Name of Chart	From	To	Descriptions
A1	Accounts Receivable	Original	C1, C2, C3	End of the month balances over time. Seasonal trends should emerge and significant deviations would be clearly apparent. Such an approach requires that a budget for receivables based on sales and collection expectations be an integral part of the entire planning process. If a change in accounts receivable appears, the disaggregation process would look first to the average turnover (Chart A2) for the average collection (Chart A3) and for the days to billing (Chart A4). The total amount of accounts receivable can increase if sales increase and still be within the control limitations set by the investment plan. Charts A2, A3, and A4 describe such control. If, however, the total accounts receivable are off, they will be disaggregated further into the accounts receivable sequence. If the problem is the absolute amount in accounts receivable, then accounts receivable will be disaggregated as described later. If the problem appears because sales are off budget, it would be necessary to move to the sales sequence shown in Chapter 13 to determine the problem.
A2	Accounts Receivable Turnover	Original	B2	Shows if accounts receivable are still in control as compared to the budget and last year's activity. The turnover is computed by dividing the annualized sales by the average investment in receivables. Your company may have a special way to compute this. This chart is a critical picture of control. Regardless of the absolute size of the accounts receivable, if the relative investment stays within the boundaries of the expected turnover, one aspect of control is in place. The components of the current month's turnover is shown in B2.
B2	N: Annualized Sales D: Average Investment in A/R	A2	A1	Relative size of annualized sales to average investment in accounts receivable. If the variance in turnover is caused by an unusual change in expected sales, then you would refer to the sales sequence for further analysis (Chapter 13). If the problem is in the total accounts receivable, refer to Chart A3 and then back to A1.

Row Col	Name of Chart	From	To	Descriptions
A3	Average Collection Period	Original	B3	Trend of the average time it takes to collect an account. If the trend is getting longer, credit action may be needed to keep the total receivables within the investment criteria. The ratio shows how many days sales are in the balance of receivables at a point in time. Seasonal trends would be shown by this chart. If a significant change in the collection period is shown, a review of B3 would show where to look for the source of the change.
B3	N: Accounts Receivable D: Average Sales Per Day	A3	A1	Relative size of account receivable to the average sales per day. If the change in the ratio is due to a change in the relative size of the average sales per day, the disaggregation would go directly to the sales sequence (Chapter 13). If the relative size of the accounts receivable is the problem, go to Chart A1 for further disaggregation of receivables.
A4	Days to Billing	Original	Freestanding	Frequency distribution that shows how long it takes from the time the product or service was actually delivered until the billing was issued to the customer. This ratio explains why the average collection period (Chart A3) and the aging (Charts C3 and D3) could both be within the investment criteria and still have a need for cash due to an increase in work in process. This chart fills a blank sometimes left open in the average budgeting cycle. The average days to billing is, in effect, an extension of the collection period and is an efficiency measurement.
C1	Account Receivable by Customer Type—Component	A1	D1	Part of the responsibility presentation showing the relative importance of the accounts receivable balances of the various customer types to the overall accounts receivable balance.
D1	Accounts Receivable by Customer Type—Item	C1	E1	Relative size of the accounts receivable balances of the customer types compared to each other and indicating where the largest amount of funds are invested. If there is a large variance from budget or prior years, further disaggregation would be required. The next chart, D1, shows the variances.

Row Col	Name of Chart	From	To	Descriptions
E1	Accounts Receivable by Customer Type—Variance	D1	System: Account Receivable, Level 1 of 2, Page 2 of 4, C1, C2, C3	Variance from plan and/or prior year by customer type. If further analysis is required, each customer type can be further disaggregated into a more detailed customer type by division, and can be aged. These sequences are further described in A/R level 2 of 2, page 2 of 4, Charts C1, C2, and C3 respectively.
C2	Accounts Receivable by Division—Component	A1	D2	Continuation of the responsibility presentation showing the relative importance of the accounts receivable balances held by the divisions to the overall A/R balance.
D2	Accounts Receivable by Division—Item	C2	E2	Relative size of the accounts receivable held by each division as compared to each other and indicating where the largest amount of funds are invested.
E2	Accounts Receivable by Division—Variance	D2	System: A/R, Level 2 of 2, 3 of 4, C1, C2, C3	Variance from plan and/or prior year by division indicating whether a further analysis of the divisional A/R should be undertaken. This data can disaggregate into additional sequences showing how each variance is caused by customer type, by the subdivision within each division, or by aging. The sequences are further described in A/R level 2 of 2, page 3 of 4, Charts C1, C2, and C3, respectively.
C3	Accounts Receivable by Aging—Component	A1	D3	The more common analysis. It is a description of the overall corporate position of receivables as described by their age. Such a view tells whether all of the components added together are within the investment criteria determined by the corporate plan. This chart shows the relative importance of the components to the total A/R. The components can be shown as 30 days, 60 days, 90 days, or whatever aging schedule is required by the individual company.
D3	Accounts Receivable by Aging—Item	C3	E3	Normal item chart providing a comparison of the individual elements one to the other. In this case, the elements are the components of receivables shown by the aging schedule. Thus this chart is a frequency distribution chart showing company A/R by days of aging.
E3	Accounts Receivable by Aging—Variance	D3	System: A/R, Level 2 of 2, Page 4 of 4, C1, C2	Variance from plan and/or prior year by the aging schedule and indicating whether a further analysis of total A/R by aging component should be undertaken. This

Row Col	Name of Chart	From	To	Descriptions
				data can be disaggregated into additional sequences showing how each variance is caused by customer type and by divisions. These sequences are further described in A/R level 2 of 2, page 4 of 4, Charts C1 and C2, respectively.

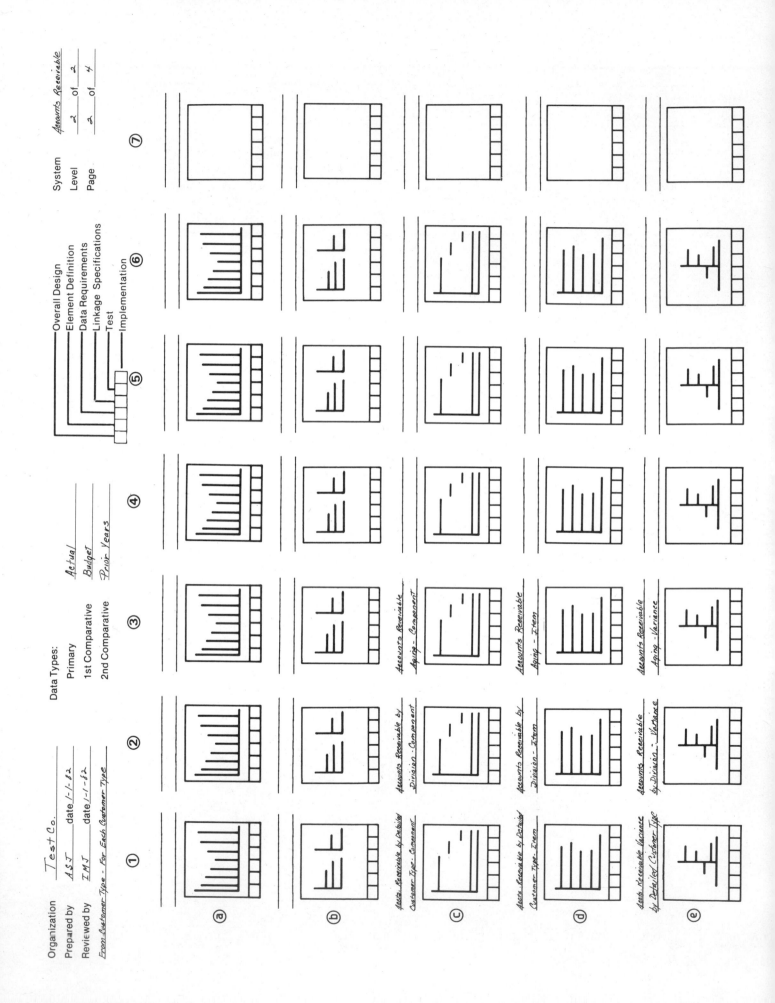

Organization Test Co.
Prepared by ASJ date 1-1-82
Reviewed by IMJ date 1-1-82
From Customer Type - For Each Customer Type

Data Types:
Primary Actual
1st Comparative Budget
2nd Comparative Prior Years

Overall Design
Element Definition
Data Requirements
Linkage Specifications
Test
Implementation

① ② ③ ④ ⑤ ⑥ ⑦

ⓐ

ⓑ

ⓒ Accts. Receivable by Detailed Customer Type - Component
Accounts Receivable by Division - Component
Accounts Receivable Aging - Component

ⓓ Accts. Receivable by Detailed Customer Type - Item
Accounts Receivable by Division - Item
Accounts Receivable Aging - Item

ⓔ Accts. Receivable Variance by Detailed Customer Type
Accounts Receivable by Division - Variance
Accounts Receivable Aging - Variance

Description of System Accounts Receivable Level 2 of 2 Page 2 Page 2 of 4

Row Col	Name of Chart	From	To	Descriptions
C1	Accounts Receivable by Detailed Customer Type—Component	System: A/R, Level 1 of 2, Page 1 of 4, Chart E1	D1	Relative importance of the detailed customer type to the total customer type. It is a detailed breakdown of accounts receivable within a customer type. If the company does not keep this detail, the sequence would not be used.
D1	Accounts Receivable Detail by Customer Type—Item	C1	E1	Relative size of the detailed customer type as compared to each other, indicating which of the detail types requires the largest investment.
E1	Accounts Receivable by Detailed Customer Type—Variance	D1	—	Variances from plan and/or prior year by detail customer type. This is the last level shown in this sequence. If further disaggregation is necessary, this sequence would disaggregate to a third level similar to C1, C2, and C3. It may be necessary to go to the detailed records.
C2	Accounts Receivable by Division—Component	A/R, Level 1 of 2, Page 1 of 4, Chart E2		Relative importance of amounts of A/R held by each division to the total A/R within the specific customer type.
D2	Accounts Receivable by Division—Item	C2	E2	Relative size of A/R held by each division within this customer type as compared to each other, showing where the largest investment is made.
E2	Accounts Receivable by Division—Variance	D2	—	Variance from plan and/or prior year for each division within the customer type. It is the last chart shown in the sequence. If further analysis is required, each division can be disaggregated into a third and subsequent level similar to C1, C2, and C3. It may also be necessary to go to the detailed records.
C3	Accounts Receivable Aging—Component	Level 1 of 2, Page 1 of 4, E3	D3	Relative importance of each element of the aging schedule to the total customer type.
D3	Accounts Receivable Aging—Item	C3	E3	Normal item chart providing a comparison of the individual elements one to the other. In this case the elements are the components of each customer type shown by the aging schedule. Thus this chart is a frequency distribution chart showing customer type A/R by days of aging.
E3	Accounts Receivable Aging—Variance	D3	—	Variances from plan and/or prior year for the customer type by each of the aging elements. This is the last level shown in this

Row Col	Name of Chart	From	To	Descriptions
				sequence. If further disaggregation is necessary, the sequence would disaggregate to a third level similar to C1, C2, and C3. It may also be necessary to go to the detailed records.

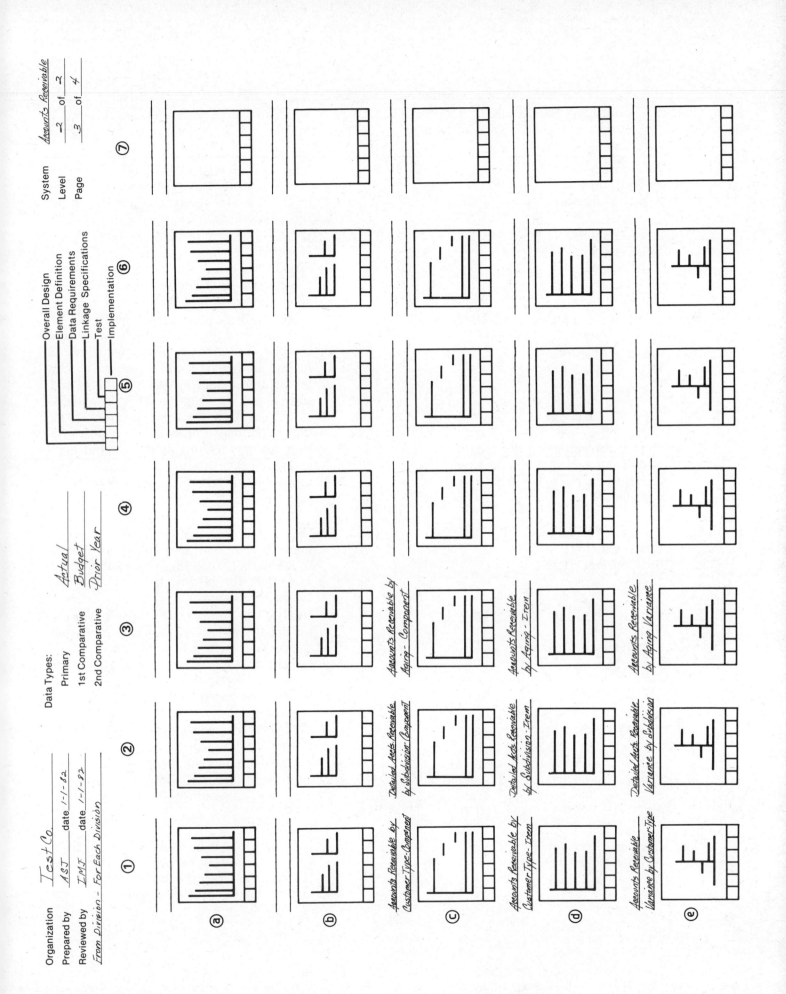

Prepared by AJJ date 1-1-82
Reviewed by IMI date 1-1-82
From Division - For Each Division

Data Types:
Primary   Actual
1st Comparative Budget
2nd Comparative Prior Year

Overall Design
Element Definition
Data Requirements
Linkage Specifications
Test
Implementation

System
Level
Page

Accounts Receivable
2 of 2
3 of 4

① ② ③ ④ ⑤ ⑥ ⑦

ⓐ
ⓑ
ⓒ Accounts Receivable by Customer-Type-Component / Detailed Accts Receivable by Subdivision-Component / Accounts Receivable by Aging-Component
ⓓ Accounts Receivable by Customer-Type-Item / Detailed Accts Receivable by Subdivision-Item / Accounts Receivable by Aging-Item
ⓔ Accounts Receivable Variance by Customer-Type / Detailed Accts Receivable Variance by Subdivision / Accounts Receivable by Aging Variance

Row Col	Name of Chart	From	To	Descriptions
C1	Accounts Receivable by Customer Type—Component	System: A/R, Level <u>1</u> of <u>2</u>, Page <u>1</u> of <u>4</u>, E2	D1	Relative importance of the accounts receivable investment by customer type to the total accounts receivable investment of this particular division.
D1	Accounts Receivable by Customer Type—Item	C1	E1	Relative size of investment in accounts receivable by customer type within the division as compared to each other, also showing where the largest accounts receivable investment was made.
E1	Accounts Receivable by Customer Type—Variance	D1	—	Variance from plan and/or prior year by customer type for each of the divisions. It is the last chart shown in the sequence. If further analysis is required, each customer type can be disaggregated into a third and subsequent level similar to C1, C2, and C3. It may also be necessary at this point to go to the detailed records.
C2	Detailed Accounts Receivable by Subdivision—Component	System: A/R, Level <u>1</u> of <u>2</u>, Page <u>1</u> of <u>4</u>, Chart D2	D2	Relative importance of the subdivision's investments in accounts receivable to the total accounts receivable investment of the division.
D2	Detailed Accounts Receivable by Subdivision—Item	C2	E2	Relative size of the subdivision's investment in accounts receivable as compared to each other, showing which subdivision has made the largest investment in accounts receivable.
E2	Detailed Accounts Receivable by Subdivision—Variance	D2	—	Variance from plan and/or prior year for the amount of receivables carried by each subdivision within the division. It is the last chart shown in the sequence. If further analysis is required, each subdivision could be disaggregated into a third and subsequent level somewhat like C1, C2, and C3. It may also be necessary to go directly to the detailed records.
C3	Accounts Receivable Aging—Component	System: A/R, Level <u>1</u> of <u>2</u>, Page <u>1</u> of <u>4</u>, Chart E2	D3	Relative importance of each element of the aging schedule to the total investment in accounts receivable for each division.
D3	Accounts Receivable Aging—Item	C3	E3	Normal item chart comparing the individual elements to each other. In this case the elements are the components of the aging schedule for the divisional accounts

Row Col	Name of Chart	From	To	Descriptions
				receivable. Thus this chart is a frequency distribution chart showing accounts receivable by days of aging for the division.
E3	Accounts Receivable Aging—Variance	D3	—	Variances from plan and/or prior year for the division by each of the aging elements. This is the last level shown in the sequence. If further disaggregation is necessary, the sequence would disaggregate to a third level for each of the aging elements similar to C1, C2, and C3. It may also be necessary at this time to go directly to the detailed records.

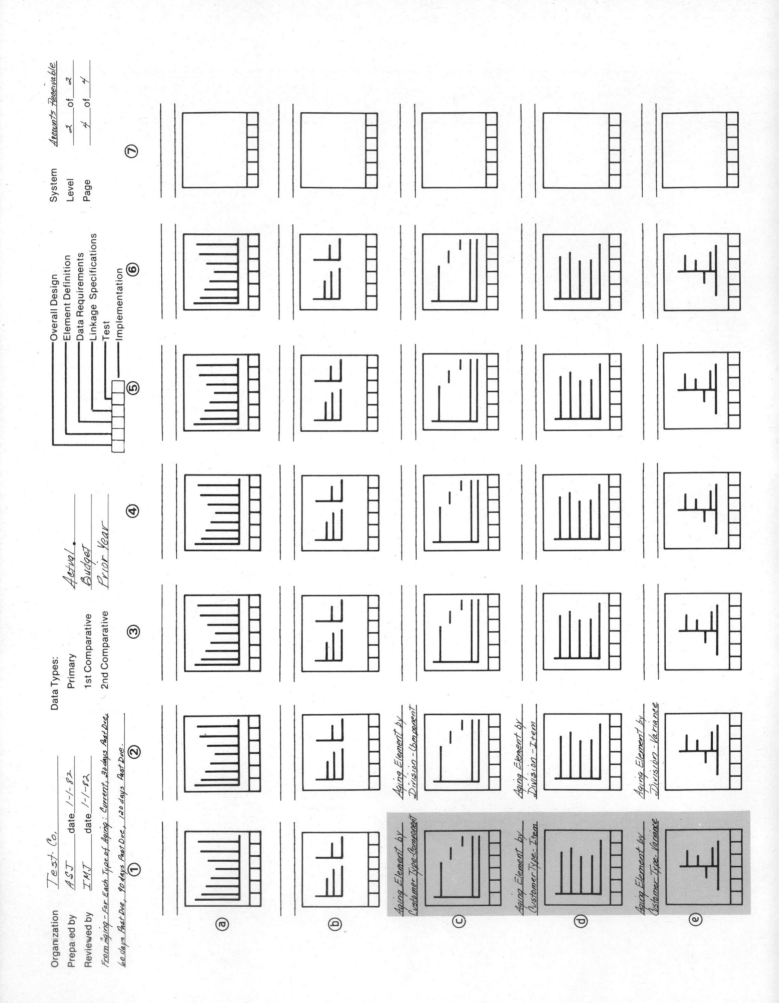

Organization   _Test Co._
Prepared by   _ASJ_   date _1-1-82_
Reviewed by   _TMJ_   date _1-1-82_

From Aging - for Each Type of Aging: Current, 30 days Past Due,
60 days Past Due, 90 days Past Due, 120 days Past Due.

Data Types:
Primary   _Actual_
1st Comparative   _Budget_
2nd Comparative   _Prior Year_

System
Level
Page

Overall Design
Element Definition
Data Requirements
Linkage Specifications
Test
Implementation

① ② ③ ④ ⑤ ⑥ ⑦

ⓐ

ⓑ

ⓒ   Aging Element by
Customer Type - Component
Aging Element by
Division - Component

ⓓ   Aging Element by
Customer Type - Item
Aging Element by
Division - Item

ⓔ   Aging Element by
Customer Type - Variance
Aging Element by
Division - Variance

For Each Aging Element:

Row Col	Name of Chart	From	To	Descriptions
C1	Aging Element by Customer Type—Component	Level 1 of 2, Page 1 of 4, Chart E3	D1	Relative importance of the investment in accounts receivable by customer type as compared to the total investment in accounts receivable for that aging element. For example, this chart would show which of the customer types made up the 30 days aging element.
D1	Aging Element by Customer Type—Item	C1	E1	Relative size of the investments in accounts receivable by customer type within the aging element as compared to each other, showing where the largest investment in accounts receivable is made for this aging element.
E1	Aging Element by Customer Type—Variance	D1	—	Variance from plan and/or prior year for the customer type within the usual aging element. It is the last level shown in this sequence. If further disaggregation is necessary, the sequence will disaggregate to a third level similar C1 and C2. It may also be necessary at this time to go to the detailed records.
C2	Aging Element by Division—Component	System A/R, Level 1 of 2, Page 1 of 4, Chart E3	D2	Relative importance of the investment in accounts receivable by division to the total investment in accounts receivable for this particular aging element. Any change in the relative size of the individual division's component from prior year or from budget would be easily noted.
D2	Aging Element by Division—Item	C2	E2	Relative size of the investment in accounts receivable by division for the particular aging element as compared to each other, showing where the largest investment in accounts receivable is made by division for this aging element.
E2	Aging Element by Division—Variance	D2		Variance from plan and/or prior year for the various divisions within a specific aging element. It is the last chart shown in this sequence. If further disaggregation is necessary, this sequence would disaggregate to a third and subsequent level similar to C1 and C2. It may also be necessary at this time to go to the detailed records.

NOTE: This sequence disaggregates each of the aging elements shown on Level 1. It does not, however, show aging by customer type or divisions. The aging for customer type and the divisions are shown as the last sequence starting with C3 in the prior two charts level 2 of 2, pages 2 of 4 and 3 of 4.

1. ACCOUNTS RECEIVABLE

Chart 10–011 shows a time series of the accounts receivable turnover through July. We can see that the ratio was significantly lower than budget in July.

Chart 10-012 shows a breakdown of the accounts receivable turnover ratio for July. The right-hand chart again tells us how much the ratio was off from budget. The left hand chart shows us:

1. The ratio is calculated by annualized sales divided by the average investment in accounts receivable.
2. The reason for the variance from budget is that the average investment in accounts receivable was higher than budget.
3. The variance in accounts receivable was $38 thousand.

The next chart in the sequence, 10-013, shows a breakdown of accounts receivable by age. The current accounts receivable represents the most significant category. Chart 10-014 is a variance chart, it shows us where the changes from budget have occurred. The major change has occurred in the current accounts receivable. The next few charts give more information about current accounts receivable.

Charts 10-015, 10-017, and 10-016 describe the current accounts receivable by customer type for July. We can see from Chart 10-015 the components of the current accounts receivable. Chart 10-017 shows us which customer types are most significant in terms of the amount of current accounts receivable they have outstanding. Chart 10-016 shows that customer types D, E, and I have the largest account differences from budget.

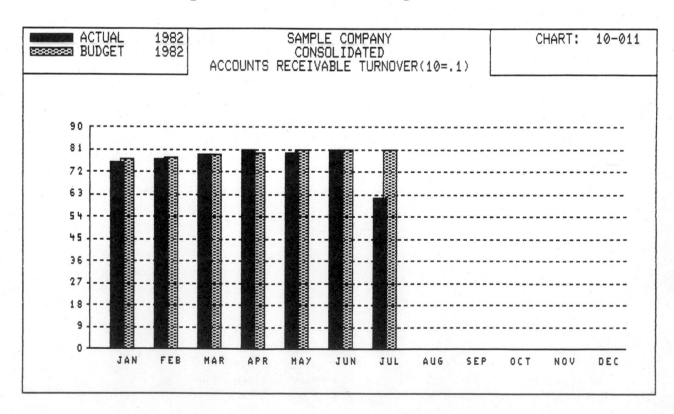

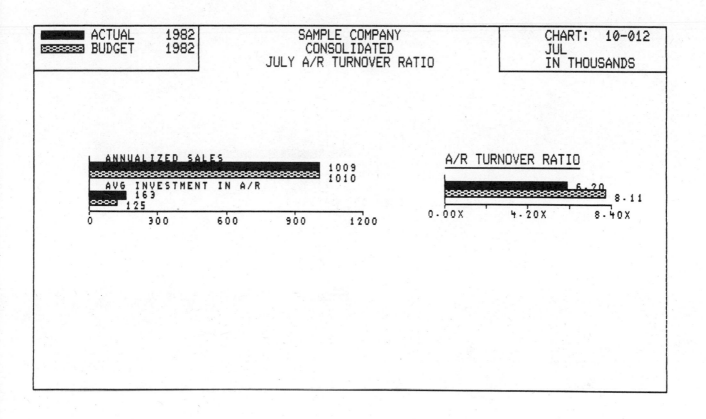

ANNUALIZED SALES
1009
1010
AVG INVESTMENT IN A/R
163
125

0   300   600   900   1200

A/R TURNOVER RATIO
6.20
8.11
0.00X   4.20X   8.40X

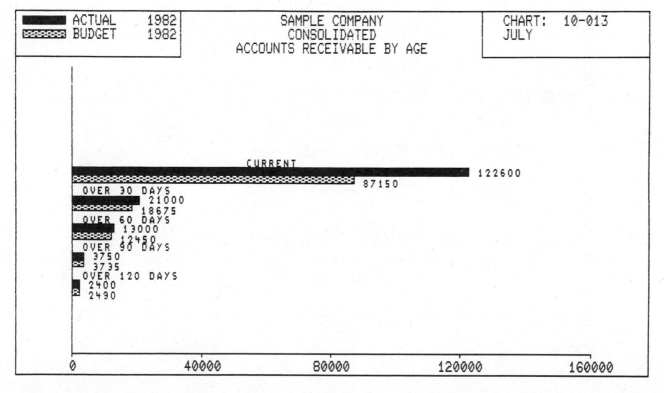

CURRENT
122600
87150
OVER 30 DAYS
21000
18675
OVER 60 DAYS
13000
12450
OVER 90 DAYS
3750
3735
OVER 120 DAYS
2400
2490

0   40000   80000   120000   160000

135

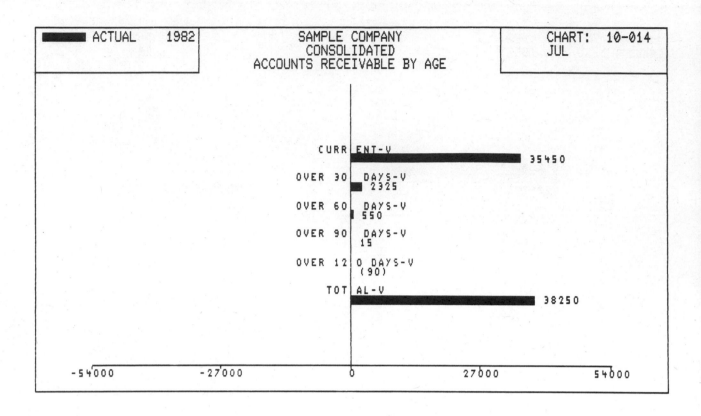

CURRENT-V   35450
OVER 30 DAYS-V
          2325
OVER 60 DAYS-V
          550
OVER 90 DAYS-V
          15
OVER 120 DAYS-V
          (90)
TOTAL-V   38250

-54000   -27000   0   27000   54000

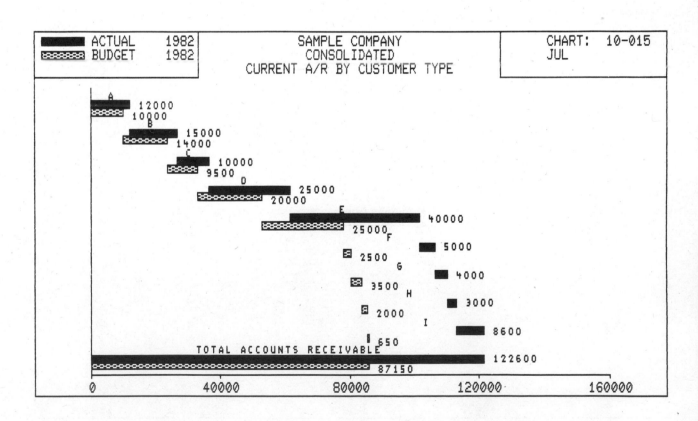

A   12000
    10000
B   15000
      14000
C   10000
     9500
D   25000
        20000
E   40000
         25000
F 5000
   2500
G   4000
    3500
H   3000
    2000
I   8600
    650

TOTAL ACCOUNTS RECEIVABLE   122600
                                 87150

0   40000   80000   120000   160000

136

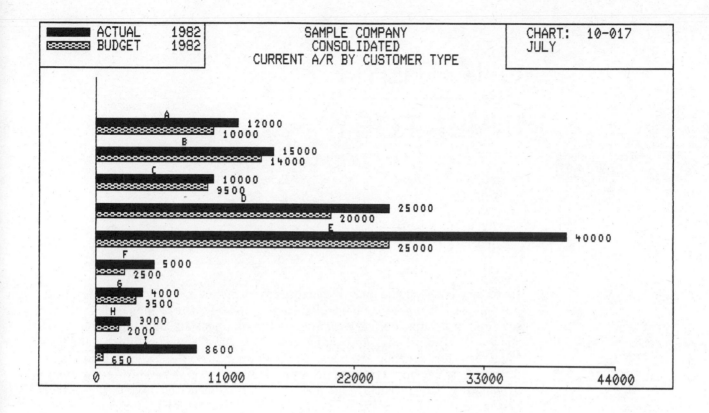

A — 12000 / 10000
B — 15000 / 14000
C — 10000 / 9500
D — 25000 / 20000
E — 40000 / 25000
F — 5000 / 2500
G — 4000 / 3500
H — 3000 / 2000
I — 8600 / 650

0   11000   22000   33000   44000

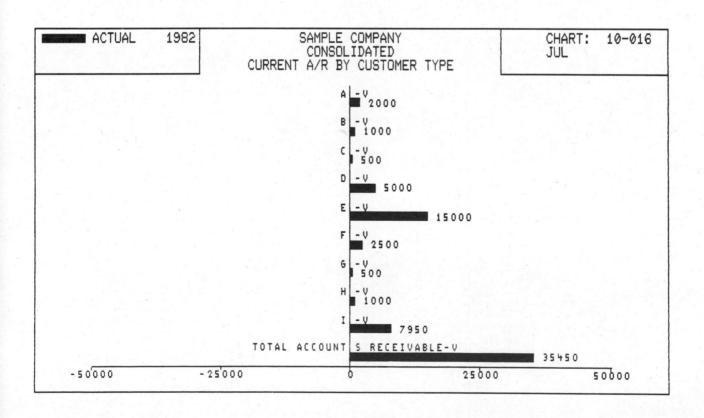

A - V 2000
B - V 1000
C - V 500
D - V 5000
E - V 15000
F - V 2500
G - V 500
H - V 1000
I - V 7950

TOTAL ACCOUNTS RECEIVABLE-V 35450

-50000   -25000   0   25000   50000

137

CHAPTER 8

INVENTORY

Inventory is one of the most important investments in many companies. The purpose of the inventory control system is to show the trends of inventory, seasonal build-ups, delivery cycles, and the balances at any point in time. As shown in Exhibit 8.1, key indicators shown are the absolute balance of inventory for the last 12 months, inventory turnover, and the average investment. The importance of inventory to liquidity is shown by the inventory to working capital ratio. The final key indicator in the inventory control system is the ABC analysis which provides the basis for understanding the control requirements for inventory. The overall balance of inventory is disaggregated into inventory by product and by location. Each of these is then

EXHIBIT 8.1

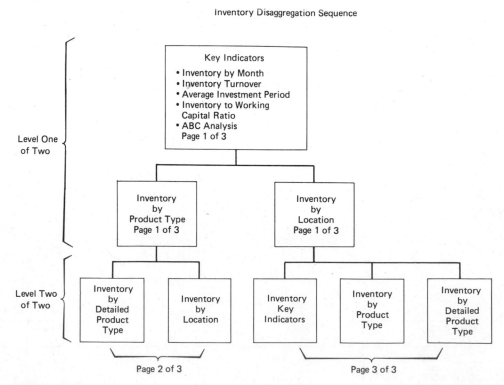

Inventory Disaggregation Sequence

138

disaggregated at a second data level. This disaggregation approach also ties into the sales/cost of goods sold/gross margin system shown in Chapter 13.

The absolute control of Inventory must occur at the detailed level. At that point, the reorder points, economic order quantity, and other specific inventory control procedures play the major role in translating corporate inventory policy into action. All of these specific control techniques must be combined with a sales forecasting system. Inventory control problems can occur at any level in the process, from sales forecast to order entry. This control system is designed to point out where the problem might be at a level low enough to take direct action.

Another possible sequence, not shown here, would be to show a sequence of co-relationship charts with inventory investment by product type and locations compared to gross margin contributions and in another sequence compared to sales contribution. The flow would be identical to the sequences described in this chapter and the resulting picture could provide a good analysis of inventory control problems.

This description of the inventory system starts with charts A2, A3, and A4, and then returns to A1 which disaggregates into the more detailed levels.

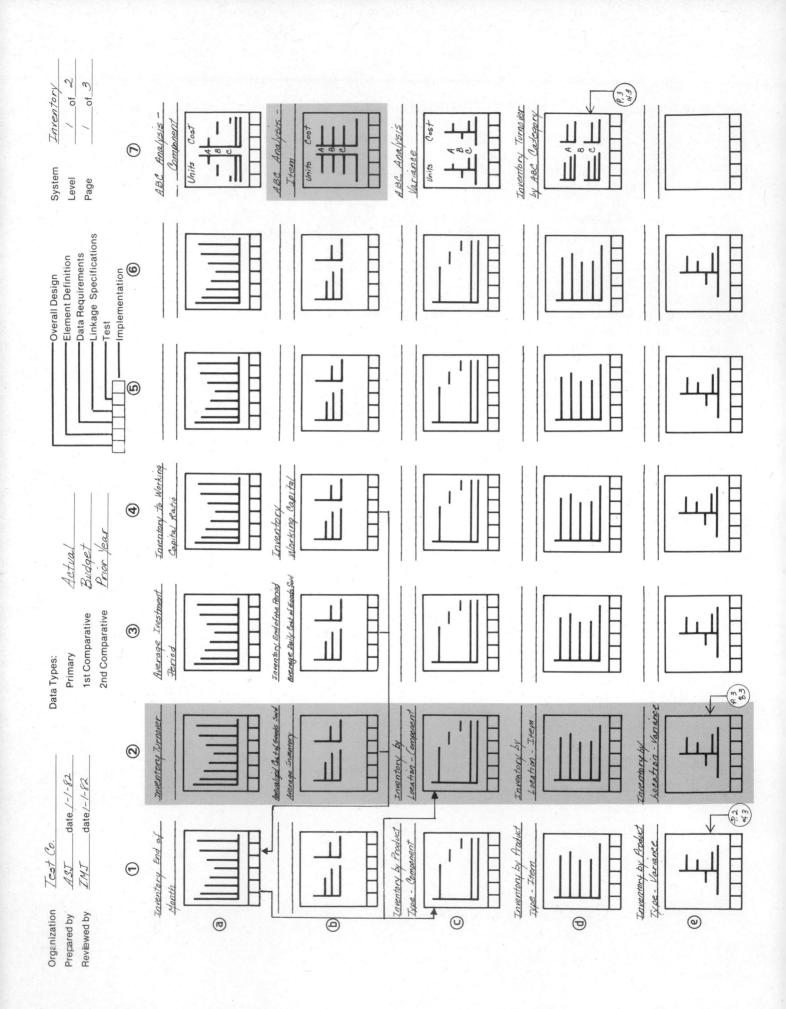

Organization _Test Co._

Prepared by _ASJ_   date _1-1-82_
Reviewed by _JMJ_   date _1-1-82_

System _Inventory_
Level _1_ of _2_
Page _1_ of _3_

Data Types:
Primary _Actual_
1st Comparative _Budget_
2nd Comparative _Prior Year_

Overall Design
Element Definition
Data Requirements
Linkage Specifications
Test
Implementation

① ② ③ ④ ⑤ ⑥ ⑦

ⓐ Inventory End of Month

ⓑ Inventory by Product Type - Component

ⓒ Inventory by Product Type - Item

ⓓ Inventory by Product Type - Item

ⓔ Inventory by Product Type - Variance

② Inventory Turnover
Annualized Cost of Goods Sold / Average Inventory

Inventory by Location - Component

Inventory by Location - Item

Inventory by Location - Variance

③ Average Investment Period
Inventory End of the Period / Average Daily Cost of Goods Sold

④ Inventory to Working Capital Ratio
Inventory / Working Capital

⑦ ABC Analysis - Component
Units Cost

ABC Analysis - Item
Units Cost

ABC Analysis - Variance
Units Cost

Inventory Turnover by ABC Category

P.3 of 3
P.3 B.3
P.2 of 3

This description of the inventory system starts with charts A2, A3, and A4, and then returns to A1 which disaggregates into the more detailed levels.

Row Col	Name of Chart	From	To	Descriptions
A2	Inventory Turnover	Original	B2	Turnover for the past 12 months as compared to the budget and prior year. This time series chart describes a seasonal variation and also shows any trend if inventory turnover is increasing or decreasing.
B2	N: Annualized Cost of Goods Sold D: Average Inventory	A2	A1	Relative size of the annualized cost of goods sold as compared to the average inventory on hand. Each company has its own way of developing the annualized cost of goods and the average inventory computation; once that procedure is established, the chart will point out any change in the ratio. If the change in turnover is due to a significant change in the relative size of the annualized cost of goods sold, then further analysis and disaggregation should occur in the cost of goods sold system, level 1 of 2, page 1 of 4, Chart A1, or the sales/gross margin system. If the change in the inventory turnover is due to a change in the relative size of the average inventory, then a further disaggregation and analysis should take place by going to Chart A1. However, before further disaggregation, Chart A3 should be reviewed.
A3	Average Investment Period	Original	B3	Time series showing how long the average inventory is kept on hand. This is another way of looking at inventory activity. This sequence is more concerned with how many days of inventory on hand is represented by the ending balance, based on the average daily cost of sales. This chart will show a relative build-up of inventory over time.
B3	N: Inventory End of the Period D: Average Daily Cost of Goods Sold	A3	A1	The numerator is the actual inventory at the end of the period and the denominator is the average daily cost of goods sold. This figure is normally computed by adding the cost of goods sold for the period and dividing by the number of sales days in that period. This ratio shows the relative size of the inventory as compared to the average daily cost of goods sold. If the change in the ratio is due to a change in the relative size of the inventory, then the

141

Row Col	Name of Chart	From	To	Descriptions
				disaggregation process and further analysis will continue by going to Chart A1. If the change in the ratio is due to a change in the relative size of the average daily cost of goods sold, then this disaggregation analysis should be continued in the cost of goods sold system, level 1 of 2, page 1 of 4, Chart A1.
A4	Inventory to Working Capital Ratio	Original	B4	Relative importance of the inventory investment over time as compared to the working capital. Seasonal changes in inventory investment would be shown and any trend in the relative importance of inventory would also be shown.
B4	N: Inventory D: Working Capital	A4	A1	Ratio showing the relative size of the inventory as compared to the working capital at any point in time. If the change in the ratio is due to a change in the relative size of the inventory, then further disaggregation would occur by going to Chart A1. If the changes in the ratio are due to a change in the relative size of the working capital, then further disaggregation and analysis would occur by going to the financial control system, level 1 of 1, page 1 of 1, Chart A4.
A1	Inventory End of Month	System: Corporate Control, Level 1 of 1, page 1 of 1, Chart A2 and from preceding Charts B2, B3, B4	C1	End of the month balance of inventory over time representing total corporate inventory and reflecting seasonal trends, showing an absolute increase or decrease in inventory. This sequence shows inventory disaggregation from the two basic views: by product over time and by location.
C1	Inventory by Product Type—Component	A1	D1	Relative importance of the various product types to the total inventory.
D1	Inventory by Product Type—Item	C1	E1	Relative size of the inventory by product type as compared to each other. It also shows the largest investment in product type.
E1	Inventory by Product Type—Variance	D1	System: Inventory, Level 2 of 2, Page 2 of 3, Charts C1 and C2	Variance from plan and/or prior year for the components of inventory by product type. If further analysis is required, each element in the chart, or product type, can be further disaggregated into detailed product type and/or location as shown in

Row Col	Name of Chart	From	To	Descriptions
				the inventory system, level 2 of 2, page 2 of 3, Charts C1 and C2.
C2	Inventory by Location— Component	A1	D2	Relative importance of the inventory as shown by location and compared to the total inventory.
D2	Inventory by Location— Item	C2	E2	Relative size of the inventory by location as compared to each other. This chart clearly shows where the largest inventory in inventory is located.
E2	Inventory by Location— Variance	D2	System: Inventory, Level 2 of 2, Page 3 of 3, Charts A1, A2, A3, A4, and A7	Variance from plan and/or prior year for the inventory investment at each location. If further analysis is required, the inventory at each location can be disaggregated into a sequence similar to this level as shown in the inventory system, level 2 of 2, page 3 of 3, Charts A1, A2, A3, A4, and A7.
A7	ABC Analysis— Component	Original	B7	Traditional ABC analysis of inventory. The co-relationship format clearly compares the number of units compared to the value of those units. A normal ABC breakdown usually shows that the A items at approximately 15% of the units account for 50–60% of the dollar value, the B items at 25–30% of the value, and the C items at 50–60% of the units account for approximately 15% of the value. This chart shows the relative number of units by ABC category as compared to the total units in inventory and the relative value of those respective units as compared to the total value of inventory.
				By using a standard percentage for the ABC breakdown such as 15, 30, and 55 (or whatever percentage is appropriate to your company), a pattern of inventory investment will appear. Control procedures should be initiated that reflect the relative value of the investment as compared to the cost of control.
B7	ABC Analysis—Item	A7	C7	Relative size of the ABC components as compared to each other by units and costs.
C7	ABC Analysis— Variance	B7	D7	Variance from plan and/or prior year of both the units and their respective dollar values. If further analysis of the inventory is required, a detailed disaggregation starts in Chart A1. However, Chart D7 might give an indication of the category of inventory where basic problems are inherent.

143

Row Col	Name of Chart	From	To	Descriptions
D7	Inventory Turnover by ABC Category	C7	System; Inventory, Level 2 of 2, Page 3 of 3, Chart A7	Turnover of inventory by ABC cateogry. If the information is available for the computation, it would provide a clear picture of the turnover mix by the various values of inventory. The A items should reflect a high turnover, B items a lesser turnover, and C items the least of all. A significant change in turnover from plan could be caused because the sales mix or manufacturing mix have changed. A more detailed view of the changing mix of inventory turnover by ABC category can be seen in the inventory system, level 2 of 2, page 3 of 3, Chart D7.

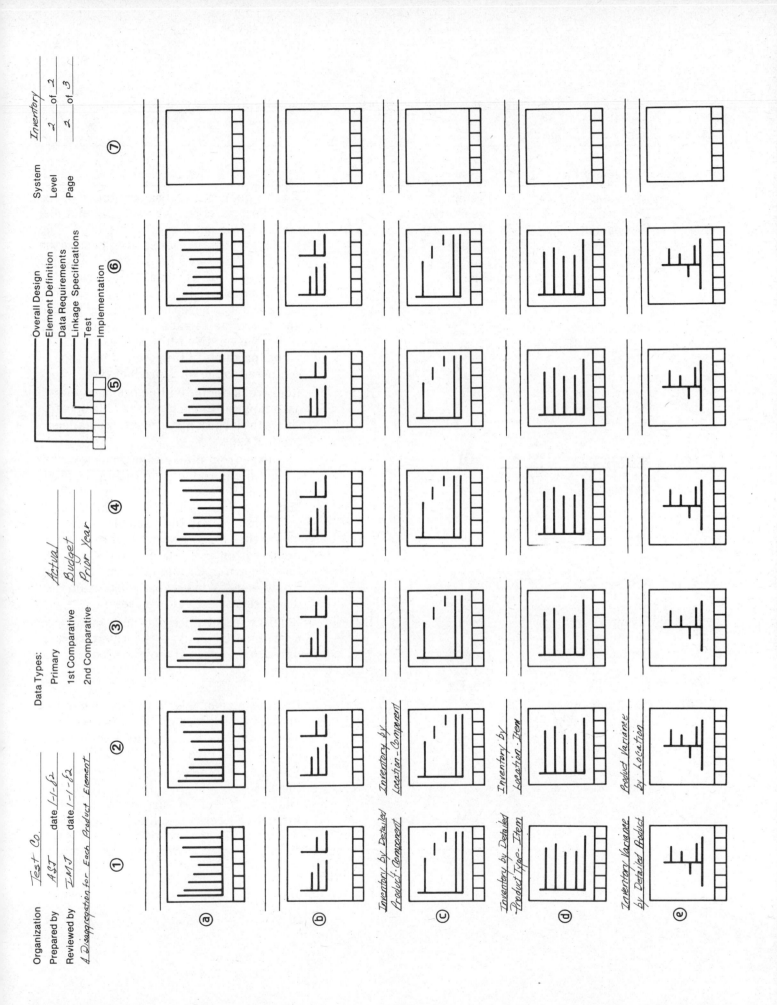

System   _Inventory_
Level   _2_ of _2_
Page   _2_ of _3_

Organization _Test Co._
Prepared by _ASJ_   date _1-1-82_
Reviewed by _IMJ_   date _1-1-82_

A Disaggregation for Each Product Element

Data Types:
Primary   _Actual_
1st Comparative   _Budget_
2nd Comparative   _Prior Year_

Overall Design
Element Definition
Data Requirements
Linkage Specifications
Test
Implementation

① ② ③ ④ ⑤ ⑥ ⑦

ⓐ

ⓑ _Inventory by Detailed Product-Component_ / _Inventory by Location-Component_

ⓒ _Inventory by Detailed Product Type-Item_ / _Inventory by Location-Item_

ⓓ _Inventory Variance by Detailed Product_ / _Product Variance by Location_

ⓔ

For Each Product Element:

Row Col	Name of Chart	From	To	Descriptions
C1	Inventory by Detailed Product— Component	System: Inventory, Level <u>1</u> of <u>2</u>, Page <u>1</u> of <u>3</u>, Chart E1	D1	First sequence in a disaggregation of the inventory variance for each product element shown on the previous level. The product type is further subdivided into the detailed product and location. The sequence starting at Chart C1 describes the detailed product and the sequence starting at C2 shows where the product is located and the value at each location. Chart C1 shows the relative importance of the individual products within the product type as compared to the total product type.
D1	Inventory by Detailed Product— Item	C1	E1	Relative size of individual product types as compared to each other. This chart shows the largest investment by detailed product type.
E1	Inventory by Detailed Product— Variance	D1	—	Variance from plan and/or prior year for the detailed product line within the product type. If further analysis is required, and depending on the remaining detailed information available, each element could be further disaggregated into specific items within the product line similar to those shown in C1 and C2. Each company would have to determine whether further disaggregation would be useful.
C2	Inventory by Location— Component	Level <u>1</u> of <u>2</u>, Page <u>1</u> of <u>3</u>, Charts D2, E2	D2	Relative importance of where the investment in product type is located as compared to the total value of the product type.
D2	Inventory by Location—Item	C2	E2	Relative size of where the investment in product type is located as compared to the other locations. It is easy to see the location of the largest investment.
E2	Inventory by Location— Variance	D2	—	Variance from plan and/or prior year for the product type by location. If further analysis is required, each element could be further disaggregated into sequences similar to that shown on this page.

146

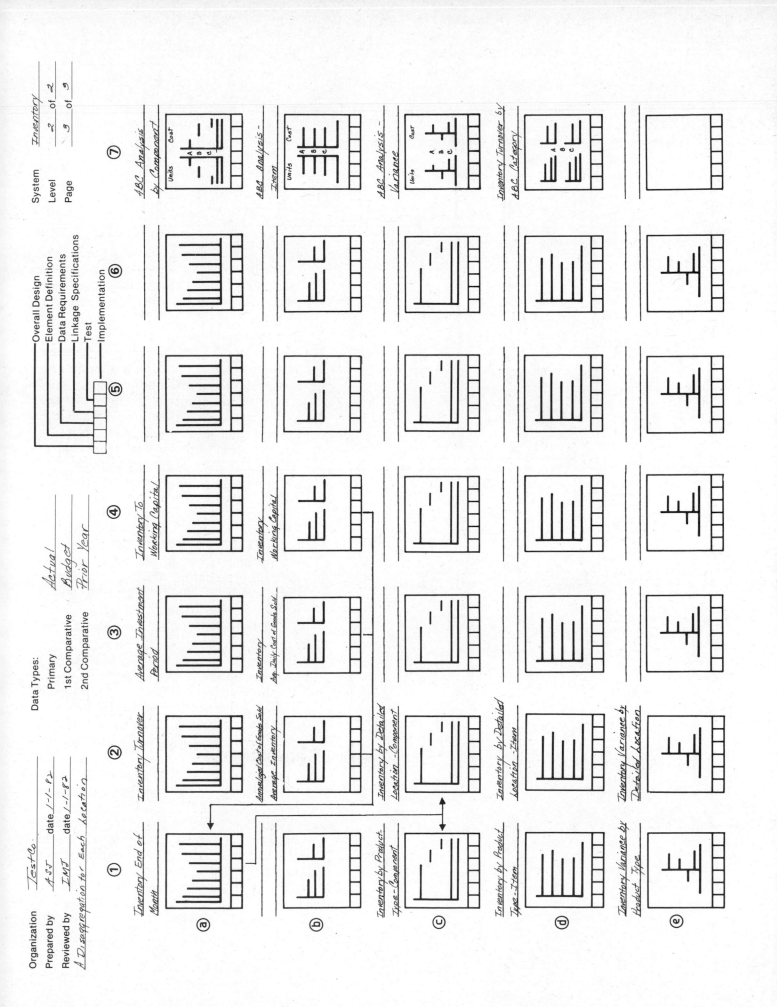

Organization _Testco_
Prepared by _ASJ_ date _1-1-82_
Reviewed by _IMJ_ date _1-1-82_
A Disaggregation for Each Location

Data Types:
Primary _Actual_
1st Comparative _Budget_
2nd Comparative _Prior Year_

System _Inventory_
Level _2_ of _2_
Page _3_ of _3_

Overall Design
Element Definition
Data Requirements
Linkage Specifications
Test
Implementation

① ② ③ ④ ⑤ ⑥ ⑦

(a) _Inventory End of Month_
Inventory Turnover
Average Investment Period
Inventory To Working Capital

(b) _Average Inventory_ / _Annualized Cost of Goods Sold_
Inventory / _Avg. Daily Cost of Goods Sold_
Inventory / _Working Capital_

(c) _Inventory by Product Type - Component_
Inventory by Detailed Location - Component

(d) _Inventory by Product Type - Item_
Inventory by Detailed Location - Item

(e) _Inventory Variance by Product Type_
Inventory Variance by Detailed Location

⑦ _ABC Analysis by Component_
ABA Analysis - Item
ABC Analysis - Variance
Inventory Turnover by ABC Category

This description of the inventory system starts with Charts A2, A3, and A4, and then returns to A1 which disaggregates into further levels.

For Each Location:

Row Col	Name of Chart	From	To	Descriptions
A2	Inventory Turnover	Original	B2	Inventory turnover for this division for the past 12 months as compared to the budget and prior year. This time series describes a seasonal variation and also shows any trend if inventory turnover is increasing or decreasing.
B2	N: Annual Cost of Goods Sold D: Average Inventory	A2	A1	Relative size of the annualized cost of goods sold as compared to the average inventory for this division. Each company has its own way of developing the annualized cost of goods sold and the average inventory and once agreed upon, they should be shown the same for each division. If the change in the turnover is due to a significant change in the relative size of the annualized cost of goods sold, then further analysis and disaggregation could occur in the cost of goods sold system, level 1 of 2, page 1 of 4, Chart A1. If the change in the inventory turnover is due to a change in the relative size of the average inventory, then a further disaggregation and analysis should take place by reviewing Charts A3 and A4, and then going to Chart A1.
A3	Average Investment Period	Original	B3	Time series showing how long, on the average, inventory is kept on hand at the division. This is another way of looking at inventory activity. This sequence shows how many days of inventory are on hand based on the average daily cost of goods sold for the division. This chart shows a relative build-up of inventory (in the division) over time.
B3	N: Inventory, End of the Period D: Average Daily Cost of Goods Sold	A3	A1	The numerator is the actual inventory at the end of the period and the denominator is the average daily cost of goods sold for this division. The average cost of goods sold figure is normally computed by adding the cost of goods sold for the period and dividing the number of sales days in that period. This result shows the relative size of the inventory as compared to the average daily cost of goods sold. If the change in the ratio

Row Col	Name of Chart	From	To	Descriptions
				is due to a change in the relative size of the inventory, then the disaggregation process and further analysis continues by going to Chart A1. If the change in the ratio is due to a change in the relative size of the average daily cost of goods sold, then the disaggregation should be continued in the cost of goods sold system, level 1 of 2, page 1 of 4, Chart A1.
A4	Inventory to Working Capital Ratio	Original	B4	Relative importance of the division's investment in inventory over time as compared to the divisional working capital. Seasonal changes in inventory investment would be shown and any trend in the relative importance of inventory to working capital would also be shown.
B4	N: Inventory D: Working Capital	A4	A1	Relative size of the inventory as compared to the working capital at any point in time. If the change in the ratio is due to a change in the relative size of the inventory, then further disaggregation would occur by going to Chart A1. If the change in the ratio is due to a change in the relative size of the working capital, then further disaggregation and analysis would occur by going to the financial control system, level 1 of 1, page 1 of 1, Chart A4.
A1	Inventory End of Month	System: Inventory, Level 1 of 2, Page 1 of 3, Chart E2	C1, C2	End of the month inventory over time. It shows the total divisional inventory, reflects seasonal trends, and shows an absolute increase or decrease in inventory. The inventory is shown in two basic views: by product line and by detailed location.
C1	Inventory by Product Type—Component	A1	D1	Relative importance of the various product types as compared to the total divisional inventory.
D1	Inventory by Product Type—Item	C1	E1	Relative importance of the various product types as compared to each other. It also shows where the largest investment for this product is located.
E1	Inventory by Product Type—Variance	D1	—	Variance from plan and/or prior year for the components of this division's inventory by product type. If further analysis is required, each element in the chart, or product type, can be further disaggregated into a more detailed product and/or location sequence as shown starting at C1 and C2.

Row Col	Name of Chart	From	To	Descriptions
C2	Inventory by Detailed Location—Component	A1	D2	Relative importance of the inventory as shown by detailed location as compared to the total inventory for the divisions.
D2	Inventory by Detailed Location—Item	C2	E2	Relative size of the inventory by detailed location as compared to each location. This chart shows the largest investment in inventory.
E2	Inventory by Detailed Location—Variance	D2	—	Variance from plan and/or prior year for the inventory investment at each detailed location. If further analysis is required, the inventory at each detailed location can be disaggregated into a sequence similar to that starting at C1 and C2
A7	ABC Analysis— Component	Original	B7	Traditional ABC analysis of inventory for divisional inventory. The co-relationship compares the number of units compared to the cost of those units. A normal ABC picture usually shows that the A items account for 15% of the units and 50-60% of the dollar value, the B inventory where 25-30% of the units account for 25-30% of the dollar value, and the C inventory where 60% of the units account for approximately 15% of the dollar value. This chart shows the relative number of units as compared to the total units in inventory, and the relative dollar value of the respective units as compared to the total value of inventory. By using a standard percentage to categorize the ABC such as 15, 30, and 55% (or whatever percentage is relative to the individual company), a pattern of divisional inventory investments occurs and the control procedures can be initiated relative to the value of the investment. Also, the divisional pattern can be compared to the total corporate pattern and the other divisions to get an overall picture of inventory values.
B7	ABC Analysis—Item	A7	C7	Relative size of the ABC units as compared to each other and the respective value of those units as compared to each other.
C7	ABC Analysis— Variance	B7	D7	Variance from plan and/or prior year of both the units and their respective dollar values. If further analysis of the inventory is required, a detailed disaggregation starts at A1. However, Chart D7 might give an indication of the ABC category where basic problems are to be found.

150

Row Col	Name of Chart	From	To	Descriptions
D7	Inventory Turnover by ABC Category	C7 and System: Inventory Level <u>1</u> of <u>2</u> Page <u>1</u> of <u>3</u> Chart D7	—	Turnover of inventory by ABC category. *If the information is available for this computation, it would provide a clear picture of the turnover by the various ABC values of inventory. The A items should reflect a high turnover, B items a lesser turnover, and C items the least. A significant change in turnover from plan could be caused because the sales within that category have changed.

1. INVENTORY

Chart 10-018 shows a time series of inventory turnover. August and September were significantly less than budgeted. A breakdown of the ratio for September (Chart 10-019) gives us more information. The right-hand chart shows how much the turnover rate was less than budget. The left-hand chart shows us that:

1. The ratio is made up of annual cost of goods sold divided by average inventory.
2. The reason for the ratio being off from budget is that average inventory was greater than budget.
3. Inventory was off approximately $15,500.

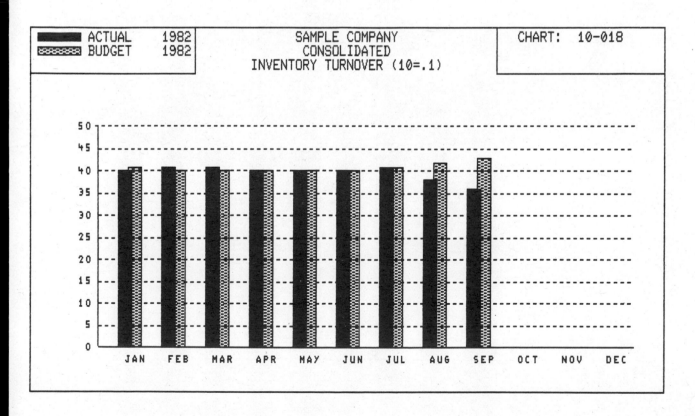

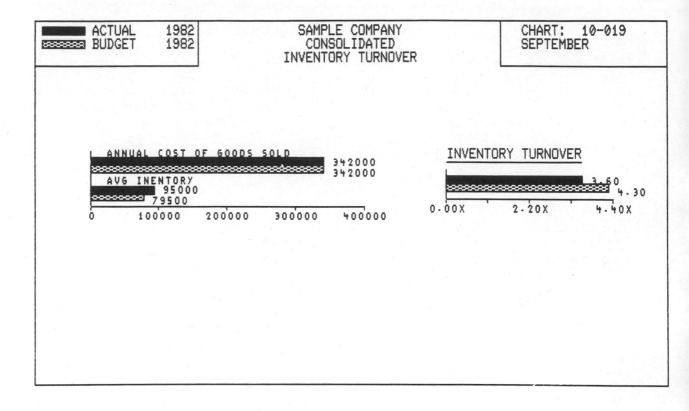

ANNUAL COST OF GOODS SOLD
342000
342000

AVG INENTORY
95000
79500

0   100000   200000   300000   400000

INVENTORY TURNOVER
3.60
4.30

0.00X   2.20X   4.40X

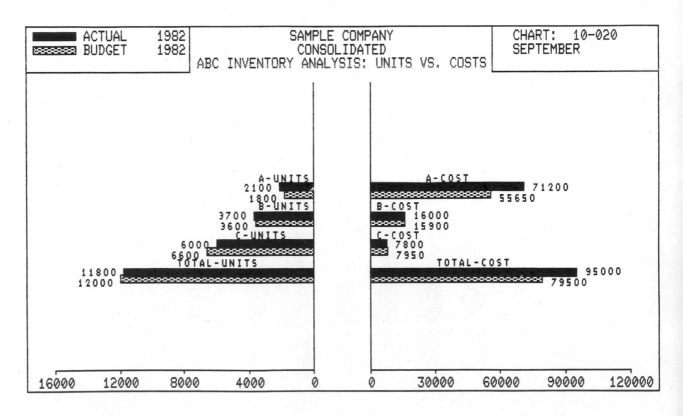

A-UNITS
2100
1800

A-COST
71200
55650

B-UNITS
3700
3600

B-COST
16000
15900

C-UNITS
6000
6600

C-COST
7800
7950

TOTAL-UNITS
11800
12000

TOTAL-COST
95000
79500

16000   12000   8000   4000   0   0   30000   60000   90000   120000

152

Chart 10-020 shows a graphic presentation of an inventory ABC analysis. The left-hand chart shows the components of inventory in units. Type C inventory contains the most units. The right-hand side shows the components in inventory by cost. Type A inventory contains the most costs. By comparing both charts we can see that a slight increase in units of A inventory was responsible for the increase in the total costs.

Charts 10-021, 10-022, and 10-023 show detailed breakdowns of Type A inventory for September. Chart 10-021 shows us that the components of Type A inventory are as budgeted, although the pattern has changed significantly. Chart 10-022 shows that the divisions with the highest values of inventory are Friedmont and Mears. Friedmont was not budgeted to have the most significant amount of inventory in the company. Chart 10-023 confirms this, as Friedmont was significantly greater than budget. Smith, Channing, and Mears were also significantly higher than budget.

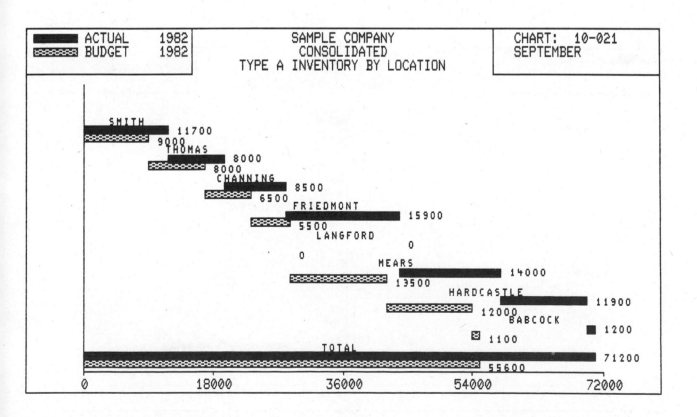

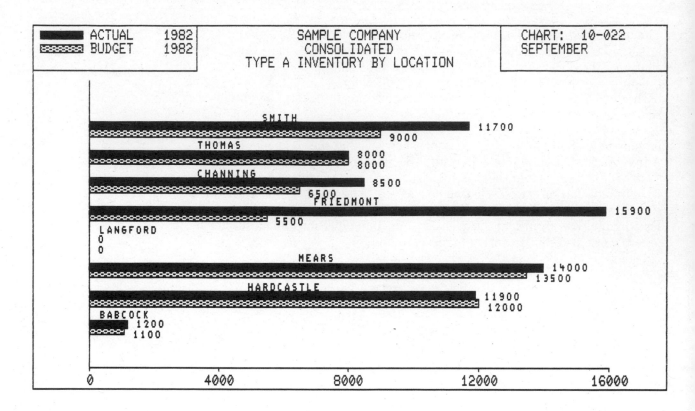

ACTUAL 1982
BUDGET 1982

SAMPLE COMPANY
CONSOLIDATED
TYPE A INVENTORY BY LOCATION

CHART: 10-022
SEPTEMBER

SMITH
11700
9000

THOMAS
8000
8000

CHANNING
8500
6500

FRIEDMONT
15900
5500

LANGFORD
0
0

MEARS
14000
13500

HARDCASTLE
11900
12000

BABCOCK
1200
1100

0   4000   8000   12000   16000

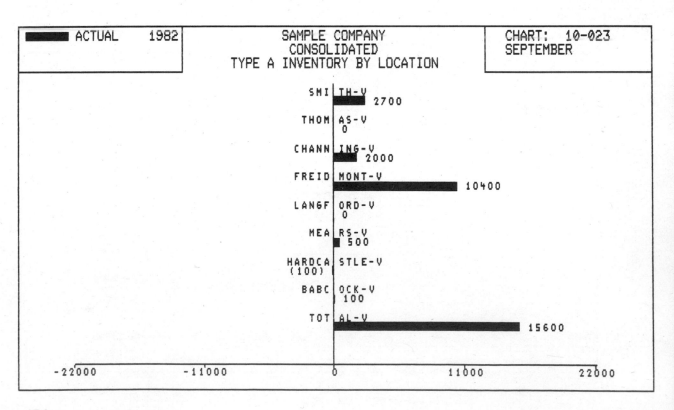

ACTUAL 1982

SAMPLE COMPANY
CONSOLIDATED
TYPE A INVENTORY BY LOCATION

CHART: 10-023
SEPTEMBER

SMITH-V
2700

THOMAS-V
0

CHANNING-V
2000

FREIDMONT-V
10400

LANGFORD-V
0

MEARS-V
500

HARDCASTLE-V
(100)

BABCOCK-V
100

TOTAL-V
15600

-22000   -11000   0   11000   22000

154

CHAPTER 9

FIXED ASSETS

Fixed assets is designed to show a system of control over the actual dollar value in assets as well as the use of the assets (accumulated depreciation) shown in the ratios. Because fixed assets are usually assignable to various divisions, a responsibility sequence is shown

As shown in Exhibit 9.1, there are a number of key indicators to fixed assets. Each of the key indicators disaggregates into either fixed assets or accumulated depreciation. Fixed assets and the corresponding accumulated depreciation is disaggregated by both location and type of fixed asset at level 1. In level 2, fixed assets and accumulated depreciation by location are further disaggregated by specific location and type of asset. Fixed assets and accumulated depreciation by type of fixed asset are disaggregated further by location.

EXHIBIT 9.1

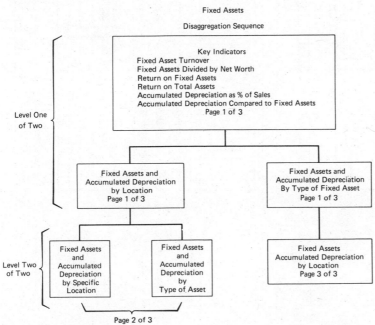

Fixed Assets

Disaggregation Sequence

| Key Indicators |
| Fixed Asset Turnover |
| Fixed Assets Divided by Net Worth |
| Return on Fixed Assets |
| Return on Total Assets |
| Accumulated Depreciation as % of Sales |
| Accumulated Depreciation Compared to Fixed Assets |
| Page 1 of 3 |

Level One of Two

Fixed Assets and Accumulated Depreciation by Location
Page 1 of 3

Fixed Assets and Accumulated Depreciation By Type of Fixed Asset
Page 1 of 3

Level Two of Two

Fixed Assets and Accumulated Depreciation by Specific Location

Fixed Assets and Accumulated Depreciation by Type of Asset

Fixed Assets Accumulated Depreciation by Location
Page 3 of 3

Page 2 of 3

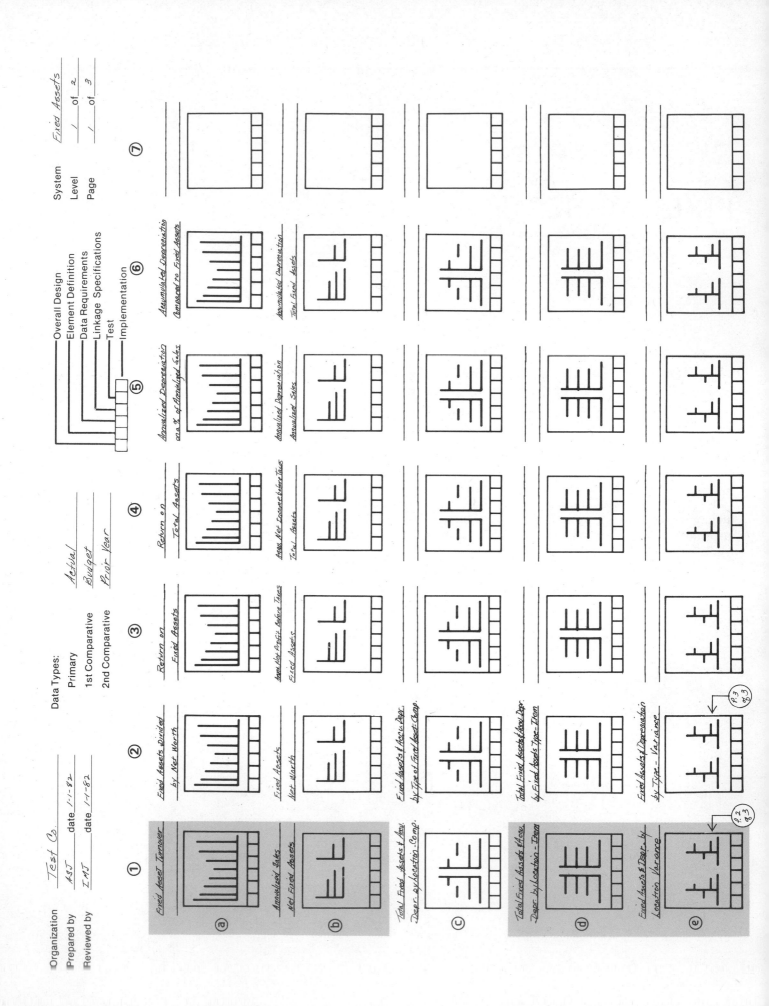

Row Col	Name of Chart	From	To	Descriptions
A1	Fixed Asset Turnover	Original	B1	Time series showing the asset turnover for the past 12 months. The chart would indicate any change in the turnover and could be one of the early indicators of future problems.
B1	N: Annualized Sales D: Net Fixed Assets	A1	C1, C2	Ratio showing the computation of the turnover ratio. The annualized sales can be computed in at least two ways, either by taking the months' sales and annualizing them, or by taking the year-to-date sales and annualizing them. Either method could be used but once chosen, a company should be consistent. The chart shows the relative size of the annualized sales as compared to the net fixed assets. If a change in the ratio is due to a change in the relative size of the annualized sales, then further analysis and disaggregation should be viewed at the sales system, level 1 of 1, Chart A1, and subsequent. If the change in ratio is due to a change in the size of the net fixed assets, then further analysis and disaggregation could occur as shown in C1 and C2. However, fixed asset turnover is only one of the important ratios shown in this system and all of the ratios should be reviewed prior to disaggregating to C1, C2.
A2	Fixed Assets Divided by Net Worth	Original	B2	Time series for the past 12 months of the ratio of fixed assets divided by net worth. This should be a fairly consistent ratio and any major changes or trends should be easily accounted for.
B2	N: Fixed Assets D: Net Worth	A2	C1, C2	Relative size of fixed assets as compared to the net worth. If the change in ratio is a change in the size of the fixed assets, then further analysis and disaggregation would take place through C1 and C2. If the change in the ratio is due to a change in the relative size of the net worth, then further analysis and disaggregation should take place in the control system, Chapter 6.
A3	Return on Fixed Assets	Original	B3	Past 12 months of return on fixed assets. It is one of the more critical performance measurements used for internal control. If fixed assets are controlled by divisions and this ratio can be shown at the division level, it could be used as a basis for allocating

157

Row Col	Name of Chart	From	To	Descriptions
				assets to various divisions. Those divisions that show a higher rate of return on fixed assets would be candidates for more money.
B3	N: Annualized Net Profit Before Taxes D: Fixed Assets	A 3	C1, C2	For the corporate ratios shown at this level, the net profit before taxes should be annualized on the same basis as the annualized sales in B1. There *must* be a consistency between those two ratios. The ratio creates an asset utilization pattern that can be used to understand the use of assets.
				At the divisional level, if net income before taxes can be computed at the divisional level, the performance template developed at the corporate level can be used to measure divisional performance. Profit contributions can also be used as the numerator for divisional performance measures. Each company will have to decide on the revenue computations at the division's level. The asset balance will also require a corporate policy for the denominator. Such questions as how corporate assets are allocated must be resolved.
				Chart B3 shows the relative size of the net profit as compared to the total fixed assets. If the change in the ratio is due to a change in the relative size of the net profit, then further disaggregation and analysis would take place in the income system. If the change in the ratio is due to a change in the relative size of the fixed assets, then further analysis and disaggregation would take place in C1 and C2.
A4	Return on Total Assets	Original	B4	Similar to A3 except that the return is shown on all assets. This is normally a ratio used at the corporate level and can not be disaggregated into the division level.
B4	N: Annualized Net Income Before Taxes D: Total Assets	A4	C1, C2	Net income before taxes should be the same as shown in B3, and the total assets will be all of the assets shown on the balance sheet. This chart shows the relative size of the net income before taxes as compared to the total assets. If the change in the ratio is due to a change in the relative size of the net profit, then further analysis and disaggregation will be shown in the income system. If the change in the ratio is

158

Row Col	Name of Chart	From	To	Descriptions
				due to a change in the relative size of the total assets, then further analysis and dis-aggregation will take place in this system starting at C1 and C2 and in the control system (chapter 5).
A5	Annualized De-preciation As a Percentage of Annualized Sales	Original	B5	Time series showing depreciation as a percentage of sales. The trend will reflect corporate investment and depreciation policy.
B5	N: Annualized Depreciation D: Annualized Sales	A5	C1, C2	The annualized depreciation should be computed on a basis consistent with that of the other annualized computations. The annualized sales should be identical to the annualized sales used in B1. The chart shows the relative size of the annualized depreciation as compared to the annual-ized sales. If the change in ratio is due to a change in the relative size of the annual-ized depreciation, then further analysis and disaggregation can take place in C1 and C2. If the change in the ratio is due to a change in the relative size of the sales, then further analysis and disaggregation should start at the sales system.
A6	Accumulated Depre-ciation Compared to Fixed Assets	Original	B6	Percentage of asset depreciation that has been matched to revenue. The larger the percentage the more likely that the assets have not been replaced and modernized. There is a limited life to most of the assets. This chart is a good indicator of the status of preventive maintenance or the rate of modernizing the equipment.
B6	N: Accumulated Depreciation D: Total Fixed Assets	A6	C1, C2	Relative size of the accumulated depreci-ation as compared to the total fixed assets. If the change in the ratio is due to a change in the relative size of the accumulated depreciation, or the relative size of the total fixed assets, then further disaggregation and analysis could take place in C1 and C2. Further disaggregation and analysis could also take place in the control sequence, Chapter 5.
C1	Total Fixed Assets and Accumulated Depreciation by Location— Component	B1, B2, B3, B4, B5, B6	D1	Co-relationship showing the relative im-portance of the accumulated depreciation by location as compared to the total depre-ciation, and the relative importance of the fixed assets by location as compared to the

Row Col	Name of Chart	From	To	Descriptions
				total fixed assets. Also, it provides some idea of the relative age of the assets in each of the locations by comparing accumulated depreciation to the respective assets.
D1	Total Fixed Assets and Accumulated Depreciation by Location—Item	C1	E1	Relative size of the accumulated depreciation as compared to other accumulated depreciation by location and the relative size of the fixed assets by location as compared to each other.
E1	Fixed Assets and Accumulated Depreciation by Location —Variance	D1	System: Fixed Assets, Level 2 of 2, Page 2 of 3, C1, C2	Variance from plan and/or prior year for the fixed assets and depreciation by location. If further analysis is required, each element can be further disaggregated into a sequence similar to C1 and C2. These sequences are described in fixed assets, level 2 of 2, page 2 of 3, C1 and C2.
C2	Fixed Assets and Accumulated Depreciation by Type of Fixed Assets —Component	B1, B2, B3, B4, B5, B6	D2	Co-relationship showing the relative importance of the accumulated depreciation by type of asset as compared to the total depreciation, and the relative importance of the cost of the asset types as compared to the total fixed assets. It also shows the relative age of each asset by comparing the asset cost of the respective depreciation.
D2	Total Fixed Assets and Accumulated Depreciation by Fixed Asset Type—Item	C2	E2	Co-relationship showing the relative importance of the accumulated depreciation by fixed assets type as compared to each other and the relative size of the fixed assets by type as compared to each other.
E2	Fixed Assets and Depreciation by Type—Variance	D2	System: Fixed Assets, Level 2 of 2, Page 3 of 3, Chart C1	Variance from plan and/or prior year for the fixed assets and the depreciation by asset type. If further analysis is required, each of the elements can be further disaggregated into a sequence similar to C1 and C2. This particular variance is further analyzed in System Fixed Assets, Level 2 of 2, Page 3 of 3, Chart C1.

160

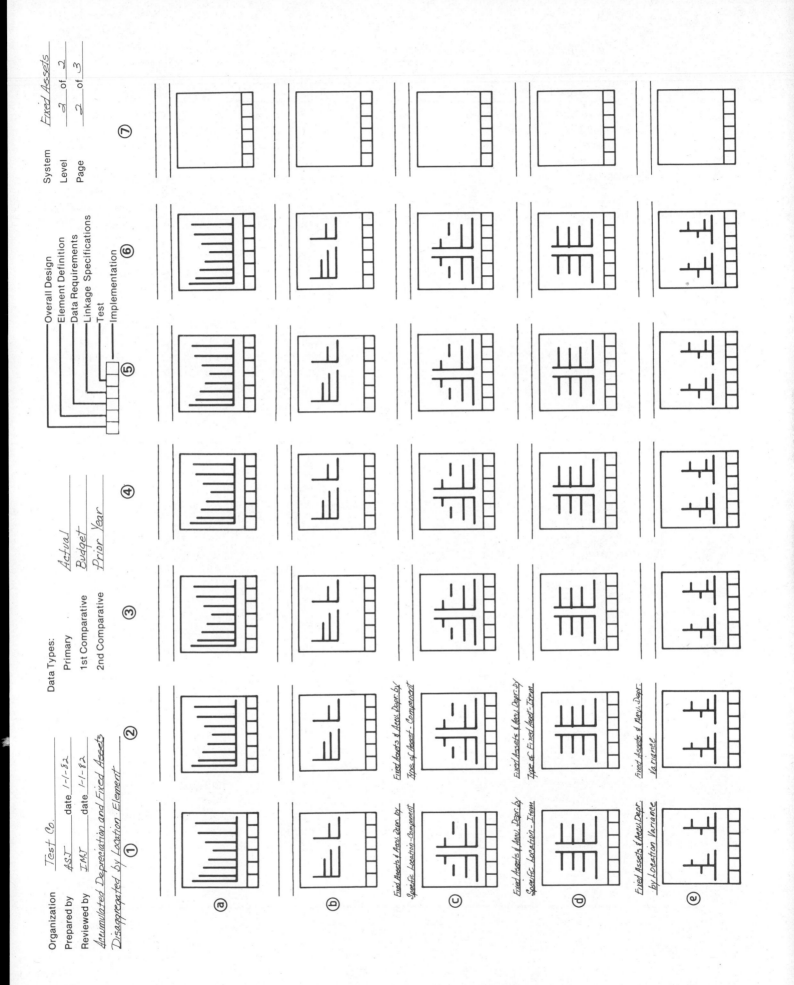

Organization   _Test Co._

Prepared by   _AST_   date _1-1-82_

Reviewed by   _IMJ_   date _1-1-82_

Accumulated Depreciation and Fixed Assets

Disaggregated by Location Element

① ②

Data Types:

Primary   _Actual_

1st Comparative   _Budget_

2nd Comparative   _Prior Year_

③ ④ ⑤ ⑥ ⑦

- Overall Design
- Element Definition
- Data Requirements
- Linkage Specifications
- Test
- Implementation

ⓐ

ⓑ

ⓒ   _Fixed Assets & Accu. Depn. by Specific Location-Component_   _Fixed Assets & Accu. Depr. by Type of Asset - Component_

ⓓ   _Fixed Assets & Accu. Depr. by Specific Location - Item_   _Fixed Assets & Accu. Depr. by Type of Fixed Asset - Item_

ⓔ   _Fixed Assets & Accu. Depr. by Location Variance_   _Fixed Assets & Accu. Depr. Variance_

Row Col	Name of Chart	From	To	Descriptions
C1	Fixed Assets and Accumulated Depreciation by Specific Location —Component	System: Fixed Assets, Level <u>1</u> of <u>2</u>, Page <u>1</u> of <u>3</u>, Chart D1, E1	D1	Co-relationship disaggregating each of the location elements shown on page 1 of 3, Charts D1 and E1 show the relative importance of the fixed assets by detailed location as compared to the total assets for that location, and the relative importance of the accumulated depreciation as compared to the total depreciation for that location. The co-relationship aspect of the two charts shows the relative age of the assets as shown by the accumulated depreciation. It will also indicate where assets have not been renovated and updated.
D1	Fixed Assets and Accumulated Depreciation by Specific Location—Item	C1	E1	Co-relationship showing the relative size of the fixed assets by specific location as compared to each other and the relative size of the accumulated depreciation of each location as compared to each other.
E1	Fixed Assets and Accumulated Depreciation by Location —Variance	D1	—	Variance between planned and/or prior year for the fixed assets and accumulated depreciation. If further analysis is required, similar sequences as shown starting at C1 and C2 could be developed. It is possible that at this point access to the book of records might be required. No further sequences are shown.
C2	Fixed Assets and Accumulated Depreciation by Type of Asset—Component	System: Fixed Assets, Level <u>1</u> of <u>1</u>, Page <u>1</u> of <u>3</u>, E1	D2	Co-relationship showing the relative importance of the fixed assets by type as compared to the total assets in this particular location, and the relative importance of the accumulated depreciation by respective fixed asset type as compared to the total depreciation for this location. It shows the relative age of the individual fixed asset types when comparing fixed assets and the accumulated depreciation.
D2	Fixed Assets and Accumulated Depreciation by Type of Fixed Asset—Item	C2	E2	Co-relationship showing the relative size of the fixed asset types as compared to each other and the relative size of the respective accumulated depreciation as compared to each other.
E2	Fixed Assets and Accumulated Depreciation—Variance	D2	—	Co-variance showing the variance from plan and/or prior year for the fixed asset type and the respective accumulated depreciation. If further analysis is required, each element could be further disaggregated into a sequence similar to that shown starting at Chart C1. No further disaggregation is shown in this example.

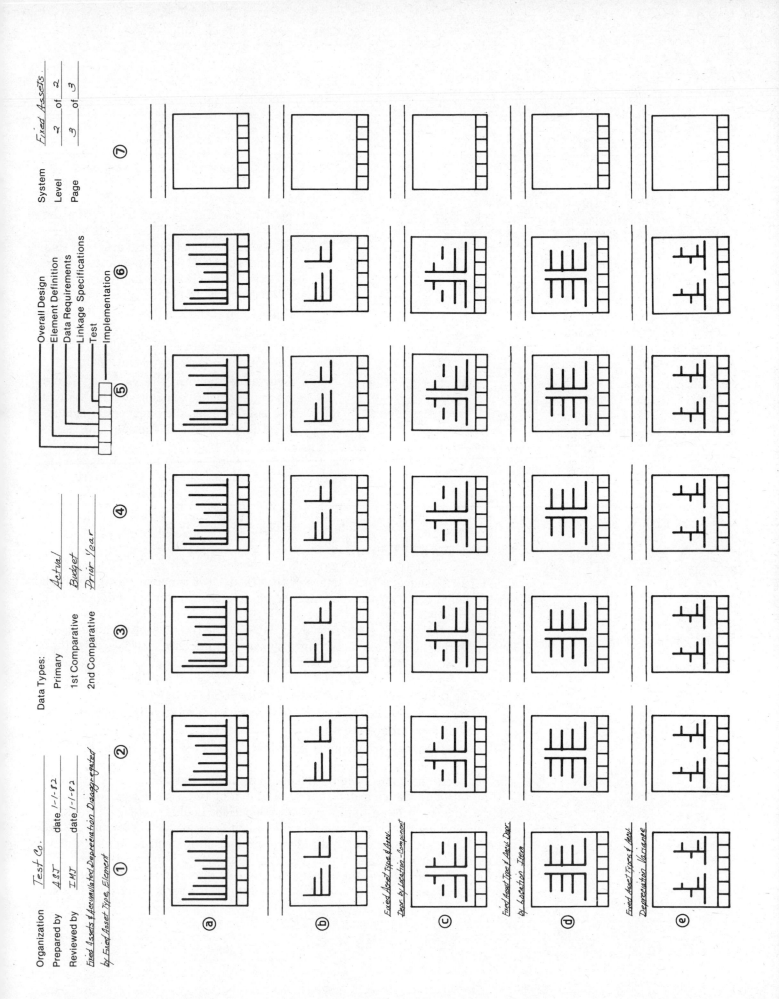

Organization _Test Co._

Prepared by _AJJ_ date _1-1-82_

Reviewed by _IMJ_ date _1-1-82_

Fixed Assets & Accumulated Depreciation Disaggregated

by Fixed Asset Type, Element

Data Types:

Primary _Actual_

1st Comparative _Budget_

2nd Comparative _Prior Year_

Overall Design
Element Definition
Data Requirements
Linkage Specifications
Test
Implementation

① ② ③ ④ ⑤ ⑥ ⑦

(a)

(b) _Fixed Asset Type & Accu._
Depr. by Location-Component

(c) _Fixed Asset Type & Accu. Depr._
by Location Item

(d) _Fixed Asset Types & Accu._
Depreciation Variance

(e)

Row Col	Name of Chart	From	To	Descriptions
C1	Fixed Asset Type and Accumulated Depreciation by Location—Component	System: Fixed Assets, Level <u>1</u> of <u>2</u>, Page <u>1</u> of <u>2</u>, Chart E2		Further disaggregation of fixed asset type showing the location of the fixed asset type, and the respective accumulated depreciation. This co-relationship chart shows the relative importance of fixed assets by location as compared to the total assets of that type and the relative importance of the respective depreciation as compared to the total depreciation for that type.
D1	Fixed Asset Type and Accumulated Depreciation by Location—Item	C1	E1	Relative size of the fixed assets by location as compared to each location and the relative importance of the accumulated depreciation for the respective locations.
E1	Fixed Asset Types and Accumulated Depreciation—Variance	D2	—	Co-variance showing the variances from plan and/or prior year for each location of fixed asset type and their respective accumulated depreciation. If further analysis is required, each of the elements could be further disaggregated to a sequence similar to that starting at C1. No further disaggregation is shown in this example.

1. FIXED ASSETS

Chart 10-032 shows a time series of the fixed asset turnover ratio through September. The turnover rate was increasing until September when the rate dropped below budget.

Chart 10-033 shows a further breakdown of the fixed asset turnover ratio for September. The chart on the right shows how much the ratio was less than budget in September. The chart on the left shows:

1. The ratio is derived from sales divided by fixed assets.
2. The reason for the change in the ratio was the relative increase in fixed assets as compared to budget.
3. Fixed assets increased $91 thousand.

The next few charts investigate the changes in fixed assets.

Chart 10-007 shows a detailed breakdown of fixed assets by location as related to accumulated depreciation by location. Looking at the right-hand side, we can see that Hardy and Shane have the largest investment in fixed assets. By looking at the accumulated depreciation for Hardy and Shane we can see what proportion of the assets have been depreciated.

Chart 10-008 shows the variance from budget for asset values and accumulated depreciation by location. Looking at the asset values, we can see

that the Hardy and Shane divisions were over budget. Accumulated depreciation variances for these divisions were negative. These divisions bought new
assets and traded them in with older depreciated assets.

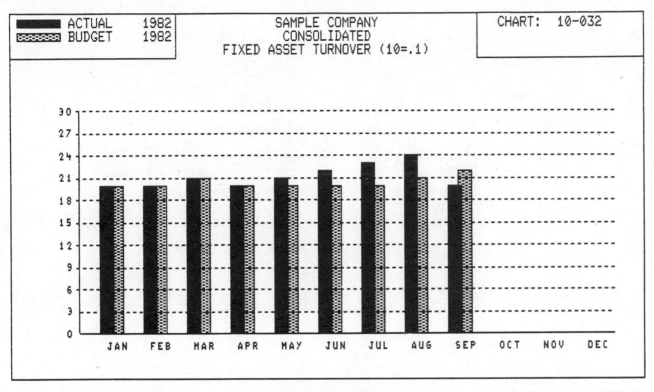

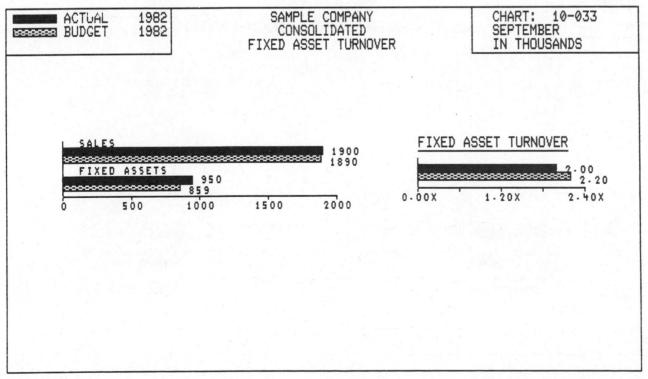

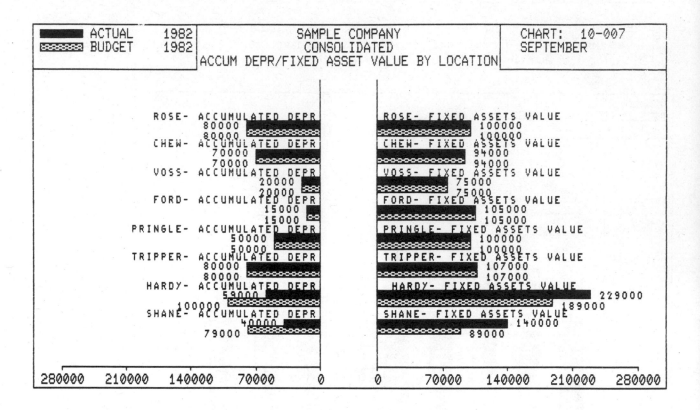

ACCUM DEPR/FIXED ASSET VALUE BY LOCATION

ROSE- ACCUMULATED DEPR
80000
80000
CHEW- ACCUMULATED DEPR
70000
70000
VOSS- ACCUMULATED DEPR
20000
20000
FORD- ACCUMULATED DEPR
15000
15000
PRINGLE- ACCUMULATED DEPR
50000
50000
TRIPPER- ACCUMULATED DEPR
80000
80000
HARDY- ACCUMULATED DEPR
59000
100000
SHANE- ACCUMULATED DEPR
40000
79000

ROSE- FIXED ASSETS VALUE
100000
100000
CHEW- FIXED ASSETS VALUE
94000
94000
VOSS- FIXED ASSETS VALUE
75000
75000
FORD- FIXED ASSETS VALUE
105000
105000
PRINGLE- FIXED ASSETS VALUE
100000
100000
TRIPPER- FIXED ASSETS VALUE
107000
107000
HARDY- FIXED ASSETS VALUE
229000
189000
SHANE- FIXED ASSETS VALUE
140000
89000

280000 210000 140000 70000 0   0 70000 140000 210000 280000

ACCUM DEPR/FIXED ASSET VALUE BY LOCATION

V-ROSE- ACCUMULATED DEPR
0
V-CHEW- ACCUMULATED DEPR
0
V-VOSS- ACCUMULATED DEPR
0
V-FORD- ACCUMULATED DEPR
0
V-PRINGLE- ACCUMULATED DEPR
0
V-TRIPPER- ACCUMULATED DEPR
0
V-HARDY- ACCUMULATED DEPR
(41000)
V-SHANE- ACCUMULATED DEPR
(39000)
V-TOTAL ACCUMULATED DEPR
(80000)

V-ROSE- FIXED ASSET VALUE
0
V-CHEW- FIXED ASSET VALUE
0
V-VOSS- FIXED ASSET VALUE
0
V-FORD- FIXED ASSET VALUE
0
V-PRINGLE- FIXED ASSET VALUE
0
V-TRIPPER- FIXED ASSET VALUE
0
V-HARDY- FIXED ASSET VALUE
40000
V-SHANE- FIXED ASSET VALUE
51000
V-TOTAL FIXED ASSET VALUE
91000

-140000 -70000 0 70000 140000   -140000 -70000 0 70000 140000

CHAPTER 10

ACCOUNTS PAYABLE

The accounts payable control system is designed to maintain the credit reputation of the corporation. Exhibit 10.1 shows the key indicators for the disaggregation sequence for accounts payable. Accounts payable are, in fact, a source of funding for the corporation and, properly controlled, can provide a significant source of working capital for the company. The basic goal of the control system is to make sure the accounts payable are not out of control and are so old the vendors are no longer willing to supply the company. That goal is accomplished by the aging of accounts payable at the data level. At the second data level, each aging element is disaggregated by vendor type and division to maintain responsibility.

Another goal of the system is to show a picture of responsibility for control. That goal is met by the disaggregation of accounts by vendor type and by the division. Each of these are further disaggregated at the second data level to provide a more detailed responsibility picture.

Finally, the counterpart of cash control and investment of cash is to control the discounts taken for accounts payable. Discounts lost as the result of poor cash control cost money and it might be wise to change the cash investment strategy to take advantage of the discounts available. Of course, each corporation will have to determine if the discounts are worth more than having the cash on hand or the other uses to which it could be put. That task is accomplished by showing the comparison of discounts taken to the discounts available at the first data level.

EXHIBIT 10.1

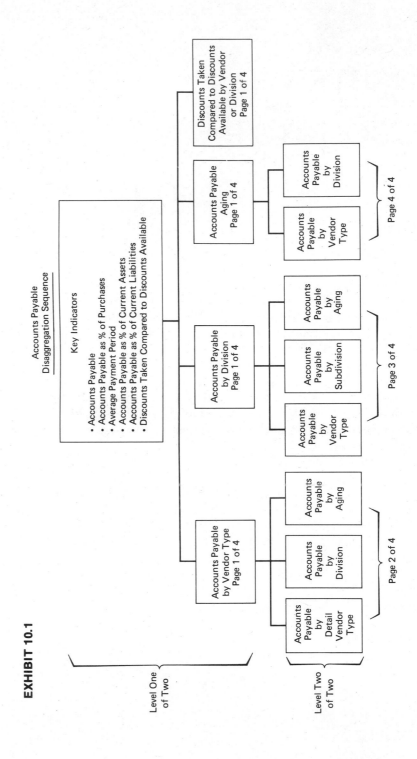

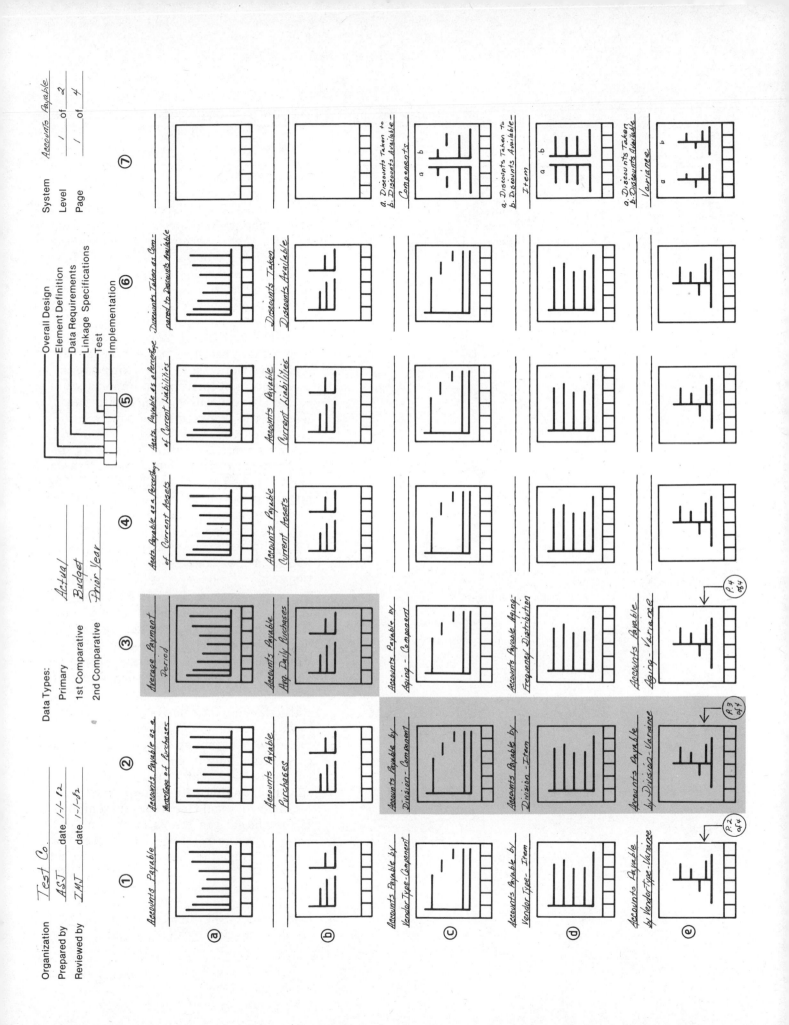

Row Col	Name of Chart	From	To	Descriptions
A1	Accounts Payable	System: Corporate Control, Level <u>1</u> of <u>2</u>, Page <u>1</u> of <u>1</u>, Chart A2, System; Financial Control, Level <u>1</u> of <u>1</u>, Page <u>1</u> of <u>1</u>, Chart B7	C1, C2, C3	Time series showing the balance of accounts payable at the end of the month over the previous 12-month period as compared to the budget and prior year. Seasonal patterns should become apparent and the trends of the actual size of accounts payable will also become apparent. The fact that accounts payable increased in total over time may not be a reflection of out of control accounts payable but may, in fact, be a reflection of the growth of the company, where accounts payable is contributing a constant share of working capital. A picture of the relative importance of accounts payable to working capital can be seen by the two ratios, accounts payable over the current assets, and accounts payable over current liabilities, Charts A4 and A5, respectively. Accounts payable as a percentage of purchase, Chart A2, shows another picture of how the total of accounts payable relates to overall corporate activity. The average payment period, Chart A3, indicates if accounts payable is still within the parameters set by the corporation.
A2	Accounts Payable as a Percentage of Purchases	Original	B2	Time series showing the percentage of accounts payable as compared to annualized purchases for the past 12 months. This percentage should remain seasonally constant over time and any change could be described by unusual events or a change in corporate policy.
B2	N: Accounts Payable D: Purchases	A2	A1	Ratio showing the relative size of accounts payable at the end of the month as compared to the annualized purchases. The corporation might choose to show purchases to date that would create a constantly changing ratio. The pattern, once established, should form a useful template. If the changes in the ratio are due to a change in the relative size of accounts payable, then the disaggregation would start with A1. If the changes in the ratio are due to a change in the relative size of purchases, either to date or on an annualized basis, then further disaggregation would take place by an examination of the

170

Row Col	Name of Chart	From	To	Descriptions
				Purchase System, Charts A1 and subsequent.
A3	Average Payment Period	Original	B3	Time series showing a 12-month average payment period. There will be seasonal variations and they should be consistent over time.
B3	N: Accounts Payable D: Average Daily Purchases	A3	A1	Ratio showing the relative size of accounts payable as divided by the average daily purchases. It shows how many days of purchases are contained in the accounts payable balance. If the change in the number of days to payment is due to a change in the relative size of accounts payable, then the disaggregation would continue by going to Chart A1. If the change in the ratio is due to a change in the relative size of the average daily purchases, then the disaggregation would continue by going to the purchase system, Charts A1 and subsequent.
A4	Accounts Payable as a Percentage of Current Assets	Original	B4	Time series showing the percentage of accounts payable as compared to current assets for the past 12 months. This ratio will exhibit seasonal variations and these should be included in the planning.
B4	N: Accounts Payable D: Current Assets	A4	A1	Ratio showing the relative size of the accounts payable to current assets. If the change in the ratio is due to a change in the relative size of the accounts payable, then further disaggregation would take place by starting at Chart A1. If the change in the ratio is due to a change in the relative size of the current assets, then further disaggregation of current assets would occur by going to Chapter 5, the corporate control system, level 1 of 1, page 1 of 1, Charts A2 and B1.
A5	Accounts Payable as a Percentage of Current Liabilities	Original	B5	Time series showing the past 12 months of accounts payable as a percentage of current liabilities. Seasonal patterns will emerge and should be accounted for in the planning cycle.
B5	N: Accounts Payable D: Current Liabilities	A6	A1	Ratio showing the relative size of accounts payable to current liabilities. If the change in the ratio is due to a change in the relative size of accounts payable, then further disaggregation would be started at Chart A1.

Row Col	Name of Chart	From	To	Descriptions
				If the change in the ratio is due to a change in the relative size of the current liabilities, further disaggregation would take place in the corporate control system, level 1 of 1, page 1 of 1, Charts A2 and B3.
A6	Discounts Taken as Compared to Discounts Available	Original	B6	Time series showing the ratio of discounts taken to the discounts available for the past 12 months. In these days of high interest rates and the need for cash on the part of most suppliers, the purchasing department can negotiate significant discounts for payment terms and this chart would reflect both the performance of the purchasing department and the performance of the comptroller's department in meeting those payment terms through proper cash management.
B6	N: Discounts Taken D: Discounts Available	A6	C7	Ratio showing the relative size of the discounts taken to the total amount of discounts available. A change can be further analyzed by the Charts C7, D7, and E7.
C7	Discounts Taken to Discounts Available— Component (by Vendor Type or by Division)	B6	D7	Co-relationship showing the relative importance of the source of discounts taken as compared to the total discounts taken, and the source of total discounts available as compared to the total discounts available.
D7	Discounts Taken to Discounts Available— Item (by Vendor Type or by Division)	C7	E7	Co-relationship showing the discounts taken on the left and the discounts available on the right. The left-hand chart shows the relative importance of the discounts taken by source as compared to each other. The chart on the right shows the total discounts available by the respective sources as compared to each other.
E7	Discounts Taken and Discounts Available— Variances	D7	—	Twin variance showing the variance from plan and/or prior year for the discounts taken by source as compared to the discounts available by source. If further analysis is required, each of the elements could be disaggregated into a sequence similar to that starting at C7. No further examples are shown in this sequence.
C1	Accounts Payable by Vendor Type— Component	A1	D1	Relative importance of the accounts payable by vendor type as compared to the total accounts payable.
D1	Accounts Payable by Vendor Type—Item	C1	E1	Relative size of the accounts payable by vendor type as compared to each other. This chart would show by the vendor type the larger balances of accounts payable.

Row Col	Name of Chart	From	To	Descriptions
E1	Accounts Payable by Vendor Type—Variance	D1	System: Accounts Payable, Level 2 of 2, Page 2 of 4, Charts C1, C2, C3	Variance from plan and/or prior year for the accounts payable by vendor type as compared to each other. If further analysis is required, each of the accounts payable by vendor type can be further disaggregated into detailed accounts payable by vendor type as shown in Accounts Payable System, Level 2 of 2, Page 2 of 4, Charts C1, C2 and C3.
C2	Accounts Payable by Division—Component	A1	D2	Relative importance of the accounts payable by each division as compared to the total accounts payable.
D2	Accounts Payable by Division—Item	C2	E2	Relative size of the accounts payable for each division as compared to each other. The division with the largest accounts payable wil be apparent.
E2	Accounts Payable by Division—Variance	D2	System: Accounts Payable, Level 2 of 2, Page 3 of 4, Charts C1, C2, C3	Variance from plan and/or prior year for the accounts payable held by each division. If further analysis is required, each division can be further disaggregated into sequences similar to those shown in Accounts Payable System, Level 2 of 2, Page 3 of 4, Charts C1, C2 and C3.
C3	Accounts Payable by Aging—Component	See C1	D3	Relative importance of accounts payable by aging category as compared to the total accounts payable.
D3	Accounts Payable Aging—Frequency Distribution	C3	E3	Age of accounts payable by accounts payable category. Any shift in the pattern from the expected template would indicate that the average payment period is shifting. Further confirmation of that shifting could be seen by reviewing the other charts in this sequence.
E3	Accounts Payable by Aging Category—Variance	D3	System: Accounts Payable, Level 2 of 2, Page 4 of 4, Charts C1, C2	Variance from plan and/or prior year for this vendor type by aging categories. If further analysis is required, each of the categories can be disaggregated into sequences similar to those starting at Charts C1, C2, and C3. Further disaggregation is shown at System: Accounts Payable, Level 2 of 2, Page 4 of 4, Charts C1 and C2.

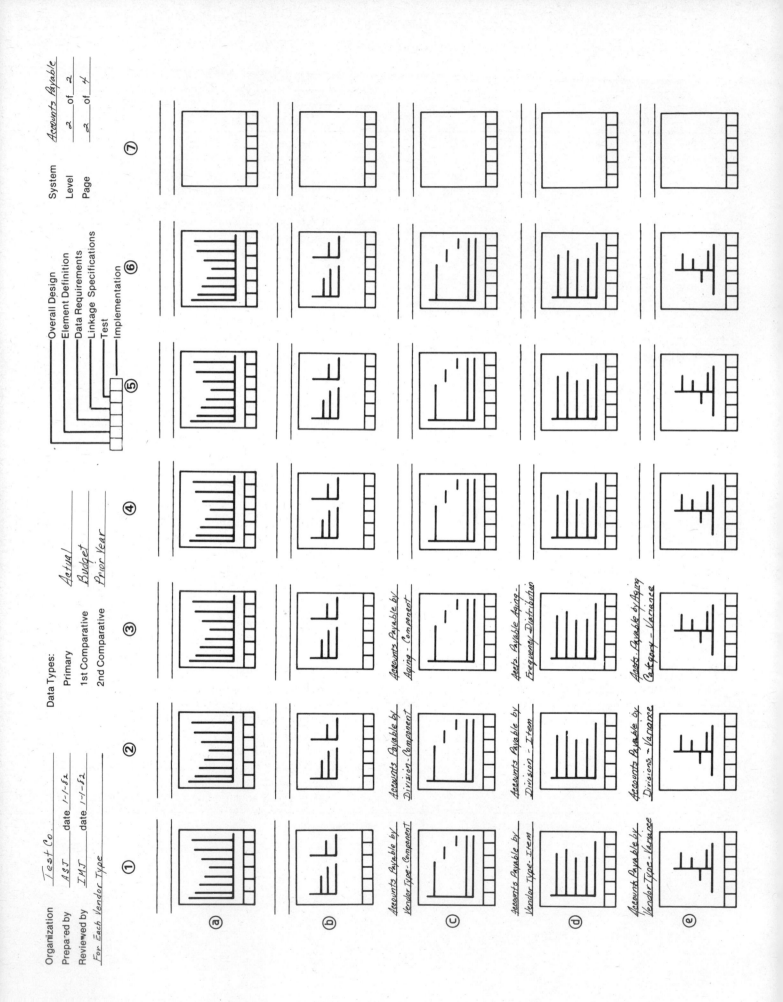

Organization _Test Co._

Prepared by _ASJ_ date _1-1-82_

Reviewed by _IMJ_ date _1-1-82_

For Each Vendor Type

Data Types:

Primary _Actual_

1st Comparative _Budget_

2nd Comparative _Prior Year_

Overall Design
Element Definition
Data Requirements
Linkage Specifications
Test
Implementation

System _Accounts Payable_

Level _2_ of _2_

Page _2_ of _4_

① ② ③ ④ ⑤ ⑥ ⑦

ⓐ

ⓑ

ⓒ _Accounts Payable by Vendor Type - Component_ / _Accounts Payable by Division - Component_ / _Accounts Payable by Aging - Component_

ⓓ _Accounts Payable by Vendor Type - Item_ / _Accounts Payable by Division - Item_ / _Accts. Payable Aging - Frequency Distribution_

ⓔ _Accounts Payable by Vendor Type - Variance_ / _Accounts Payable by Divisions - Variance_ / _Accts. Payable by Aging Category - Variance_

Row Col	Name of Chart	From	To	Descriptions
C1	Accounts Payable by Vendor Type—Component	System: Accounts Payable, Level <u>1</u> of <u>2</u>, Page <u>1</u> of <u>4</u>, Chart E1	D1	Relative importance of the accounts payable by detailed vendor type as compared to the total accounts payable for this vendor type.
D1	Accounts Payable by Vendor Type—Item	C1	E1	Relative size of the accounts payable by detailed vendor type as compared to each other for this vendor type. This chart would show by detailed vendor type the larger balances of accounts payable.
E1	Accounts Payable by Vendor Type—Variance	D1	—	Variance from plan and/or prior year for the accounts payable by detailed vendor type as compared to each other for this vendor type. If further analysis is required, each of the accounts payable by vendor can be further disaggregated into detailed accounts payable vendor similar to the charts starting at C1, C2, and C3.
C2	Accounts Payable by Division—Component	See C1	D2	Relative importance of the accounts payable for this vendor type held by each division as compared to the total accounts payable for this vendor type.
D2	Accounts Payable by Division—Item	C2	E2	Relative size of the accounts payable for this vendor type held by each division as compared to each other. The division with the largest accounts payable will be apparent.
E2	Accounts Payable by Division—Variance	D2	—	Variance from plan and/or prior year for the accounts payable of this vendor type as held by each division. If further analysis is required, each division can be further disaggregated into sequences similar to those starting at Charts C1, C2, and C3.
C3	Accounts Payable by Aging—Component	See C1	D3	Relative importance of accounts payable for this vendor type by aging category as compared to the total accounts payable.
D3	Accounts Payable Aging—Frequency Distribution	C3	E3	Age of accounts payable by accounts payable category for this vendor type. Any shift in the pattern from the expected template would indicate that the average payment period is shifting for this vendor type. Further confirmation of that shifting could be seen by reviewing the other charts in this sequence.

175

Row Col	Name of Chart	From	To	Descriptions
E3	Accounts Payable by Aging Category— Variance	D3	System: Accounts Payable, Level $\underline{2}$ of $\underline{2}$, Page $\underline{4}$ of $\underline{4}$, Charts C1, C2	Variance from plan and/or prior year for this vendor type by aging categories. If further analysis is required, each of the categories can be disaggregated into sequences similar to those starting at Charts C1, C2, and C3. Further disaggregation is shown at System: Accounts Payable, Level $\underline{2}$ of $\underline{2}$, Page $\underline{4}$ of $\underline{4}$, Charts C1 and C2.

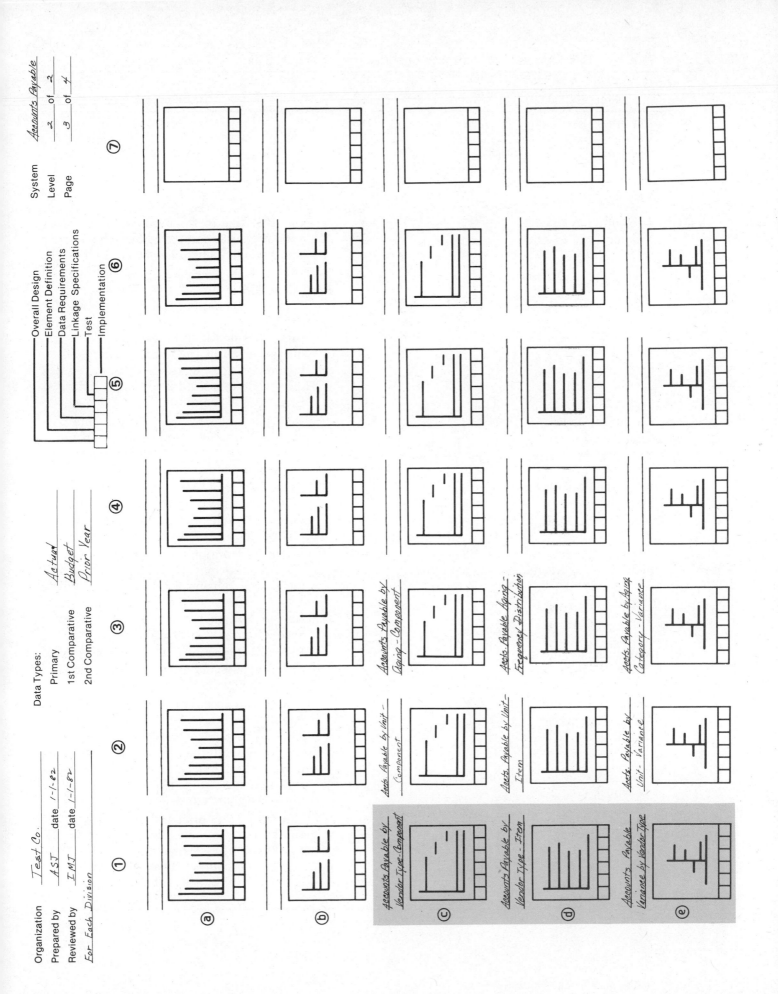

Row Col	Name of Chart	From	To	Descriptions
C1	Accounts Payable by Vendor Type—Component	System, Accounts Payable, Level <u>1</u> of <u>2</u>, Page <u>1</u> of <u>4</u>, Chart E2	D1	Relative importance of the accounts payable by vendor type as compared to the total accounts payable for this division.
D1	Accounts Payable by Vendor Type—Item	C1	E1	Relative size of the accounts payable by vendor type as compared to each other for this division. This chart would show the vendor types, with the larger balance of accounts payable for this division.
E1	Accounts Payable by Vendor Type—Variance	D1	—	Variance from plan and/or prior year for the accounts payable by vendor type for this division. If further analysis is required, each of the accounts payable by vendor type can be further disaggregated into sequences similar to those starting at Charts C1, C2, and C3.
C2	Accounts Payable by Unit—Component	See C1	D2	Relative importance of the accounts payable held by each detailed unit within the division as compared to the total accounts payable for this division.
D2	Accounts Payable by Unit—Item	C2	E2	Relative size of the accounts payable held by each unit within the division as compared to each other. The unit with the largest accounts payable will be apparent.
E2	Accounts Payable by Unit—Variance	D2	—	Variance from plan and/or prior year for the accounts payable held by each unit within the division. Most likely this will be the lowest level of disaggregation by location and further analysis might require access to the books of record.
C3	Accounts Payable by Aging—Component	See C1	D3	Relative importance of accounts payable by aging category as compared to the total accounts payable for this division.
D3	Accounts Payable Aging—Frequency Distribution	C3	E3	Age of the accounts payable by accounts payable category for this division. Any shift in the pattern from the expected would indicate that the average payment period is shifting. Further confirmation of that shifting could be seen by reviewing the other charts in this sequence.
E3	Accounts Payable by Aging Category—Variance	D3	—	Variance from plan and/or prior year for the aging categories for this division. If further analysis is required, each of the categories can be disaggregated into a sequence similar to that shown starting at Charts C1, C2, and C3.

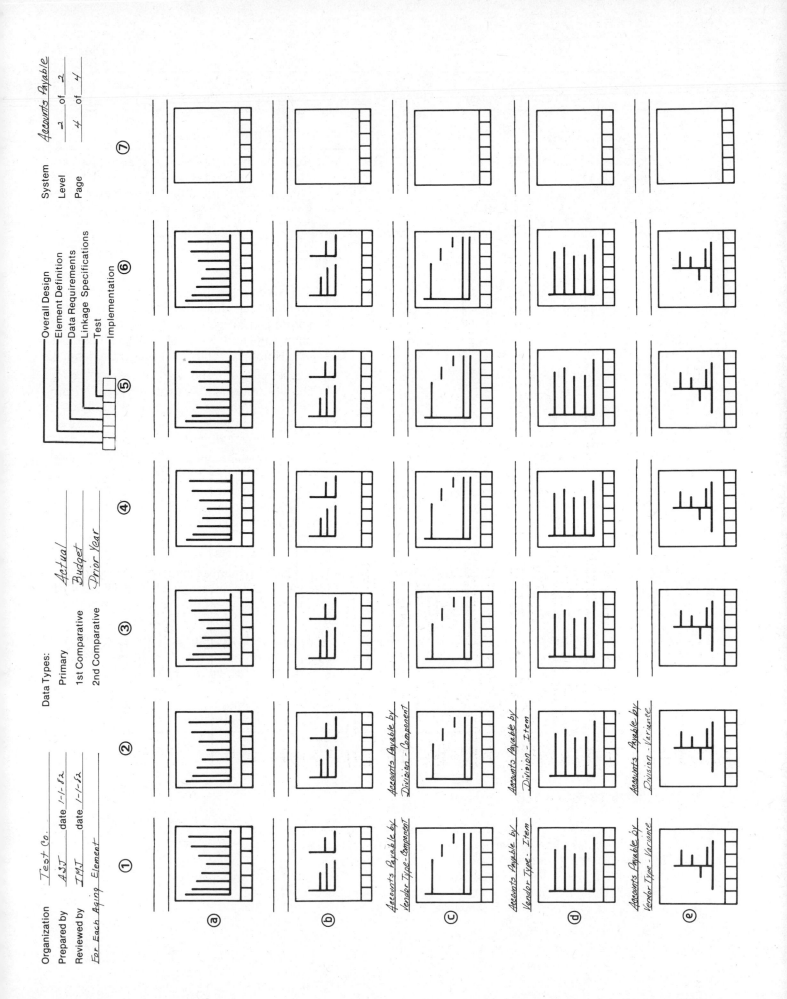

Organization _Test Co._
Prepared by   _ASJ_ date _1-1-82_
Reviewed by   _TMJ_ date _1-1-82_

For Each Aging Element

Data Types:
Primary   _Actual_
1st Comparative _Budget_
2nd Comparative _Prior Year_

Overall Design
Element Definition
Data Requirements
Linkage Specifications
Test
Implementation

① ② ③ ④ ⑤ ⑥ ⑦

ⓐ

ⓑ

ⓒ
Accounts Payable by Vendor Type - Component
Accounts Payable by Division - Component

ⓓ
Accounts Payable by Vendor Type - Item
Accounts Payable by Division - Item

ⓔ
Accounts Payable by Vendor Type - Variance
Accounts Payable by Division - Variance

Description of System <u>Accounts Payable</u>   Level <u>2</u> of <u>2</u>   Page <u>4</u> of <u>4</u>

Row Col	Name of Chart	From	To	Descriptions
C1	Accounts Payable by Vendor Type—Component	System: Accounts Payable, Level <u>1</u> of <u>2</u>, Page <u>1</u> of <u>4</u>, Chart E3	D1	Relative importance of the accounts payable by vendor type as compared to the total accounts payable for the aging category.
D1	Accounts Payable by Vendor Type—Item	C1	E1	Relative size of the accounts payable by vendor type for this aging category as compared to each other. This chart would show, by vendor type, the larger balances of accounts payable for this aging category.
E1	Accounts Payable by Vendor Type—Variance	D1	—	Variance from plan and/or prior year for the accounts payable by vendor type within this aging category. If further analysis is required, each of the accounts payable by vendor type can be further disaggregated into sequences similar to that shown starting at Charts C1 and C2.
C2	Accounts Payable by Division—Component	See C1	D2	Relative importance of the accounts payable held by each division as compared to the total accounts payable for this aging category.
D2	Accounts Payable by Division—Item	C2	E2	Relative size of the accounts payable held by each division as compared to each other for this aging category. The division with the largest accounts payable within this aging category will be apparent.
E2	Accounts Payable by Division—Variance	D2	—	Variance from plan and/or prior year for the accounts payable as held by each division for this aging category. If further analysis is required, each division can be further disaggregated into sequences similar to those starting at Charts C1 and C2.

1. ACCOUNTS PAYABLE

Chart 10-024 shows a time series through September of the average payment period. You can see that in September the average payment period was significantly greater than budget.

Chart 10-025 shows a further breakdown of the ratio for September. The chart on the right shows how much the average payment period was greater than budget. The chart on the left shows us:

1. The ratio is made up of accounts payable divided by the average daily purchases.
2. The reason for the variance in the ratio was the variance in accounts payable.
3. Accounts payable was greater than budget by $52 thousand.

The next step is to look at Charts 10-026, 10-027, and 10-028 which show a breakdown of accounts payable by division for September. Chart 10-026 shows us that the general pattern of accounts payable has changed from budget. Chart 10-027 shows us which divisions have the significant accounts payable; namely, Sweeny, Finney, and Lincoln. Chart 10-028 shows us where the variances in accounts payable from budget have occurred. Lincoln has had the most significant variance from budget.

Charts 10-029, 10-030, and 10-031 show a further breakdown of accounts payable for Lincoln for September by type of accounts payable. Chart 10-029 shows us that there are three components of accounts payable, and they have changed dramatically. Chart 10-030 shows us that type C payables are now the most significant. Chart 10-032 shows even more clearly that accounts payable for Lincoln were higher than budget because of the increases in type A and C payables.

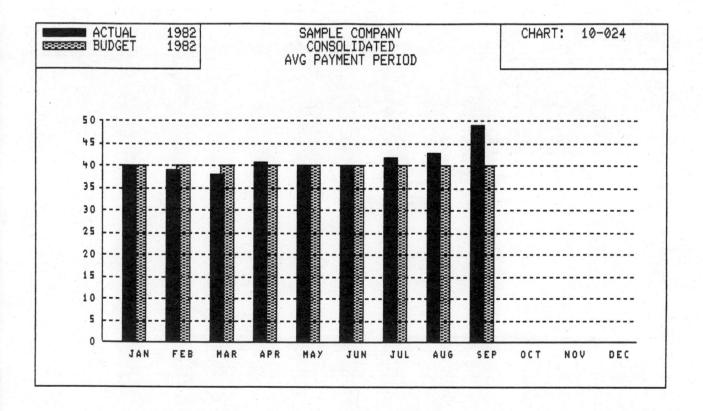

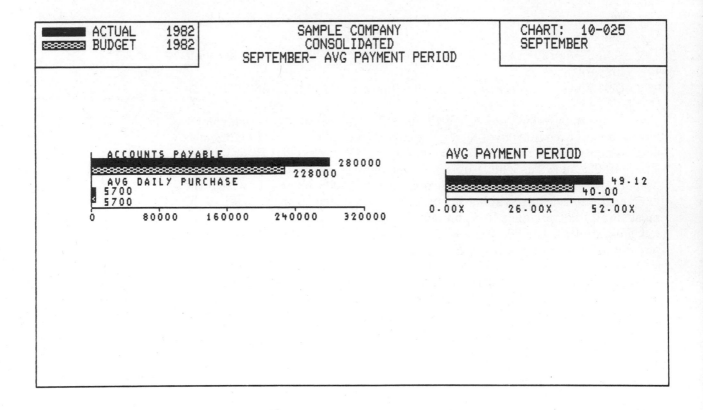

| ACTUAL | 1982 |
| BUDGET | 1982 |

SAMPLE COMPANY
CONSOLIDATED
SEPTEMBER- AVG PAYMENT PERIOD

CHART: 10-025
SEPTEMBER

ACCOUNTS PAYABLE   280000
                                    228000
AVG DAILY PURCHASE
5700
5700

0   80000   160000   240000   320000

AVG PAYMENT PERIOD
                              49-12
                          40.00
0.00X   26.00X   52.00X

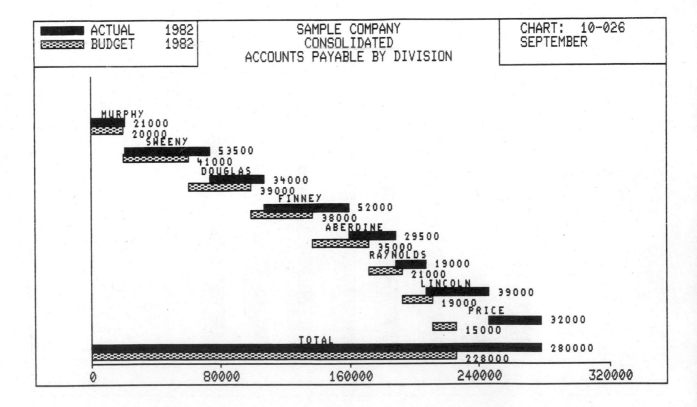

| ACTUAL | 1982 |
| BUDGET | 1982 |

SAMPLE COMPANY
CONSOLIDATED
ACCOUNTS PAYABLE BY DIVISION

CHART: 10-026
SEPTEMBER

MURPHY
21000
20000
SWEENY   53500
41000
DOUGLAS   34000
39000
FINNEY   52000
38000
ABERDINE   29500
35000
RA7NOLDS   19000
21000
LINCOLN   39000
19000
PRICE   32000
15000
TOTAL   280000
                                228000

0   80000   160000   240000   320000

182

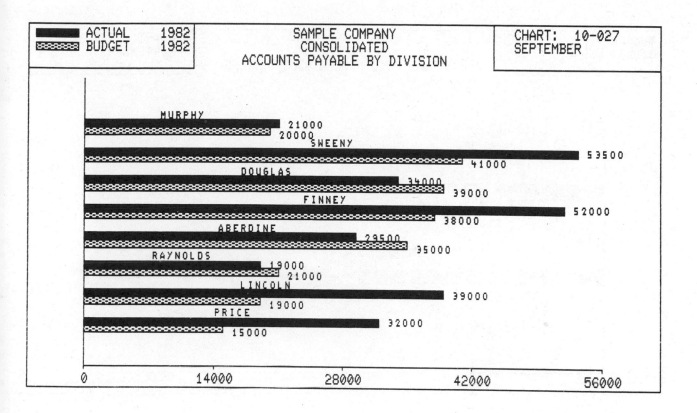

MURPHY 21000
20000
SWEENY 53500
41000
DOUGLAS 34000
39000
FINNEY 52000
38000
ABERDINE 29500
35000
RAYNOLDS 19000
21000
LINCOLN 39000
19000
PRICE 32000
15000

0   14000   28000   42000   56000

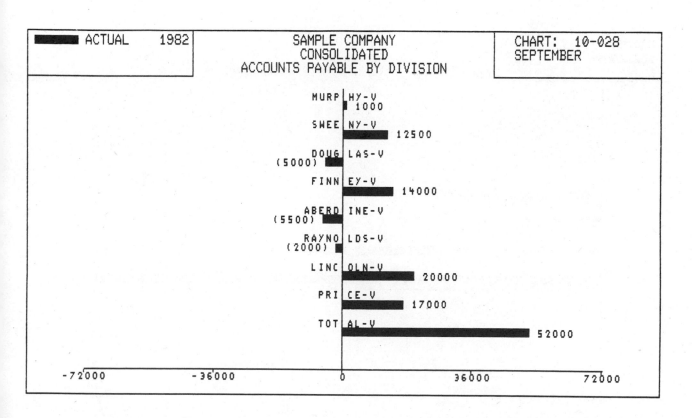

MURPHY-V 1000
SWEENY-V 12500
DOUGLAS-V (5000)
FINNEY-V 14000
ABERDINE-V (5500)
RAYNOLDS-V (2000)
LINCOLN-V 20000
PRICE-V 17000
TOTAL-V 52000

-72000   -36000   0   36000   72000

183

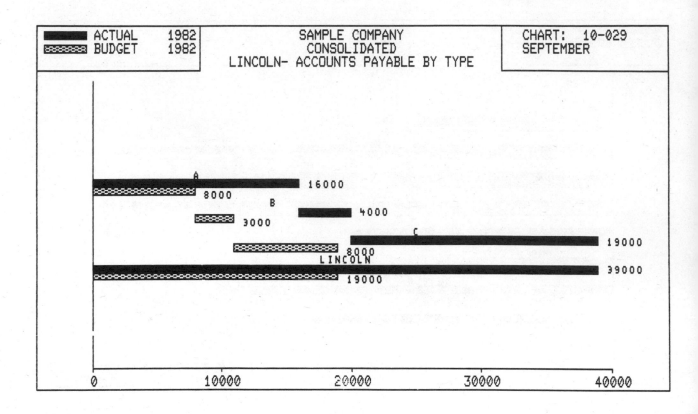

A 16000
8000
B
4000
3000
C 19000
8000
LINCOLN 39000
19000

0   10000   20000   30000   40000

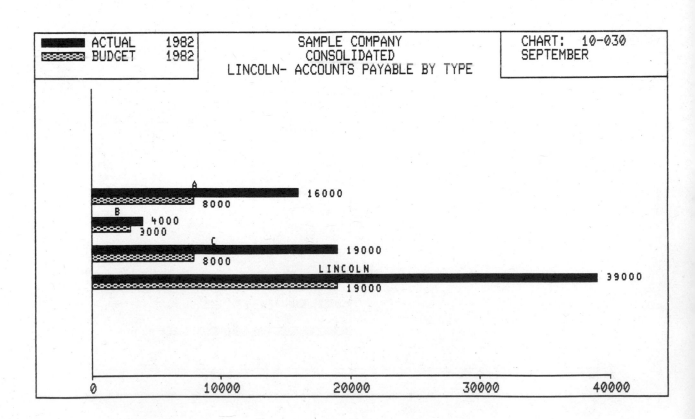

A 16000
8000
B 4000
3000
C 19000
8000
LINCOLN 39000
19000

0   10000   20000   30000   40000

184

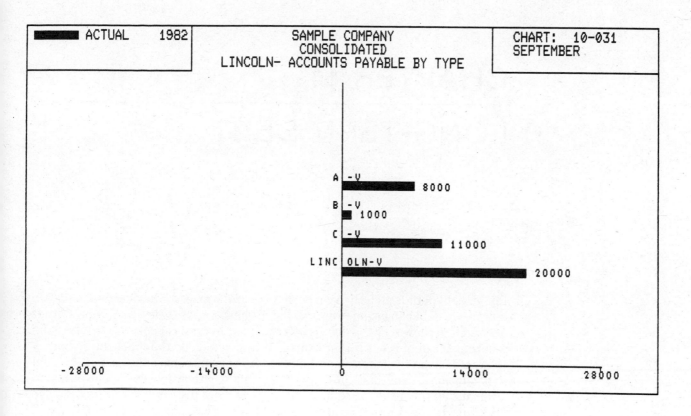

CHAPTER 11

LONG-TERM DEBT

Long-term debt is strictly a corporate control process. The decision to obtain long-term debt can be made only at the highest corporate levels. This system is designed to show how the debt is affecting the overall corporate activities and whether the debt is within the control standards set by the corporation and by the external analysts. Two components of that control are the cost of the debt and relationship of the long-term debt to net worth or leverage. The external analysts use the three ratios shown as indicators of proper control. As shown in Exhibit 11.1, the indicators are further disaggregated into long-term debt and interest by debt type for internal corporate control.

EXHIBIT 11.1

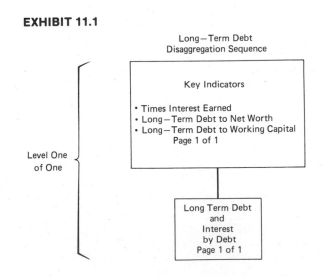

Long—Term Debt
Disaggregation Sequence

Key Indicators

• Times Interest Earned
• Long—Term Debt to Net Worth
• Long—Term Debt to Working Capital
Page 1 of 1

Level One
of One

Long Term Debt
and
Interest
by Debt
Page 1 of 1

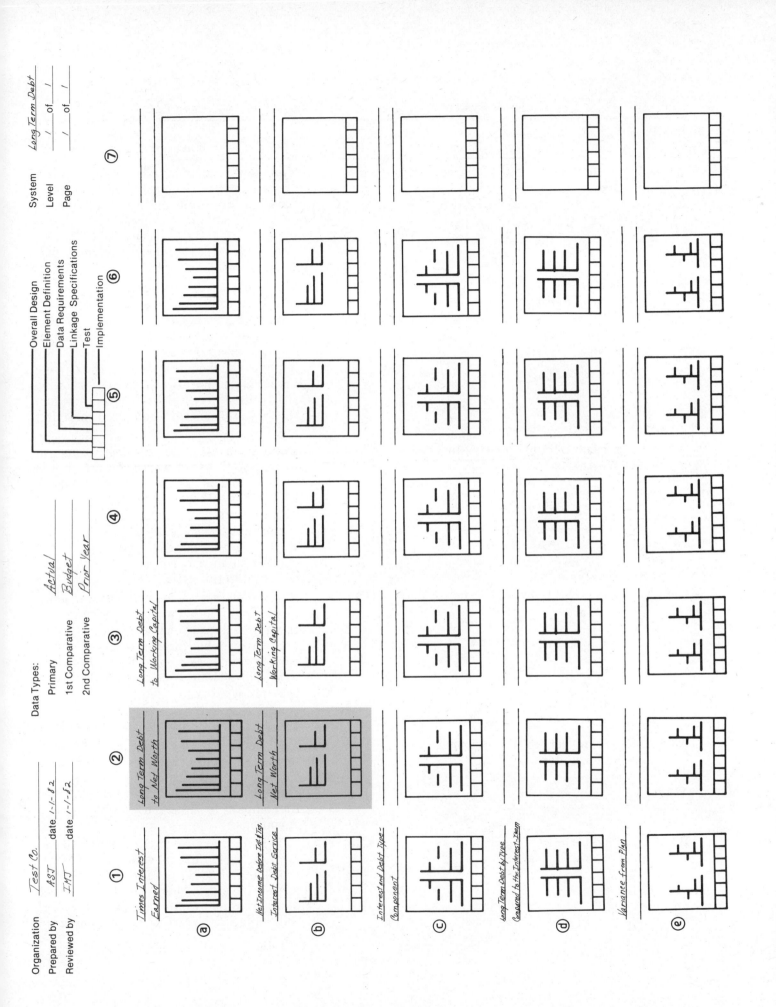

Row Col	Name of Chart	From	To	Descriptions
A1	Times Interest Earned	Original	B1	Time series showing the times interest earned for the previous 12 months as compared to budget and prior year. If the ratio shown is too low or decreasing, it might indicate that debt service is becoming excessive for the revenue generating power of the assets.
B1	N: Net Income Before Interest and Taxes D: Interest Debt Service	A1	C1	Relative size of the net income before interest and income taxes to the debt service. If the change in the ratio is due to a change in the net income before taxes, then further disaggregation would occur by going to the income system. If the change in the ratio is due to a change in the relative size of the interest debt service, then further disaggregation would occur starting at C1.
A2	Long-Term Debt to Net Worth	Original	B2	Time series showing the last 12-month ratio of debt to net worth. As the debt is reduced and as the net worth is increased, the ratio should tend to increase over time. Major activities that would extend the size of the debt service, extend the value of net worth, or any major changes that affect the net worth of the corporation would be reflected in this ratio.
B2	N: Long-Term Debt D: Net Worth	A2	C1	Ratio showing the relative size of long-term debt to the net worth. If the change in the ratio is due to a change in the size of the long-term debt, further disaggregation would occur in sequence C1. If the change in the ratio is due to a change in the size of the net worth, further disaggregation would occur at the equity system, level 1 of 1, page 1 of 1, Charts A1 and subsequent.
A3	Long-Term Debt to Working Capital	Original	B3	Time series showing the ratio of the long-term debt to the working capital. This ratio is one of the critical ratios used by outside analysts to determine the ability of the company to withstand unusual seasonal variations.
B3	N: Long-Term Debt D: Working Capital	A3	C1	This ratio chart shows the relative size of the long-term debt to working capital. If the change in the ratio is due to a change in the size of the long-term debt, further disaggregation would take place at C1. If the change in the ratio is due to a change in

Row Col	Name of Chart	From	To	Descriptions
				the size of the working capital, further disaggregation would take place in the financial control system, level 1 of 1, page 1 of 1, Charts A3 and A4.
C1	Interest and Debt Type—Component	B1, B2, B3	D1	Sequence showing the long-term debt on the right and the interest for the respective debt type on the right. This first chart shows the relative importance of the long-term debt by debt type as compared to the total long-term debt on the right. The left side shows the relative importance of the interest by debt type as compared to the overall interest paid by the corporation.
D1	Long-Term Debt by Type Compared to the Interest—Item	C1	E1	Right side shows the relative size of the long-term debt by type as compared to each other; left side shows the relative importance of the interest paid for each of the debt types as compared to each other. This chart will show the size of the debt and the amount of interest that debt is incurring in proportion to all of the other interest types paid.
E1	Variance from Plan	D1	—	Variance from plan and/or prior year for the debt and the interest by long-term debt type. If further analysis is required, each debt type could be further disaggregated similar to the sequence starting in C1. No further descriptions of this sequence are shown.

1. LONG-TERM DEBT

Chart 10-036 shows a time series of the long-term debt to net worth ratio for the past 10 years ending with 1982. In 1982 (and 1981) long-term debt to net worth was higher than budget. Chart 10-037 shows a further breakdown of the ratio. The chart on the right again shows that the ratio was higher than budget. The chart on the left shows:

1. The ratio is made up of long-term debt divided by net worth.
2. The variance in the ratio is due to long-term debt being higher than budget.
3. Long-term debt was higher than budget by $296 thousand.

Charts 10-038, 10-039, and 10-040 show a further breakdown of long-term debt by debt type. It appears that convertible bonds–15% and mortgage–15% have changed the makeup of total long-term debt. Chart 10-039 shows that 10%

bonds and convertible bonds–15% are the more significant loan amounts. Mortgage debt at 15% has increased in significance. Chart 10-040 shows where the variances from budget have occurred; as pointed out already, the changes are due to increases in convertible bonds–15% and mortgage–15% debt.

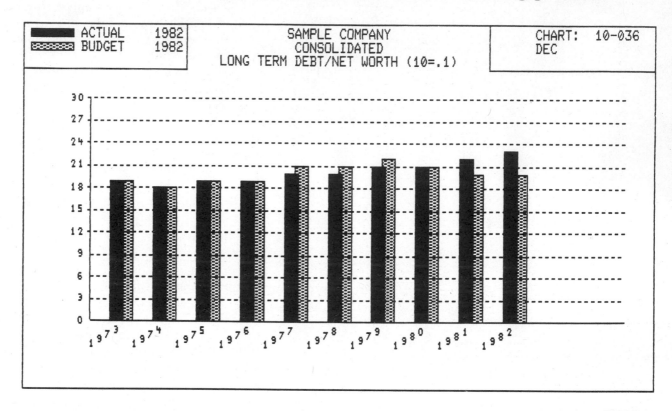

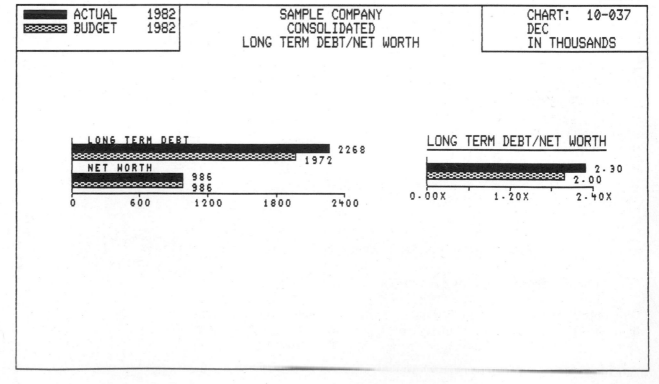

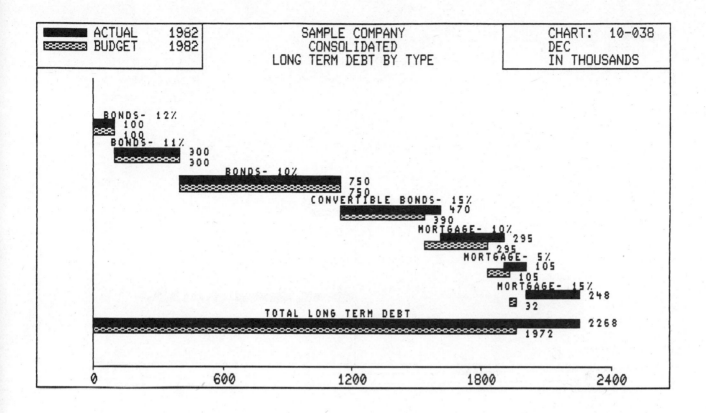

ACTUAL 1982
BUDGET 1982

SAMPLE COMPANY
CONSOLIDATED
LONG TERM DEBT BY TYPE

CHART: 10-038
DEC
IN THOUSANDS

BONDS- 12%
100
100

BONDS- 11%
300
300

BONDS- 10%
750
750

CONVERTIBLE BONDS- 15%
470
390

MORTGAGE- 10%
295
295

MORTGAGE- 5%
105
105

MORTGAGE- 15%
248
32

TOTAL LONG TERM DEBT
2268
1972

0   600   1200   1800   2400

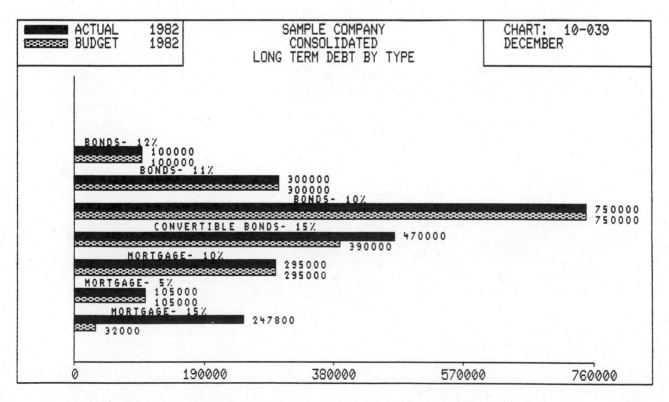

ACTUAL 1982
BUDGET 1982

SAMPLE COMPANY
CONSOLIDATED
LONG TERM DEBT BY TYPE

CHART: 10-039
DECEMBER

BONDS- 12%
100000
100000

BONDS- 11%
300000
300000

BONDS- 10%
750000
750000

CONVERTIBLE BONDS- 15%
470000
390000

MORTGAGE- 10%
295000
295000

MORTGAGE- 5%
105000
105000

MORTGAGE- 15%
247800
32000

0   190000   380000   570000   760000

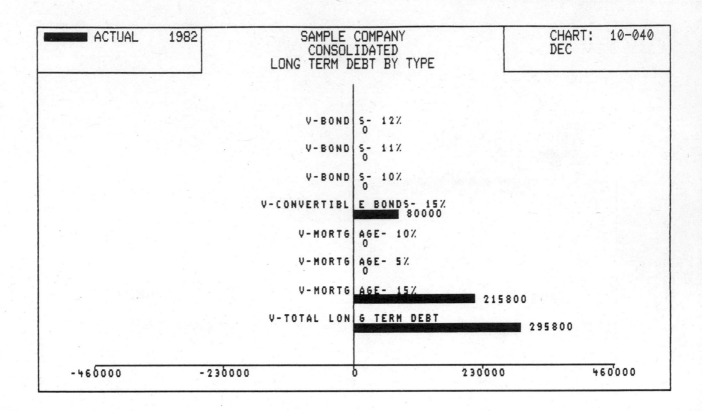

CHAPTER 12

NET WORTH: EQUITY

Equity is the net result of all the other activities of the firm. Analysis of equity gives some indication of how well the firm is doing in providing a return for the stockholders and the picture of the relative effectiveness of the equity investment in the corporate activities. As shown in Exhibit 12.1, the overall description of the equity performance is provided in a series of ratios with a disaggregation of equity by type. The source of all of these ratios is the income statement, balance sheet and the statement of changes in financial position.

EXHIBIT 12.1

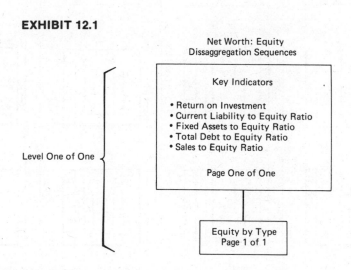

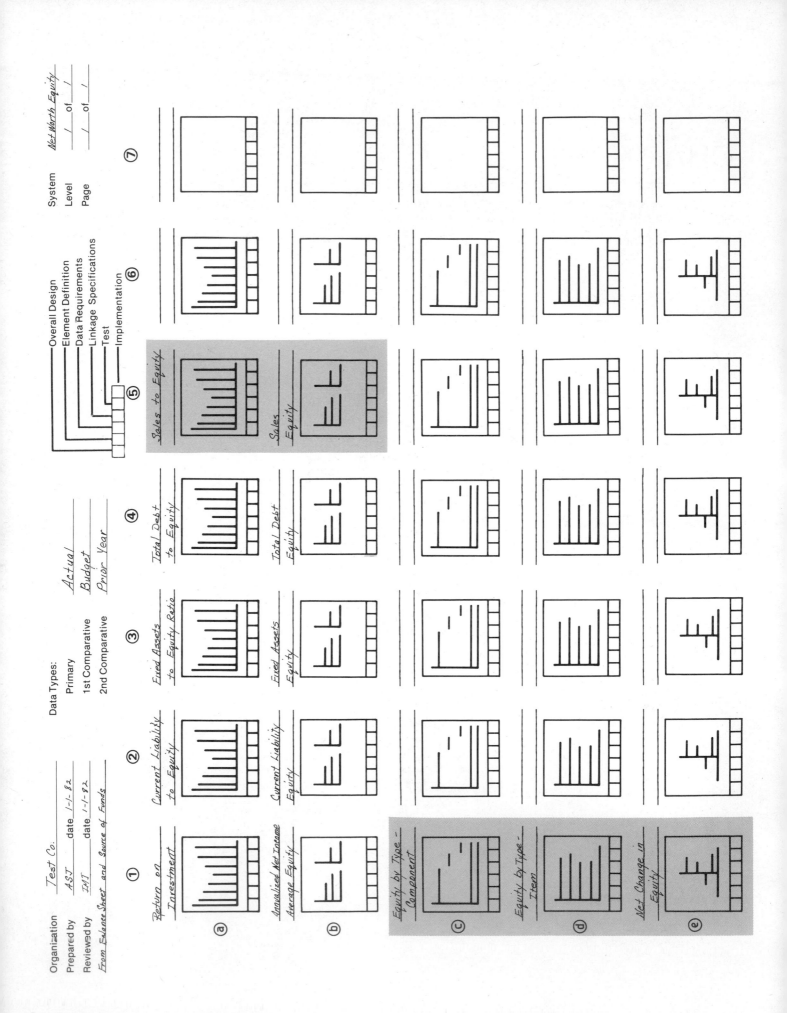

Row Col	Name of Chart	From	To	Descriptions
A1	Return on Investment	Original	B1	One of the most significant charts used by outside investors to determine the investment potential of the corporation. The DuPont ratios build to the return on investment. The DuPont ratios are shown in Chapter 16. The time series shows the return on investment for the prior 12 months (or the prior periods set by the corporation). It is an important comparison to see how the ratio is performing as compared to the budget and the prior year. Major deviations should be explained.
B1	N: Annualized Net Income D: Average Equity	A1	C1	Relative size of the annualized net income as compared to the average equity investment in the firm. If the change in the return on investment is due to a change in the size of the net income, then further aggregation or analysis would take place in the income system. If the change in the return on income is due to a change in the equity, then further disaggregation or analysis would take place in C1 and in the corporate control system.
A2	Current Liability to Equity	Original	B2	Time series showing the relative importance of funding from liabilities as compared to equity. The lower the ratio, to a point, the better the equity position is reflected by the chart.
B2	N: Current Liability D: Equity	A2	C1	Ratio chart showing the relative size of current liabilities as compared to the equity. If the change in the ratio is due to a change in the relative size of current liabilities, then further analysis would take place in the balance sheet (corporate control), financial control systems, and in the accounts payable system. If the change in the ratio is due to a change in the size of the equity, then further disaggregation and analysis would take place at C1.
A3	Fixed Assets to Equity Ratio	Original	B3	Time series showing the ratio of fixed assets to equity for the past 12 periods.
B3	N: Fixed Assets D: Equity	A3	C1	Ratio chart showing the relative size of the fixed assets compared to equity. One way to interpret this chart is to see how much of the fixed assets were supplied by the equity investment. If the change in the ratio is due to a change in the fixed assets, further analysis and disaggregation would occur

195

Row Col	Name of Chart	From	To	Descriptions
				in the fixed assets system. If the change in the ratio is due to a change in the size of the equity, then further disaggregation and analysis would take place in C1.
A4	Total Debt to Equity	Original	B4	Total debt to equity over a standard period of time. This ratio describes the importance of the debt and the equity.
B4	N: Total Debt D: Equity	A4	C1	Relative size of the total debt as compared to equity. If the change in ratio is due to the change in the total debt, the balance sheet and the overall control systems should be reviewed. If the change in ratio is due to a change in the size of equity, further disaggregation and analysis starts in C1.
A5	Sales to Equity	Original	B5	This ratio over time gives an indication of the efficiency of the use of equity in creating sales. It is a useful comparative to other organizations and firms in the same industry.
B5	N: Sales D: Equity	A5	C1	Relative size of sales as compared to equity. If the change in ratio is due to a change in the size of sales, then further analysis and disaggregation would occur in the sales system. If the change in the ratio is due to a change in equity, further analysis and disaggregation would take place at C1.
C1	Equity by Type—Component	B1–B5	D1	Relative importance of the various types of equity as compared to the total equity. Unusual equity patterns might suggest further analysis when compared to other organizations in the same industry.
D1	Equity by Type—Item	C1	E1	Relative size of the individual components and the individual types of equity compared to each other. This chart also shows the largest source of equity funding.
E1	Net Change in Equity	D1	—	Variance from plan and/or prior year by the individual types of equity. If further analysis is required, each of the equity types could be further disaggregated and analyzed through sequences such as that starting at C1. No further examples of this sequence are provided.

EQUITY

Chart 10-073 shows the sales/equity ratio for the 10-year period ending with 1982. In 1982 the ratio was higher than budget. Chart 10-074 shows more information about the ratio. The right-hand chart shows how much the ratio was above budget. The left-hand chart shows:

1. The ratio is calculated by sales divided by equity.
2. The ratio increased because equity was less than budget.
3. Equity was $55 thousand less than budget.

Charts 10-075, 10-076, and 10-077 show further information about equity. Chart 10-075 shows that although the same components make up the whole, there have been some significant changes in the amounts of some components. Chart 10-076 shows that Preferred–12% is not the largest item as budgeted. Common Class B is also a larger item than budgeted. Chart 10-077 shows that the major changes in equity occurred in a decrease in Preferred–12% stock and an increase in Common Class B stock.

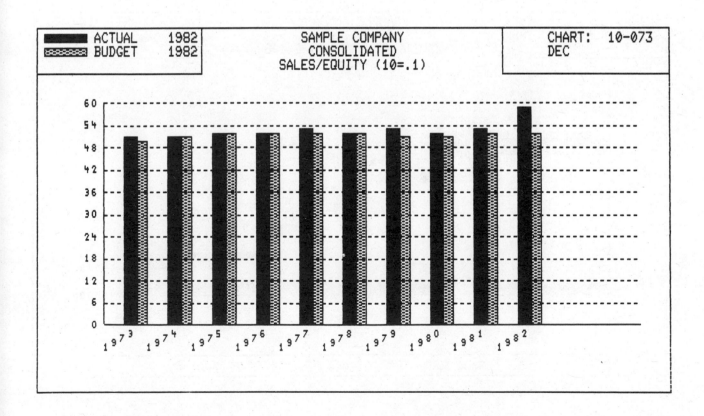

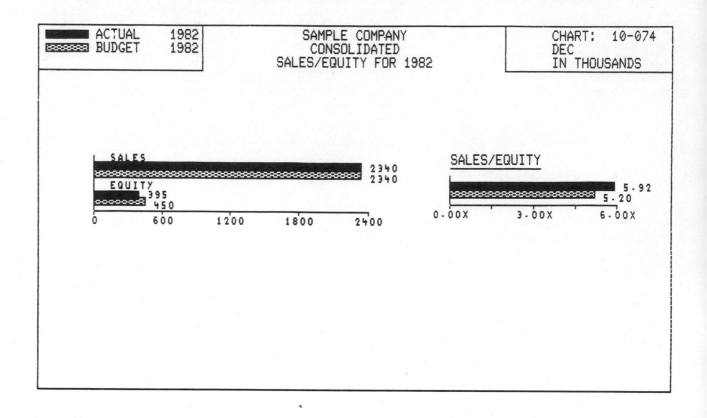

ACTUAL 1982
BUDGET 1982

SAMPLE COMPANY
CONSOLIDATED
SALES/EQUITY FOR 1982

CHART: 10-074
DEC
IN THOUSANDS

SALES
2340
2340

EQUITY
395
450

0   600   1200   1800   2400

SALES/EQUITY
5.92
5.20

0.00X   3.00X   6.00X

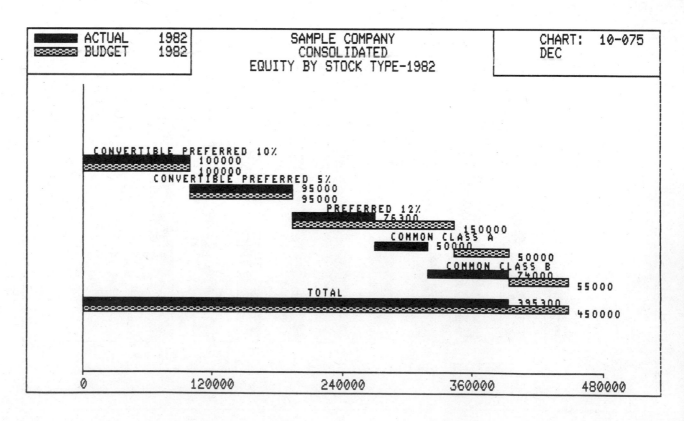

ACTUAL 1982
BUDGET 1982

SAMPLE COMPANY
CONSOLIDATED
EQUITY BY STOCK TYPE-1982

CHART: 10-075
DEC

CONVERTIBLE PREFERRED 10%
100000
100000

CONVERTIBLE PREFERRED 5%
95000
95000

PREFERRED 12%
76300
150000

COMMON CLASS A
50000
50000

COMMON CLASS B
74000
55000

TOTAL
395300
450000

0   120000   240000   360000   480000

198

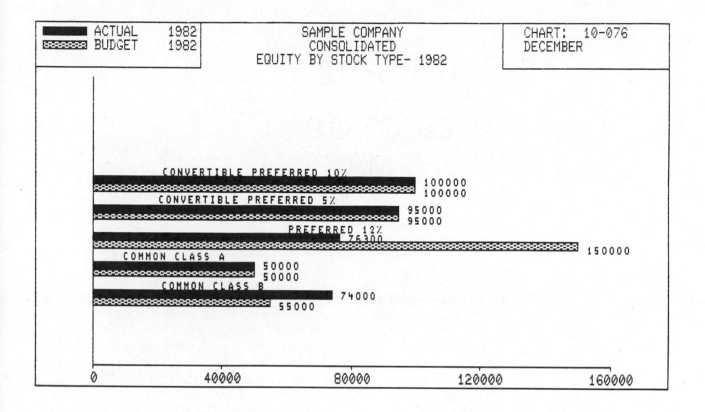

ACTUAL 1982
BUDGET 1982

SAMPLE COMPANY
CONSOLIDATED
EQUITY BY STOCK TYPE- 1982

CHART: 10-076
DECEMBER

CONVERTIBLE PREFERRED 10%
100000
100000
CONVERTIBLE PREFERRED 5%
95000
95000
PREFERRED 12%
76300
150000
COMMON CLASS A
50000
50000
COMMON CLASS B
74000
55000

0   40000   80000   120000   160000

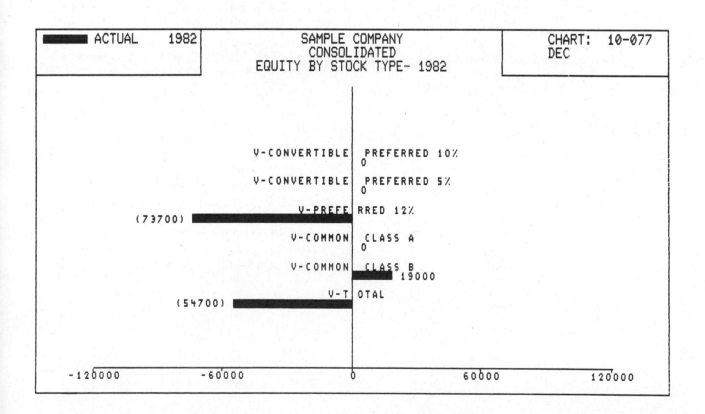

ACTUAL 1982

SAMPLE COMPANY
CONSOLIDATED
EQUITY BY STOCK TYPE- 1982

CHART: 10-077
DEC

V-CONVERTIBLE PREFERRED 10%
0
V-CONVERTIBLE PREFERRED 5%
0
V-PREFERRED 12%
(73700)
V-COMMON CLASS A
0
V-COMMON CLASS B
19000
V-TOTAL
(54700)

-120000   -60000   0   60000   120000

199

CHAPTER 13

SALES/COGS/ GROSS MARGIN

This chapter describes four systems that show the various relationships of sales, cost of goods sold, and gross margin. Three of the systems show only single relationships: sales, cost of goods sold, and gross margin. One system shows the co-relationships: sales—cost of goods sold; sales—gross margin. The purpose of showing the systems in four separate system flows is to provide communication links for those managers who see the various relationships from the perspective of their function in the organization and still show the co-relationships between the mix of revenue sources and their costs, a picture so important for understanding and learning about the company's profit behavior. When these co-relationships are depicted, the impact on profit of sales mix, volume mix, price changes, and cost changes are clearly shown by the defined sequences. Only two systems, sales and the sales/cost of goods sold/gross margin system, are described in the text. The cost of goods sold and gross margin systems follow the exact same format as the sales system and the same descriptions apply.

SALES

The sales sequence is perhaps the most commonly used sequence in the GMIS. As shown in Exhibit 13-1, there are three key indicators in this sequence: sales by month, gross margin, and return on sales. Sales is then disaggregated into the three common approaches to controlling sales: by customer type, product type, and division. Each of these is then disaggregated further at the second data level. For example, each customer type is disaggregated into sales by detailed customer type (or customer if applicable), sales by product type, and sales by division.

EXHIBIT 13.1

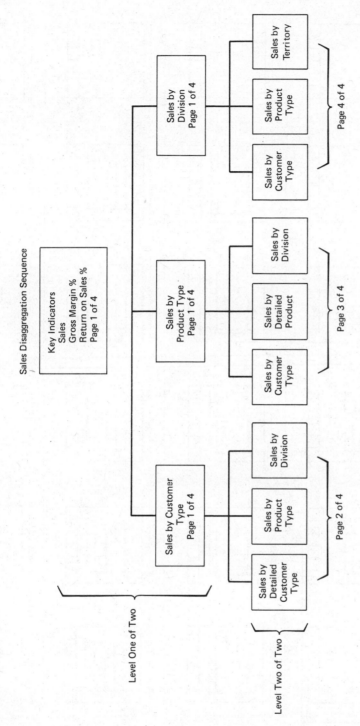

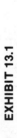

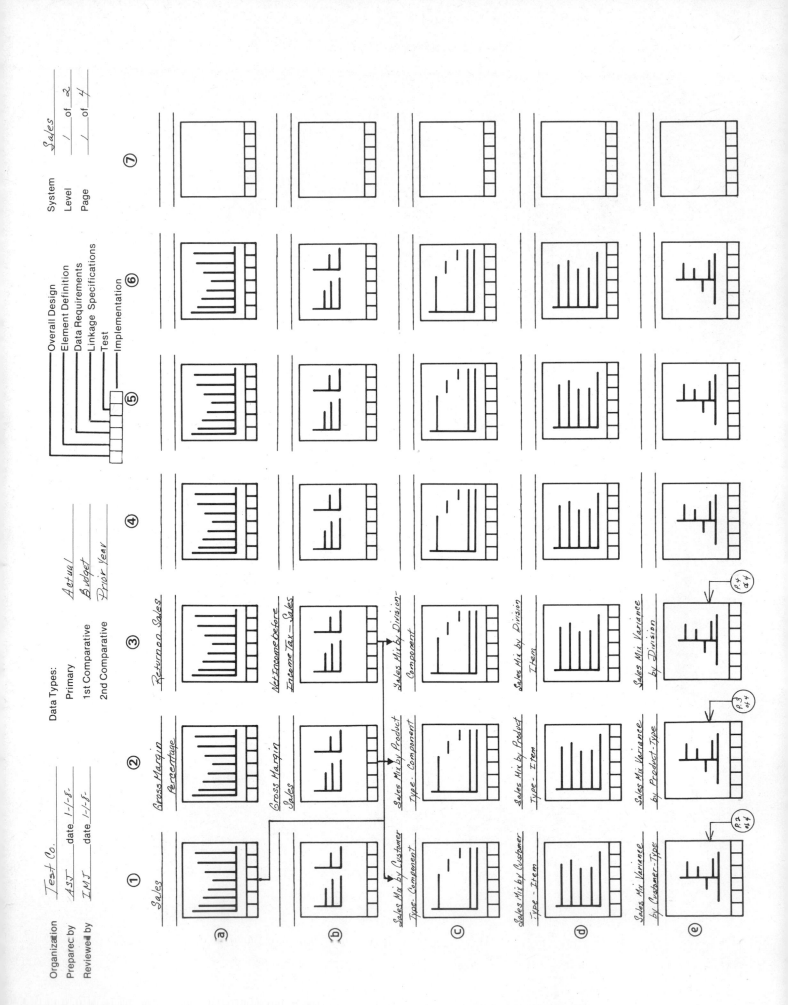

Row Col	Name of Chart	From	To	Descriptions
A1	Sales	Original	C1, C2, C3	Time series showing the actual sales values for the previous 12 months as compared to budget and prior year. Seasonal trends will emerge and variances therefrom can be seen. This chart provides a view most commonly seen by management.
A2	Gross Margin Percentage	Original	B2	Time series showing the net effect of the changing relationship between cost of goods sold and sales, and the gross margin received by the company for its goods and services. The gross margin percentage is the complement of the cost of goods sold percentage. The picture shown by this chart will reflect the effect of the changing product/cost of goods sold mix.
B2	N: Gross Margin D: Sales	A2	C1, C2, C3	Ratio showing the relative size of gross margin as compared to sales. If the change in the ratio is due to a change in the relative size of the gross margin, the disaggregation would take place either by reviewing the changes in the cost of goods sold system, or by reviewing the separate gross margin system. The path taken would depend strictly on the audience reviewing the charts. The pathway would be chosen to enhance communication depending on the functional responsibilities of those reviewing the charts. If the change in ratio is due to the relative size of the sales, the disaggregation would follow Charts C1 through C3.
A3	Return on Sales	Original	B2	Time series showing the net income before taxes as compared to sales providing an overall indication of the final result of corporate activity before taxes. Any drastic changes in the bottom line would be seen by reviewing the income system, the cost of goods sold system, and/or the gross margin system. The changing relationships will be reflected on the bottom line. A further analysis of operating expenses and administrative expenses would be required to see the whole picture, but certainly a major contribution to the change in the net income would be a change in gross margin. You can see changing gross margins and sales mix activity in the sales/COGS/GM System

Row Col	Name of Chart	From	To	Descriptions
				providing, at the same time, a view of cause and result. If the cost of goods sold and gross margin are right on target, the operating expenses and administrative expenses systems should be reviewed to determine why return on sales is down. This return on sales chart is shown in a number of systems and is one of the more critical ratios for reviewing overall corporate performance.
B3	N: Net Income Before Income Tax D: Sales	A3	C1, C2, C3	Net income before income tax as compared to sales. If the change in the ratio is due to a change in the relative size of the net income before income tax, then a disaggregation of the entire income process should be reviewed, including a review of the income system, the cost of goods sold system, the operating expenses, and administrative expense systems. If the change in the ratio is due to a change in the relative size of the sales, then disaggregation and analysis could take place through Charts C1 through C3 in this series.
C1	Sales Mix by Customer Type—Component	A1, B2, B3	D1	Relative importance of sales by customer type as compared to total sales. This is a primary view of the complex relationships between the sales mix and profit.
D1	Sales Mix by Customer Type—Item	C1	E1	Relative size of the sales by customer type as compared to each other. A change in the pattern should indicate a policy change toward the mix of sales to customer type. The pattern should represent the policy pattern of the corporation toward the sales to customer type. Selling more to one customer type, for example, might require more service that could result in a lower profit.
E1	Sales Mix by Customer Type—Variance	D1	System: Sales Level 2 of 2 Page 2 of 4, A1, A2	Sales mix variance from plan and/or prior year. This picture of sales mix variance is one of the most important in showing where further analysis should occur. It does not explain *why* variances have occurred, but it does point out where to look for the causes. If further analysis is required, each of the elements can be further disaggregated to sequences the same as those shown starting at C1, C2, and C3 and as described in the sales system, level 2 of 2, page 2 of 4, Charts A1 and A2.

Row Col	Name of Chart	From	To	Descriptions
C2	Sales Mix by Product Type—Component	A1, B2, B3	D2	Relative importance of sales by product type as compared to the total sales. A change in the pattern should be a reflection of policy change, such as new products, and would be an indicator that further disaggregation is required.
D2	Sales Mix by Product Type—Item	C2	E2	Relative size of the sales by product type as compared to the other product types. As in Chart C2, the patterns should be similar from year to year unless there was a change in policy. Any change from policy—budget—as reflected by the patterns would indicate further analysis.
E2	Sales Mix by Product Type—Variance	D2	System: Sales, Level 2 of 2, Page 3 of 4,	Variance from plan and/or prior year for the sales by product type. The important picture shown is the magnitude of the changing sales mix. Further analysis will be required to fully understand *why* change occurred. If further analysis is required, a further disaggregation similar to that shown starting at C1 through C3 can be shown. Also, see system sales, level 2 of 2, page 3 of 4, Charts A1 and A2.
C3	Sales Mix by Division—Component	A1, B2, B3	D3	Relative importance of sales by division as compared to the total sales. The pattern should reflect corporate policy. If there are any variances from the expected pattern, further analysis would be required.
D3	Sales by Division—Item	C3	E3	Relative importance of the sales by division as compared to the other divisions. A major change in the pattern of sales by division would indicate further analysis should be completed.
E3	Sales Mix by Division—Variance	D3	System: Sales, Level 2 of 2, Page 4 of 4, A1, A2	Sales mix variance by division. Any major shifts in variances would indicate which divisions should be analyzed to find the reasons for the variances. Further analysis for each element can be shown in sequences similar to those starting at C1, C2, and C3 as shown in system sales, level 2 of 2, page 4 of 4, Charts A1 and A2.

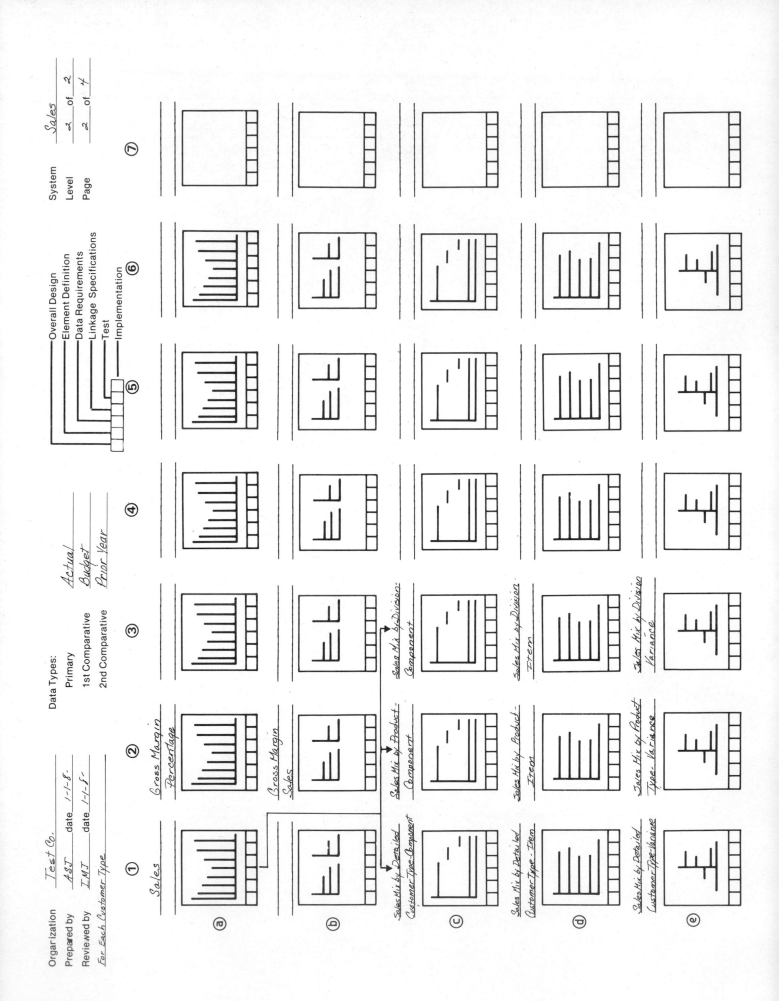

Organization _Test Co._

Prepared by _ASJ_ date _1-1-8-_

Reviewed by _IMJ_ date _1-1-5-_

For Each Customer Type

Data Types:

Primary _Actual_

1st Comparative _Budget_

2nd Comparative _Prior Year_

Overall Design
Element Definition
Data Requirements
Linkage Specifications
Test
Implementation

① ② ③ ④ ⑤ ⑥ ⑦

② _Gross Margin Percentage_

Gross Margin Sales

① _Sales_

ⓐ

ⓑ

ⓒ _Sales Mix by Detailed Customer Type-Component_   _Sales Mix by Product-Component_   _Sales Mix by Division-Component_

ⓓ _Sales Mix by Detailed Customer Type-Item_   _Sales Mix by Product-Item_   _Sales Mix by Division-Item_

ⓔ _Sales Mix by Detailed Customer Type-Variance_   _Sales Mix by Product Type-Variance_   _Sales Mix by Division-Variance_

NOTE: This sequence of charts is almost identical to that shown in level one, except for the return on sales ratios. The difference is that sales for a single customer type is disaggregated to show sales within a customer type (perhaps even by customer), sales by type of product sold to a single customer type, and sales by a division or geographical area to a single customer type.

Row Col	Name of Chart	From	To	Descriptions
A1	Sales	System: Sales, Level <u>1</u> of <u>2</u>, Page <u>1</u> of <u>4</u>, E1	C1, C2 C3	Time series showing the actual sales values for a single customer type for the previous 12 months as compared to budget and prior year. Seasonal trends will emerge and variances therefrom can be seen. This chart provides a view most commonly seen by management, and shows the seasonal behavior of a customer type plus trend.
A2	Gross Margin Percentage	Same as A1	B2	Time series showing the net effect of the changing relationship between cost of goods sold and sales, the gross margin received by the company for its goods and service sold to this customer type. The gross margin percentage is the complement of cost of goods sold percentage. The picture shown by this chart will reflect the effect of the changing product/cost of goods sold mix sold to a customer type.
B2	N: Gross Margin D: Sales	A2	C1, C2, C3	Ratio showing the relative size of gross margin for this customer type as compared to sales. If the change in the ratio is due to a change in the relative size of the gross margin, the disaggregation would take place either by reviewing the changes in the cost of goods sold system, or by reviewing the separate gross margin system. The path taken would depend strictly on the audience reviewing the charts. The pathway would be chosen to enhance communication depending on the functional responsibilities of those reviewing the Charts. If the change in the ratio is due to the relative size of the sales, the disaggregation would follow Charts C1 through C3.
C1	Sales Mix by Detailed Customer Type—Component	A1, B2	D1	Relative importance of sales by detailed customer type, perhaps even as detailed as specific customers, as compared to the total sales for the customer type shown. This view of the complex sales mix by customer type provides the first picture of

207

Row Col	Name of Chart	From	To	Descriptions
				which detailed customer type or customers might be singled out for review.
D1	Sales Mix by Detailed Customer Type—Item	C1	E1	Relative size of the sales by detailed customer type as compared to each other. The pattern should represent the policy pattern of the corporation for sales to the customer type, not a pattern of uncontrolled changes.
E1	Sales Mix by Detailed Customer Type—Variances	D1	—	Sales mix variances from plan and/or prior year for the sales to the detailed customer type. This picture of mix variances is one of the most important in showing where further analysis should occur. It does not explain why variances have occurred, but it does point out where to look for the causes. If further analysis is required, each of the elements can be further disaggregated to sequences the same as those shown starting at C1, C2, and C3. At this point it may be necessary to go to the detailed books of record.
C2	Sales Mix by Product Type—Component	A1, B2	D2	Relative importance of sales by product type for this customer type as compared to the total sales.
D2	Sales by Product Type—Item	C2	E2	Relative size of the sales to this customer type by product type as compared to the other product types sold. It also shows another picture of the relationship between the sales to this customer type by product type and their respective cost of goods sold. As in Chart C2, the patterns should be similar from year to year unless there are new products or a change in the sales strategy. Any change in this relationship as reflected by the patterns would indicate further analysis is necessary.
E2	Sales Mix by Product Type—Variance	D2	—	Variance from plan and/or prior year for the sales to this customer type by product type. The important picture is the size of the changing product sales mix to this customer type. If further analysis is required, a further disaggregation similar to that shown starting at C1 through C3 can be shown. It may be necessary to go directly to the books of record.
C3	Sales Mix by Division—Component	A1, B2	D3	Relative importance of sales to this customer type by division as compared to the total sales.

Row Col	Name of Chart	From	To	Descriptions
D3	Sales Mix by Division—Item	C3	E3	Relative importance of the sales to this customer type by division as compared to the other divisions. Any major change in the pattern of sales by division for this customer type would indicate further analysis is necessary.
E3	Sales Mix by Division—Variance	D3	—	Divisional sales mix variance. Any major shifts in the relative size of the variances would indicate the need for further divisional analysis. Further analysis for each element can be shown in sequences similar to those starting at C1, C2, and C3.

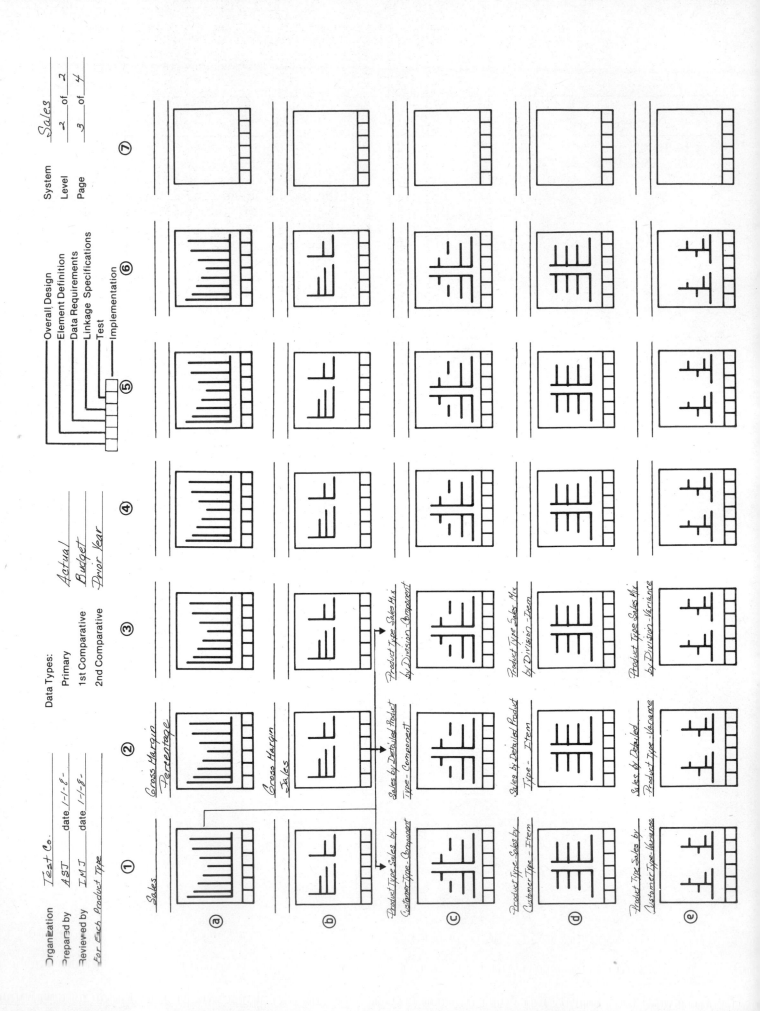

NOTE: This sequence of charts is almost identical to that shown in level 1 (except for the return on sales ratio). The difference is sales, cost of goods sold, and gross margin for a single product type is disaggregated to show gross profit contribution in detail within a product type, perhaps even by product, gross margin contribution by this product type to various customer types, and the gross profit performance of this product type by division. This complex view of performance by product type is seldom seen.

Row Col	Name of Chart	From	To	Descriptions
A1	Sales	System: Sales, Level 1 of 2, Page 1 of 4, Chart E2	C1, C2, C3	Time series showing the actual sales values for a product type for the previous 12 months as compared to budget and/or prior year. Seasonal trends will emerge and variances therefrom can be seen. This chart provides a view most commonly seen by management, and shows the seasonal behavior of a product type plus its trend.
A2	Gross Margin Percentage	Same as A1	B2	Time series showing the net effect of the changing relationship between the sales mix, the cost of goods sold, and the resulting gross margin received by the company for this product type. The gross margin is the complement of the cost of goods sold percentage. The picture shown by this chart will reflect the effect of the changing mix of related items for a product type. The gross margin is the complement of the cost of goods sold percentage. The picture shown by this chart will reflect the effect of the changing mix of related items for a product type.
B2	N: Gross Margin D: Sales	A2	C1, C2, C3	Relative size of gross margin for this product type as compared to sales. If the change in the ratio is due to a change in the relative size of the gross margin, the disaggregation would take place either by reviewing the changes in the cost of goods sold system or by reviewing the separate gross margin system. The path taken would depend strictly on the audience reviewing the charts. The pathway would be chosen to enhance communication depending on the functional responsibilities of those reviewing the charts. If the change in the ratio is due to the relative size of the sales, the disaggregation would follow Charts C1 through C3.

Row Col	Name of Chart	From	To	Descriptions
C1	Product Type Sales by Customer Type—Component	A1, B2, B3	D1	Relative importance of the product type sales and respective gross margin to the various customer types as compared to total product type sales and total gross margin.
D1	Product Type Sales by Customer Type—Item	C1	E1	Relative size of the product type sales and respective gross margin by customer type as compared to each other. A change in the pattern should indicate a policy change toward sales to a customer type. The pattern should represent the policy pattern of the corporation for this product type, not a pattern of uncontrolled changes.
E1	Product Type Sales by Customer Type—Variance	D1	—	Mix variances from plan and/or prior year for product type sales and respective gross margin to the customer types. This picture of mix variances is one of the most important for showing where the significant mix variances occurred. It does not explain *why* variances have occurred, but it does point out where to look for the causes. If further analysis is required, each of the elements can be further disaggregated to sequences the same as those shown starting at C1, C2, and C3.
C2	Sales by Detailed Product Type—Component	A1-B2	D2	Relative importance of sales and respective gross margin by detailed product type as compared to the total product type. A change in the pattern would be an indicator that further disaggregation is required.
D2	Sales by Detailed Product Type—Item	C2	E2	Relative size of the sales and respective gross margin by detailed product type as compared to the other detailed product types. As in Chart C2, the patterns should be similar from year to year. Any change to the patterns would indicate further analysis.
E2	Sales by Detailed Product Type—Variance	D2	—	Variance from plan and/or prior year for the sales mix and respective gross margin mix by detailed product type. The important picture is the changing sales mix. If further analysis is required, a further disaggregation similar to that shown starting at C1 through C3 can be shown. At this point it may be necessary to go to the original books of record.

Row Col	Name of Chart	From	To	Descriptions
C3	Product Type Sales Mix by Division—Component	A1–B2	D3	Relative importance of this product type sales and respective gross margin by division as compared to the total product type sales. Changes from prior year or expected pattern would indicate further analysis.
D3	Product Type Sales Mix by Division—Item	C3	E3	Shows two important relationships for this product type by the divisions. The first is the relative importance of the product type sales by each of the divisions as compared to the other divisions, and the second is the related gross margin by division as compared to the other divisions. Any major change in the pattern of sales and gross margin by division would indicate further analysis should be completed.
E3	Product Type Sales Mix by Division—Variance	D3	—	Relative size of the sales and respective gross margin variances by divisions. Any major shifts in the variances indicate that a further divisional analysis should be undertaken. Further analysis for each element can be shown in sequences similar to those starting at C1, C2, and C3.

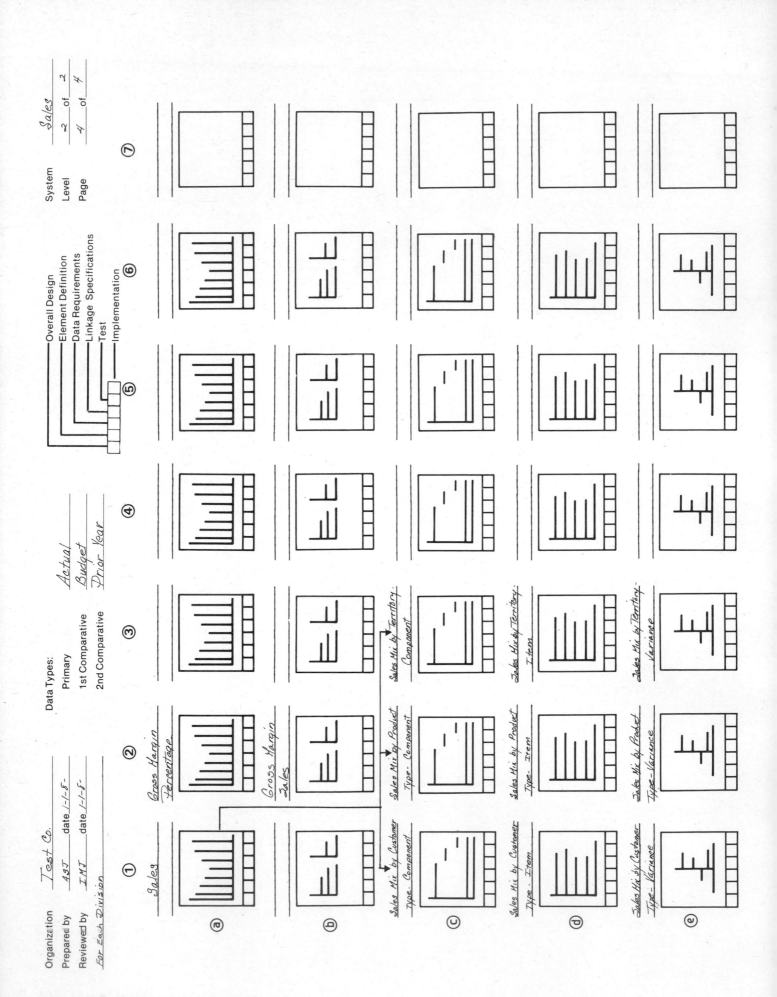

NOTE: This sequence of charts is almost identical to that shown in level 1 (except for the return on sales ratio). The difference is sales for a single product type, perhaps even by product, sales of this product type to the customer types, and the sales of this product type by division.

Row Col	Name of Chart	From	To	Descriptions
A1	Sales	System: Sales, Level 1 of 2, Page 1 of 4, Chart E3	C1, C2, C3	Time series showing the actual sales for this division for the previous 12 months as compared to budget and prior year. Seasonal trends will emerge and variances therefrom can be seen. This chart provides a view most commonly seen by management.
A2	Gross Margin Percentage	Same as A1	B2	Time series showing the net effect of the changing relationship between sales, cost of goods sold, and the resulting gross margin for this division. The gross margin is the complement of the cost of goods sold percentage. The picture shown by this chart will reflect the effect of the changing mix of related items for this division.
B2	N: Gross Margin D: Sales	A2	C1, C2, C3	Relative size of gross margin as compared to sales for this division. If the change in the ratio is due to a change in the relative size of the gross margin, the disaggregation would take place either by reviewing the changes in the cost of goods sold or by reviewing the separate gross margin system. The path taken would depend strictly on the audience reviewing the charts. The pathway would be chosen to enhance communication depending on the functional responsibilities of those reviewing the charts. If the change in the ratio is due to the relative size of the sales, the disaggregation could also follow Charts C1 through C3 in this system.
C1	Sales Mix by Customer Type—Component	A1, B2	D1	Relative importance of sales by customer type as compared to total sales.
D1	Sales Mix by Customer Type—Item	C1	E1	Relative size of the sales for this division by customer type as compared to each other. A change in the pattern should indicate a policy change toward the sales to a customer type. The pattern should represent the policy pattern of the corporation, not a pattern of uncontrolled change at the division level.

Row Col	Name of Chart	From	To	Descriptions
E1	Sales Mix by Customer Type—Variance	D1	—	Mix Variances from plan and/or prior year for the sales by customer type for this division. This picture of mix variances is one of the most important for showing where the significant mix variances have occurred. It does not explain *why* variances have occurred, but it does point out where to look for the causes. If further analysis is required, each of the elements can be further disaggregated to sequences the same as those shown starting at C1, C2, and C3.
C2	Sales Mix by Product Type—Component	A1-B2	D2	Relative importance of sales by product type as compared to the total sales for the division. A change in the pattern would be an indicator that further disaggregation is required.
D2	Sales Mix by Product Type—Item	C2	E2	Relative size of the sales by product type for the division as compared to the other product types. As in Chart C2, the pattern should be similar from year to year. Any major change reflected by the changing patterns would indicate further analysis.
E2	Sales Mix by Product Type—Variance	D2	—	Variance from plan and/or prior year for the sales by product type for this division. The important picture is the size of changing sales mix within this division. Further analysis will be required to fully understand *why* changes occurred. If further analysis is required, a further disaggregation similar to that shown starting at C1 through C3 can be shown.
C3	Sales Mix by Territory—Component	A1-B2	D3	Relative importance of sales by territory within a division as compared to the total sales for the division.
D3	Sales Mix by Territory—Item	C3	E3	Relative importance of the sales by territory within a division as compared to other territories. Any major change in the pattern of sales by territory would indicate further analysis is necessary.
E3	Sales Mix by Territory—Variance	D3	—	Sales mix variance by territory within a division. Any major shifts in the variances indicate further analysis is necessary. Further analysis for each element can be shown in sequences similar to those starting at C1, C2, and C3. At this point it may be necessary to go directly to the books of record.

1. COST OF GOODS SOLD AND GROSS MARGIN

As noted earlier, the charts and the disaggregation sequence for the cost of goods sold and gross margin systems are exactly the same as for the sales sequence. For example, cost of goods sold could be disaggregated by customer type, product type, and division. These would be further disaggregated as in the Sales sequence. The key indicators for cost of goods sold by month and cost of goods sold as a percentage of sales. The key indicators for gross margin would be the gross margin percentage and gross margin as a percentage of sales.

A. Sales/Cost of Goods Sold/Gross Margin

The sales/cost of goods sold/gross margin system is both a control and a responsibility accounting system. The relationships between customer mix, product mix, and division mix is shown by the systems as a co-relationship between sales and their respective cost of goods sold and the same sales and their respective gross margin. This view should enhance communication between the functional groups about their efforts and should encourage a sharing of information about how to improve profit performance.

As shown in Exhibit 13.2, the sales/cost of goods sold/gross margin system is a combination of two systems, sales/cost of goods sold and sales/gross margin. The key indicators can be disaggregated into either system. The breakdown of both systems shows that each system is parallel to the sales system described earlier in the chapter. Sales/cost of goods sold is disaggregated by customer type, product type, and division. The same disaggregation occurs for the sales/gross margin comparison.

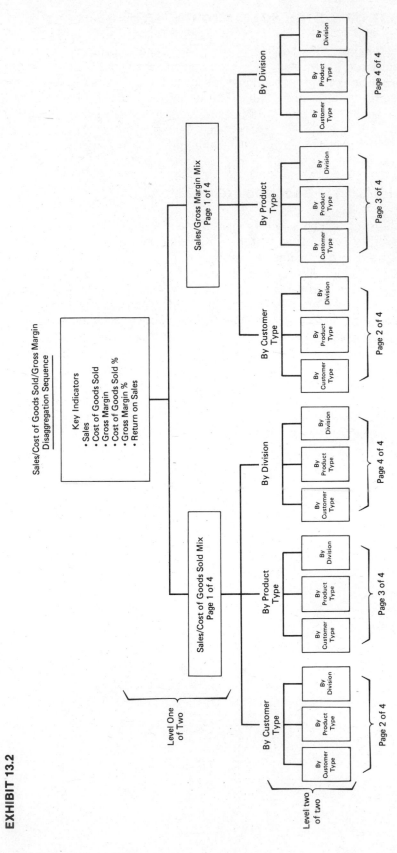

EXHIBIT 13.2

218

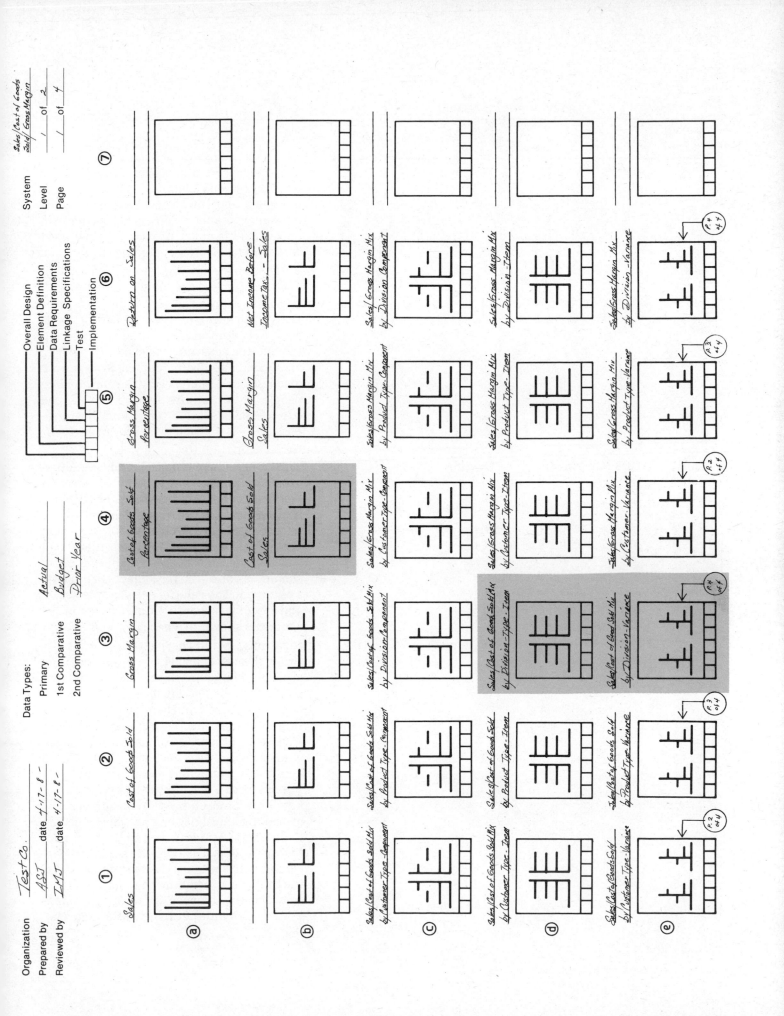

Row Col	Name of Chart	From	To	Descriptions
A1	Sales	Original	C1–C6	Time series showing the actual sales values for the previous 12 months as compared to budget and prior year. Seasonal trends will emerge and variances therefrom can be seen. This chart provides a view most commonly seen by management.
A2	Cost of Goods Sold	Original	C1, C2, C3	Time series showing the actual cost of goods sold for the previous 12-month period as compared to budget and prior year. Depending on the way cost of goods sold are computed in the acocunting system, the seasonal patterns will emerge and variances from that pattern can be discussed and analyzed by the appropriate people. In a manufacturing business, the cost of goods sold system could disaggregate the information through variances for each production line.
A3	Gross Margin	Original	C4, C5, C6	Time series showing 12 months actual gross margin as compared to budget and prior year. Seasonal trends and patterns will relate to and are the product of the first two Charts, A1 and A2. Seasonal patterns, trends, and variations therefrom will soon become apparent. This net chart should be one of the first charts to indicate a change in the relationship between sales and cost of goods sold. A further view of the change is shown by charts A4 and A5.
A4	Cost of Goods Sold Percentage	Original	B4	Relationship for the past 12 months between the cost of goods sold as a percentage of sales. The changing relationships over time as described by this chart are extremely complex and cannot be seen from a single comparison. Yet if the cost of goods sold as a percentage of sales is going up, then obviously the gross margin is going down and that could have a direct impact on the bottom line. This chart is a key indicator chart that describes the overall productivity of a number of people including the sales force and the manufacturing process. Disaggregation of this percentage throughout the system provides the basis for describing the complex interrelationship between sales mix, production mix, manufacturing costs, and cus-

Row Col	Name of Chart	From	To	Descriptions
				tomer response to product. Learning curve expectations would also be clearly reflected through this disaggregation process. In short, this chart could be one of the key indicators in the management instrument panel.
B4	N: Cost of Goods Sold D: Sales	A4	C1, C2, C3	Relative size of the cost of goods sold as compared to sales for the current period, and both are compared to budget and/or prior year. If the change in the ratio is due to a change in the relative size of the cost of goods sold, then the disaggregation would occur starting with chart C1, C2, and/or C3; for a separate analysis of cost of goods sold alone, you could use the cost of goods sold system and disaggregate without showing the co-relationship to sales. If the change seen in the ratio is due to a change in the relative size of sales, the disaggregation could occur by going to charts C1, C2 or C3, or by going to the sales system where sales can be disaggregated without showing the corelationship to cost of goods sold.
A5	Gross Margin Percentage	Original	B5	Time series showing the net effect of the changing relationship between cost of goods sold and sales, and the gross margin received by the company for its goods and services. The gross margin percentage is the complement of the cost of goods sold percentage. The picture shown by this chart will reflect the effect of the changing product/cost of goods sold mix.
B5	N: Gross Margin D: Sales	A5	C4–C6	Relative size of gross margin as compared to sales. If the change in the ratio is due to a change in the relative size of the gross margin, the disaggregation would take place either by reviewing the changes in the cost of goods sold, by reviewing the separate gross margin system, or by following Charts C4, C5, and C6. The path taken would depend strictly on the audience reviewing the charts. The pathway would be chosen to enhance communication depending on the functional responsibilities of those reviewing the charts. If the change in the ratio is due to the relative size of the

Row Col	Name of Chart	From	To	Descriptions
A6	Return on Sales	Original	B6	sales, the disaggregation would follow Charts C1 through C6 in the sales system. Time series showing net income before taxes as compared to sales. It provides an overall indication of the final result of corporate activity before taxes. Any drastic changes in the bottom line would be seen by reviewing charts A1 through A5. The changing relationships will be reflected on the bottom line. A further analysis of operating expenses and administrative expenses would be required to see the whole picture, but certainly a major contribution to the change in the net income would be a change in gross margin. You can see changing gross margins and sales mix activity providing, at the same time, a view of cause and result. If however, the cost of goods sold and gross margin were right on target, the operating expenses and administrative expense systems should be reviewed to determine why return on sales was down. This chart is shown in a number of systems and is one of the more critical ratios for reviewing overall corporate performance.
B6	N: Net Income before Income Tax D: Sales	A6	C1–C6	Ratio showing the net income before income tax as compared to sales. If the change in the ratio is due to a change in the relative size of the net income before income tax, then a disaggregation of the entire income process should be reviewed, including a review of the income, cost of goods sold, operating expenses, and administrative expense systems. If the change in the ratio is due to a change in the relative size of the sales, then disaggregation and analysis could take place through the sales system or through charts C1 through C6 in this series.
C1	Sales/Cost of Goods Sold Mix by Customer Type—Component	A1, A2 B4, B6	D1	Relative importance of sales by customer type as related to the corresponding cost of goods sold by customer type. The relative importance of sales by customer type is compared to total sales and the relative importance of the cost of goods sold by customer type as compared to the total cost of goods sold. This view of the complex relationships between the sales mix and

222

Row Col	Name of Chart	From	To	Descriptions
				cost of goods sold mix by customer type provides the first inkling of what sales efforts and/or cost controls might be needed.
D1	Sales/Cost of Goods Sold Mix by Customer Type—Item	C1	E1	Relative size of the sales by customer type as compared to each other and the relative size of the cost of goods sold as compared to each other. Both are related to their respective customer type, showing the complex co-relationship between the sales ad cost of goods sold. The *patterns* for the two sides should be similar. A change in one of the patterns should indicate a policy change toward the relationship between sales price and cost of goods sold. The pattern should represent the policy pattern of the corporation, not a pattern of uncontrolled change of pricing policies, a change in the productivity of the plants, or a change in the effectiveness of the purchasing department.
E1	Sales/Cost of Good Sold by Customer Type—Variance	D1	System: Sales/ COGS/Gross Margin, Level 2 of 2, Page 2 of 4, Charts A1–A5 and/or System: Sales, Level 1 of 2, Page 1 of 4, Charts A1–A3 and/or System: Cost of Goods Sold, Level 1 of 2, Page 1 of 4, Charts A1–A5	Twin variance showing the mix of variances from plan and/or prior year for sales and the respective cost of goods sold. This picture of mix variances is one of the most important in showing where the significant mix variances in sales and cost of goods sold occurred. It does not explain *why* variances have occurred, but it does point out where to look for the causes. If further analysis is required, each of the elements can be further disaggregated to sequences the same as those shown starting at C1, C2, and C3 and as described in the Sales/ COGS/Gross Margin System, level 2 of 2, page 2 of 4, Charts A1–A5.
C2	Sales/Cost of Goods Sold Mix by Product Type—Component	A1, A2 B4, B6	D2	Relationship between sales and cost of goods sold by product types, as well as the relative importance of sales by product type to the total sales, and the relative importance of the cost of goods sold by product type to the total cost of goods sold. This co-relationship should have similar patterns assuming a consistent relationship between sales and cost of goods sold by product type. A change in the pattern would be an indicator that further disaggregation is required.

Row Col	Name of Chart	From	To	Descriptions
D2	Sales/Cost of Goods Sold by Product Type—Item	C2	E2	Relative size of the sales by product type as compared to the other product types and the relative size of cost of goods sold by product type as compared to the other cost of goods sold, as well as the relationship between the sales by product type and their respective cost of goods sold. As in Chart C2, the patterns should be similar from year to year assuming a consistent relationship between sales and cost of goods sold. Any change in this relationship as reflected by the patterns would indicate a need for further analysis.
E2	Sales/Cost of Goods Sold by Product Type—Variance	D2	System: Sales/COGS/Gross Level 2 of 2, Page 3 of 4, Charts A1-A5	Twin variance showing the variance from plan and/or prior year for the sales and cost of goods sold by product type. Two distinct pictures are produced by this chart: the twin pattern of the sales and cost of goods sold mix variance and the changing relationship between the sales mix and the cost of goods sold mix. At this point, the picture of cause and affect can first be seen. Further analysis will be required to fully understand *why* change occurred. If further analysis is required, a further disaggregation similar to that shown starting at C1 through C3 can be shown. Also, see System Sales/COGS/Gross Margin, level 2 of 2, page 3 of 4, Charts A1 through A5.
C3	Sales/Cost of Goods Sold Mix by Division—Component	A1, A2 B4, B6	D3	Relative importance of sales by division as compared to the total sales, and the related cost of goods sold as compared to the total cost of goods sold, as well as the related pattern of sales and cost of goods sold. Assuming a standard relationship between sales and cost of goods sold, the patterns should remain consistent between sales and cost of goods sold over the years. If there are any variances in that pattern over time, it would be reflected by assuming that last year's sales are included as one of the comparatives. If last year's figures are not included, then the budget would show the expected pattern and changes from budget would indicate if further analysis is required.

Row Col	Name of Chart	From	To	Descriptions
D3	Sales/Cost of Goods Sold Mix by Division—Item	C3	E3	Relative importance of the sales by division as compared to the other divisions, and the related cost of goods sold by division as compared to the other divisions. A major change in the pattern of sales and cost of goods sold by division would indicate further analysis should be completed.
E3	Sales/Cost of Goods Sold Mix by Division—Variance	D3	System Sales/COGS/ Gross Margin, Level 2 of 2, Page 4 of 4, Charts A1–A5	Twin variance showing the sales mix variance and the cost of goods sold mix variance by division. It also shows the relative size of the variances between sales and cost of goods sold. Any major shifts in the variances indicate that a further divisional analysis should be undertaken to find the reasons for these variances. Further analysis for each element can be shown in sequences similar to those starting at C1, C2, and C3 as shown in system—sales/COGS/gross margin, level 2 of 2, page 4 of 4, Charts A1 through A6.
C4	Sales/Gross Margin Mix by Customer Type—Component	A1, A3, B5, B6	D4	Relationship between sales and gross margin. The right side of the chart, gross margin, is the complement of the cost of goods chart shown in C1. As noted in C1, the pattern for both sides should be similar assuming the relationship between sales and gross margin is the same. Two important relationships are shown: the relative importance of sales by customer type as compared to the total sales and the relative importance of the gross margin by customer type as compared to gross margin, and also, the relationship between sales and gross margin as compared to total gross margins.
D4	Sales/Gross Margin Mix by Customer Type—Item	C4	E4	Relative importance of sales by customer type as compared to each other, the same as Chart D1. The chart also shows the complement of the cost of goods sold chart by showing the relative importance of gross margin contribution by customer type as compared to each other. In addition, it shows the relative amount of sales contributed by each customer type as compared to the relative size of the gross margin contributed by that same customer type. The patterns of sales contributions by

Row Col	Name of Chart	From	To	Descriptions
				customer type should be similar over time. Any change in the pattern would indicate that further analysis is necessary. These sequences of charts could also be used as a preliminary indicator of whether a customer type is a candidate for being dropped as a market or if a different pricing policy should be implemented for certain customer types. Further analysis should be made prior to any policy changes, but this chart does provide a picture of imbalance.
E4	Sales/Gross Margin Mix by Customer—Variance	D4	System: Sales/COGS/ Gross Margin, Level 2 of 2, Page 2 of 4, Charts A1–A5.	Twin variance showing the sales mix and gross margin mix variances from budget and/or prior year, as well as the relative size of the sales as compared to the relative change in gross margin. You would expect an increase in sales to reflect an increase in gross margin. Although the differences may not be significant, the patterns of variances should be similar. If further analysis is required, further disaggregation could occur for each element similar to Charts C4 through C6 and as shown in sales/COGS/gross margin, level 2 of 2, page 2 of 4, Charts A1 through A5.
C5	Sales/Gross Margin Mix by Product Type—Component	A1, A3, B5, B6	D5	Relative importance of sales by product type as compared to the total sales (also shown in C2) and the relative importance of gross margin for each of the product types as compared to the total gross margin (the complement of the cost of goods sold shown in C2). It also compares sales by product type to the respective gross margins. Such a view shows imbalances in either sales and/or gross margin contributions. Any change in the patterns of the gross margin contribution or sales would require further analysis.
D5	Sales/Gross Margin Mix by Product Type—Item	C5	E5	Relative importance of sales by product type as compared to each other similar to that shown in D1, and the relative importance of the gross margin contributions by product types as compared to each other (the complement of the cost of goods sold shown in C2). It also shows the relationship between sales by product type and gross margin contribution by product type. The

Row Col	Name of Chart	From	To	Descriptions
				relationship between the two should provide a consistent pattern.
E5	Sales/Gross Margin Mix by Product Type—Variance	D5	System: Sales/ COGS/Gross Margin, Level 2 of 2, Page 3 of 4, A1–A5	Twin variance showing the variance from plan and/or prior year for sales and gross margin, as well as the relationship of those variances as compared to each other. The relative size of the variances should produce a consistent pattern. If further analysis is required, each of the product types can be further broken into charts similar to those shown in C4, C5, and C6, and in system sales/COGS/gross margin, level 2 of 4, page 3 of 4, Charts A1 through A5.
C6	Sales/Gross Margin Mix by Division—Component	A1, A3, B5, B6	D6	Relative importance of the sales by division as compared to total sales (identical to that shown in Chart C3) and the relative importance of the gross margin contribution by division as compared to total gross margin contribution, the complement of the cost of goods sold pattern shown in C3. It also shows the relative size of sales by division and the corresponding size of the gross margin contribution for each division. The patterns of the sales and gross margin contribution should be similar. A change in the pattern would indicate that additional analysis may be required.
D6	Sales/Gross Margin Mix by Division—Item	C6	E6	Relative importance of the sales by division as compared to the other divisions (identical to that shown in chart D3) and the relative importance of the gross margin contribution by division as compared to the other divisions, the complement of the cost of goods sold pattern in Chart D3. It also shows the relative size of sales as compared to the relative size of its related gross margin contribution by division. Such a picture provides an indication of performance and productivity by division.
E6	Sales/Gross Margin Mix by Division—Variance	D6	System: Sales/ COGS/Gross Margin, Level 2 of 2, Page 4 of 4, A1–A5	Relative size of the variance from plan and/or prior year by division for both sales and gross margin, as well as the relative importance of the change in the actual size of variances between sales and gross margin. We assume that if the cost of goods sold is approximately the same for various

Row Col	Name of Chart	From	To	Descriptions
				sales volumes, then the margin would increase or decrease at approximately the same rate as sales. If further analysis is required, each of the divisions can be broken into a sequence similar to that starting at C4, C5, and C6. Also, see sales/COGS/gross margin, level 2 of 2, page 4 of 4, Charts A1 through A6.

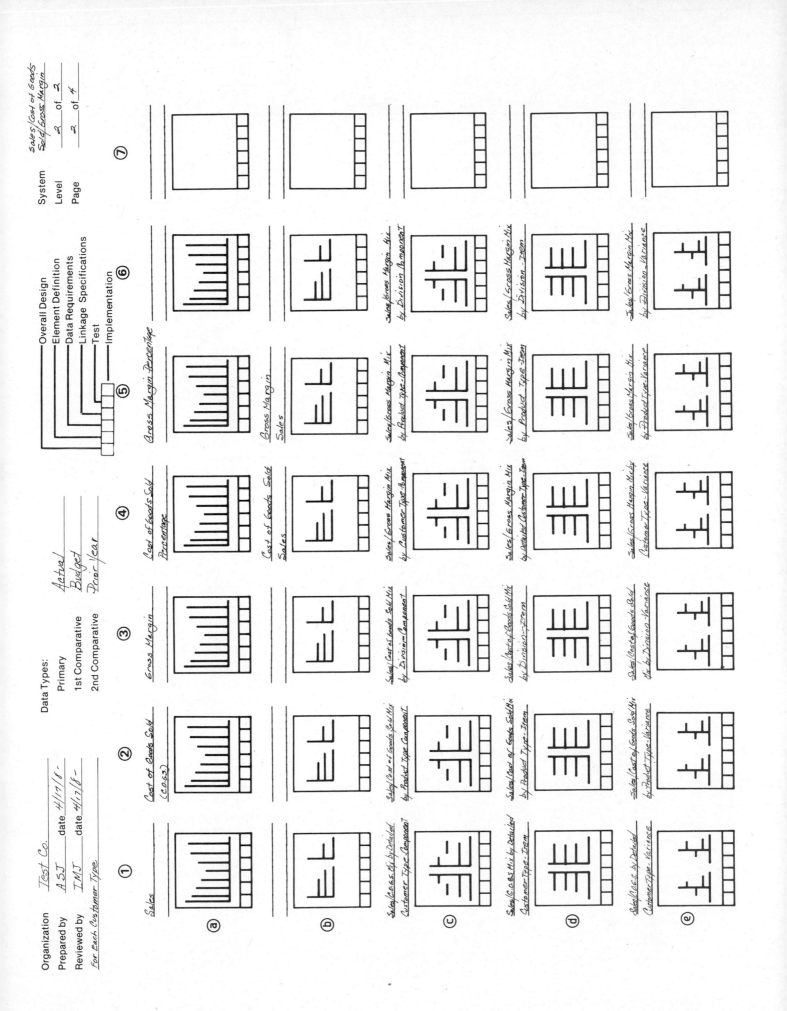

Organization Test Co. date 4/17/8-
Prepared by ASJ date 4/17/8-
Reviewed by IMJ
For Each Customer Type

Data Types:
Primary — Actual
1st Comparative — Budget
2nd Comparative — Prior Year

System
Level
Page

Overall Design
Element Definition
Data Requirements
Linkage Specifications
Test
Implementation

① ② ③ ④ ⑤ ⑥ ⑦

Row a:
- Sales
- Cost of Goods Sold (C.O.G.S.)
- Gross Margin
- Cost of Goods Sold Percentage
- Gross Margin Percentage
- Sales
- Gross Margin
- Cost of Goods Sold

Row b:
- Sales/C.O.G.S. Mix by Detailed Customer Type-Component
- Sales/Cost of Goods Sold Mix by Product Type-Component
- Sales/Cost of Goods Sold Mix by Division-Component

Row c:
- Sales/Gross Mix by Detailed Customer Type-Item
- Sales/Cost of Goods Sold Mix by Product Type-Component
- Sales/Cost of Goods Sold Mix by Division-Component
- Sales/Gross Margin Mix by Customer Type-Component
- Sales/Gross Margin Mix by Product Type-Component
- Sales/Gross Margin Mix by Division-Component

Row d:
- Sales/C.O.G.S. Mix by Detailed Customer Type-Item
- Sales/Cost of Goods Sold Mix by Product Type-Item
- Sales/Cost of Goods Sold Mix by Division-Item
- Sales/Gross Margin Mix by Detailed Customer Type-Item
- Sales/Gross Margin Mix by Product Type-Item
- Sales/Gross Margin Mix by Division-Item

Row e:
- Sales/C.O.G.S. by Detailed Customer Type-Variance
- Sales/Cost of Goods Sold Mix by Product Type-Variance
- Sales/Cost of Goods Sold Mix by Division-Variance
- Sales/Gross Margin Mix by Customer Type-Variance
- Sales/Gross Margin Mix by Product Type-Variance
- Sales/Gross Margin Mix by Division-Variance

Row Col	Name of Chart	From	To	Descriptions
A1	Sales	System: Sales/ COGS Gross Margin, Level <u>1</u> of <u>2</u>, Page <u>1</u> of <u>4</u>, Charts E1 & E4	C1–C6	Time series showing the actual sales values for a single customer type for the previous 12 months as compared to budget and prior year. Seasonal trends will emerge and variances therefrom can be seen. This chart provides a view most commonly seen by management, and shows the seasonal behavior of a customer type plus trend.
A2	Cost of Goods Sold	See A1	C1, C2, C3	Time series showing the actual cost of goods sold for the sales of this customer type for the previous 12-month period as compared to budget and prior year. Depending on the way the cost of goods sold are computed in the accounting system, the seasonal patterns will emerge and variances from that pattern can be discussed and analyzed by the appropriate people. When compared to other customer types, this chart should indicate any differences in the product mix that woud make one customer type more profitable than another.
A3	Gross Margin	See A1	C4, C5, C6	Time series showing 12 months' actual gross margin for this customer type as compared to budget and prior year. Seasonal trends and patterns will relate to and are the product of the first two charts, A1 and A2. Seasonal patterns, trends, and variations therefrom will soon become apparent. This net chart should be one of the first charts to indicate change in the relationship between the sales and cost of goods sold within the customer type. A further view of the change is shown by Charts A4 and A5.
A4	Cost of Goods Sold Percentage	See A1	B5	Relationship for the first 12 months between the cost of goods sold as a percent of sales for a single customer type. The changing relationships over time as described by this chart are extremely complex and cannot be seen from a single comparison. Yet if the cost of goods sold as a percentage of sales is going up, then obviously the gross margin is going down and that could have a direct impact on the bottom line. This is a key indicator chart

Row Col	Name of Chart	From	To	Descriptions
				that describes the overall profitability of a customer type. Disaggregation of this percentage throughout the system provides the basis for describing the complex interrelationship between sales mix, production mix, manufacturing costs, and customer response to product. A comparison of this chart with the same chart for all of the customer types would provide a clear picture of the relative changes in customer profitability and would provide a key indicator to further analysis.
B4	N: Cost of Goods Sold D: Sales	A4	C1–C3	Ratio showing the relative size of the cost of goods sold as compared to sales to this customer type for the current period; both are compared to budget and/or prior year. If the change in the ratio is due to a change in the relative size of the cost of goods sold, then the disaggregation would occur starting with Charts C1, C2, and/or C3; for a separate analysis of cost of goods sold alone, you could use the cost of goods sold system and disaggregate without showing the correlation to sales. If the change seen in the ratio is due to a change in the relative size of sales the disaggregation could occur by going to Chart C1, C2, and/or C3, or by going to the sales system where sales can be disaggregated without showing the correlationship to cost of goods sold.
A5	Gross Margin Percentage	See A1	B5	Time series showing the net effect of the changing relationship between cost of goods sold and sales, the gross margin received by the company for its goods and services sold to this customer type. The gross margin percentage is the complement of cost of goods sold percentage. The picture shown by this chart will reflect the effect of the changing product/cost of goods sold mix sold to a customer type.
B5	N: Gross Margin D: Sales	A5	C4–C6	Ratio showing the relative size of gross margin for this customer type as compared to sales. If the change in the ratio is due to a change in the relative size of the gross margin, the disaggregation would take place either by reviewing the changes in

Row Col	Name of Chart	From	To	Descriptions
				the cost of goods sold, by reviewing the separate gross margin system, or by following Charts C4, C5, and C6. The path taken would depend strictly on the audience reviewing the charts. The pathway would be chosen to enhance communication depending on the functional responsibilities of those reviewing the charts. If the change in the ratio is due to the relative size of the sales, the disaggregation would follow Charts C1 through C6 in the sales system.
C1	Sales/Cost of Goods Sold Mix by Detailed Customer Type—Component	A1, A2, B4	D1	Co-relationship showing the relative importance of sales by detailed customer type, perhaps even as detailed as specific customers, as related to the corresponding cost of goods sold. The relative importance of sales by detailed customer type is compared to total sales for the customer type shown; the relative importance of the cost of goods sold by detailed customer type is compared to the total cost of goods sold for the customer type shown. This view of the complex relationships between sales mix and cost of goods sold mix by customer type provides the first inkling of what sales efforts and/or cost controls might be needed for this customer type. Specific customers might be singled out for review.
D1	Sales/Cost of Goods Sold Mix by Detailed Customer Type—Item	C1	E1	Relative size of the sales by detailed customer type as compared to each other and the relative size of the corresponding cost of goods sold as compared to each other. Both are related to their respective detailed customer type, showing the complex co-relationship between the sales and cost of goods sales. The *patterns* for the two sides should be similar. A change in one of the patterns should indicate a policy change toward the relationship between sales price and cost of goods sold. The pattern should represent the policy pattern of the corporation for the customer type, not a pattern of uncontrolled changes.
E1	Sales/Cost of Goods Sold by Detailed Customer Type—Variance	D1	—	Twin variance showing the mix variances from plan and/or prior year for the sales and the respective cost of goods sold for the detailed customer type. This picture of mix

232

Row Col	Name of Chart	From	To	Descriptions
				variances is one of the most important in showing where the significant mix variances in sales and cost of goods sold occurred. It does not explain why variances have occurred but it does point out where to look for the causes. If further analysis is required, each of the elements can be further disaggregated to sequences the same as those shown starting at C1, C2, and C3. At this point, it may be necessary to go to the detailed books of record.
C2	Sales/Cost of Goods Sold Mix by Product Type—Component	A1, A2, B4	D2	Co-relationship showing the relationship between product sales to this customer type and the respective cost of goods sold, and the relative importance of sales for this customer type by product type as compared to the total sales and the relative importance of the cost of goods sold for the respective product type as compared to the total cost of goods sold. This co-relationship should show similar patterns assuming the consistent relationship between sales and cost of goods sold by product type. A change in the pattern would be an indicator that further disaggregation is required.
D2	Sales/Cost of Goods Sold Mix by Product Type—Item	C2	E2	Co-relationship showing the relative size of the sales to this customer type by product type as compared to the other product types sold and the relative size of the cost of goods sold by the respective product type as compared to the other cost of goods sold, and the relationship between the sales to this customer type by product type and their respective cost of goods sold. As in Chart C2, the patterns should be similar from year to year assuming a consistent relationship between sales and cost of goods sold. Any change in this relationship as reflected by the patterns would indicate further analysis is needed.
E2	Sales/Cost of Goods Sold Mix by Product Type—Variance	D2	—	Twin variance showing the variance from plan and/or prior year for the sales to this customer type and cost of goods sold mix by product type. Two distinct pictures are produced by this chart: a twin pattern of the sales mix and the cost of goods sold variance for this customer type, and the changing relationship between the sales

Row Col	Name of Chart	From	To	Descriptions
				mix and the cost of goods sold mix. At this point, the picture of cause and effect can be seen. If further analysis is required, a further disaggregation similar to that shown starting at C1 through C3 can be shown.
C3	Sales/Cost of Goods Sold Mix by Division— Component	A1, A2, B4	D3	Co-relationship showing the relative importance of sales to this customer type by division as compared to the total sales and the relative cost of goods sold by division as compared to the total cost of goods sold, and the related pattern of sales and cost of goods sold to this customer type for the various divisions. Assuming a standard relationship between sales and cost of goods sold, the patterns should remain consistent between sales and cost of goods sold over the years. If there are any variances in that pattern over time, it would be reflected assuming that last year's divisional sales to this customer type are included as one of the comparatives. If last year's figures are not included, then the budget would show the expected pattern and changes from budget would indicate if further analysis were required.
D3	Sales/Cost of Goods Sold Mix by Division—Item	C3	E3	Co-relationship showing the relative importance of the sales to this customer type by division as compared to the other divisions, and the related cost of goods sold by division as compared to the other divisions. Any major change in the pattern of sales and cost of goods sold by division for this customer type would indicate further analysis should be completed.
E3	Sales/Cost of Goods Sold Mix by Division— Variance	D3	—	Twin variance showing the sales mix variance and the cost of goods sold mix variance by division, and the relative size of the variances between sales and cost of goods sold. Any major shifts in the relative size of the variances indicate that a further divisional analysis should be undertaken to find the reasons for these variances. Further analysis for each element can be shown in sequences similar to those starting at C1, C2, and C3.
C4	Sales/Gross Margin Mix by Customer Type—Component	A1, A3, B5	D4	Relationship between sales to this customer type by detailed customer type, perhaps even customer, and gross margin. The

234

Row Col	Name of Chart	From	To	Descriptions
				right side of the chart, gross margin, is the complement of the cost of goods chart shown in C1. As noted in C1, the pattern for both sides should be similar assuming the relationship between sales and gross margin is the same. Two important relationships are shown: the relative importance of sales by detailed customer type as compared to the total sale for this customer type and the relative importance of the gross margin by detailed customer type as compared to total gross margin, and the relationship between detailed customer type sales and their respective gross margins.
D4	Sales/Gross Margin Mix by Detailed Customer Type—Item	C4	E4	Co-relationship chart showing the relative importance of sales by detailed customer type as compared to each other, the same as in Chart D1, and the complement of the cost of goods sold in Chart D1 by showing the relative importance of gross margin contribution by detailed customer type as compared to each other. It also shows the relative amount of sales contributed for this customer type by detailed customer type as compared to the relative size of the respective gross margin contribution. The patterns of sales contributions by detailed customer type should be similar over time. Any change in the pattern would indicate that further analysis is necessary. These sequences of charts could also be used as a preliminary indicator of whether the detailed customer type is a candidate for being dropped or if a different pricing policy should be implemented for certain customers. Further analysis should be made prior to any policy changes, but this chart does provide a picture of imbalance.
E4	Sales/Gross Margin Mix by Customer Type—Variance	D4	—	Twin variance chart showing the sales mix and gross margin mix variances from budget and/or prior year, and the relative size of the sales mix variances as compared to the relative change in gross margin mix variances. You would expect an increase in sales to reflect an increasing gross margin. Although the differences may not be significant, the patterns of variances should be similar. If further analysis is required, it might be necessary to go to the detailed books of record.

235

Row Col	Name of Chart	From	To	Descriptions
C5	Sales/Gross Margin Mix by Product Type—Component	A1, A3, B5	D5	Co-relationship showing the relative importance of sales to this customer type by product type as compared to the total sales to this customer type (also shown in C2), but then it shows the relative importance of gross margin for the respective product types as compared to the total gross margin for this customer type—the complement of the cost of goods sold shown in C2. It also compares sales to this customer type by product type to the respective gross margins. Such a view shows imbalances in either sales and/or gross margin contributions. Any change in the patterns of the gross margin contributions or sales would require further analysis.
D5	Sales/Gross Margin Mix by Product Type—Item	C5	E5	Co-relationship showing the relative importance of sales to this customer type by product type as compared to each other similar to that shown in D2, but also showing the relative importance of the gross margin contributions by product type as compared to each other—the complement of the cost of goods sold shown in D2. It also shows the relationship between sales to this customer type by product type and the respective gross margin contribution. The relationship between the two should provide a consistent pattern.
E5	Sales/Gross Margin Mix by Product Type—Variance	D5	—	Twin variance showing the variance from plan and/or prior year for sales and gross margin and the relationship of those variances as compared to each other. The relative size of the variances should produce a consistent pattern. If further analysis is required, each of the product types can be further broken into charts similar to those shown in C4, C5, and C6.
C6	Sales/Gross Margin Mix by Division—Component	A1, A3, B5	D6	Co-relationship showing the relative importance of the sales to this customer type by division as compared to total sales for the customer type (identical to that shown in Chart C3), and the relative importance of the gross margin contribution for this customer type to the various divisions as compared to total gross margin contribution—the complement of the cost of goods sold pattern shown in C3. It also shows the

Row Col	Name of Chart	From	To	Descriptions
				relative size of sales to this customer type by division and the corresponding size of gross margin contribution for each division. The patterns of the sales and gross margin contribution should be similar. A change in the pattern would indicate that additional analysis may be required.
D6	Sales/Gross Margin Mix by Division—Item	C6	E6	Co-relationship showing the relative importance of the sales to this customer type by division as compared to the other divisions (identical to that shown in Chart D3) and the relative importance of the respective gross margin contributions to each division as compared to the other divisions—the complement of the cost of goods sold pattern in Chart D3. It also shows the relative size of the divisional sales to this customer type as compared to the respective gross margin contribution. Such a picture provides an indication of performance and productivity by division.
E6	Sales/Gross Margin Mix by Division—Variance	D6	—	Twin variance comparing the relative size of the variance from plan and/or prior year by division for both sales and gross margin. It also shows the relative importance of the change in the actual size of variances between sales and gross margin. We assume that if the cost of goods sold is approximately the same for various sales volumes, then the gross margin would increase or decrease at approximately the same rate as sales. If further analysis is required, each of the divisions can be broken into a sequence similar to that starting at C4, C5, and C6.

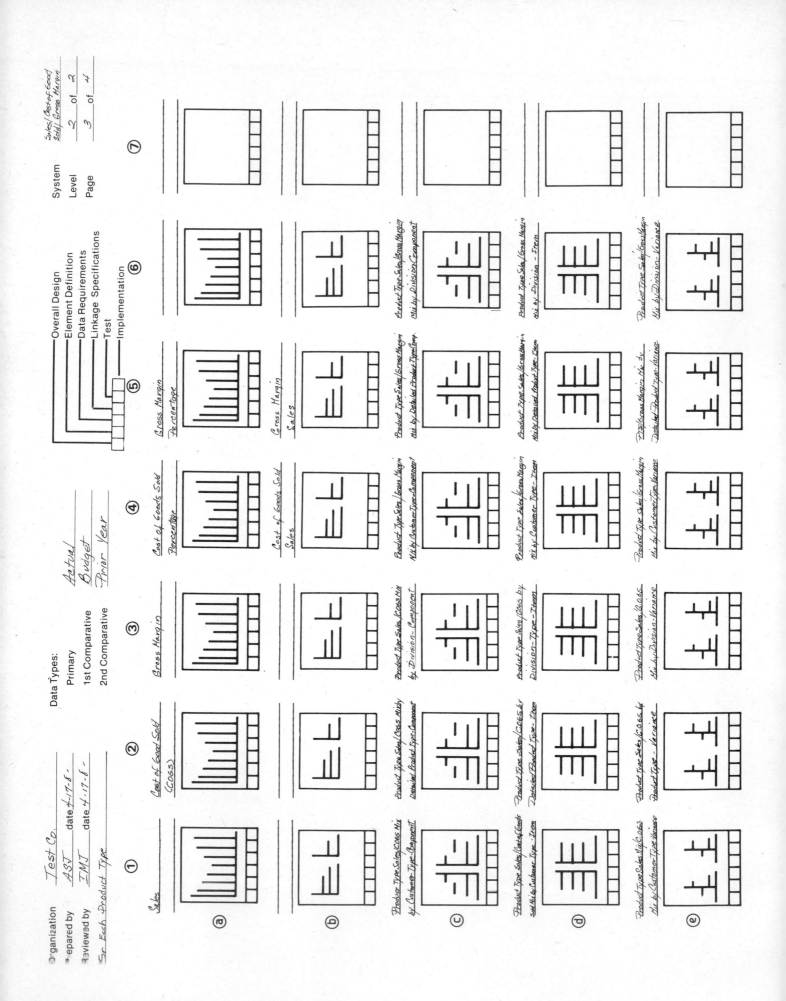

Row Col	Name of Chart	From	To	Descriptions
A1	Sales	System: Sales/CGS/ Gross Margin, Level <u>1</u> of <u>2</u>, Page <u>1</u> of <u>4</u>, Charts E2, E5	C1–C6	Time series showing the actual sales values for a product type for the previous 12 months as compared to budget and/or prior year. Seasonal trends will emerge and variance therefrom can be seen. This chart provides a view most commonly seen by management, and shows the seasonal behavior of a product type plus trends.
A2	Cost of Goods Sold	See A1	C1, C2, C3	Time series showing the actual cost of goods sold for a product type for the previous 12-month period as compared to budget and/or prior year. Depending on the way the cost of goods sold is computed in the accounting system, the seasonal patterns will emerge and variances from that pattern can be discussed and analyzed by the appropriate people. When compared to other product types, this chart should indicate any differences in the cost of goods that would make one product type more profitable than another.
A3	Gross Margin	See A1	C4, C5, C6	Time series showing 12 months' actual gross margin for a single product type as compared to budget and/or prior year. Seasonal trends and patterns will relate to and are the product of the first two charts, A1 and A2. Seasonal patterns, trends, and variations therefrom will soon become apparent. This net chart should be one of the first charts to indicate change in the relationship between sales and cost of goods sold for a product type. A further view of the change is shown by Charts A4 and A5.
A4	Cost of Goods Sold Percentage	See A1	B4	Relationship for the first 12 months between the cost of goods sold as a percentage of sales for a single product type. The changing relationships over time as described by this chart are extremely complex and cannot be seen from a single comparison. Yet if the cost of goods sold as a percentage of sales is going up, then obviously the gross margin is going down and that could have a direct impact on the bottom line. This chart is a key indicator chart that describes the overall profitability of a product type. Disaggregation of

239

Row Col	Name of Chart	From	To	Descriptions
				this percentage throughout the system provides the basis for describing the complex interrelationship between sales mix, production mix, manufacturing costs, and customer response to product. A comparison of this chart with the same chart for all of the product types would provide a clear picture of the relative changes in product profitability and would provide a key indicator to further analysis.
B4	N: Cost of Goods Sold D: Sales	A4	C1–C3	Ratio showing the relative size of the cost of goods sold as compared to sales of this product type for the current period, and both compared to budget and/or prior year. If the change in the ratio is due to a change in the relative size of the cost of goods sold, then the disaggregation would occur starting with Charts C1, C2, and/or C3; for a separate analysis of cost of goods sold alone, you could use the cost of goods sold system and disaggregate without showing co-relationship to sales. If the change seen in the ratio is due to a change in the relative size of sales, the disaggregation could occur by going to Charts C1, C2, and/or C3, or by going to the sales system where sales can be disaggregated without showing the co-relationship to cost of goods sold.
A5	Gross Margin Percentage	See A1	B5	Time series showing the net effect of the changing relationship between cost of goods sold, sales, and the gross margin received by the company for this product type. The gross margin is the complement of the cost of goods sold percentage. The picture shown by this chart will reflect the effect of the changing cost of goods sold for a product type.
B5	N: Gross Margin D: Sales	A5	C4–C6	Ratio showing the relative size of gross margin for this product type as compared to sales. If the change in the ratio is due to a change in the relative size of the gross margin, the disaggregation would take place either by reviewing the changes in the cost of goods sold, by reviewing the separate gross margin system, or by following Charts C4, C5, and C6. The path taken would depend strictly on the audi-

Row Col	Name of Chart	From	To	Descriptions
				ence reviewing the charts. The pathway would be chosen to enhance communication depending on the functional responsibilities of those reviewing the charts. If the change in the ratio is due to the relative size of the sales, the disaggregation would follow Charts C1 through C6 in the sales system.
C1	Product Type Sales/ Cost of Goods Sold Mix by Customer Type—Component	A1, A2, B4	D1	Co-relationship showing the relative importance of the sales of the product type to the various customer types, as related to the corresponding cost of goods sold by customer type. The relative importance of sales for each customer type is compared to total product type sales and the relative importance of the cost of goods sold for each customer type is compared to the total cost of goods sold for the product type. This view of the complex relationship between sales mix and cost of goods sold mix by customer type provides the first inkling of what sales efforts and/or cost controls might be needed for this product type.
D1	Product Type Sales/ Cost of Goods Sold Mix by Customer Type—Item	C1	E1	Relative size of the product type sales by customer type as compared to each other and the relative size of the respective cost of goods sold as compared to each other. The *patterns* for the two sides should be similar. A change in one of the patterns should indicate a policy change toward the relationship between sales price and cost of goods sold. The pattern should represent the policy pattern of the corporation for this product type, not a pattern of uncontrolled changes.
E1	Product Type Sales Mix/Cost of Goods Sold Mix by Customer Type—Variance	D1	—	Twin variance showing the mix variances from plan and/or prior year for product type sales and the respective cost of goods sold. This picture of mix variances is one of the most important in showing where the significant mix variances in sales and cost of goods sold occurred. It does not explain *why* variances have occurred but it does point out where to look for the causes. If further analysis is required, each of the elements can be further disaggregated to sequences the same as those shown starting at C1, C2, and C3.

Row Col	Name of Chart	From	To	Descriptions
C2	Product Type Sales/ Cost of Goods Sold Mix by Detailed Product Type— Component	A1, A2, B4	D2	Co-relationship showing the relationship between detailed product sales and their respective cost of goods sold, and the relative importance of sales by detailed product type as compared to the total product type sales, as well as the relative importance of the cost of goods sold by detailed product type as compared to the total product type cost of goods sold. This co-relationship should have similar patterns assuming a consistent relationship between sales and cost of goods sold by detailed product type. A change in the pattern would be an indicator that further disaggregation is required.
D2	Product Type Sales/ Cost of Goods Sold by Detailed Product Type—Item	C2	E2	Co-relationship showing the relative size of the sales by detailed product type as compared to the other detailed product types and the relative size of the cost of goods sold by detailed product type as compared to the other cost of goods sold. It also shows the relationship between the sales by detailed product type and their respective cost of goods sold. As in Chart C2, the pattern should be similar from year to year assuming a consistent relationship between sales and cost of goods sold. Any change in this relationship as reflected by the patterns would indicate further analysis.
E2	Product Type Sales/ Cost of Goods Sold by Product Type— Variance	D2	—	Twin variance showing the variance from plan and/or prior year for the sales and cost of goods sold mix by detailed product type. Two distinct pictures are produced by this chart: a twin pattern of the sales mix and the cost of goods sold mix variance, and the changing relationship between the sales mix and the cost of goods sold mix. At this point the picture of cause and affect can be seen. If further analysis is required, a further disaggregation similar to that shown starting at C1 through C3 can be shown.
C3	Product Type Sales/ Cost of Goods Sold Mix by Division— Component	A1, A2, B4	D3	Co-relationship showing the relative importance of this product type sales by division as compared to the total product type sales, and the relative cost of goods sold as compared to the total cost of goods

Row Col	Name of Chart	From	To	Descriptions
				sold for the product type. It also shows the related pattern of product type sales and cost of goods sold. Assuming a standard relationship between sales and cost of goods sold, the patterns should remain consistent between sales and cost of goods sold over the years. If there are any variances in that pattern over time, it would be reflected, assuming that last year's sales are included as one of the comparatives. If last year's figures are not included, then the budget would show the expected pattern and changes from budget would indicate if further analysis is required.
D3	Product Type Sales/ Cost of Goods Sold by Division—Item	C3	E3	Co-relationship showing the relative importance of the product type sales by each of the divisions as compared to the other divisions, and the related cost of goods sold by division as compared to the other divisions. Any major change in the pattern of sales and cost of goods sold by division would indicate further analysis should be completed.
E3	Product Type Sales/ Cost of Goods Sold Mix by Division— Variance	D3	—	Twin variance showing the sales mix variance and the cost of goods sold mix variance by division. It also shows the relative size of the variances between sales and cost of goods sold. Any major shifts in the variances indicate that a further divisional analysis should be undertaken to find the reasons for these variances. Further analysis for each element can be shown in sequences similar to those starting at C1, C2, and C3.
C4	Product Type Sales/ Gross Margin Mix by Customer Type— Component	A1, A3, B5	D4	Relationship between product type sales by customer type and the respective gross margin. The right side of the chart, gross margin, is the complement of the cost of goods chart shown in C1. As noted in C1, the pattern for both sides should be similar assuming the relationship between sales and gross margin is the same. Two important relationships are shown: the relative importance of product type sales by customer type as compared to the total product type sales and the relative importance of gross margin by customer type as compared to total product type gross margin,

243

Row Col	Name of Chart	From	To	Descriptions
				and the relationship between product type sales by customer type and the respective gross margin.
D4	Product Type Sales/ Gross Margin Mix by Customer Type— Item	C4	E4	Co-relationship showing the relative importance of this product type sales to each customer type as compared to each other, the same as in Chart D1, and the complement of the cost of goods sold chart by showing the relative importance of gross margin contribution for this product type by customer type as compared to each other. It also shows the relative amount of sales this product type contributes to each customer type as compared to the relative size of the gross margin it contributes to that same customer type. The pattern of sales and gross margin contributions by customer type should be similar over time. Any change in the pattern would indicate that further analysis is necessary. These sequences of charts could also be used as a preliminary indicator of whether a customer type should be sold this product type, or if a different pricing policy should be implemented for this product type to certain customer types. Further analysis should be made prior to any policy changes, but this chart does provide a picture of imbalance.
E4	Product Type Sales/ Gross Margin Mix by Customer Type— Variance	D4	—	Twin variance showing the sales mix and gross margin mix variance from budget and/or prior year. It also shows the relative size of the sales variances as compared to the relative change in gross margin mix variances. You would expect an increase in sales to reflect an increasing gross margin. Although the differences may not be significant, the patterns of variances should be similar. If further analysis is required, further disaggregation could occur for each element similar to charts C4 through C6.
C5	Product Type Sales/ Gross Margin Mix by Detailed Product Type—Component	A1, A3, B5	D5	Co-relationship showing the relative importance of detailed product type sales as compared to the total product type sales (also shown in C2), and the relative importance of gross margin for each detailed product type as compared to the total gross margin for this product type, the comple-

244

Row Col	Name of Chart	From	To	Descriptions
				ment of the cost of goods sold shown in C2. It also shows the relative importance of sales by detailed product type as compared to their respective gross margins. Such a view shows imbalances in either sales and/or gross margin contributions. Any change in the patterns of the gross margin contributions or sales would require further analysis.
D5	Product Type Sales/ Gross Margin Mix by Detailed Product Type—Item	C5	E5	Co-relationship showing the relative importance of product sales by detailed product type as compared to each other, similar to that shown in D1, and the relative importance of the detailed product type gross margin contribution as compared to each other, the complement of the cost of goods sold shown in D2. It also shows the relationship between sales by detailed product type and their respective gross margin contribution. The relationship between the two should provide a consistent pattern.
E5	Product Type Sales/ Gross Margin Mix by Detailed Product Type—Variance	D5	—	Twin variance showing the variance from plan and/or prior year for detailed product type sales and the respective gross margins, and the relationship of those variances as compared to each other. The relative size of the variances should produce a consistent pattern. If further analysis is required, it may be necessary to go to the detailed records.
C6	Product Type Sales/ Gross Margin Mix by Division— Component	A1, A3, B5	D6	Co-relationship showing the relative importance of the product type sales by division as compared to total product type sales (identical to that shown in Chart C3), and the relative importance of the product type gross margin contribution to each division as compared to total product type gross margin contribution, the complement of the cost of goods sold pattern shown in C3. It also shows the relative size of product type sales by division and the corresponding size of gross margin contribution for each division. The patterns of the product type sales and gross margin contribution should be similar. A change in the pattern would indicate that additional analysis may be required.

245

Row Col	Name of Chart	From	To	Descriptions
D6	Product Type Sales/ Gross Margin Mix by Division—Item	C6	E6	Co-relationship showing the relative importance of the product type sales by division as compared to the other divisons (identical to that shown in Chart D3) and the relative importance of the product type gross margin contribution by division as compared to the other divisions, the complement of the cost of goods sold pattern in Chart D3. It also shows the relative size of the product type sales as compared to their respective gross margin contribution by division. Such a picture provides an indication of division performance for this product type.
E6	Product Type Sales/ Gross Margin Mix by Division— Variance	D6	—	Twin variance comparing two important mix variances and showing their relationships. It shows the relative size of the variance from plan and/or prior year by division for both product type sales and their respective gross margins. It also shows the relative importance of the change in the actual size of variances between product type sales and gross margin. We assume that if the cost of goods sold is approximately the same for various sales volumes, then the gross margin would increase or decrease at approximately the same rate as sales. If further analysis is required, each of the divisions can be broken down into a sequence similar to that starting at C4, C5, and C6.

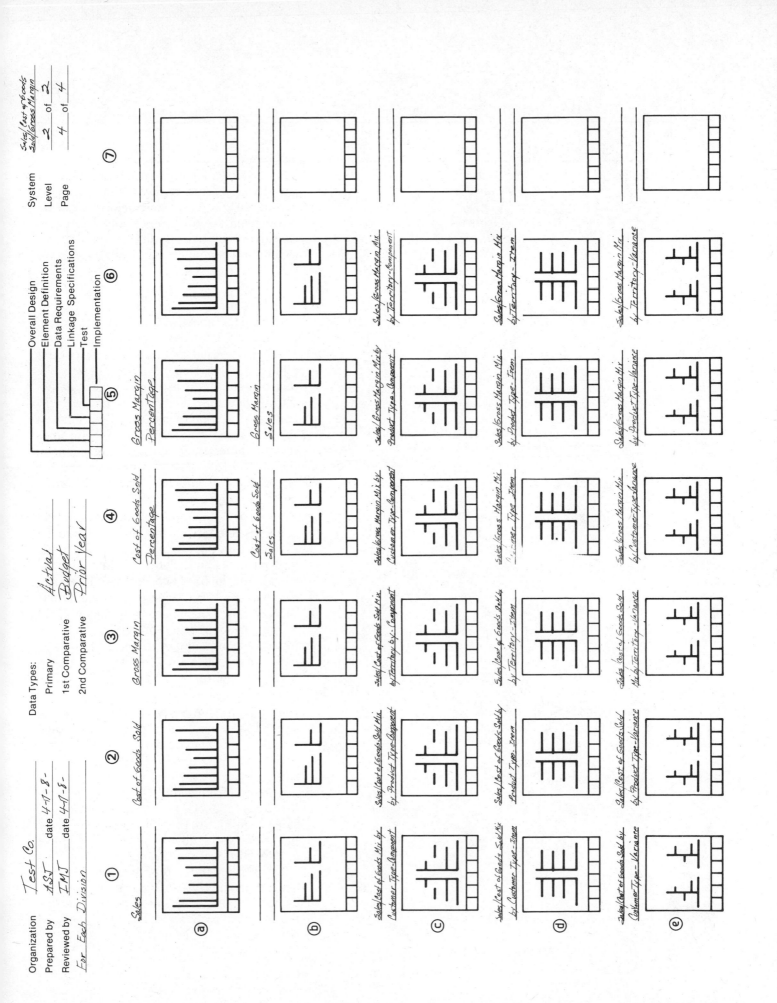

Organization _Test Co._

Prepared by _ASJ_ date _4-17-8-_

Reviewed by _IMJ_ date _4-9-8-_

For Each Division

Data Types:

Primary _Actual_

1st Comparative _Budget_

2nd Comparative _Prior Year_

Overall Design
Element Definition
Data Requirements
Linkage Specifications
Test
Implementation

① ② ③ ④ ⑤ ⑥ ⑦

(a) Sales | Cost of Goods Sold | Gross Margin | Cost of Goods Sold Percentage | Gross Margin Percentage

(b) | Cost of Goods Sold | Sales | Cost of Goods Sold | Sales | Gross Margin

(c) Sales/Cost of Goods Mix by Customer Type-Component | Sales/Cost of Goods Sold Mix by Product Type-Component | Sales/Cost of Goods Sold Mix by Territory by-Component | Sales/Gross Margin Mix by Customer Type-Component | Sales/Gross Margin Mix by Product Type-Component | Sales/Gross Margin Mix by Territory-Component

(d) Sales/Cost of Goods Sold Mix by Customer Type-Item | Sales/Cost of Goods Sold by Product Type- Item | Sales/Cost of Goods Sold Mix by Territory-Item | Sales/Gross Margin Mix by Customer Type- Item | Sales/Gross Margin Mix by Product Type- Item | Sales/Gross Margin Mix byTerritory- Item

(e) Sales/Cost of Goods Sold by Customer Type-Variance | Sales/Cost of Goods Sold by Product Type-Variance | Sales/Cost of Goods Sold Mix by Territory-Variance | Sales/Gross Margin Mix by Customer Type-Variance | Sales/Gross Margin Mix by Product Type-Variance | Sales/Gross Margin Mix by Territory-Variance

Row Col	Name of Chart	From	To	Descriptions
A1	Sales	System: Sales/ COGS/ Gross Margins, Level <u>1</u> of <u>2</u>, Page <u>1</u> of <u>4</u>, Charts E3 & E6	C1–C6	Time series showing the actual sales for this division for the previous 12 months as compared to budget and prior year. Seasonal trends will emerge and variances therefrom can be seen. This chart provides a view most commonly seen by management.
A2	Cost of Goods Sold	See A1	C1, C2, C3	Time series showing the actual cost of goods sold for the division for the previous 12-month period as compared to budget and prior year. Depending on the way the cost of goods sold is computed in the accounting system, the seasonal patterns will emerge and variances from that pattern can be discussed and analyzed by the appropriate people. In a manufacturing business, the cost of goods sold system would disaggregate the information through variances for each production line.
A3	Gross Margin	See A1	C4, C5, C6	Time series showing the 12 months' actual gross margin for this division as compared to budget and prior year. Seasonal trends and patterns will relate to and are the product of the first two charts, A1 and A2. Seasonal patterns, trends, and variations therefrom will soon become apparent. This net chart should be one of the first charts to indicate some change in the relationship between the sales and cost of goods sold. A further view of the change is shown by Charts A4 and A5.
A4	Cost of Goods Sold Percentage	See A1	B4	Relationship for the past 12 months between the cost of goods sold as a percentage of sales for this division. The changing relationships over time as described by this chart are extremely complex and cannot be seen from a single comparison. Yet, if the cost of goods sold as a percentage of sales is going up, then obviously the gross margin is going down and that could have a direct impact on the bottom line. This chart is a key indicator that describes the overall productivity of a number of people, especially the sales force, as well as the manufacturing process. Disaggregation of this percentage throughout the system pro-

248

Row Col	Name of Chart	From	To	Descriptions
				vides the basis for describing the complex inter-relationship between sales mix and production mix, manufacturing costs, and customer response to product at the division level.
B4	N: Cost of Goods Sold D: Sales	A4	C1–C3	Relative size of the cost of goods sold as compared to sales for this division for the current period as compared to budget and/or prior year. If the change in the ratio is due to a change in the relative size of the cost of goods sold, then the disaggregation would occur in Charts C1, C2, and/or C3; for a separate analysis of cost of goods sold, the cost of goods sold system could be used and disaggregated without showing the relationship to sales. If the change seen in the ratio is due to a change in the relative size of sales, the disaggregation could occur by going to Charts C1, C2, and/or C3, or by going to the sales system where sales can be disaggregated without showing the co-relationship to cost of goods sold.
A5	Gross Margin Percentage	See A1	C4–C6	Time series showing the net effect of the changing relationship between cost of goods sold and sales of the gross margin for this division. The gross margin is the complement of the cost of goods sold percentage. The picture shown by this chart will reflect the effect of the changing product/cost of goods sold mix.
B5	N: Gross Margin D: Sales	A5	C4–C6	Ratio showing the relative size of gross margin as compared to sales for this division. If the change in the ratio is due to a change in the relative size of the gross margin, the disaggregation would take place either by reviewing the changes in the cost of goods sold, by reviewing the separate gross margin system, or by following Charts C4, C5, and C6. The path taken would depend strictly on the audience reviewing the charts. The pathway would be chosen to enhance communication depending on the functional responsibilities of those reviewing the charts. If the change in the ratio is due to the relative size of the sales, the disaggregation could also follow Charts C1 through C6 in the sales system.

Row Col	Name of Chart	From	To	Descriptions
C1	Sales/Cost of Goods Sold Mix by Customer Type—Component	A1, A2, B4	D1	Co-relationship showing the relative importance of this division's sales by customer type as related to the corresponding cost of goods sold. The relative importance of sales by customer type is compared to total sales and the relative importance of the cost of goods sold by customer type is compared to the total cost of goods sold. This view of the complex relationship between the sales mix and cost of goods sold mix by customer type provides the first inkling of where sales efforts and/or cost controls might be needed.
D1	Sales/Cost of Goods Sold Mix by Customer Type—Item	C1	E1	Relative size of the sales for this division by customer type as compared to each other and the relative size of the respective cost of goods sold as compared to each other. The *patterns* for the two sides should be similar. A change in one of the patterns should indicate a policy change toward the relationship between sales price and cost of goods sold. The pattern should represent the policy pattern of the corporation, not a pattern of uncontrolled change of pricing policies at the division level.
E1	Sales/Cost of Goods Sold by Customer Type—Variance	D1	—	Twin variance showing the mix variances from plan and/or prior year for the sales and the respective cost of goods sold for this division. This picture of mix variances is one of the most important in showing where the significant mix variances in sales and cost of goods sold occurred. It does not explain *why* variances have occurred, but it does point out where to look for the causes. If further analysis is required, each of the elements can be further disaggregated to sequences the same as those shown starting at C1, C2, and C3.
C2	Sales/Cost of Goods Sold Mix by Product Type—Component	A1, A2, B4	D2	Co-relationship showing the relationship between sales and the respective cost of goods sold for this division by product types, and the relative importance of sales by product type as compared to the total sales for the division and the relative importance of the cost of goods sold by product type as compared to the total cost of goods sold for this division. This co-relationship should have similar patterns assuming a

Row Col	Name of Chart	From	To	Descriptions
				consistent relationship between sales and cost of goods sold by product type. A change in the pattern would be an indicator that further disaggregation is required.
D2	Sales/Cost of Goods Sold by Product Type—Item	C2	E2	Co-relationship showing the relative size of the sales by product type for the division as compared to the other product types and the relative size of the cost of goods sold by product type for the division as compared to the other cost of goods sold. It also shows the relationship between the sales by product type and their respective cost of goods sold for the division. As in Chart C2, the patterns should be similar from year to year assuming a consistent relationship between sales and cost of goods sold. Any change in this relationship as reflected by the patterns would indicate further analysis.
E2	Sales/Cost of Goods Sold by Product Type—Variance	D2	—	Twin variance showing the variance from plan and/or prior year for the sales and cost of goods sold by product type for this division. Two distinct pictures are produced by this chart: a twin pattern of the cost of goods sold and sales variance for this division, and the changing relationship between the sales mix and the cost of goods sold mix within this division. At this point the picture of cause and effect can be seen. Further analysis will be required to fully understand *why* changes occurred. If further analysis is required, a further disaggregation similar to that shown starting at C1 through C3 can be shown.
C3	Sales/Cost of Goods Sold Mix by Territory—Component	A1, A2, B4	D3	Co-relationship showing the relative importance of sales by territory within a division as compared to the total sales for the division and the respective cost of goods sold as compared to the total cost of goods sold. It also shows the related pattern of sales and cost of goods sold. Assuming a standard relationship between sales and cost of goods sold, the pattern should remain consistent between sales and cost of goods sold over the years. If there are any variances in that pattern over time, it would be reflected by assuming that last year's sales are included as one of the

Row Col	Name of Chart	From	To	Descriptions
				comparatives. If last year's figures are not included, then the budget would show the expected pattern and changes from budget that would indicate if further analysis is required.
D3	Sales/Cost of Goods Sold by Territory—Item	C3	E3	Co-relationship showing the relative importance of the sales by territory within a division as compared to the other territories, and the related cost of goods sold by territory within a division as compared to the other territories. Any major change in the pattern of sales and cost of goods sold by division would indicate further analysis.
E3	Sales/Cost of Goods Sold Mix by Territory—Variance	D3	—	Twin variance showing the sales mix variance and the cost of goods sold mix variance by territory within a division. It also shows the relative size of the variances between sales and cost of goods sold for each territory. Any major shifts in the variances indicate that a further analysis should be undertaken to find the reasons for these variances. Further analysis for each element can be shown in sequences similar to those starting at C1, C2, and C3.
C4	Sales/Gross Margin Mix by Customer Type—Component	A1, A3, B5	D4	Relationship between sales and gross margin for this division's margin. The right side of the chart, gross margin, is the complement of the cost of goods chart shown in C1. As noted in C1, the pattern for both sides should be similar assuming the relationship between sales and gross margin is the same. Two important relationships are shown: the relative importance of sales by customer type for this division as compared to the total sales and the relative importance of gross margin by customer type as compared to gross margin, and also the relationship between sales and their respective gross margin.
D4	Sales/Gross Margin Mix by Customer Type—Item	C4	E4	Co-relationship showing the relative importance of sales by customer type within this division as compared to each other, the same as in Chart D1, and the complement of the cost of goods sold chart by showing the relative importance of gross margin contribution by customer type as compared to each other for this division. It also shows the relative amount of sales contributed by

252

Row Col	Name of Chart	From	To	Descriptions
				each customer type as compared to the relative size of the gross margin contributed by that same customer type for the division. The patterns of sales contributions by customer type should be similar over time. Any change in the pattern would indicate that further analysis is necessary. This sequence of charts could also be used as a preliminary indicator of whether a customer type is a candidate for being dropped as a market, or if a different pricing policy should be implemented for certain customer types. Further, analysis should be made prior to any policy changes, but this chart does provide a picture of imbalance.
E4	Sales/Gross Margin Mix by Customer Type—Variance	D4	—	Twin variance showing the mix variance of sales and gross margin from budget and/or prior year for this division, and the relative size of the sales variances as compared to the relative change in gross margin for the division. You would expect an increase in sales to reflect an increase in gross margin. Although the differences may not be significant, the patterns of variances should be similar. If further analysis is required, further disaggregation could occur for each element similar to Charts C4 through C6.
C5	Sales/Gross Margin Mix by Product Type—Component	A1, A3, B5	D5	Co-relationship showing the relative importance of sales by product type as compared to the total sales for the division, the same as shown in C2, and the relative importance for gross margin for each of the product types for the division as compared to the total gross margin, the complement of the cost of goods sold shown in C2. It also shows the relative importance of sales by product type as compared to the respective gross margins by product type. Such a view shows imbalances in either sales and/or gross margin contributions. Any change in the patterns of the gross margin contributions or sales would require further analysis.
D5	Sales/Gross Margin Mix by Product Type—Item	C5	E5	Co-relationship showing the relative importance of sales by product type for the division as compared to each other, the

Row Col	Name of Chart	From	To	Descriptions
				same as that shown in D1, but it also shows the relative importance of the gross margin contributions by product types as compared to each other, the complement of the cost of goods sold shown in D2. In addition, it shows the relationship between sales by product type and the gross margin contribution by product type to the division. The relationship between the two provides a critical pattern.
E5	Sales/Gross Margin Mix by Product Type—Variance	D5	—	Twin variance showing the mix variance from plan and/or prior year for sales and gross margin for the division by product type, and the relationship of those variances as compared to each other. The relative size of the variances should produce a consistent pattern. If further analysis is required, each of the product types can be further broken into charts similar to those shown in C4, C5, and C6.
C6	Sales/Gross Margin Mix by Territory—Component	A1, A3, B5	D6	Co-relationship showing the relative importance of the sales by territory within a division as compared to total sales for the division (identical to that shown in Chart C3), and the relative importance of the gross margin contribution by territory within a division as compared to total gross margin contribution, the complement of the cost of goods sold pattern shown in C3. It also shows the relative size of sales by territory within a division and the corresponding size of gross margin contribution for each territory. The patterns of the sales and gross margin contribution should be similar. A change in the pattern would indicate that additional analysis may be required.
D6	Sales/Gross Margin Mix by Territory—Item	C6	E6	Co-relationship showing the relative importance of the sales by territory within a division as compared to the other territories (identical to that shown in Chart D3) and the relative importance of the gross margin contribution by territory as compared to the other territories, the complement of the cost of goods sold pattern in Chart D3. It also shows the relative size of

Row Col	Name of Chart	From	To	Descriptions
				the sales as compared to the relative size of its related gross margin contribution for each territory. Such a picture provides an indication of performance and productivity by territory within a division.
E6	Sales/Gross Margin Mix by Territory— Variance	D6	—	Twin variance comparing two important mix variances and their relationships. It shows the relative size of the variance from plan and/or prior year by territory for both sales and gross margin, and the relative importance of the change in the actual size of variances between sales and gross margin for each territory. We assume that if the cost of goods sold is approximately the same for various sales volumes, then the gross margin would increase or decrease at approximately the same rate as sales. If further analysis is required, each of the territories can be broken into a sequence similar to that starting at C4, C5, and C6. It might also be time to go to the detailed records.

2. COST OF GOODS SOLD/SALES

Chart 10-041 shows the cost of goods sold percentage through October on a time series. In October the cost of goods sold percentage was higher than budgeted. Chart 10-042 shows a further breakdown of the cost of goods sold percentage for October. The right-hand chart shows by how much the cost of goods sold percentage was higher than budgeted. The left-hand chart shows:

1. The cost of goods sold percentage is calculated as cost of goods sold divided by sales.
2. The reason for the change was a mixture of cost of goods sold and sales being greater than budget.
3. The variances from budget were $212 thousand and $200 thousand for cost of goods sold and sales, respectively.

Charts 10-044 and 10-045 give more information about cost of goods sold as related to sales. Chart 10-044 shows a comparison of the significance of each division's cost of goods sold related to the other division's cost of goods sold, and to each division's sales. For example, Suggs' cost of goods sold was the largest of all divisions, but its sales was the second largest! Chart 10-045 shows the variances from budget for cost of goods sold (the variance chart on the left) and sales (the variance chart on the right) by division for October. Barnes has had the largest increase in cost of goods sold, and in sales. Suggs' increase in cost of goods sold was greater than its increase in sales.

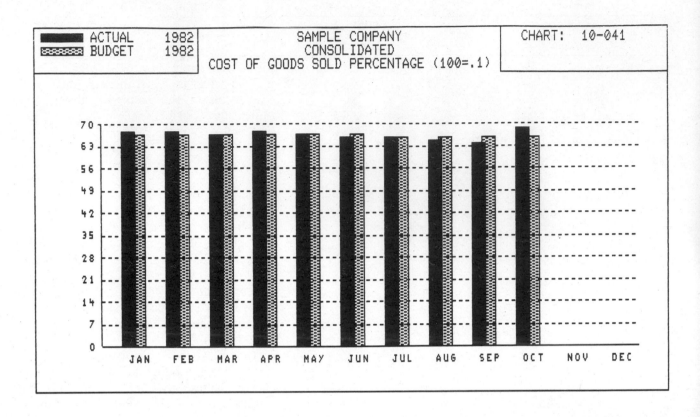

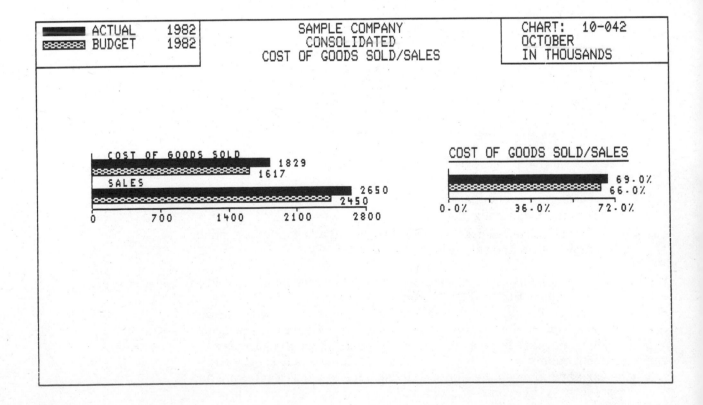

256

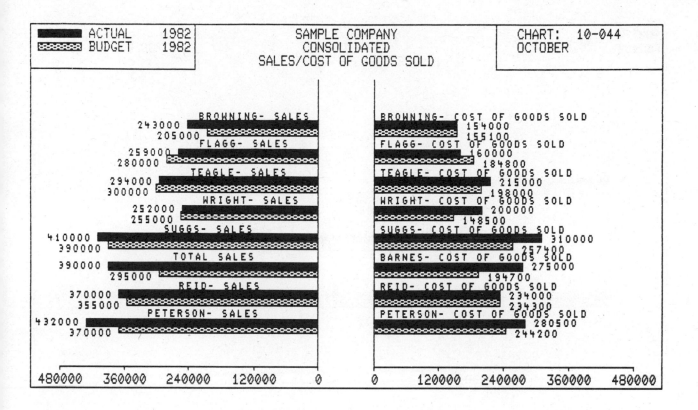

Chart 10-044: SAMPLE COMPANY CONSOLIDATED SALES/COST OF GOODS SOLD — OCTOBER

Legend: ACTUAL 1982, BUDGET 1982

BROWNING- SALES: 243000 / 205000
FLAGG- SALES: 259000 / 280000
TEAGLE- SALES: 294000 / 300000
WRIGHT- SALES: 252000 / 255000
SUGGS- SALES: 410000 / 390000
TOTAL SALES: 390000 / 295000
REID- SALES: 370000 / 355000
PETERSON- SALES: 432000 / 370000

BROWNING- COST OF GOODS SOLD: 154000 / 155100
FLAGG- COST OF GOODS SOLD: 160000 / 184800
TEAGLE- COST OF GOODS SOLD: 215000 / 198000
WRIGHT- COST OF GOODS SOLD: 200000 / 148500
SUGGS- COST OF GOODS SOLD: 310000 / 257400
BARNES- COST OF GOODS SOLD: 275000 / 194700
REID- COST OF GOODS SOLD: 234000 / 234300
PETERSON- COST OF GOODS SOLD: 280500 / 244200

Sales axis: 480000 360000 240000 120000 0
Cost of goods sold axis: 0 120000 240000 360000 480000

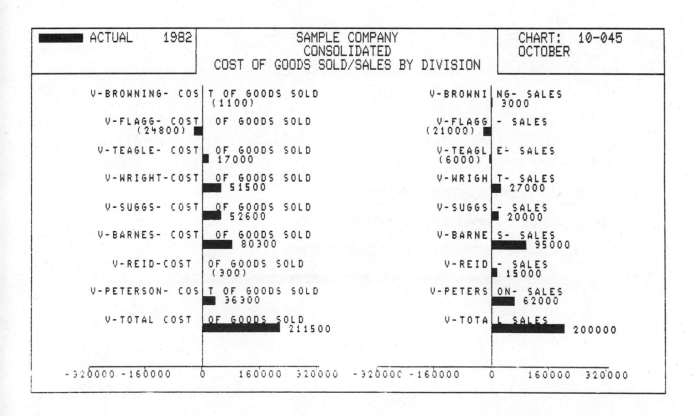

Chart 10-045: SAMPLE COMPANY CONSOLIDATED COST OF GOODS SOLD/SALES BY DIVISION — OCTOBER

Legend: ACTUAL 1982

V-BROWNING- COST OF GOODS SOLD: (1100)
V-FLAGG- COST OF GOODS SOLD: (24800)
V-TEAGLE- COST OF GOODS SOLD: 17000
V-WRIGHT-COST OF GOODS SOLD: 51500
V-SUGGS- COST OF GOODS SOLD: 52600
V-BARNES- COST OF GOODS SOLD: 80300
V-REID-COST OF GOODS SOLD: (300)
V-PETERSON- COST OF GOODS SOLD: 36300
V-TOTAL COST OF GOODS SOLD: 211500

V-BROWNING- SALES: 3000
V-FLAGG- SALES: (21000)
V-TEAGLE- SALES: (6000)
V-WRIGHT- SALES: 27000
V-SUGGS- SALES: 20000
V-BARNES- SALES: 95000
V-REID- SALES: 15000
V-PETERSON- SALES: 62000
V-TOTAL SALES: 200000

Axis: -320000 -160000 0 160000 320000   -320000 -160000 0 160000 320000

257

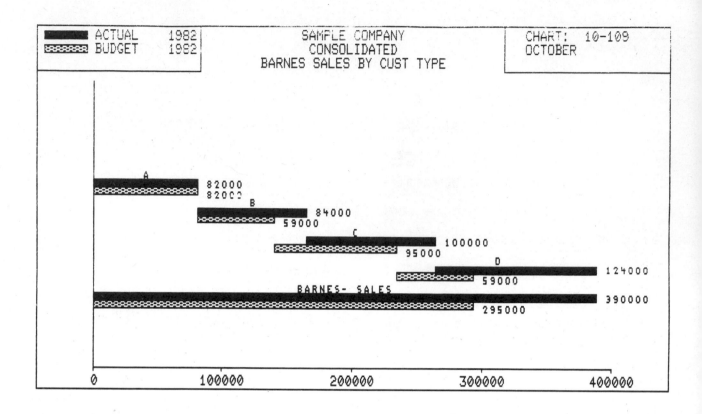

ACTUAL 1982
BUDGET 1982

SAMPLE COMPANY
CONSOLIDATED
BARNES SALES BY CUST TYPE

CHART: 10-109
OCTOBER

A
82000
82000
B
84000
59000
C
100000
95000
D
124000
59000
BARNES- SALES
390000
295000

0   100000   200000   300000   400000

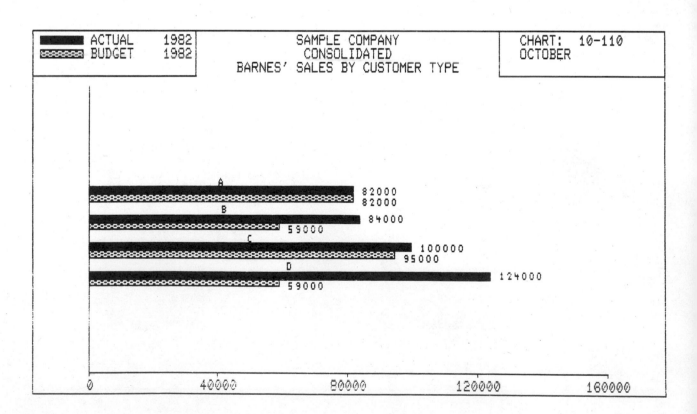

ACTUAL 1982
BUDGET 1982

SAMPLE COMPANY
CONSOLIDATED
BARNES' SALES BY CUSTOMER TYPE

CHART: 10-110
OCTOBER

A
82000
82000
B
84000
59000
C
100000
95000
D
124000
59000

0   40000   80000   120000   160000

258

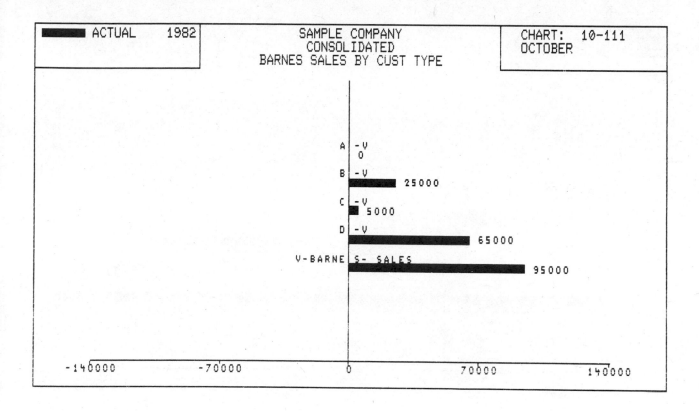

Charts 10-109, 10-110, and 10-111 show more information about sales for Barnes for October. Chart 10-109 shows that the components of sales for Barnes are the same as budgeted, although individual items have changed. Chart 10-110 shows that customer type D has bought the most product, even though it was not budgeted to have the highest sales. Chart 10-111 shows clearly that the major increases in sales were to customer types D and B.

Charts 10-106, 10-107, and 10-108 show more information about Suggs' cost of goods sold by customer type for October. Chart 10-106 shows that the components of cost of goods sold are the same as budgeted. Chart 10-107 shows which customer types have the largest cost of goods sold and Chart 10-108 shows that the costs of sales to customer types A and B have increased significantly.

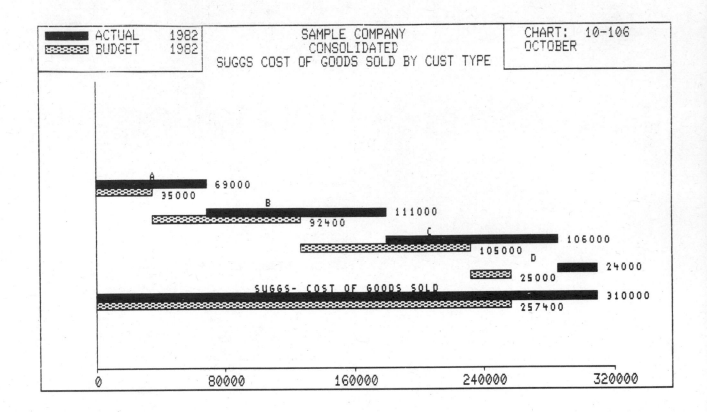

A 69000
35000
B 111000
92400
C 106000
105000
D 24000
25000

SUGGS- COST OF GOODS SOLD 310000
257400

0   80000   160000   240000   320000

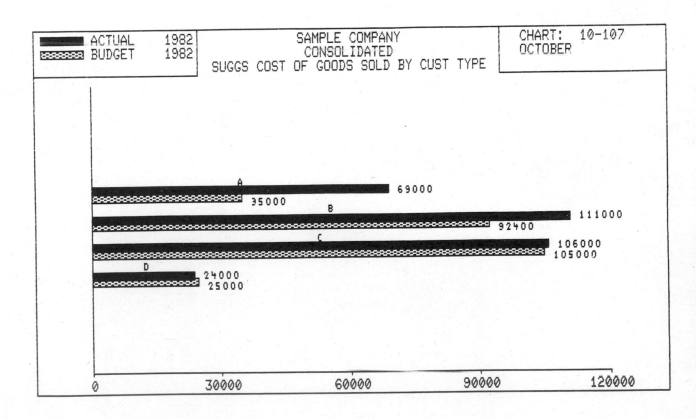

A 69000
35000
B 111000
92400
C 106000
105000
D 24000
25000

0   30000   60000   90000   120000

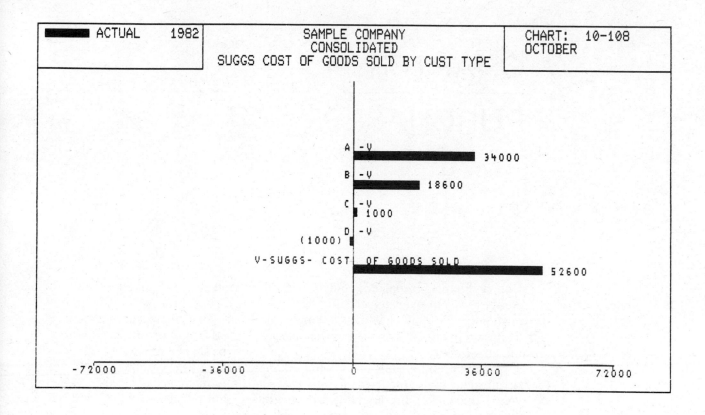

CHAPTER 14

PURCHASES

One of the most important control points in business is purchasing. In many companies, however, purchasing is considered an overhead with little, if any, authority. The purchasing system displayed in this sequence of charts is designed to give an overview of the profit potential from a properly controlled purchasing system. It will *not* show if the prices paid are correct, but will give a picture of timely performance. There are two basic comparisons made throughout the sequences: the purchases actually made are compared to last year's purchases and/or budgeted purchases, and purchase orders that are open at any given point in time are compared to last year's or budgeted open purchase orders. The pattern of disaggregation is shown in Exhibit 14.1

Open purchase orders are further analyzed showing those that are past due and those that are open for future delivery dates. The past due performance provides a picture of vendor performance, and the future dates give a picture of commitments by month, quarter, or company production period. Comparisons *can* be made between actual purchase orders committed and expected (budgeted) purchases for future dates to give an indication of open commitments yet to be made. In many instances, commitments not made are as important as commitments that are overmade—not having material can stop production lines. This particular system shows purchase information by product type, by division, and by vendor type. Most quality purchase order systems keep this kind of information and it is easily obtainable.

Finally, note that a special section has been added under vendor type to control vendor performance.

EXHIBIT 14.1

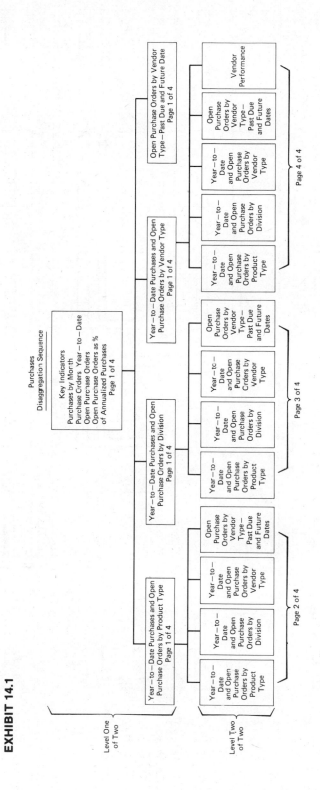

263

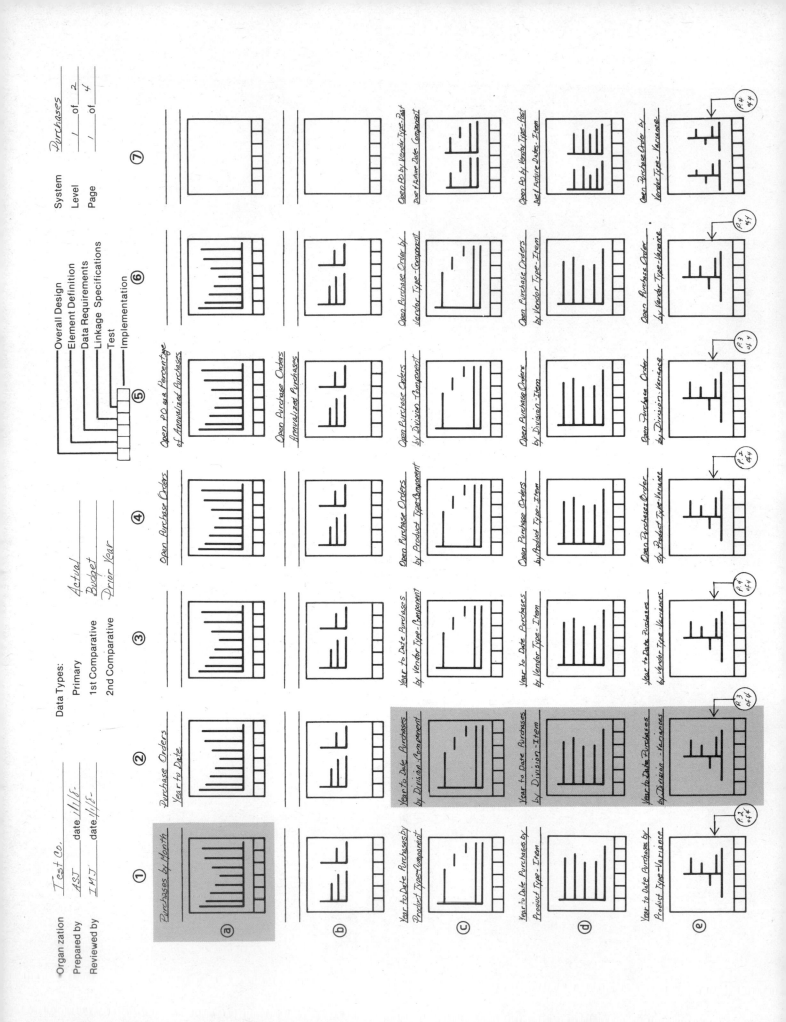

Row Col	Name of Chart	From	To	Descriptions
A1	Purchases by Month	Original	C1, C2, C3	Time series showing the actual purchases made for the past 12 months as compared to the prior year and to budget. Seasonal purchases would be reflected in the patterns and changes from those patterns shown.
A2	Purchase Orders Year to Date	Original	C1, C2, C3	Time series showing the purchase orders year-to-date for this month each year for the prior three to five years. The time line depends on what your firm feels is an important number of years of history for the firm. If major changes in year-to-date have occurred within the last three years due to defineable and permanent events, then only the pertinent years of information should be shown. However, if a similar purchasing strategy has been used for the past five years or more, the longer time frame should be shown. Your organization will have to decide the number of years to show. Word of warning—the fact that the last five years look the same may, in fact, be bad! Five consistent years of bad buying is not good.
A4	Open Purchase Orders	Original	C4–C7	Time series showing the open purchase orders at the end of the month for the past 12 months. It shows a pattern of open purchase orders over time as compared to budget and/or prior year. There should be a relationship between the amount of open purchase orders over time, the buying patterns, and the delivery patterns of the vendors. Once that pattern has been established, variances should be easily identified for further analysis.
A5	Open Purchase Orders as a Percentage of Annualized Purchases	Original	B5	Time series ratio showing the changing importance of open purchase orders as a relationship to annualized purchases. Seasonal variances should occur as well as a pattern of relationship between the open purchase orders and the annualized purchases. This pattern could be used as a leveling effect to predict the pattern that should be occurring. Any change in this pattern can be further analyzed by disaggregating through Chart B5.

265

Row Col	Name of Chart	From	To	Descriptions
B5	N: Open Purchase Orders D: Annualized Purchases	A5	C4–C7	Relative size of open purchase orders at any period to annualized purchases. Assuming there is a pattern to the business activity and the size of purchases, and an expected pattern of the relative growth of open purchase orders, this ratio normalizes the relationship and major changes from expected budget are readily apparent. If a change in the ratio is due to a change in the relative size of the open purchase orders, then further disaggregation and analysis would take place through Charts C4–C7. If the change in the ratio is due to a change in the relative size of the annual purchases, then the further disaggregation and analysis would occur starting at C1 through C3.
C1	Year-to-Date Purchases by Product Type—Component	A1–B5	D1	Relative importance of the purchases for each product type as compared to the total purchases for the year. Note that the information shown is for year-to-date only. By showing the year-to-date purchases, monthly variances because of a single large order can be somewhat leveled. Leveling of purchases on a year-to-date basis gives a more balanced expression of how purchases are going this year as compared to budget and the previous years.
D1	Year-to-Date Purchases by Product Type—Item	C1	E1	Relative size of the purchases to date by product type as compared to each product type. This chart shows where the largest purchases are being made and for what product type. Comparing this sequence of charts with the gross margin by product type in the sales/cost of goods sold system would provide an interesting picture and might help ask the question, "Are we paying too much—or charging too little?"
E1	Year-to-Date Purchases by Product Type—Variance	D1	System: Purchases, Level 2 of 2, Page 2 of 4, Charts A1–A5	Variance from plan and/or prior year for the year-to-date purchases for each product type. If further analysis is required, each product type can be further disaggregated into sequences similar to those shown starting at C1, C2, and C3. These sequences are further disaggregated as described in system purchases, level 2 of 2, page 2 of 4, Charts A1 through A5 and subsequent.

Row Col	Name of Chart	From	To	Descriptions
C2	Year-to-Date Purchases by Division —Component	B5	D2	Relative importance of the purchases by each division as compared to the total purchases to date.
D2	Year-to-Date Purchases by Division —Item	C2	E2	Relative size of the purchases for each division as compared to the other divisions. This chart also gives a clear indication of where the large division purchases are made. Comparing this sequence to the sales/cost of goods sold/gross margin sequence for the divisions would provide a useful picture.
E2	Year-to-Date Purchases by Division —Variance	D2	System: Purchases, Level 2 of 2, Page 3 of 4, Charts A1–A5	Variance from plan and/or prior year for purchases for each division. If further analysis is required, each division can be further disaggregated into sequences similar to C1 through C3. These sequences are further described in system purchases, level 2 of 2, page 3 of 4, Charts A1 through A5.
C3	Year-to-Date Purchases by Vendor Type—Component	B5	D3	Relative importance of the purchases by vendor type to the total purchases for the year to date. This is the first chart in a sequence that gives some indication of vendor performance. Further discussion of vendor performance would be found in the discussion of system purchases, level 2 of 2, page 2 of 4.
D3	Year-to-Date Purchases by Vendor Type—Item	C3	E3	Relative size of the purchases by vendor type compared to each other. The largest amount of purchases from a vendor type would be apparent. Assuming a relationship between vendor type and product type, this sequence would also be useful to the system sales/cost of goods sold to compare the gross margin contribution by product types to see how the product types are performing.
E3	Year-to-Date Purchases by Vendor Type—Variance	D3	System: Purchases, Level 2 of 2, Page 4 of 4, Charts C1, C2, C3	Variance from plan and/or prior years for the purchases by vendor type. If further analysis is required, each of the year-to-date purchases by vendor type can be further disaggregated into a sequence similar to that shown in C1, C2, and C3. These sequences are further described in system purchases, level 2 of 2, page 4 of 4. In addition, at that level, vendor performance is specifically described.

Row Col	Name of Chart	From	To	Descriptions
C4	Open Purchase Orders by Product Type—Component	B5	D4	Relative importance of the open purchase orders by product type at a given point in time as compared to the total amount of open purchase orders at that point. This chart is the first in a series to analyze the situation of commitments through picturing purchase orders.
D4	Open Purchase Orders by Product Type—Item	C4	E4	Relative size of the open purchase orders by product type compared to the other product types. This chart shows the largest amount of open purchase orders. This chart can be an indicator that action is required if products are needed now for production or resale or there is an excess of inventory on hand for a particular product.
E4	Open Purchase Orders by Product Type—Variance	D4	System: Purchases, Level 2 of 2, Page 2 of 4, Charts A4, A5	Variance from plan and/or prior year for the open purchase orders by product type. If further analysis is required, each of the open purchase orders by product type can be disaggregated in a sequence similar to that of C4 through C7. These sequences are further described in system purchases, Level 2 of 2, Page 2 of 4, Charts A4 and A5. This chart requires that a purchase budget be established showing open purchase orders. The budget system should consider the time cycles for vendor delivery, safety stock requirements, the cost of the money, and so on.
C5	Open Purchase Orders by Division —Component	B5	D5	Relative importance of the open purchase orders by division as compared to the total open purchase orders.
D5	Open Purchase Orders by Division —Item	C5	E5	Relative size of the open purchase orders by division as compared to the other divisions. Any unusual patterns would require further analysis.
E5	Open Purchase Orders by Division—Variance	D5	System: Purchases, Level 2 of 2, Page 3 of 4, Charts A4, A5	Variance from plan and/or prior year for the open purchase orders by division. If further analysis is required, each division can be further disaggregated into a sequence similar to that starting at A4 and A5. These sequences are described in system purchases, level 2 of 2, page 3 of 4, Charts A4 and A5.
C6	Open Purchase Orders by Vendor Type—Component	B5	D6	Relative importance of the open purchase orders by vendor type to the total open purchase orders at a given point in time. This is the first sequence that leads to

268

Row Col	Name of Chart	From	To	Descriptions
				actual vendor performance. The changing patterns might indicate further review.
D6	Open Purchase Orders by Vendor Type—Item	C6	E6	Relative size of the open purchase orders by vendor type as compared to the other vendor types.
E6	Open Purchase Orders by Vendor Type—Variance	D6	System: Purchases, Level 2 of 2, Page 4 of 4, Charts A4, A5	Variance from plan and/or prior years for the open purchase orders by vendor type. If further analysis is required, each of the variances by vendor type can be further disaggregated into sequences starting at A4 and A5. This sequence leads directly into vendor performance, page 4 of 4. These sequences are further described in the system purchases, level 2 of 2, page 4 of 4, Charts A4 and A5.
C7	Open Purchase Orders by Vendor Type, Past Due and Future Dates—Component	B5	D7	Sample sequence of potential presentations of the open purchase orders by product, by division, and by vendor type. This twin chart format shows total open purchase orders divided among those that are past due and those that are for future dates. This presentation may be more desirable for certain presentations and it could be a separate sequence shown with each of the other sequences shown at C4, C5, C6, and subsequent. Another formatting presentation could be to put all three views on one page, for example, showing the total open purchase orders by vendor type, past due, and those for the future. There are a number of ways to show this information, but for this sample the open purchase orders by vendor type are shown as an example. This first chart shows those items that are past due. It shows the relative importance of the open purchase orders past due by vendor type as compared to the total past due open purchase orders. The second chart shows the relative importance of the open purchase orders by vendor type due at future dates compared to the total open purchase orders due at a future date. Another way of showing this chart would be to show them by aging categories. Such a presentation would show those open that are past due 30, 60, and 90 days and the future purchase orders due in whatever timeframe is useful for planning purposes.

Row Col	Name of Chart	From	To	Descriptions
D7	Open Purchase Orders by Vendor Type, Past Due and Future Dates—Item	C7	C7	Relative size of the past due purchase orders by vendor type as compared to the other vendor types and the relative size of the future purchase orders outstanding by vendor type as compared to the vendor types.
E7	Open Purchase Orders by Vendor Type—Variance	D7	System: Purchases, Level $\underline{2}$ of $\underline{2}$, Page $\underline{4}$ of $\underline{4}$, Charts C7 and subsequent	Variance from prior year of the past due purchase orders by vendor type (this comparison will give an idea of the consistent performance of vendor types over time) and the variance from plan and/or prior year of the vendor type for future purchases. If further analysis is required, each of the vendor types can be further disaggregated into a sequence similar to that shown in C7 or one that might be designed by the individual corporation. Further discussion of such a sequence is shown in system purchases, level 2 of 2, page 4 of 4, Charts C7 and subsequent.

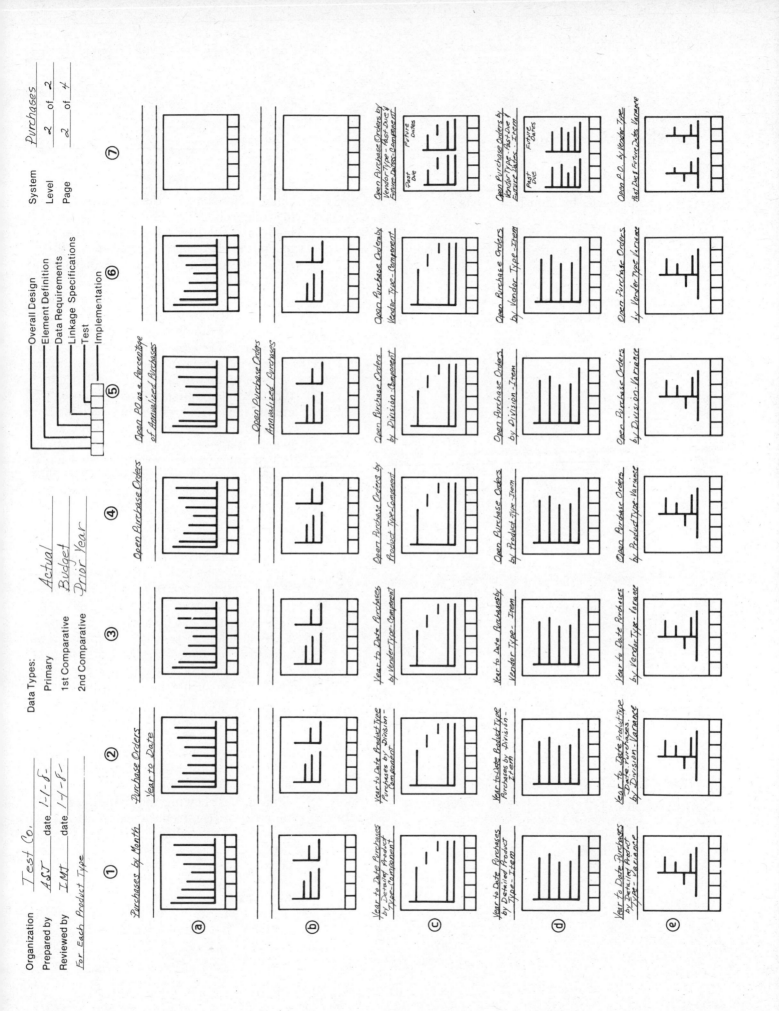

Organization *Test Co.*

Prepared by *ASJ* date *1-1-8-*

Reviewed by *IMJ* date *1-1-8-*

For Each Product Type

Data Types:

Primary *Actual*

1st Comparative *Budget*

2nd Comparative *Prior Year*

System *Purchases*

Level 2 of 2

Page 2 of 4

— Overall Design
— Element Definition
— Data Requirements
— Linkage Specifications
— Test
— Implementation

① ② ③ ④ ⑤ ⑥ ⑦

(a) *Purchases by Month* / *Purchase Orders Year to Date* / *Open Purchase Orders* / *Open PO as a Percentage of Annualized Purchases*

(b) *Year to Date Purchases by Detailed Product Type-Component* / *Year to Date Product Type Purchases by Division-Component* / *Year to Date Purchases by Vendor Type-Component* / *Open Purchase Orders by Product Type-Component* / *Open Purchase Orders by Division-Component* / *Open Purchase Orders by Vendor Type-Component* / *Open Purchase Orders by Vendor Type-Past-Due & Future Dates-Component*

(c) *Year to Date Purchases by Detailed Product Type-Item* / *Year to Date Product Type Purchases by Division-Item* / *Year to Date Purchases by Vendor Type-Item* / *Open Purchase Orders by Product Type-Item* / *Open Purchase Orders by Division-Item* / *Open Purchase Orders by Vendor Type-Item* / *Open Purchase Orders by Vendor Type-Past-Due & Future Dates-Item*

(d) *Year to Date Purchases by Detailed Product Type-Item* / *Year to Date Product Type Purchases by Division-Item* / *Year to Date Purchases by Vendor Type-Item* / *Open Purchase Orders by Product Type-Item* / *Open Purchase Orders by Division-Item* / *Open Purchase Orders by Vendor Type-Item* / *Open P.O. by Vendor Type-Past Due & Future Date Variance*

(e) *Year to Date Purchases by Detailed Product Type-Variance* / *Year to Date Product Type Purchases by Division-Variance* / *Year to Date Purchases by Vendor Type-Variance* / *Open Purchase Orders by Product Type-Variance* / *Open Purchase Orders by Division-Variance* / *Open Purchase Orders by Vendor Type Variance* / *Open P.O. by Vendor Type Past Due & Future Date Variance*

Past Due   Future Dates

For Each Product Type:

Row Col	Name of Chart	From	To	Descriptions
A1	Purchases by Month	Original	C1, C2, C3	Time series showing the actual purchases for this product type made for the past 12 months as compared to the prior year and to budget. Seasonal purchases would be reflected in the patterns and changes from those patterns shown.
A2	Purchase Orders Year-to-Date	Original	C1, C2, C3	Time series showing the purchase orders year-to-date for this product type compared to year-to-date for the prior three to five years. The time line depends on what your firm feels is an important number of years of history to present for this product type. If major changes in year-to-date purchases have occurred within the last few years due to defineable and permanent events, then only the pertinent years of information should be shown. However, if a similar purchasing strategy has been used for the past five years or more, the longer timeframe should be shown. Your organization will have to decide the number of years to show. Word of warning—the fact that the last five years look the same may, in fact, be bad! Five consistent years of bad buying is not good.
A4	Open Purchase Orders	Original	C4–C7	Time series showing the open purchase orders for this product type at the end of the month for the past 12 months. It shows a pattern of open purchase orders over time as compared to budget and/or prior year. There should be a relationship between the amount of open purchase orders over time, the buying patterns, and the delivery patterns of the vendors for this product type. Once that pattern has been established, variances should be easily identified for further analysis.
A5	Open Purchase Orders as a Percentage of Annualized Purchases	Original	B5	Time series showing the changing importance of open purchase orders as a relationship to annualized purchases for this product type. Seasonal variances should occur as well as a pattern of relationship between the open purchase orders and the annualized purchases. This pattern could be used as a leveling effect to predict the pattern that should be occurring. Any

272

Row Col	Name of Chart	From	To	Descriptions
				change in this pattern can be further analyzed by disaggregating through Chart B5.
B5	N: Open Purchase Orders D: Annualized Purchases	A5	C4-C7	Ratio chart showing the relative size of open purchase orders at any period for this product type as compared to annualized purchases. Assuming there is a pattern to the business and the size of purchases for this product type, and an expected pattern of the relative growth of open purchase orders, this ratio normalizes the relationship and major changes from expected budget are readily apparent. If a change in the ratio is due to a change in the relative size of the open purchase orders for this product type, then further disaggregation and analysis would take place through Charts C4 through C7. If the change in the ratio is due to a change in the relative size of the annual purchases, then the further disaggregation and analysis would occur starting at C1, C2, and C3.

This sequence, C1 through E1, assumes that the corporation has several levels of product categorization. Smaller companies might show this sequence for specific products.

Row Col	Name of Chart	From	To	Descriptions
C1	Year-to-Date Purchases by Detailed Product Type—Component	A1–B5	D1	Relative importance of the purchases for each detailed product type as compared to the total product type purchases for the year. Note that the information shown is for year-to-date only. By showing the year-to-date purchases, monthly variances because of a single large order can be somewhat leveled. Leveling of purchases on a year-to-date basis gives a more balanced expression of how purchases are going this year as compared to budget and the previous years.
D1	Year-to-Date Purchases by Detailed Product Type—Item	C1	E1	Relative size of the purchases to date by product type as compared to the other detailed product type. This chart shows where the largest detailed product type purchases are being made. Comparing this sequence of charts with the gross margin by detailed product type in the sales/cost of goods sold system would provide an interesting picture and might help ask the question, "Are we paying too much—or charging too little?"

Row Col	Name of Chart	From	To	Descriptions
E1	Year-to-Date Purchases by Detailed Product Type—Variance	D1	—	Variance from plan and/or prior year for the year-to-date purchases for each detailed product type. If further analysis is required, each detailed product type can be further disaggregated into sequences similar to those shown starting at C1, C2, and C3.
C2	Year-to-Date Product Type Purchases by Division—Component	B5	D2	Relative importance of the purchases of this product type by each division as compared to the total purchases to date.
D2	Year-to-Date Product Type Purchases by Division—Item	C2	E2	Relative size of the purchases by each division of this product type as compared to the other divisions. It also gives a clear indication of which division is buying the most of this product type. Comparing this sequence to the sales/cost of goods sold/gross margin sequence for the divisions and similar product type would provide a useful picture.
E2	Year-to-Date Product Type Purchases by Division—Variance	D2	System Purchases, Level 2 of 2, Page 3 of 4, Charts A1–A5, D3	Variance from plan and/or prior year for this product type purchases by each division. If further analysis is required, each division can be further disaggregated into sequences similar to C1, C2, and C3, or to purchases, level 2 of 2, page 3 of 4.
C3	Year-to-Date Purchases by Vendor Type—Component	A5	D3	Relative importance of the purchases from each vendor type for this product type compared to the total product type purchases for the year to date. This is the second sequence that gives some indication of vendor performance. Further discussion of vendor performance would be found in the discussion of system purchases, level 2 of 2, page 4 of 4, Charts C5, C6, and C7.
D3	Year-to-Date Purchases by Vendor Type—Item	C3	E3	Relative size of the purchases of this product type from each vendor type compared to each of the vendor types. The largest amount of product type purchases from a vendor type would be apparent. Assuming a relationship between vendor type and product type, this sequence would also be useful to compare to the system sales/cost of goods sold to compare the gross margin contribution by respective product types to see how the product types are performing.
E3	Year-to-Date Purchases by Vendor Type—Variances	D3	—	Variance from plan and/or prior years for purchases of this product type from each vendor type. If further analysis is required,

Row Col	Name of Chart	From	To	Descriptions
				each of the year-to-date purchases by vendor type can be further disaggregated into a sequence similar to that shown in C1, C2, and C3.
C4	Open Purchase Orders by Product Type—Component	B5	D4	Relative importance of the open purchase orders by detailed product type at a given point in time as compared to the total amount of purchase orders open at that point for the product type.
D4	Open Purchase Orders by Product Type—Item	C4	E4	Relative size of the open purchase orders by detailed product type compared to the other detailed product types. This chart shows the largest amount of open purchase orders for detailed product type, and can be an indicator that action is required if detailed products are needed now for production or resale or there is an excess of inventory on hand for a particular product.
E4	Open Purchase Orders by Product Type—Variance	D4	—	Variance from plan and/or prior year for the open purchase orders by detailed product type. If further analysis is required, each of the open purchase orders by detailed product type can be disaggregated in a sequence similar to that of C4 through C7.
C5	Open Purchase Orders by Division—Component	B5	D5	Relative importance of the open purchase orders for this product type by division as compared to the total open purchase orders for this product type.
D5	Open Purchase Orders by Division—Item	C5	E5	Relative size of the open purchase orders for this product type by division as compared to the other divisions. Any unusual patterns would require further analysis.
E5	Open Purchase Orders by Division—Variance	D5	—	Variance from plan and/or prior year for the open purchase orders for this product type by division. If further analysis is required, each division can be further disaggregated into a sequence similar to that starting at A4 and A5.
C6	Open Purchase Orders by Vendor Type—Component	B5	D6	Relative importance of the open purchase orders by vendor type as compared to the total open purchases for this product type. This is the second sequence that leads to actual vendor performance. The changing patterns might indicate further review.
D6	Open Purchase Orders by Vendor Type—Item	C6	E6	Relative size of the open purchase orders for this product type by vendor type as compared to the other vendor types.

Row Col	Name of Chart	From	To	Descriptions
E6	Open Purchase Orders by Vendor Type—Variance	D6	—	Variance from plan and/or prior years for the open purchase orders for this product type shown by vendor type. If further analysis is required, each of the product type variances by vendor type can be further disaggregated into sequences starting at A4 and A5. This sequence leads directly into vendor performance, page 4 of 4.
C7	Open Purchase Orders by Vendor Type, Past Due and Future Dates—Component	B5	D7	Sample sequence of potential presentations of the open purchase orders for this product type, by product, by division, and by vendor type. The twin chart format shows total open purchase orders for this product type divided among those that are past due and those that are for future dates by vendor type. This presentation may be more desirable for certain presentations and it could be a separate sequence shown with each of the other sequences shown at C4, C5, C6, and subsequent. Another format presentation could be to put all three views on one page, for example, showing the total open purchase orders for this product type by vendor type, those past due, and those for the future. There are a number of ways to show this information, but this sample uses the open purchase orders for this product type by vendor type. The first chart shows those items that are past due. It shows the relative importance of the open purchase orders past due by vendor type as compared to the total past due purchase orders for this product type. The second chart shows the relative importance of the open purchase orders by vendor type due at future dates compared to the total open purchase orders due at a future date for this product type. Another way of showing this chart would be to show them by aging categories. Such a presentation would show those open that are past due 30, 60, and 90 days and the future purchase orders due in whatever timeframe is useful for planning purposes.
D7	Open Purchase Orders by Vendor Type, Past Due and Future Dates—Item	C7	E7	Relative size of the past due purchase orders for this product type by vendor type as compared to the other vendor types and the relative size of the future purchase orders outstanding for this product type by

Row Col	Name of Chart	From	To	Descriptions
				vendor type as compared to the other vendor types.
E7	Open Purchase Orders by Vendor type, Past Due and Future Dates—Variance	D7	—	Variance from prior year of the past due purchase orders for this product type by vendor type. It is assumed there is no budget for past due purchase orders. This comparison will give an idea of the consistent performance of vendor types over time. The second variance chart shows the variance from plan and/or prior year of the vendor type for future purchases of this product type. If further analysis is required, each of the vendor types can be further disaggregated into a sequence similar to that shown in C7 or one that might be designed by the individual corporation.

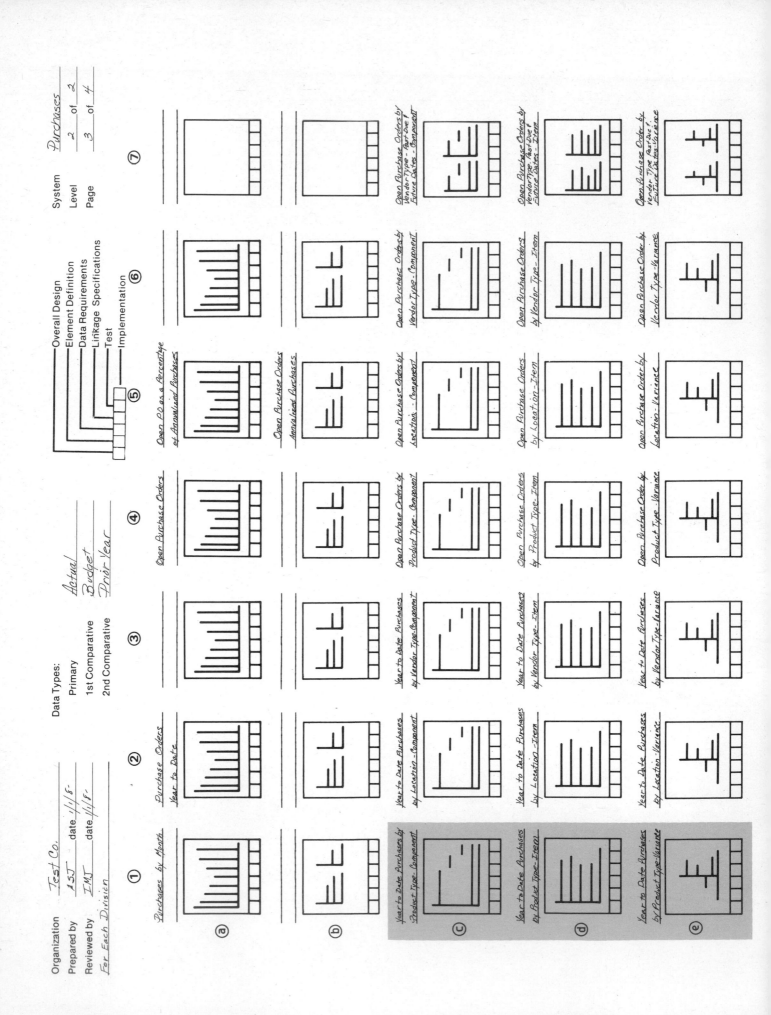

For Each Division:

Row Col	Name of Chart	From	To	Descriptions
A1	Purchases by Month	Original	C1, C2, C3	Time series showing the actual purchases made by this division for the past 12 months as compared to the prior year and to budget. Seasonal purchases would be reflected in the patterns and changes from those patterns shown.
A2	Purchase Orders Year-to-Date	Original	C1, C2, C3	Time series showing the purchase orders year-to-date for this division through the current month each year for the prior three to five years. The time line depends on what your firm feels is an important number of years of history for the firm. If major changes in year-to-date purchases have occurred within the last three years due to defineable and permanent events, then only the pertinent years of information should be shown. However, if a similar purchasing strategy has been used for the past five years or more, the longer time-frame should be shown. Your organization will have to decide the number of years to show. Word of warning—the fact that the last five years look the same may, in fact, be bad! Five consistent years of bad buying is not good.
A4	Open Purchase Orders	Original	C4–C7	Time series showing the open purchase orders for this division at the end of the month for the past 12 months. It shows a pattern of open purchase orders over time as compared to budget and/or prior year. There should be a relationship between the amount of purchase orders over time, the buying patterns, and the delivery patterns of the vendors. Once that pattern has been established, variances should be easily identified for further analysis.
A5	Open Purchase Orders as a Percentage of Annualized Purchases	Original	B5	Time series ratio showing the changing importance of open purchase orders as a relationship to annualized purchases for this division. Seasonal variances should occur as well as a pattern of relationships between the open purchase orders and the annualized purchases. This pattern could be used as a leveling effect to predict the pattern that should be occurring. Any change in this pattern can be further

Row Col	Name of Chart	From	To	Descriptions
				analyzed by disaggregating through Chart B5.
B5	N: Open Purchase Orders D: Annualized Purchases	A5	C4–C7	Ratio showing the relative size of open purchase orders at any period to annualized purchases for this division. Assuming there is a pattern to the division activity and the size of purchases, and an expected pattern of the relative growth of open purchase orders, this ratio normalizes the relationship and major changes from expected budget are readily apparent. If a change in the ratio is due to a change in the relative size of the open purchase orders, then further disaggregation and analysis would take place through Charts C4 through C7. If the change in the ratio is due to a change in the relative size of the annual divisional purchases, then the further disaggregation and analysis would occur starting at C1 through C3.
C1	Year-to-date Purchases by Product Type—Component	A1, A2	D1	Relative importance of the purchases for each product type purchases by the divisions as compared to the total divisional purchases for the year. Note that the information shown is for year-to-date only. By showing the year-to-date purchases, monthly variances because of a single large order can be somewhat leveled. Leveling of purchases on a year-to-date basis gives a more balanced expression of how purchases are going this year as compared to budget and the previous years.
D1	Year-to-Date Purchases by Product Type—Item	C1	E1	Relative size of the purchases to date by product type for this division as compared to the other product types. This chart shows which of the product types is being purchased most often by this division. Comparing this sequence of charts with the gross margin by product type for the respective division in the sales/cost of goods sold system would provide an interesting picture and might help ask the question, "Are we paying too much—or charging too little?"
E1	Year-to-Date Purchase by Product Type—Variance	D1	—	Variance from plan and/or prior year for the year-to-date purchases for each product type by this division. If further analysis is required, each product type can be further disaggregated into sequences sim-

Row Col	Name of Chart	From	To	Descriptions
				ilar to those shown starting at C1, C2, and C3.
C2	Year-to-Date Purchases by Location—Component	B5	D2	Relative importance of the purchases by location within this division as compared to the total divisional purchases to date.
D2	Year-to-Date Purchases by Location—Item	C2	E2	Relative size of the purchases for each location within the division as compared to the other locations giving a clear indication of where the large purchases are made within the division. Comparing this sequence to the sales/cost of goods sold/gross margin sequence for the respective locations would provide a useful picture.
E2	Year-to-Date Purchases by Location—Variance	D2	—	Variance from plan and/or prior year for purchases for each location within the division. If further analysis is required, each location could be further disaggregated into sequences similar to C1 through C3.
C3	Year-to-Date Purchases by Vendor Type—Component	B5	D3	Relative importance of the purchases by vendor type to the total purchases for the year-to-date for this division.
D3	Year-to-Date Purchases by Vendor Type—Item	C3	E3	Relative size of the purchases from each vendor type for the division as compared to the other vendor types. The largest amount of purchases from a vendor type would be apparent.
E3	Year-to-Date Purchases by Vendor Type—Variance	D3	—	Variance from plan and/or prior years for the purchases from each vendor type for this division. If further analysis is required, each of the year-to-date purchases by vendor type can be further disaggregated into a sequence similar to that shown in C1, C2, and C3.
C4	Open Purchase Orders by Product Type—Component	B5	D4	Relative importance of the open divisional purchase orders by product type at a given point in time as compared to the total amount of open purchase orders at that point. This chart is one in a series that analyzes the situation of commitments by picturing purchase orders.
D4	Open Purchase Orders by Product Type—Item	C4	E4	Relative size of the open purchase orders within this division by product type compared to the other product types showing the largest amount of open purchase orders. This chart can be an indicator that action is required if the division needs products now for production or resale, or

281

Row Col	Name of Chart	From	To	Descriptions
				there is an excess of inventory on hand for a particular product type.
E4	Open Purchase Orders by Product Type—Variance	D4	—	Variance from plan and/or prior year for the open purchase orders within this division by product type. If further analysis is required, each of the open purchase orders by product type can be disaggregated in a sequence similar to that of C4 through C7.
C5	Open Purchase Orders by Location —Component	B5	D5	Relative importance of the open purchase orders by location within the division as compared to the total open purchase orders.
D5	Open Purchase Orders by Location —Item	C5	E5	Relative size of the open purchase orders by location within the division as compared to other locations. Any unusual patterns would require further analysis.
E5	Open Purchase Orders by Location —Variance	D5	—	Variance from plan and/or prior year for the open purchase orders by location. If further analysis is required, each location can be further disaggregated into a sequence similar to that starting at A4 and A5.
C6	Open Purchase Orders by Vendor Type—Component	B5	D6	Relative importance of the open purchase orders within this division by vendor type to the total open purchase orders for this division.
D6	Open Purchase Orders by Vendor Type—Item	C6	E6	Relative size of the open purchase orders by vendor type for this division as compared to the other vendor types.
E6	Open Purchase Orders by Vendor Type—Variance	D6	—	Variance from plan and/or prior years for the open purchase orders within this division by vendor type. If further analysis is required, each of the variances by vendor type can be further disaggregated into sequences starting at A4 and A5.
C7	Open Purchase Orders by Vendor Type, Past Due and Future Dates—Component	B5	D7	Sample sequence of potential presentations of the open purchase orders by product, by division, and by vendor type. This twin chart format shows total open purchase orders divided among those that are past due and those that are for future dates for this division. This may be more desirable for certain presentations and it could be a separate sequence used with each of the other sequences shown at C4, C5, C6, and subsequent. Another formatting presentation could be to put all three views on one page, for example, showing the total open

Row Col	Name of Chart	From	To	Descriptions
				purchase orders for this division by vendor type, past due, and those for the future. There are a number of ways to show this information, but this example uses the open purchase orders within this division by vendor type. This first chart shows those items that are past due. It shows the relative importance of the open purchase orders for this division that are past due by vendor type as compared to the total divisional past due open purchase orders. The second chart shows the relative importance of the open purchase orders by vendor type due at future dates compared to the total open purchase orders due at a future date. Another way of showing this chart would be to show them by aging categories. Such a presentation would show those open that are past due 30, 60, and 90 days and the future purchase orders due in whatever timeframe is useful for planning purposes.
D7	Open Purchase Orders by Vendor Type, Past Due and Future Dates—Item	C7	E7	Relative size of the past due purchase orders for this division by vendor type as compared to the other vendor types and the relative size of the future purchase orders outstanding for this division by vendor type as compared to the vendor types.
E7	Open Purchase Orders by Vendor Type, Past Due and Future Dates—Variance	D7	—	Variance from prior year of the past due purchase orders by vendor type for this division. This comparison will give an idea of the consistent performance of vendor types over time. The second variance chart shows the variance from plan and/or prior year of the vendor type for future purchases. If further analysis is required, each of the vendor types can be further disaggregated into a sequence similar to that shown in C7 or one that might be designed by the individual corporation.

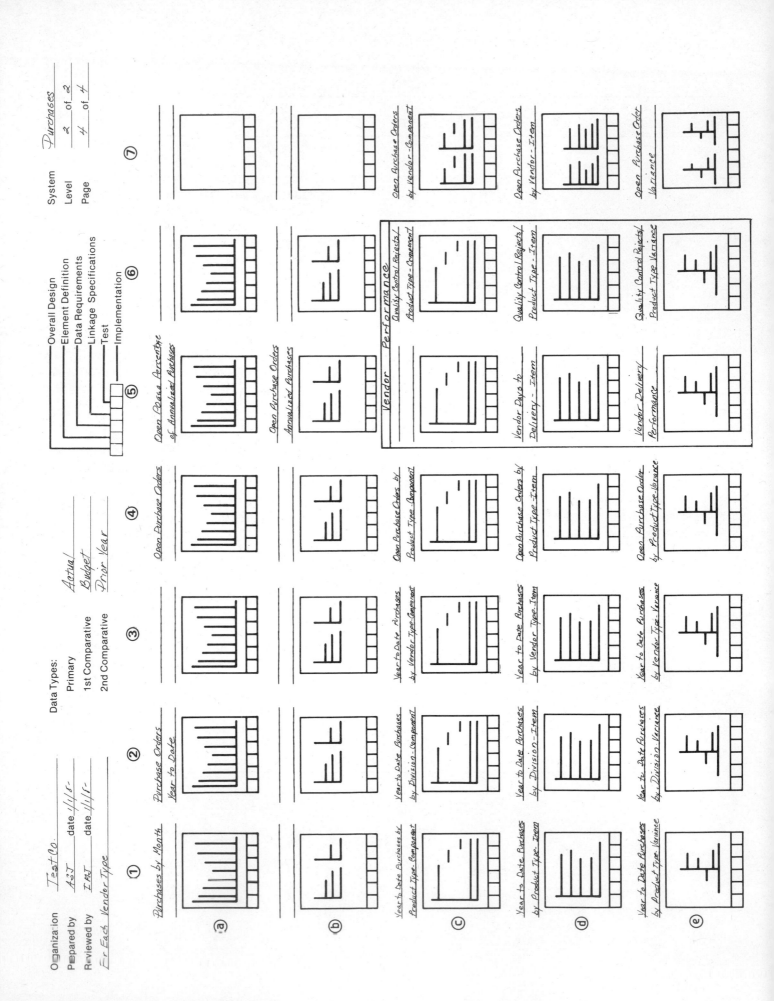

Organization _Test Co._
Prepared by _AJJ_ date _1/1/8-_
Reviewed by _IHJ_ date _1/1/8-_
For Each Vendor Type

Data Types:
Primary   _Actual_
1st Comparative _Budget_
2nd Comparative _Prior Year_

Overall Design
Element Definition
Data Requirements
Linkage Specifications
Test
Implementation

① ② ③ ④ ⑤ ⑥ ⑦

(a) _Purchases by Month_ | _Purchase Orders Year to Date_ | | _Open Purchase Orders_ | _Open Data Percentge of Annualized Purchases_ | |

(b) _Year to Date Purchases by Product Type-Component_ | _Year to Date Purchases by Division-Component_ | _Year to Date Purchases by Vendor Type-Component_ | _Open Purchase Orders by Product Type-Component_ | _Open Purchase Orders Annualized Purchases_ |

Vendor Performance

(c) _Year to Date Purchases by Product Type-Item_ | _Year to Date Purchases by Division-Item_ | _Year to Date Purchases by Vendor Type-Item_ | _Open Purchase Orders by Product Type-Item_ | _Vendor Days to Delivery-Item_ | _Quality Control Rejects/ Product Type-Component_ | _Open Purchase Orders by Vendor-Component_

(d) _Year to Date Purchases by Product Type-Item_ | _Year to Date Purchases by Division-Item_ | _Year to Date Purchases by Vendor Type-Item_ | _Open Purchase Orders by Product Type-Item_ | _Vendor Delivery Performance_ | _Quality Control Rejects/ Product Type-Item_ | _Open Purchase Orders by Vendor-Item_

(e) _Year to Date Purchases by Product Type Variance_ | _Year to Date Purchases by Division Variance_ | _Year to Date Purchases by Vendor Type-Variance_ | _Open Purchase Order by Product Type-Variance_ | | _Quality Control Rejects/ Product Type Variance_ | _Open Purchase Order Variance_

For Each Vendor:

Row Col	Name of Chart	From	To	Descriptions
A1	Purchases by Month	Original	C1, C2, C3	Time series showing the actual purchases made from this vendor type for the past 12 months as compared to the prior year and budget. Seasonal purchases would be reflected in the patterns and changes from those patterns shown.
A2	Purchase Orders Year-to-Date	Original	C1, C2, C3	Time series showing the purchase orders year-to-date for this vendor type for the prior three to five years. The time line depends on what your firm feels is an important number of years of history for the firm. If major changes in year-to-date purchases have occurred within the last three years due to defineable and permanent events, then only the pertinent years of information should be shown for this vendor type. However, if a similar purchasing strategy has been used for the past five years or more, the longer timeframe should be shown. Your organization will have to decide the number of years to show. Word of warning—the fact that the last five years looks the same may, in fact, be bad! Five consistent years of bad buying is not good.
A4	Open Purchase Orders	Original	C4–C7	Time series showing the past 12 months' open purchase orders at the end of the month for this vendor type. It shows a pattern of open purchase orders over time as compared to budget and/or prior year. There should be a relationship between the amount of open purchase orders over time, the buying patterns, and the delivery patterns of this vendor type. Once that pattern has been established, variance should be easily identified for further analysis.
A5	Open Purchase Orders as a Percentage of Annualized Purchases	Original	B5	Time series ratio showing the changing importance of open purchase orders as a relationship to annualized purchases for this vendor type. Seasonal variances should occur and a pattern of relationship between the open purchase orders and the annualized purchases for this vendor type will occur. This pattern could be used as a leveling effect to predict the pattern that should be occurring for this vendor type.

285

Row Col	Name of Chart	From	To	Descriptions
				Any change in this pattern can be further analyzed by disaggregating through Chart B5.
B5	N: Open Purchase Orders D: Annualized Purchases	A5	C1–C7	Ratio showing the relative size of open purchase orders at any period to annualized purchases for this vendor type. Assuming there is a pattern to the business activity and the size of purchases, and an expected pattern of the relative growth of open purchase orders, this ratio normalizes the relationship and major changes from expected budget are readily apparent. If a change in the ratio is due to a change in the relative size of the open purchase orders, then further disaggregation and analysis would take place through Charts C4 and subsequent. If the change in the ratio is due to a change in the relative size of the annual purchases, then the further disaggregation and analysis would occur starting at C1 through C3.
C1	Year-to-Date Purchases by Product Type—Component	A1, A2	D1	Relative importance of the purchases for each product type from this vendor type as compared to the total purchases for the year. Note that the information shown is for year-to-date only. By showing the year-to-date purchases, monthly variances because of a single large order can be somewhat leveled. Leveling of purchases on a year-to-date basis gives a more balanced expression of how purchases are going this year as compared to budget and previous years.
D1	Year-to-Date Purchases by Product Type—Item	C1	E1	Relative size of the purchases to date from this vendor type by product type as compared to each product type. This chart shows the largest volume of product type purchases from this vendor type. Comparing this sequence of charts with the gross margin by product type in the sales/cost of goods sold system for the respective product types would provide an interesting picture and might help ask the question, "Are we paying too much—or charging too little?"
E1	Year-to-Date Purchases by Product Type—Variance	D1	—	Variance from plan and/or prior year for the year-to-date purchases from this vendor type for each product type. If further analysis is required, each product type can

Row Col	Name of Chart	From	To	Descriptions
				be further disaggregated into sequences similar to those shown starting at C1, C2, and C3.
C2	Year-to-Date Purchases by Division—Component	B5	D2	Relative importance of the purchases of this product type for each division as compared to the total product type purchases to date.
D2	Year-to-Date Purchases by Division—Item	C2	E2	Relative size of the purchases for this product type by each division as compared to the other divisions, giving a clear indication of where the large product type purchases are made by division. Comparing this sequence to the sales/cost of goods sold/gross margin sequence for the divisions would provide a useful picture.
E2	Year-to-Date Purchases by Division—Variance	D2	—	Variance from plan and/or prior year of purchases for this product type for each division. If further analysis is required, each division can be further disaggregated into sequences similar to C1 through C3.
C3	Year-to-Date Purchases by Vendor Type—Component	B5	D3	Relative importance of the purchases by vendor to the total purchases for the year-to-date for this vendor type. This is the third sequence that gives some indication of vendor performance. Further discussion of vendor performance is shown starting at C5, C6, and C7.
D3	Year-to-Date Purchases by Vendor Type—Item	C3	E3	Relative size of the purchases by vendor within this vendor type compared to each other. The largest amount of purchases from a vendor would be apparent.
E3	Year-to-Date Purchases by Vendor Type—Variance	D3	—	Variance from plan and/or prior years for the purchases by vendor within this vendor type. If further analysis is required, it may be necessary to go to the books of record.
C4	Open Purchase Orders by Product Type—Component	B5	D4	Relative importance of the open purchase orders for this vendor type by product type at a given point in time as compared to the total amount of vendor type open purchase orders at that point.
D4	Open Purchase Orders by Product Type—Item	C4	E4	Relative size of the open purchase orders for this vendor type by product type compared to the other product types, showing the largest amount of open purchase orders. This chart can be an indicator that action is required if products are needed now for production or resale, or there is an excess of inventory on hand for a particular product.

Row Col	Name of Chart	From	To	Descriptions
E4	Open Purchase Orders by Product Type—Variance	D4	—	Variance from plan and/or prior year for the open purchase orders for this vendor type by product type. If further analysis is required, each of the open purchase orders by product type can be disaggregated in a sequence similar to that starting at C4.

NOTE: Special Insert—Vendor Performance. This special insert is designed to show how vendor performance might be evaluated. The proposed information is available in most good vendor/account payable/purchase order systems.

For Each Vendor Type:

Row Col	Name of Chart	From	To	Descriptions
D5	Vendor Days to Delivery	Original	E5	Number of days in aging categories from purchase order issue until merchandise receipt. The elements show the frequency distribution of vendor shipping performance. The actual performance could be matched to last year and to an acceptable performance template to assist evaluation.
E5	Vendor Delivery Performance	D5	—	Variance providing an invaluable vendor performance template to measure individual vendor performance and vendor type performance, and enhancing comparisons between vendors.
C6	Quality Control Rejects/Product Type—Component	Original	D6	Relative value of quality control rejects from a vendor by product type compared to total vendor rejects. The pattern can be compared to last year's performance and acceptable performance templates. Any change in patterns would be noticeable.
D6	Quality Control Rejects/Product Type—Item	C6	E6	Relative value of quality control rejects from a vendor by product type as compared to the various product types.
E6	Quality Control Rejects/Product Type—Variance	D6	—	Variance from acceptable and/or last year's quality performance for this vendor by product type.
C7	Open Purchase Orders by Vendor —Component	Original	D7	Twin component comparing the relative value of open purchase orders from this vendor for product types between open purchase orders that are late (on the left) to open purchase orders for the future (on the right). Both charts show the relative values by product compared to the total past due and total future due. If you see a lot of past due purchase orders and a lot of future

Row Col	Name of Chart	From	To	Descriptions
				purchase orders for a product type and you need the material, corrective action may be required. This sequence could have shown the open purchase orders by aging categories.
D7	Open Purchase Orders by Vendor —Item	C7	E7	Twin component comparing the relative value of open purchase orders from this vendor for product types between open purchase orders that are late (on the left) to open purchase orders for the future (on the right). Both charts show the relative values by product type compared to other product types.
E7	Open Purchase Orders by Vendor —Variance	D7	—	The first variance chart, on the left, shows the variance from prior year (perhaps an acceptable past due plan could be used) for past due purchase orders by product type. The second variance chart, on the right, shows the variance from plan and/or prior year for future purchase orders due from this vendor by product type. The variance shown in these two charts could be an indicator that new negotiations would be appropriate.

1. PURCHASES

Chart 10-089 shows a time series of the purchases month-to-date through September. August purchases seem to have been much higher than budgeted.

Chart 10-090 shows the component of August purchases by division to add up to total purchases for August. The components, or overall make-up, have remained the same compared to budget, although individual items have changed.

Chart 10-091 compares each division's purchases to the other divisions. Conrad certainly has made the most purchases in August.

A look at Chart 10-092 shows the variances from budget in August purchases by division. Conrad has had the biggest variance from budget. (Dickens' and Keats' divisions also purchases more than budgeted.)

The next set of charts gives further information about the Conrad division purchases for August. The purchases are categorized by product type.

Chart 10-093 shows the components of purchases in Conrad's division.

A look at Chart 10-094 and 10-095 shows us that the variance in purchases in product type E was responsible for the variance from budget for Conrad.

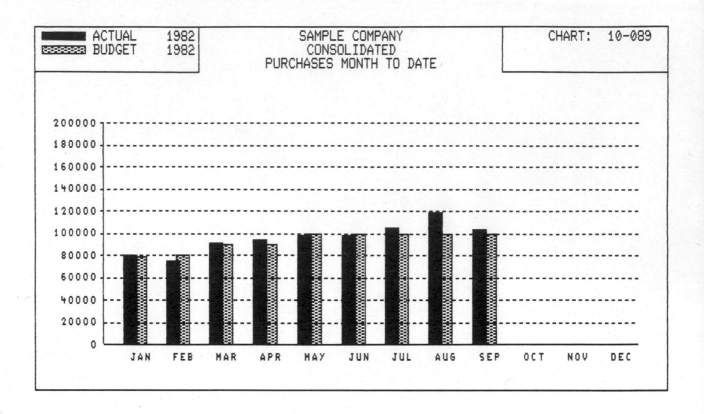

ACTUAL 1982
BUDGET 1982

SAMPLE COMPANY
CONSOLIDATED
PURCHASES MONTH TO DATE

CHART: 10-089

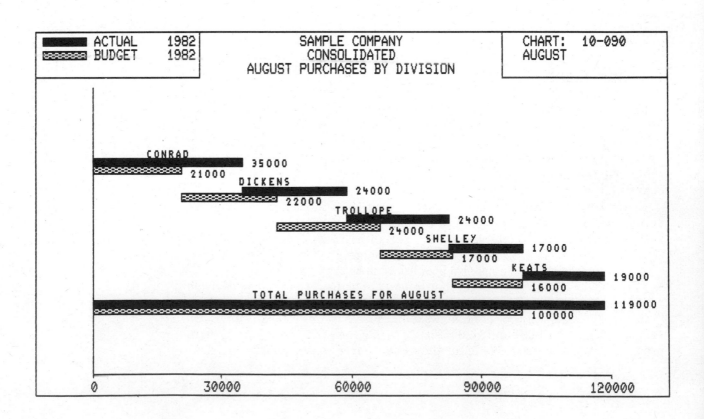

ACTUAL 1982
BUDGET 1982

SAMPLE COMPANY
CONSOLIDATED
AUGUST PURCHASES BY DIVISION

CHART: 10-090
AUGUST

CONRAD 35000
21000
DICKENS 24000
22000
TROLLOPE 24000
24000
SHELLEY 17000
17000
KEATS 19000
16000
TOTAL PURCHASES FOR AUGUST 119000
100000

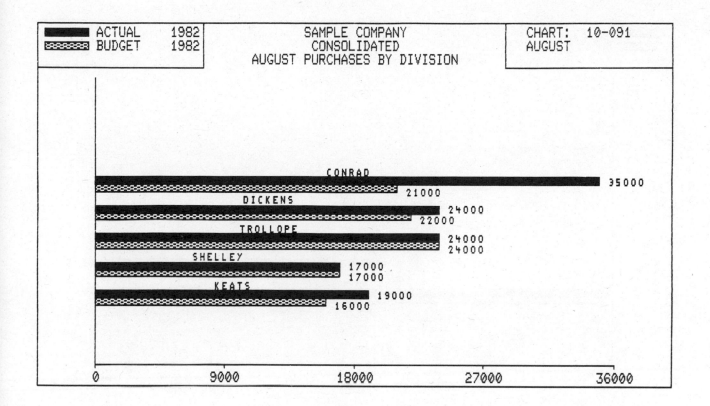

ACTUAL 1982
BUDGET 1982

SAMPLE COMPANY
CONSOLIDATED
AUGUST PURCHASES BY DIVISION

CHART: 10-091
AUGUST

CONRAD
35000
21000

DICKENS
24000
22000

TROLLOPE
24000
24000

SHELLEY
17000
17000

KEATS
19000
16000

0   9000   18000   27000   36000

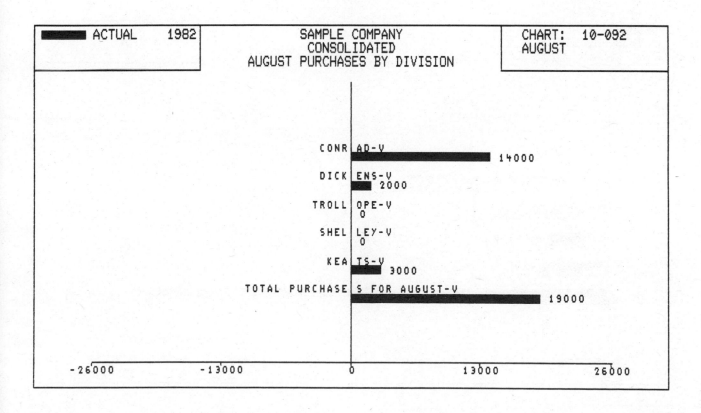

ACTUAL 1982

SAMPLE COMPANY
CONSOLIDATED
AUGUST PURCHASES BY DIVISION

CHART: 10-092
AUGUST

CONRAD-V
14000

DICKENS-V
2000

TROLLOPE-V
0

SHELLEY-V
0

KEATS-V
3000

TOTAL PURCHASES FOR AUGUST-V
19000

-26000   -13000   0   13000   26000

291

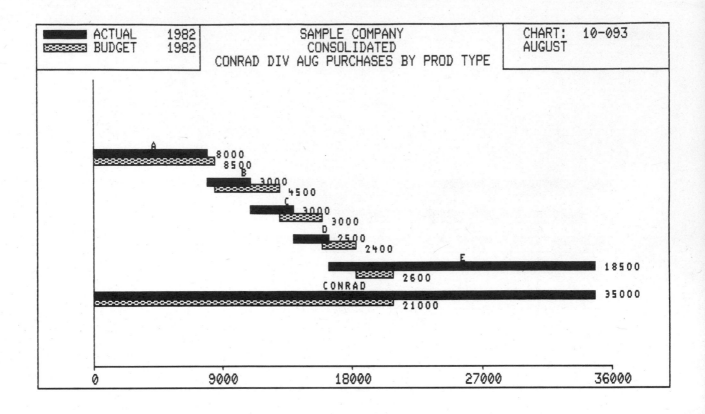

ACTUAL 1982
BUDGET 1982
SAMPLE COMPANY
CONSOLIDATED
CONRAD DIV AUG PURCHASES BY PROD TYPE
CHART: 10-093
AUGUST

A 8000
8500
B 3000
4500
C 3000
3000
D 2500
2400
E 18500
2600
CONRAD 35000
21000

0   9000   18000   27000   36000

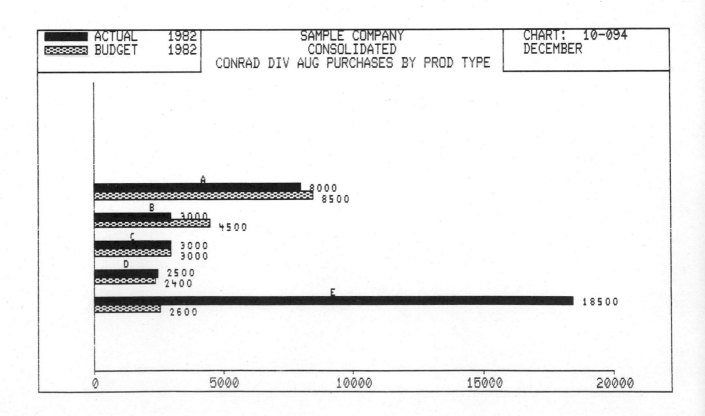

ACTUAL 1982
BUDGET 1982
SAMPLE COMPANY
CONSOLIDATED
CONRAD DIV AUG PURCHASES BY PROD TYPE
CHART: 10-094
DECEMBER

A 8000
8500
B 3000
4500
C 3000
3000
D 2500
2400
E 18500
2600

0   5000   10000   15000   20000

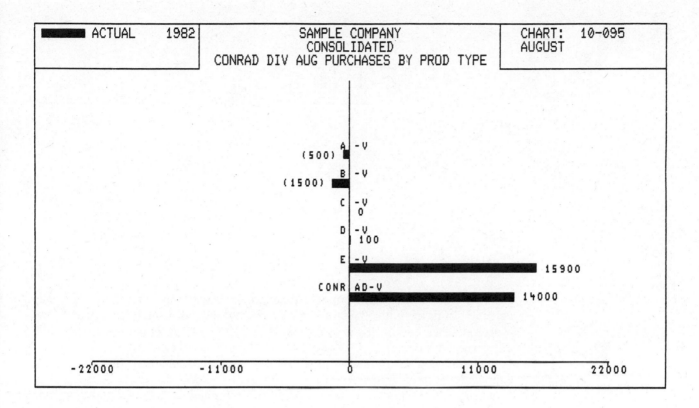

CHAPTER 15

PAYROLL

Payroll is one of the more important control points in any organization. Each company will have its own specific way to view payroll control. There are two systems described in this chapter. The first, Payroll System A, shows payroll activities by division, the type of job, and the type of employee. All of these views are tied to both responsibility control by responsibility area and corporate control by line item.

Exhibit 15.1 shows the disaggregation sequence for this system. Note that the key indicators relate the payroll expense to revenues and the average number of employees. The system carries this relation throughout the disaggregation sequence.

EXHIBIT 15.1

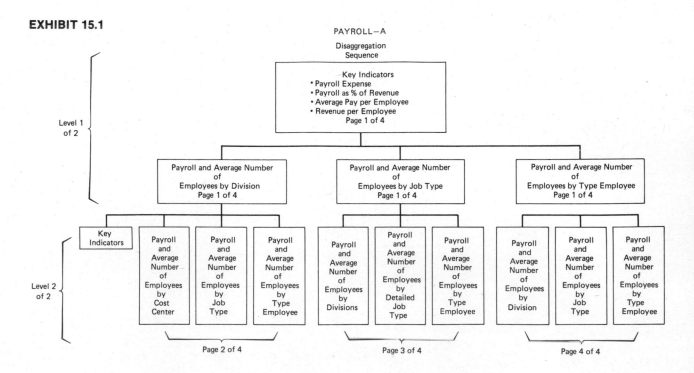

PAYROLL—A

Disaggregation Sequence

The second system, Payroll-B, shows the relationship between the various components of payroll such as straight time, overtime pay and the hours of pay by division, by type of job, and type of employee versus the total hours. In addition there is a break between billable and productive pay as a percentage of the total pay, a figure that is most useful in determining how many hours are nonbillable or nonproductive. Nonbillable hours are also shown as a percentage of total pay and disaggregated. The relationships between billable and productive hours, and nonbillable and nonproductive hours form a picture of business that could lead to considerable analysis.

Exhibit 15.2 lists the key indicators for this system. Note that in this chapter only one data level is shown and described for Payroll System B. When the information in Payroll System B is desired, the data described in this chapter will be shown for each data level used in Payroll System A. For example, Payroll System A is described in two levels and four pages. If required, Payroll System B would be shown for both data levels as described in all four pages.

Payroll—B

For Each Data Level—Each Key Indicator
Is Disaggregated

Key Indicators
• Overtime Pay as % of Total Pay
• Overtime Hours as % of Total Hours
• Billable/Productive Pay as % of Total Pay
• Nonbillable/Nonproductive Pay as % of Total Pay
• Billable/Productive Hours as % of Total Hours
• Nonbillable/Nonproductive Hours as % of Total Hours

EXHIBIT 15.2

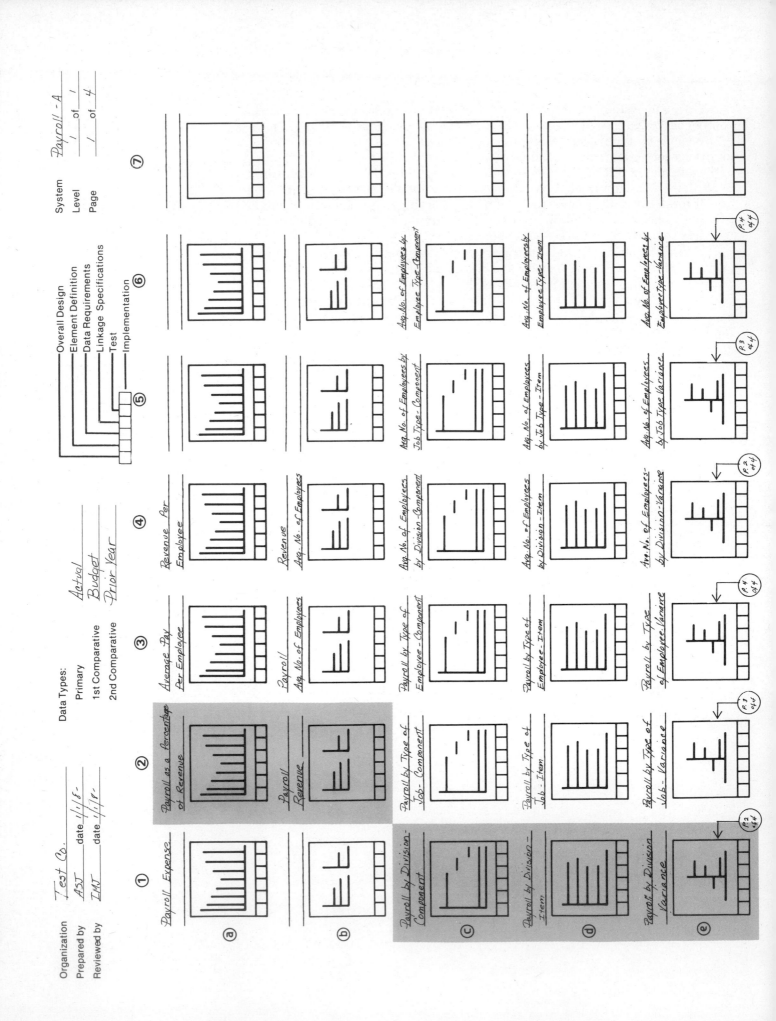

Row Col	Name of Chart	From	To	Descriptions
A1	Payroll Expense	Original	C1, C2, C3	Time series showing the total payroll for the past 12 months as compared to budget and prior year. Seasonal patterns and variations should be apparent.
A2	Payroll as a Percentage of Revenue	Original	B2	Twelve-month time series showing the payroll as a percentage of revenues. Any seasonal patterns will be reflected in this chart and major changes in the amount of payroll as a relationship to revenue will be apparent. Further disaggregation would show why the change occurred.
B2	N: Payroll D: Revenue	A2	C1, C2, C3	Ratio showing the relative size of payroll as compared to the total revenues of the firm. If the change in the ratio is due to a change in the payroll expenses, then a further disaggregation would occur by going to Charts C1 and C3. If the change in the ratio is due to a change in the size of the revenues, then further disaggregation would occur by going to the income system.
A3	Average Pay per Employee	Original	B3	Time series of the past 12 periods showing the changing rates of pay to the average employee. This chart most likely will show an increasing trend over time and would be indicative of the inflationary period we are experiencing. However, good investments in equipment could show the employee productivity increasing (see Chart A4). Another way to show this chart is with the figures normalized to a base year.
B3	N: Payroll D: Average Number of Employees	A3	C1–C6	Ratio showing the relative size of payroll as compared to the average number of employees in the firm. If the change in the ratio is due to a change in the relative size of the payroll, then further disaggregation and analysis would take place by following the sequences in this payroll system. If the change in ratio is due to a change in the relative size of the number of employees, the disaggregation starting at C4 through C6 would help explain the change.
C1	Payroll by Division—Component	A1, B2, B3	D1	Relative importance of the payroll for each division as compared to the total payroll of the firm.
D1	Payroll by Division—Item	C1	E1	Relative size of the payroll for each division as compared to the other divisions. It shows the location of the largest payroll.

Row Col	Name of Chart	From	To	Descriptions
E1	Payroll by Division—Variance	D1	System: Payroll-A, Level 2 of 2, Page 2 of 4	Variance from plan and/or prior year for the payroll by divisions. If further analysis is required, each divisional payroll can be further disaggregated into the sequences similar to that shown on this page. The additional sequences are described in system Payroll-A, level 2 of 2, page 2 of 4.
C2	Payroll by Type of Job—Component	A1, B2, B3, B4	D2	Relative importance of the payroll paid by type of job as compared to the total payroll.
D2	Payroll by Type of Job—Item	C2	E2	Relative importance of the payroll by type of job as compared to each of the types of jobs. This analysis shows which type of job receives the most payroll.
E2	Payroll by Type of Job—Variance	D2	System: Payroll-A, Level 2 of 2, Page 3 of 4	Variance from plan and/or prior year for the payroll by type of job. If further analysis is required, each type of job can be further disaggregated to a sequence similar to that shown on this page. The sequences are further described in the system Payroll-A, level 2 of 2, page 3 of 4.
C3	Payroll by Type of Employee—Component	B1, B2, B3	D3	Relative importance of the payroll by type of employee as compared to the total payroll.
D3	Payroll by Type of Employee—Item	C3	E3	Relative size of the payroll by type of employee as compared to the other types of employees. The largest payroll for a type of employee would be shown, as would a change in the mix of employees by type.
E3	Payroll by Type of Employee—Variance	D3	System: Payroll-A, Level 2 of 2, Page 4 of 4	Variance from plan and/or prior year for the payroll by type of employee. If further analysis is required, each payroll by type of employee can be further disaggregated into sequences similar to that shown on this page. These sequences are further described in system Payroll-A, level 2 of 2, page 4 of 4.
A4	Revenue per Employee	Original	B4	A leveling ratio when compared to A3. This chart shows the average contribution each employee is making to the overall revenue of the firm. This ratio will most likely remain fairly stable or increase if productivity is increasing. Even though the average pay per employee may be going up, the average revenue per employee could be going up even faster.
B4	N: Revenue D: Average Number of Employees	A4	C4, C5, C6	Ratio showing the relative size of the revenue divided by the average number of employees. If the change in the ratio is due

298

Row Col	Name of Chart	From	To	Descriptions
				to a change in the relative size of the revenue, then further disaggregation will take place by reviewing the revenue sequence in the income or sales system. If the change in the ratio is due to the change in the relative size of the average number of employees, then further disaggregation would take place as shown in Charts C4 through C6.
C4	Average Number of Employees by Division—Component	B3, B4	D4	Relative importance of the average number of employees by division as compared to the total number of employees in the firm.
D4	Average Number of Employees by Division—Item	C4	E4	Relative size of the average number of employees by division compared to the other divisions. The division with the largest number of employees would be shown as would any change in the mix of employees by division.
E4	Average Number of Employees by Division—Variance	D4	System: Payroll-A, Level 2 of 2, Page 2 of 4	Variance from plan and/or prior year for the average number of employees by division. If further analysis of the variance is required, each division can be fully disaggregated in the sequences similar to those shown in C4 through C6. These sequences are fully described in system Payroll-A, level 2 of 2, page 2 of 4.
C5	Average Number of Employees by Job Type—Component	B3, B4	D5	Relative importance of the average number of employees by job type as compared to the total number of employees.
D5	Average Number of Employees by Job Type—Item	C5	E5	Relative size of the average number of employees by job type as compared to all of the other job types. Any change in the mix of the job types would, over time, become apparent in this chart.
E5	Average Number of Employees by Job Type—Variance	D5	Payroll-A, Level 2 of 2, Page 3 of 4	Variance from plan and/or prior year for each of the job types. If further analysis is required, each of the average number of employees by job type can be further disaggregated into sequences similar to those shown in C4 through C6. These sequences are fully described in system Payroll-A, level 2 of 2, page 3 of 4.
C6	Average Number of Employees by Type of Employee—Component	B3, B4	D6	Relative importance of the average number of employees by type of employee as compared to the total number of employees.

Row Col	Name of Chart	From	To	Descriptions
D6	Average Number of Employees by Type of Employee—Item	C6	E6	Relative size of the average number of employees by type of employee as compared to all of the other types of employees. Any change in the mix of the employee types would, over time, become apparent in this chart.
E6	Average Number of Employees by Type of Employee—Variance	D6	System Payroll-A, Level 2 of 2, Page 4 of 4	Variance from plan and/or prior year. If further analysis is required, each of the types of employees can be fully disaggregated into sequences similar to those shown at C4 through C6. These sequences are fully described in system Payroll-A, level 2 of 2, page 4 of 4.

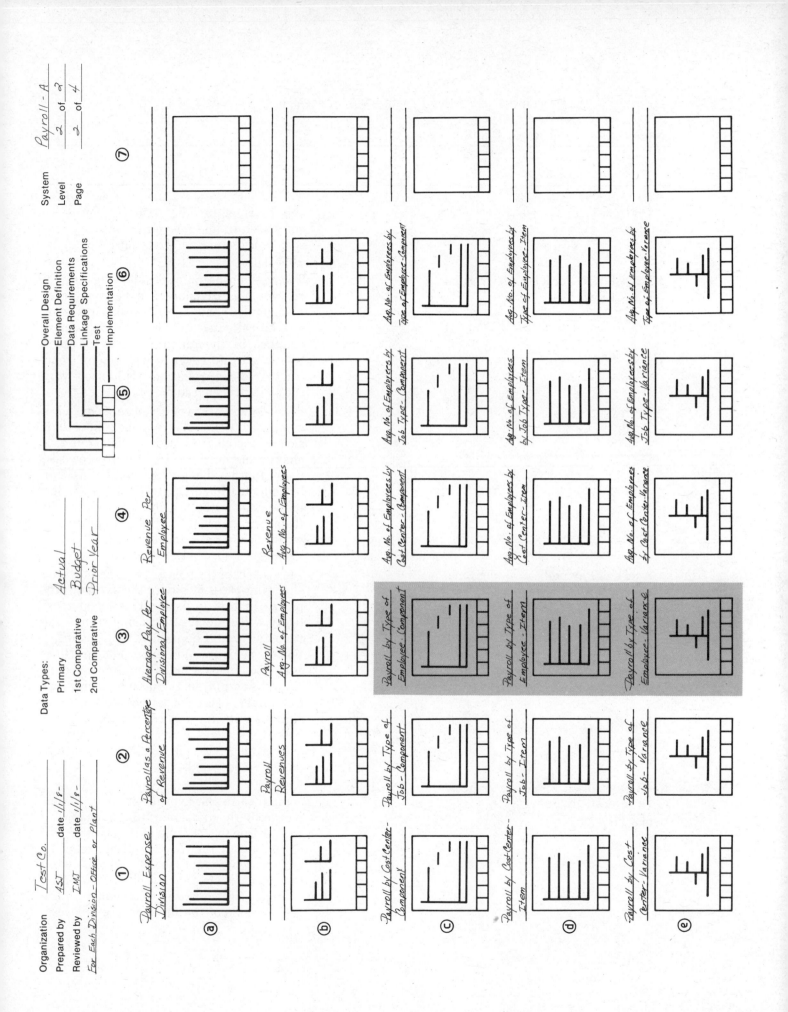

System   _Payroll - A_
Level   2 of 2
Page   2 of 4

Organization   _Test Co._

Prepared by   _ASJ_   date _1/1/8-_

Reviewed by   _JMJ_   date _1/1/8-_

For Each Division - Office or Plant

Data Types:

Primary   _Actual_

1st Comparative   _Budget_

2nd Comparative   _Prior Year_

Overall Design
Element Definition
Data Requirements
Linkage Specifications
Test
Implementation

① ② ③ ④ ⑤ ⑥ ⑦

(a) _Payroll Expense - Division_   _Payroll as a Percentage of Revenue_   _Average Pay per Divisional Employee_   _Revenue Per Employee_

(b) _Payroll by Cost Center - Component_   _Payroll Revenues_   _Payroll Avg. No. of Employees_   _Revenue Avg. No. of Employees_

(c) _Payroll by Cost Center - Component_   _Payroll by Type of Job - Component_   _Payroll by Type of Employee - Component_   _Avg. No. of Employees by Cost Center - Component_   _Avg. No. of Employees by Job Type - Component_   _Avg. No. of Employees by Type of Employee - Component_

(d) _Payroll by Cost Center - Item_   _Payroll by Type of Job - Item_   _Payroll by Type of Employee - Item_   _Avg. No. of Employees by Cost Center - Item_   _Avg. No. of Employees by Job Type - Item_   _Avg. No. of Employees by Type of Employee - Item_

(e) _Payroll by Cost Center - Variance_   _Payroll by Type of Job - Variance_   _Payroll by Type of Employee - Variance_   _Avg. No. of Employees by Cost Center - Variance_   _Avg. No. of Employees by Job Type - Variance_   _Avg. No. of Employees by Type of Employee - Variance_

For Each Division—Office Or Plant:

Row Col	Name of Chart	From	To	Descriptions
A1	Payroll Expense— Division	Original	C1, C2, C3	Time series showing the total payroll for this division for the past 12 months as compared to budget and prior year. Seasonal patterns and variations should be apparent.
A2	Payroll as a Percentage of Revenue	Original	B2	Twelve-month time series showing the payroll for this division as a percentage of divisional revenues. Any seasonal patterns will be reflected in this chart and major changes in the amount of payroll as a relationship to revenue will be apparent. Further disaggregation would show why the change occurred.
B2	N: Payroll D: Revenues	A2	C1, C2, C3	Ratio showing the relative size of payroll as compared to the total revenues of the division. If the change in the ratio is due to a change in the division payroll expenses, then a further disaggregation would occur by going to Charts C1 and C3. If the change in the ratio is due to a change in the size of the revenues, then further disaggregation would occur by going to the appropriate income system for this division.
A3	Average Pay per Divisional Employee	Original	B3	Time series of the past 12 periods shows the changing rates of pay to the average employee in this division. This chart most likely will show an increasing trend over time and would be indicative of the inflationary period we are experiencing. However, good investments in equipment could show the employee productivity increasing (see Chart A4). Another way to show this chart is with the figures normalized to a base year. This chart for all divisions should be reviewed together to see any unexplained trends.
B3	N: Payroll D: Average Number of Employees	A3	C1-C6	Ratio showing the relative size of payroll as compared to the average number of employees in the division. If the change in the ratio is due to a change in the relative size of the payroll, then further disaggregation and analysis would take place by following the sequences in the payroll system. If the change in ratio is due to a change in the relative size of the number of employees,

302

Row Col	Name of Chart	From	To	Descriptions
				the disaggregation starting at C4 through C6 would help explain the change. This chart is useful when compared to other divisions and the overall firm.
C1	Payroll by Cost Center—Component	A1, B2 to B3	D1	Relative importance of the payroll for each cost center within this division as compared to the total payroll of the division.
D1	Payroll by Cost Center—Item	C1	E1	Relative size of the payroll for each cost center within this division as compared to the other cost centers. It shows the location of the largest payroll in this division.
E1	Payroll by Cost Center—Variance	D1	—	Variance from plan and/or prior year for the payroll by cost center within this division. If further analysis is required, each cost center payroll can be further disaggregated into the sequence similar to that shown on this page.
C2	Payroll by Type of Job—Component	A1, B2, B3, B4	D2	Relative importance of the payroll paid by type of job in this division as compared to the total divisional payroll.
D2	Payroll by Type of Job—Item	C2	E2	Relative importance of the payroll by type of job in this division as compared to each of the other types of jobs. This analysis shows which type of job receives the most payroll in their division and is a good chart to compare to other divisions.
E2	Payroll by Type of Job—Variance	D2	—	Variance from plan and/or prior year for the divisional payroll by type of job. If further analysis is required, each type of job can be further disaggregated to a sequence similar to that shown on this page.
C3	Payroll by Type of Employee—Component	B1, B2, B3	D3	Relative importance of the payroll by type of employee for this division as compared to the total divisional payroll.
D3	Payroll by Type of Employee—Item	C3	E3	Relative size of the payroll by type of employee for this division as compared to the other types of employees. The largest payroll for a type of employee would be shown as would a change in the mix of employees by type in this division.
E3	Payroll by Type of Employee—Variance	D3	—	Variance from plan and/or prior year for the payroll by type of employee in this division. If further analysis is required, each payroll by type of employee can be further disaggregated into sequences similar to that shown on this page.

Row Col	Name of Chart	From	To	Descriptions
A4	Revenue per Employee	Original	B4	Leveling ratio when compared to A3. This sequence assumes that this division is a profit center. If it is a cost center, this ratio is not used. This chart shows the average contribution each employee is making to the overall revenue of the division. This ratio will most likely remain fairly stable or increase if productivity is increasing. Even though the average pay per employee may be going up, the average revenue per employee could be going up even faster.
B4	N: Revenue D: Average Number of Employees	A4	C4, C5, C6	Ratio showing the relative size of the divisional revenue divided by the average number of employees. (As noted in A4, if this division is a cost center, this chart is not used.) If the change in the ratio is due to a change in the relative size of the revenue, then further disaggregation will take place by reviewing the revenue sequence in the income or sales system for this division. If the change in the ratio is due to the change in the relative size of the average number of employees, then further disaggregation would take place as shown in Charts C4 through C6.
C4	Average Number of Employees by Cost Center—Component	B3, B4	D4	Relative importance of the average number of employees by cost center within this division as compared to the total number of employees in the division.
D4	Average Number of Employees by Cost Center—Item	C4	E4	Relative size of the average number of employees by cost center within this division compared to the other cost centers. The cost center with the largest number of employees would be shown as would any change in the mix of employees by cost center.
E4	Average Number of Employees by Cost Center—Variance	D4	—	Variance from plan and/or prior year for the average number of employees by cost center within this division. If further analysis of the variance is required, each division can be fully disaggregated in the sequences similar to those shown in C4 through C6.
C5	Average Number of Employees by Job Type—Component	B3, B4	D5	Relative importance of the average number of employees by job type as compared to the total number of employees for this division.

Row Col	Name of Chart	From	To	Descriptions
D5	Average Number of Employees by Job Type—Item	C5	E5	Relative size of the average number of employees by job type as compared to all of the other job types for this division. Any change in the mix of the job types, would, over time, become apparent in this chart.
E5	Average Number of Employees by Job Type—Variance	D5	—	Variance from plan and/or prior year for each of the job types in this division. If further analysis is required, each of the job types can be further disaggregated into sequences similar to those shown in C4 through C6.
C6	Average Number of Employees by Type of Employee—Component	B3, B4	D6	Relative importance of the average number of employees by type of employee as compared to the total number of employees.
D6	Average Number of Employees by Type of Employee—Item	C6	E6	Relative size of the average number of employees by type of employee as compared to all of the other types of employees. Any change in the mix of the employee types would, over time, become apparent in this chart.
E6	Average Number of Employees by Type of Employee—Variance	D6	—	Variance from plan and/or prior year for the average number of employees by type of employee within this division. If further analysis is required, each of the types of employees can be fully disaggregated into sequences similar to those shown at C4 through C6.

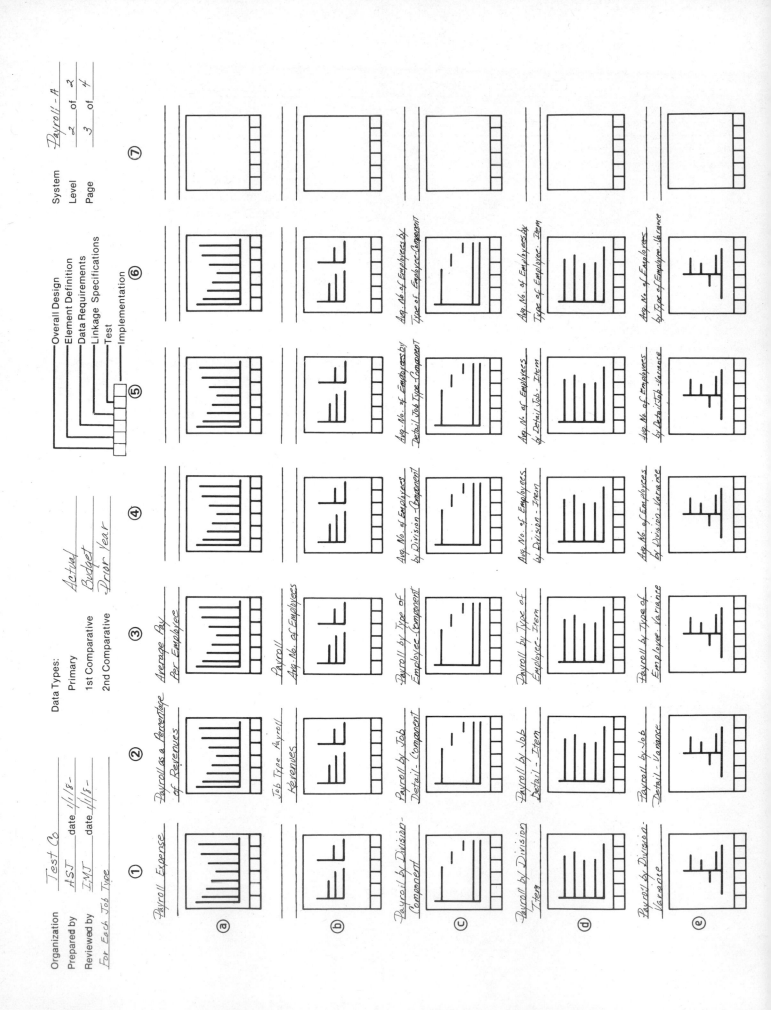

Organization Test Co
Prepared by HSJ date 1/18-
Reviewed by IMJ date 1/18-
For Each Job Type

Data Types:
Primary Actual
1st Comparative Budget
2nd Comparative Prior Year

Legend (⑤):
Overall Design
Element Definition
Data Requirements
Linkage Specifications
Test
Implementation

Column headings: ① ② ③ ④ ⑤ ⑥ ⑦

Row ⓐ:
① Payroll Expense
② Payroll as a Percentage of Revenues
③ Average Pay Per Employee

Row ⓑ:
② Job Type Payroll Revenues
③ Payroll Avg. No. of Employees

Row ⓒ:
① Payroll by Division - Component
② Payroll by Job Detail - Component
③ Payroll by Type of Employee - Component
④ Avg. No. of Employees by Division - Component
⑤ Avg. No. of Employees by Detail Job Type - Component
⑥ Avg. No. of Employees by Type of Employee - Component

Row ⓓ:
① Payroll by Division - Item
② Payroll by Job Detail - Item
③ Payroll by Type of Employee - Item
④ Avg. No. of Employees by Division - Item
⑤ Avg. No. of Employees by Detail Job - Item
⑥ Avg. No. of Employees by Type of Employee - Item

Row ⓔ:
① Payroll by Division - Variance
② Payroll by Job Detail - Variance
③ Payroll by Type of Employee Variance
④ Avg. No. of Employees by Division - Variance
⑤ Avg. No. of Employees by Detail Job Variance
⑥ Avg. No. of Employees by Type of Employee Variance

For Each Job Type:

Row Col	Name of Chart	From	To	Descriptions
A1	Payroll Expense	Original	C1, C2, C3	Time series showing the total payroll for the past 12 months as compared to budget and prior year for this job type. Seasonal patterns and variations should be apparent.
A2	Payroll as a Percentage of Revenue	Original	B2	12-month time series showing the payroll for this job type as a percentage of corporate revenues (or revenues for this job type, if available). Any seasonal patterns will be reflected in this chart and major changes in the amount of payroll for this job type in relationship to revenue will be apparent. Further disaggregation would show why the change occurred.
B2	N: Job Type Payroll D: Revenues	A2	C1, C2, C3	Ratio showing the relative size of payroll for this job type as compared to the total revenues of the firm (or for this job type, if available). If the change in the ratio is due to a change in the payroll expenses, then a further disaggregation would occur by going to Charts C1 and C3. If the change in the ratio is due to a change in the size of the revenues, then further disaggregation would occur by going to the income system.
A3	Average Pay per Employee	Original	B3	Time series of the past 12 periods showing the changing rates of pay paid to the average employee in this job type. This chart most likely will show an increasing trend over time and would be indicative of the inflationary period we are experiencing. However, good investments in equipment could show the employee productivity increasing (see Chart A4). Another way to show this chart is with the figures normalized to a base year.
B3	N: Payroll D: Average Number of Employees	A3	C1-C6	Ratio showing the relative size of payroll for this job type as compared to the average number of employees in the job type. If the change in the ratio is due to a change in the relative size of the payroll, then further disaggregation and analysis would take place by following the sequences in this payroll system. If the change in ratio is due to a change in the relative size of the number of employees, the disaggregation

307

Row Col	Name of Chart	From	To	Descriptions
				starting at C4 through C6 would help explain the change.
C1	Payroll by Division —Component	A1, B2, B3	D1	Relative importance of the payroll for this job type within each division as compared to the total payroll of this job type.
D1	Payroll by Division —Item	C1	E1	Relative size of the payroll for this job type in each of the divisions as compared to the other divisions. It shows the location of the largest payroll for this job type.
E1	Payroll by Division —Variance	D1	—	Variance from plan and/or prior year for the payroll of this job type by divisions. If further analysis is required, each divisional payroll can be further disaggregated into the sequence similar to that shown on this page.
C2	Payroll by Job Detail—Component	A1, B2, B3, B4	D2	Relative importance of the payroll paid by detail job as compared to the total payroll for this job type.
D2	Payroll by Job Detail—Item	C2	E2	Relative importance of the payroll by detail job as compared to the other detail jobs. This analysis shows which detail job receives the most payroll for this job type.
E2	Payroll by Job Detail—Variance	D2	—	Variance from plan and/or prior year for the payroll for this job type by detail job. At this point, it may be necessary to directly go to the books of record for further analysis.
C3	Payroll by Type of Employee— Component	B1, B2, B3	D3	Historically, a number of employee types will be used to perform various job types. This sequence is designed to show the mix of employee types performing this job. This chart shows the relative importance of payroll by type of employee as compared to the total payroll for this job type.
D3	Payroll by Type of Employee—Item	C3	E3	Relative size of the payroll by type of employee working in this job type as compared to the other types of employees. The changing mix of employees assigned to this job type will be shown.
E3	Type of Employee —Variance	D3	—	Variance from plan and/or prior year for this type of job by type of employee. If further analysis is required it may be necessary to go to the books of record.
C4	Average Number of Employees by Division—Component	B3, B4	D4	Relative importance of the average number of employees in this job type who work in each division as compared to the total number of employees in this job type.

308

Row Col	Name of Chart	From	To	Descriptions
D4	Average Number of Employees by Division—Item	C4	E4	Relative size of the average number of employees in this job type who work in each division compared to the other divisions. The division with the largest number of employees in this job type would be shown as would any change in the mix by division.
E4	Average Number of Employees by Division—Variance	D4	—	Variance from plan and/or prior year for the average number of employees in this job type who work in each division. If further analysis of the variance is required, it might be necessary to go to the original books of record.
C5	Average Number of Employees by Detail Job Type—Component	B3, B4	D5	Relative importance of the average number of employees by detail job as compared to the total number of employees in this job type.
D5	Average Number of Employees by Detail Job Type—Item	C5	E5	Relative size of the average number of employees by detail job as compared to all of the other jobs. Any change in the mix of the detail jobs will be shown over time.
E5	Average Number of Employees by Detail Job Type—Variance	D5	—	Variance from plan and/or prior year for each of the detail job types. If further analysis is required, it might be necessary to go directly to the original books of record.
C6	Average Number of Employees by Type of Employee—Component	B4	D6	Relative importance of the average number of employees by type of employee as compared to the total number of employees.
D6	Average Number of Employees by Type of Employee—Item	C6	E6	Relative size of the average number of employees by type of employee as compared to all of the other types of employees. Any change in the mix of the employee types would, over time, become apparent in this chart.
E6	Average Number of Employee by Type of Employee—Variance	D6	—	Variance from plan and/or prior year for the average number of employees in this job type by type of employee. If further analysis is required, it might be necessary to go directly to the original books of record.

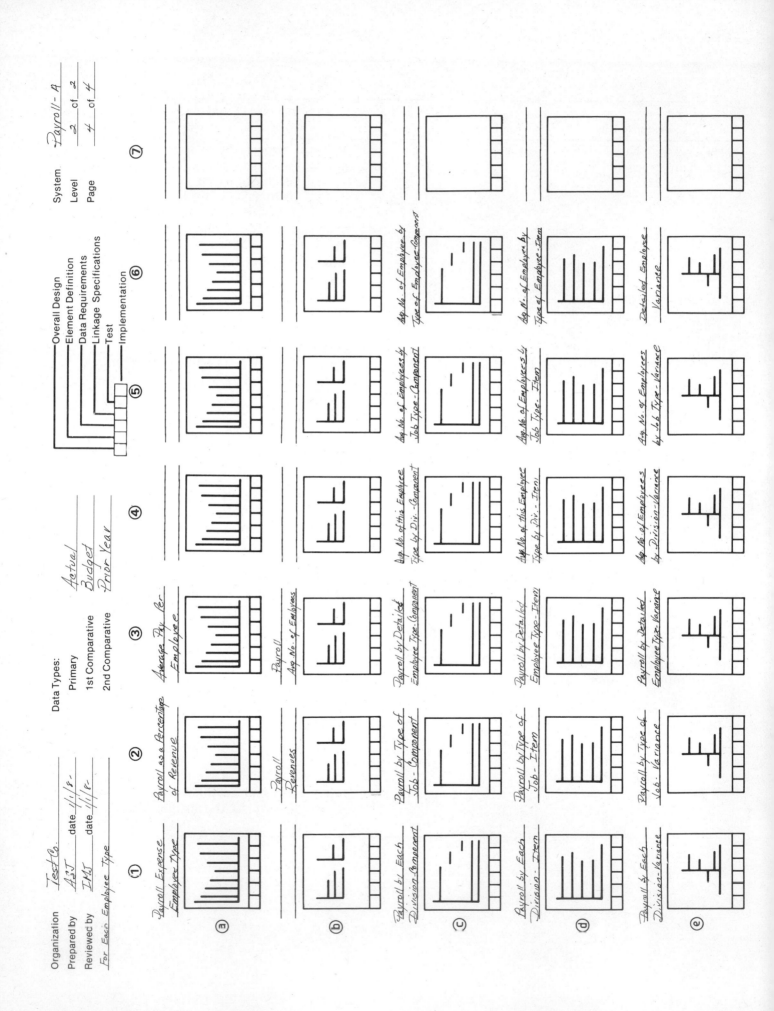

For Each Employee Type:

Row Col	Name of Chart	From	To	Descriptions
A1	Payroll Expense— Employee Type	Original	C1, C2, C3	Time series showing the total payroll for this employee type for the past 12 months as compared to budget and prior year. Seasonal patterns and variations should be apparent.
A2	Payroll as a Percentage of Revenue	Original	B2	Twelve-month time series showing the payroll for this employee type as a percentage of revenues. Any seasonal patterns will be reflected in this chart and major changes in the amount of payroll as a relationship to revenue will be apparent. Further disaggregation would show why the change occurred.
B2	N: Payroll D: Revenues	A2	C1, C2, C3	Ratio showing the relative size of payroll for this employee type as compared to the total revenues of the firm. If the change in the ratio is due to a change in the payroll expenses, then a further disaggregation would occur by going to Charts C1 and C3. If the change in the ratio is due to a change in the size of the revenues, then further disaggregation would occur by going to the income system.
A3	Average Pay per Employee	Original	B3	Time series of the past 12 periods showing the changing rates of pay paid to the average employee in this employee type. This chart most likely will show an increasing trend over time and would be indicative of the inflationary period we are experiencing.
B3	N: Payroll D: Average Number of Employees	A3	C1-C6	Ratio showing the relative size of payroll for the employee type as compared to the average number of employees in the employee type. If the change in the ratio is due to a change in the relative size of the payroll, then further disaggregation and analysis would take place by following the sequences in this payroll system. If the change in the ratio is due to a change in the relative size of the number of employees, the disaggregation starting at C4 through C6 would help explain the change.
C1	Payroll by Each Division— Component	A1, B2, B3	D1	Relative importance of the payroll for the employee type for each division as compared to the total payroll for this employee type.

311

Row Col	Name of Chart	From	To	Descriptions
D1	Payroll by Each Division—Item	C1	E1	Relative size of the payroll for this employee type paid by each division as compared to the other divisions. It shows the location of the largest payroll for this employee type.
E1	Payroll by Each Division—Variance	D1	—	Variance from plan and/or prior year for the payroll for this employee type by divisions. If further analysis is required, each divisional payroll for this employee type can be further disaggregated into the sequences similar to that shown on this page.
C2	Payroll by Type of Job—Component	A1, B2, B3, B4	D2	Relative importance of the payroll paid for this employee type by type of job worked as compared to the total employee type payroll. This analysis shows where this type of job this employee type works most often is located.
D2	Payroll by Type of Job—Item	C2	E2	Relative importance of the payroll paid this employee type for the type of job worked as compared to each of the job types.
E2	Payroll by Type of Job—Variance	D2	—	Variance from plan and/or prior year of where this employee type actually worked compared to the job type he or she was expected to work. If further analysis is required, each type of job for this employee type can be further disaggregated to a sequence similar to that shown on this page.
C3	Payroll by Detailed Employee Type—Component	B1, B2, B3	D3	NOTE: This sequence is shown because in large companies the employee type can be categorized at several levels of detail, for example, Level 1: hourly, salaried, classified; Level 2; machinist operator to the electrician; Level 3: machinist 1, 2, 3, and so on. This chart shows the relative importance of the payroll by detailed employee type as compared to total payroll for this employee type.
D3	Payroll by Detailed Employee Type—Item	C3	E3	Relative size of the payroll by detailed employee type as compared to the other detailed employee types within this employee type.
E3	Payroll by Detailed Employee Type—Variance	D3	—	Variance from plan and/or prior year for the payroll by detailed employee type for this employee type. If further analysis is required, it might be necessary to go to the detailed books of record.
C4	Average Number of	B3, B4	D4	Relative importance of the average num-

Row Col	Name of Chart	From	To	Descriptions
	Employees Type by Division—Component			ber of this employee type working in each division as compared to the total number of this employee type.
D4	Average Number of Employees Type by Division—Item	C4	E4	Relative size of the average number of this employee type working in each division compared to the other divisions. The division with the largest number of this employee type would be shown as would any change in the mix of this employee type working amongst the divisions.
E4	Average Number of Employees Type by Division—Variance	D4	—	Variance from plan and/or prior year for the average number of this employee type working at each division. If further analysis of the variance is required, each division can be fully disaggregated in the sequences similar to those shown in C4 through C6.
C5	Average Number of Employees by Job Type—Component	B3, B4	D5	Relative importance of the average number of this employee type working at each of the job types as compared to the total number of this employee type.
D5	Average Number of Employees by Job Type—Item	C5	E5	Relative size of the average number of this employee type working at each of the job types as compared to the other job types. Any change in the mix of the job types worked by this employee type would, over time, become apparent in this chart.
E5	Average Number of Employees by Job Type—Variance	D5	—	Variance from plan and/or prior year for each of the job types worked by this employee type. If further analysis is required, each of the average number of employees by job type can be further disaggregated into sequences similar to those shown in C4 through C6.
C6	Average Number of Employees by type of Employee—Component	B3, B4	D6	Relative importance of the average number of employees by type of employee as compared to the total number of employees.
D6	Average Number of Employees by Type of Employee—Item	C6	E6	Relative size of the average number of employees by type of employee as compared to all of the other types of employees. Any change in the mix of the employee types would, over time, become apparent in this chart.
E6	Detailed Employee —Variance	D6	—	Variance from plan and/or prior year for the average number of employees by detailed employee type. If further analysis is required, it might be necessary to go to the books of record.

1. PAYROLL—EXAMPLE 1

Chart 10-060 shows the payroll divided by revenue percentage through October. September and October have been significantly higher than budget. Chart 10-061 shows a further breakdown of the ratio for September. The right-hand chart shows how much higher the ratio was in September than budgeted. The left-hand chart shows that:

1.   The percentage is calculated by payroll divided by revenues.
2.   The ratio was higher than budget because payroll was higher than budget.
3.   Payroll was $93 thousand higher than budget.

Charts 10-062, 10-063, and 10-064 show a further breakdown of payroll for September by division. Chart 10-062 shows that the make-up of payroll is the same as budgeted, although the magnitude has changed and there are individual differences. Chart 10-063 shows Richfield, Carson, and Swift as having the highest payrolls, even though they were not budgeted to be this much higher than the other divisions. Chart 10-064 shows that Swift, Richfield, and Carson's divisions were responsible for the majority of the variance in payroll from budget.

Chart 10-065 shows a further breakdown of the payroll for the Richfield Division for September. The same components make up the total payroll: however, there have been significant changes in the proportion and amounts tha each type of employee type has compared to budget. Charts 10-066 and 10-067 show that the major changes have occurred in manager and staff payrolls.

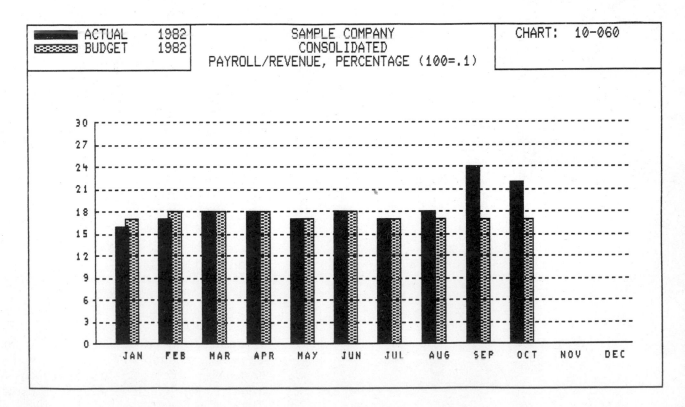

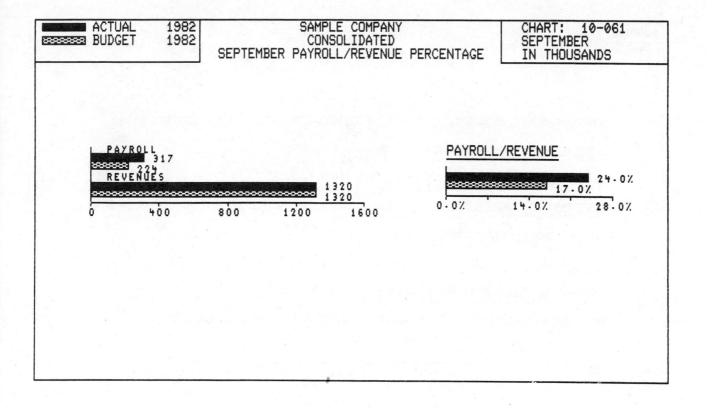

SAMPLE COMPANY
CONSOLIDATED
SEPTEMBER PAYROLL/REVENUE PERCENTAGE

CHART: 10-061
SEPTEMBER
IN THOUSANDS

PAYROLL
317
224
REVENUES
1320
1320

0   400   800   1200   1600

PAYROLL/REVENUE
24.0%
17.0%

0.0%   14.0%   28.0%

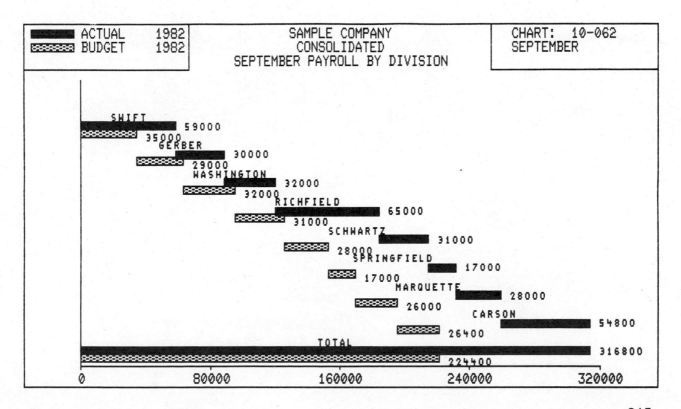

| ACTUAL | 1982 |
| BUDGET | 1982 |

SAMPLE COMPANY
CONSOLIDATED
SEPTEMBER PAYROLL BY DIVISION

CHART: 10-062
SEPTEMBER

SWIFT
59000
35000
GERBER
30000
29000
WASHINGTON
32000
32000
RICHFIELD
65000
31000
SCHWARTZ
31000
28000
SPRINGFIELD
17000
17000
MARQUETTE
28000
26000
CARSON
54800
26400
TOTAL
316800
224400

0   80000   160000   240000   320000

315

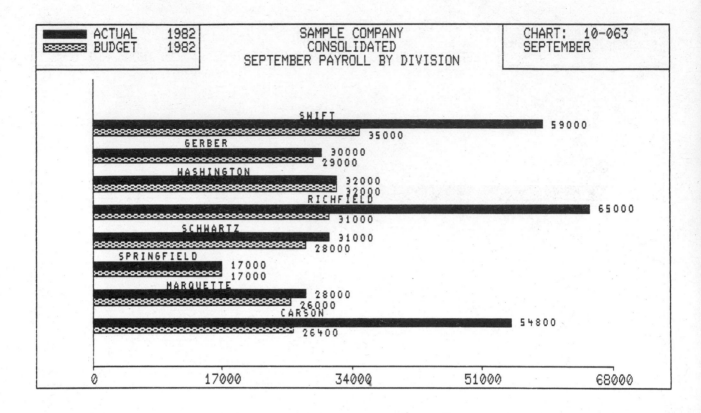

ACTUAL 1982
BUDGET 1982

SAMPLE COMPANY
CONSOLIDATED
SEPTEMBER PAYROLL BY DIVISION

CHART: 10-063
SEPTEMBER

SWIFT 59000
35000
GERBER 30000
29000
WASHINGTON 32000
32000
RICHFIELD 65000
31000
SCHWARTZ 31000
28000
SPRINGFIELD 17000
17000
MARQUETTE 28000
26000
CARSON 54800
26400

0   17000   34000   51000   68000

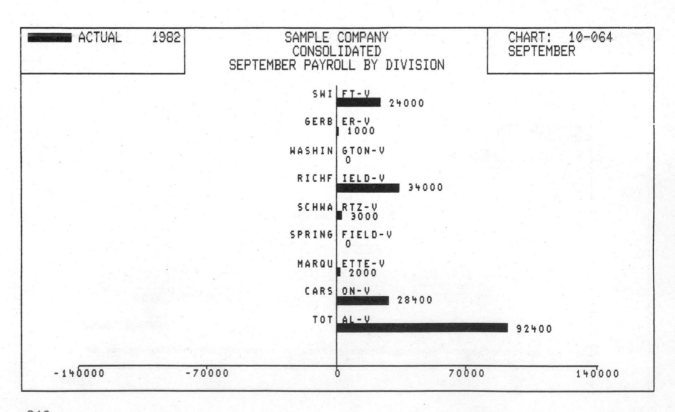

ACTUAL 1982

SAMPLE COMPANY
CONSOLIDATED
SEPTEMBER PAYROLL BY DIVISION

CHART: 10-064
SEPTEMBER

SWIFT-V 24000
GERBER-V 1000
WASHINGTON-V 0
RICHFIELD-V 34000
SCHWARTZ-V 3000
SPRINGFIELD-V 0
MARQUETTE-V 2000
CARSON-V 28400
TOTAL-V 92400

-140000   -70000   0   70000   140000

316

| ACTUAL | 1982 |
| BUDGET | 1982 |

SAMPLE COMPANY
CONSOLIDATED
RICHFIELD DIV PAYROLL BY EMPLOYEE TYPE

CHART: 10-065
SEPTEMBER

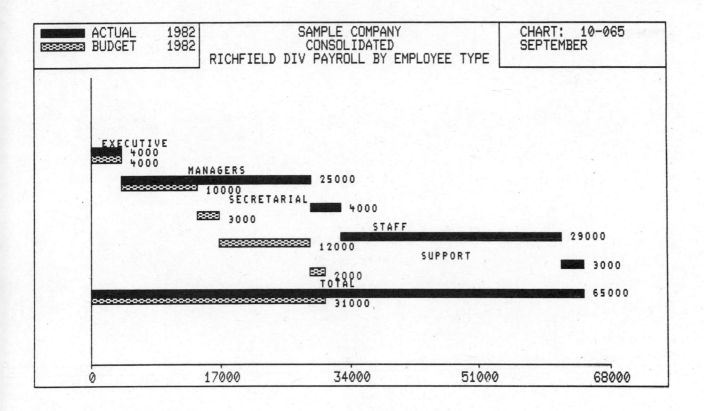

| ACTUAL | 1982 |
| BUDGET | 1982 |

SAMPLE COMPANY
CONSOLIDATED
RICHFIELD DIV PAYROLL BY EMPLOYEE TYPE

CHART: 10-066
SEPTEMBER

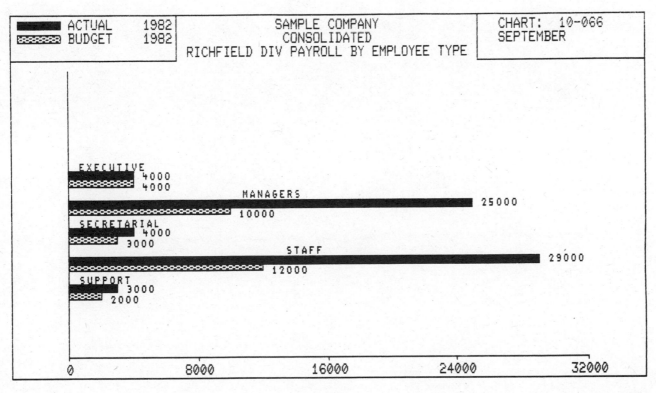

317

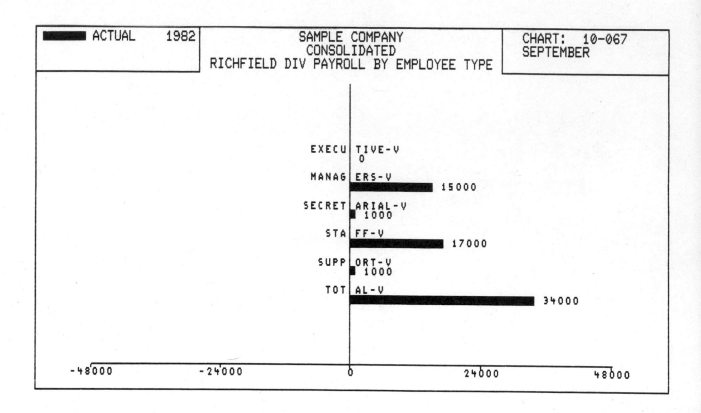

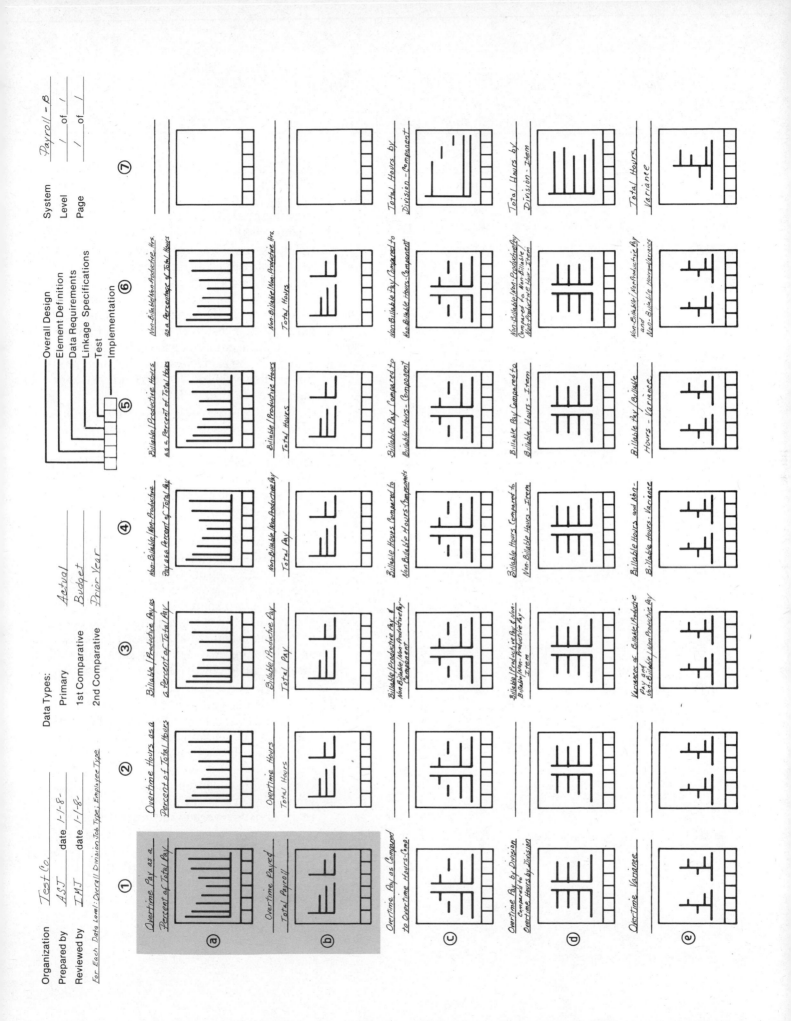

Organization *Test Co.*
Prepared by *ASI* date *1-1-8-*
Reviewed by *IMI* date *1-1-8-*

For Each Data Level: Overall Division Job Type; Employee Type

Data Types:
Primary *Actual*
1st Comparative *Budget*
2nd Comparative *Prior Year*

Overall Design
Element Definition
Data Requirements
Linkage Specifications
Test
Implementation

① ② ③ ④ ⑤ ⑥ ⑦

System *Payroll - B*
Level *1* of *1*
Page *1* of *1*

① (a) Overtime Pay as a Percent of Total Pay
(b) Overtime Payed / Total Payroll

② (a) Overtime Hours as a Percent of Total Hours
(b) Overtime Hours / Total Hours

③ (a) Billable / Productive Pay as a Percent of Total Pay
(b) Billable / Productive Pay / Total Pay

④ (a) Non-Billable Non-Productive Pay as a Percent of Total Pay
(b) Non-Billable Non-Productive Pay / Total Pay

⑤ (a) Billable / Productive Hours as a Percent of Total Hours
(b) Billable / Productive Hours / Total Hours

⑥ (a) Non-Billable Non-Productive Hrs. as a Percentage of Total Hours
(b) Non-Billable Non-Productive Hrs. / Total Hours

(c) ① Overtime Pay as Compared to Overtime Hours-Comp.
② —
③ Billable / Productive Pay & Non-Billable Non-Productive Pay - Component
④ Billable Hours Compared to Non-Billable Hours-Component
⑤ Billable Pay Compared to Billable Hours - Component
⑥ Non-Billable Non-Productive Pay Compared to Non-Billable Non-Productive Hour - Component
⑦ Total Hours by Division - Component

(d) ① Overtime Pay by Division Compared to Overtime Hours by Division
③ Billable / Productive Pay and Non-Billable Non-Productive Pay - Item
④ Billable Hours Compared to Non-Billable Hours - Item
⑤ Billable Pay Compared to Billable Hours - Item
⑥ Non-Billable Non-Productive Pay Compared to Non-Billable Non-Productive Pay - Item
⑦ Total Hours by Division - Item

(e) ① Overtime Variance
③ Variances of Billable / Productive Pay and Non-Billable Non-Productive Pay
④ Billable Hours and Non-Billable Hours - Variance
⑤ Billable Pay / Billable Hours - Variance
⑥ Non-Billable Nonproductive Pay and Non-Billable Hours Variance
⑦ Total Hours Variance

Row Col	Name of Chart	From	To	Descriptions
A1	Overtime Pay as a Percentage of Total Pay	Original	B1	Percentage of overtime pay compared to total payroll for the past 12 months. A significant change in overtime pay would become readily apparent.
B1	N: Overtime Pay D: Total Payroll	A1	C1	Relative size of overtime pay as compared to the total payroll. If the change in the ratio is due to a change in the relative size of overtime pay, then further analysis could be made by reviewing the disaggregated sequences shown at C1 and subsequent. If the change in the ratio is due to a change in the relative size of the total pay, further analysis and disaggregation would take place at system Payroll-A.
C1	Overtime Pay as Compared to Overtime Hours— Component	B1	D1	Co-relationship showing the relationship between the overtime pay and the overtime hours. The left-hand side of the chart shows the relative importance of overtime pay by division as compared to the total overtime pay for the corporation. The chart on the right-hand side makes a similar comparison of the respective overtime hours as shown to the total overtime hours. Note the disaggregation is by division only. The same types of disaggregation could take place for job type or employee type. The other two sequences should be available within the system and will be available to management as they see fit. Repeat: on this page, we are only showing the disaggregation by *division* as an example.
D1	Overtime Pay by Division Compared to Overtime Hours by Division—Item	C1	E1	Co-relationship showing the overtime pay by division as compared to the other divisions, and the respective overtime hours as compared to the other divisions. The pattern shown by both charts should be the same. A change in patterns might indicate that a higher percentage of higher paid employees are working overtime in one or more divisions versus the other divisions.
E1	Overtime—Variance	E1	Required Level	Twin variance showing the variance between plan and/or prior year for the overtime pay and overtime hours. If further analysis is required, each of the variances can be further disaggregated in a sequence similar to those starting at C1.

320

Row Col	Name of Chart	From	To	Descriptions
A2	Overtime Hours as a Percentage of Total Hours	Original	B2	Relationship of the overtime hours as a percentage of total hours for the past 12 months as compared to budget and/or prior year. Seasonal variations should become apparent and any change in the expected performance would be clearly indicated over time.
B2	N: Overtime Hours D: Total Hours	A2	C1	Ratio showing the relative size of the overtime hours as compared to the total hours worked. If the change in the ratio is due to the change in the relative size of the overtime hours, further disaggregation would occur similar to that shown on this page. If the change in the ratio is due to the change in the relative size of the total hours worked, then further disaggregation would take place in a sequence similar to that shown starting at A5 and A6 on this page.
A3	Billable/Productive Pay as a Percentage of Total Pay	Original	B3	Time series showing the percentage of billable/productive pay to the total payroll. The percentage should remain fairly high except for seasonal patterns. A change in this particular ratio is a critical indicator of a change in overall productivity performance.
B3	N: Billable/ Productive Pay D: Total Pay	A3	C3 and Subsequent	Ratio showing the billable/productive pay as compared to the total pay. If the change in the ratio is due to a change in the billable/productive pay, then the disaggregation would start at Chart C3 and subsequent. If the change in the ratio is due to a change in the total pay, see system Payroll–A.
C3	Billable/Productive Pay and Nonbillable/ Nonproductive Pay —Component	B3	D3	Co-relationship showing the billable/productive pay by divisions as compared to the nonbillable/nonproductive pay by respective divisions. The left side shows the relative importance of the billable pay by division as compared to the total billable pay paid by the company. The right side shows the relative importance of the nonbillable pay paid by division as compared to the total nonbillable pay for the corporation. This chart should give a picture of the relative productivity of each of the divisions.

Row Col	Name of Chart	From	To	Descriptions
D3	Billable/Productive Pay and Nonbillable/Nonproductive Pay —Item	C3	E3	Co-relationship showing the relative importance of the billable/productive pay by division as compared to the other divisions, and the respective nonbillable/nonproductive pay for each of the divisions as compared to the other divisions. Any change in the pattern would indicate further analysis is required.
E3	Variances of Billable/Productive Pay and Nonbillable/Nonproductive Pay	D3	Required Level	Twin variance showing the variance from plan and/or prior year for the productive/billable pay and nonproductive/nonbillable pay by division. If further analysis is required, each of the divisions can be further disaggregated into sequences similar to that shown on these pages starting at Charts C3 to C6, and subsequent.
A4	Nonbillable/Nonproductive as a Percentage of Total Pay	Original	B4	Time series showing the percentage of nonproductive payroll to the payroll, and the trend of nonbillable or nonproductive pay as compared to the total payroll. An upward trend would indicate problems might be occurring and would require further analysis.
B4	N: Nonbillable/Nonproductive pay D: Total Pay	A4	C4, C6	Ratio showing the relative size of the nonbillable/nonproductive pay as compared to the total payroll of the corporation. If the change in ratio is due to a change in the relative size of the nonbillable pay, then further disaggregation would occur as shown in the sequences C4 and subsequent. If the change in the ratio is due to a change in the relative size of the total pay, then further disaggregation would occur as shown in the system Payroll–A.
C4	Billable Hours Compared to Nonbillable Hours—Component	B5	D4	Co-relationship showing the billable hours on the left by division versus the nonbillable hours on the right by respective divisions. The left-hand side shows the relative importance of the billable hours by division as compared to the total billable hours. The right-hand side shows the relative importance of the nonbillable hours by division as compared to the total amount of nonbillable hours.
D4	Billable Hours Compared to Nonbillable Hours—Item	C4	E4	Co-relationship showing the billable hours on the left versus the nonbillable hours on the right for the respective divisions. The left-hand chart shows the relative impor-

322

Row Col	Name of Chart	From	To	Descriptions
				tance of the billable hours by division as compared to the other divisions and the right-hand chart shows the relative importance of the nonbillable hours as compared to the nonbillable hours for the respective divisions.
E4	Billable Hours and Nonbillable Hours—Variance	D4	Required Level	Twin variance showing the variance from plan and/or prior year for the billable hours and the nonbillable hours by division. If further analysis is required, each of the divisions can be disaggregated in the system similar to those shown starting at C3 and subsequent.
A5	Billable/Productive Hours as a Percentage of Total Hours	Original	B5	Time series showing the percentage of productive hours to total hours. In Chart A3, you see the actual dollars for productive work as compared to the total payroll and in this chart you see the same ratios except in terms of productive hours versus the total hours. Viewing Charts A3 and A5 together might show a picture worth pursuing.
B5	N: Billable/Productive Hours D: Total Hours	A5	C4, C5	Ratio chart showing the relative size of the billable/productive hours as compared to total hours worked in the corporation. If the change in the ratio is due to a change in the relative size of the billable hours, then further analysis and disaggregation would start at sequences C4 and C5. If a change in the ratio is due to a change in the relative size of the total hours worked, further analysis and disaggregation would start at A2, A5, and A6.
C5	Billable Pay Compared to Billable Hours—Component	B5	D5	Co-relationship showing the billable pay by division as compared to the billable hours by respective division. The left-hand side of the chart shows the relative importance of the billable pay as compared to the total billable pay for the firm. The right-hand side shows the total billable hours by their respective divisions as compared to the total billable hours of the firm. The relative patterns of both sides should stay the same. Any change in the relative size of the pattern would indicate that one division was paying more or less for the billable hours than the other divisions.

Row Col	Name of Chart	From	To	Descriptions
D5	Billable Pay Compared to Billable Hours—Item	C5	E5	Co-relationship showing the relationship between the billable pay and the billable hours by division. The left-hand side shows the relative importance of the billable pay per division as compared to the other divisions. The right-hand side shows the relative importance of the billable hours by divisions as compared to the other divisions.
E5	Billable Pay/Billable Hours—Variance	D5	Required	Twin variance showing the variance from plan and/or prior year of billable pay and billable hours. If further analysis is required, each of the divisions can be disaggregated in sequences similar to those shown on this page.
A6	Nonbillable/Nonproductive Hours as a Percentage of Total Hours	Original	B6	Time series showing the percentage of nonbillable hours as compared to total hours worked in the firm. Any increase in this percentage would indicate a trend that required review.
B6	N: Billable/Nonproductive Hours D: Total Hours	A6	C6, C7	Ratio showing the relative size of the nonbillable/nonproductive hours as compared to the total hours worked in the firm. If a change in the ratio is due to a change in the relative size of the nonbillable hours, further analysis would take place per the disaggregation shown at C6 and subsequent. If the change in the ratio is due to a change in the relative size of the total hours worked, further analysis could be performed by reviewing the disaggregation at C7.
C6	Nonbillable Pay Compared to Nonbillable Hours—Component	B4, B6	D6	Co-relationship showing the nonbillable pay by division as compared to the nonbillable hours by the respective division. The left-hand side shows the relative importance of the nonbillable pay by divisions as compared to the total nonbillable pay of the firm. The right-hand side shows the relative importance of the nonbillable hours by the respective divisions as compared to the total amount of nonbillable hours worked in the firm.
D6	Nonbillable/Nonproductive Pay Compared to Nonbillable/Nonproductive Hours—Items	C6	E6	Co-relationship showing the relationship between the nonbillable/nonproductive pay by division as compared to the respective nonbillable/nonproductive hours by division. The left-hand side shows the non-

Row Col	Name of Chart	From	To	Descriptions
				billable/nonproductive pay by division as compared to the other divisions, whereas the right-hand side shows the relative importance of the nonbillable hours of the respective divisions as compared to the other division.
E6	Nonbillable/Non-productive Pay and Nonbillable Hours —Variance	D6	Required Level	Twin variance showing the variance from plan and/or previous year for the nonbillable/nonproductive pay and the nonbillable/nonproductive hours. If further analysis is required, each of the divisions can be further disaggregated into sequences similar to those shown on the page.
C7	Total Hours by Division—Component	B2, B5, B6	D7	Relative importance of the total hours worked by divisions as compared to the total hours worked by the firm.
D7	Total Hours by Division—Item	C7	E7	Relative size of total hours worked by division as compared to the other divisions. This chart would show which of the divisions consistently works the largest number of hours.
E7	Total Hours—Variance	D7	—	Variance from plan and/or previous year for the individual divisions. If further analysis is required for each of the divisions, they can be further disaggregated into sequences similar to those shown at C7.

2. PAYROLL—EXAMPLE 2

Chart 10-068 shows a time series of the ratio overtime pay divided by total pay for the past year. In January and February there were very large differences between the budgeted ratio and the actual ratio. Chart 10-069 shows a further breakdown of the ratio for January. The chart on the right shows how much the ratio was higher than budget. The chart on the left shows:

1. The ratio shown is calculated as overtime pay divided by total pay.
2. The ratio was higher than budget because overtime pay increased at a higher rate than total pay. (By looking at the bars, you can see that overtime pay was about twice as great as budgeted. The total pay was about one-tenth larger than budget.)
3. Overtime pay was $10 thousand higher than budget and total pay was $9 thousand higher than budget.

Charts 10-070, 10-071, and 10-072 show a further breakdown of overtime pay and total pay by employee type. By looking at Chart 10-070, we can see on the

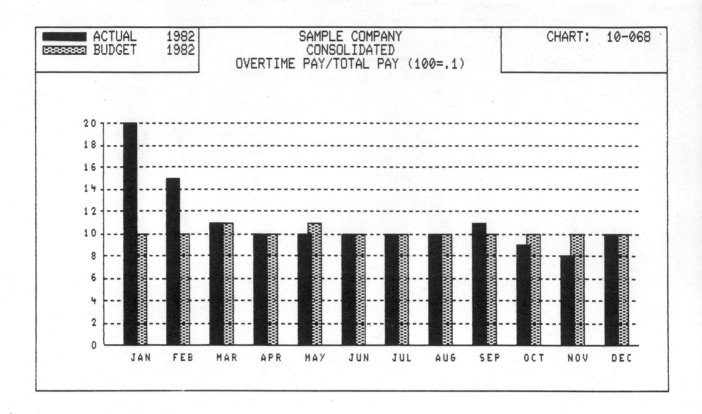

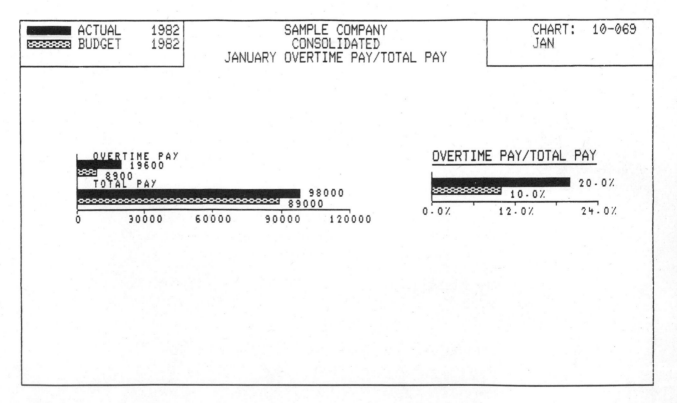

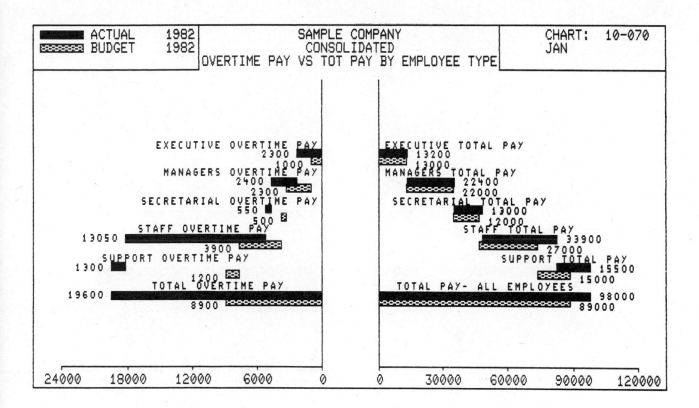

```
┌──────────────────────┬─────────────────────────────┬──────────────────────┐
│ ▬▬▬▬  ACTUAL    1982 │        SAMPLE COMPANY       │  CHART:  10-070      │
│ ▨▨▨▨  BUDGET    1982 │         CONSOLIDATED        │  JAN                 │
│                      │ OVERTIME PAY VS TOT PAY BY EMPLOYEE TYPE           │
└──────────────────────┴─────────────────────────────┴──────────────────────┘
```

EXECUTIVE OVERTIME PAY 2300 / 1000
MANAGERS OVERTIME PAY 2400 / 2300
SECRETARIAL OVERTIME PAY 550 / 500
STAFF OVERTIME PAY 13050 / 3900
SUPPORT OVERTIME PAY 1300 / 1200
TOTAL OVERTIME PAY 19600 / 8900

EXECUTIVE TOTAL PAY 13200 / 13000
MANAGERS TOTAL PAY 22400 / 22000
SECRETARIAL TOTAL PAY 13000 / 12000
STAFF TOTAL PAY 33900 / 27000
SUPPORT TOTAL PAY 15500 / 15000
TOTAL PAY- ALL EMPLOYEES 98000 / 89000

24000 18000 12000 6000 0   0 30000 60000 90000 120000

left that the make-up of overtime pay has changed dramatically from budget,
particularly in staff overtime pay. The right-hand side of the chart shows that
the make-up of total pay appears about the same, although there have been
some changes in individual items. Charts 10-071 and 10-072 show that staff
overtime pay has experienced the most significant change. A further breakdown of staff pay would show the reason for this unusual trend.

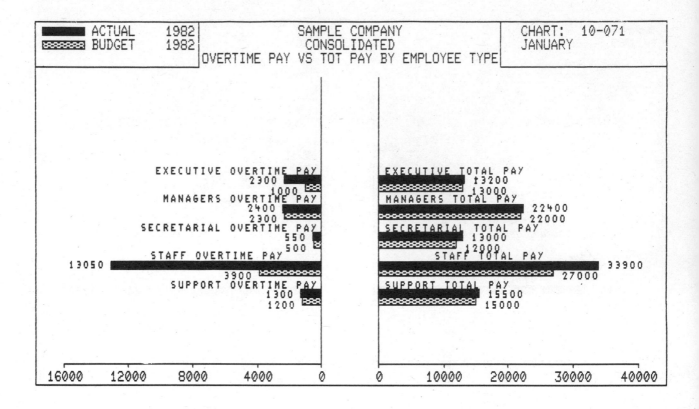

OVERTIME PAY VS TOT PAY BY EMPLOYEE TYPE

EXECUTIVE OVERTIME PAY
2300
1000

MANAGERS OVERTIME PAY
2400
2300

SECRETARIAL OVERTIME PAY
550
500

STAFF OVERTIME PAY
13050
3900

SUPPORT OVERTIME PAY
1300
1200

EXECUTIVE TOTAL PAY
13200
13000

MANAGERS TOTAL PAY
22400
22000

SECRETARIAL TOTAL PAY
13000
12000

STAFF TOTAL PAY
33900
27000

SUPPORT TOTAL PAY
15500
15000

16000 12000 8000 4000 0   0 10000 20000 30000 40000

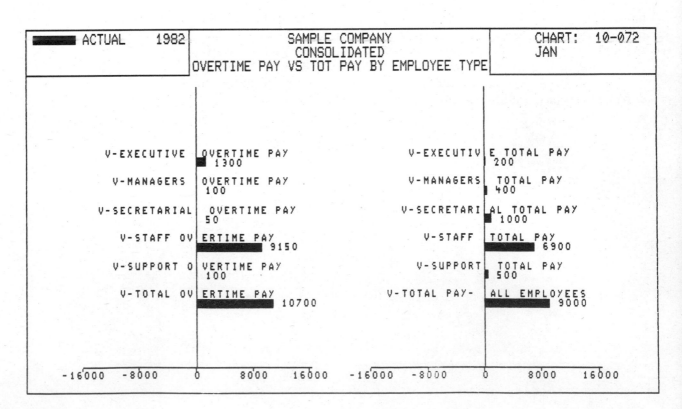

OVERTIME PAY VS TOT PAY BY EMPLOYEE TYPE

V-EXECUTIVE OVERTIME PAY
1300

V-MANAGERS OVERTIME PAY
100

V-SECRETARIAL OVERTIME PAY
50

V-STAFF OVERTIME PAY
9150

V-SUPPORT OVERTIME PAY
100

V-TOTAL OVERTIME PAY
10700

V-EXECUTIVE TOTAL PAY
200

V-MANAGERS TOTAL PAY
400

V-SECRETARIAL TOTAL PAY
1000

V-STAFF TOTAL PAY
6900

V-SUPPORT TOTAL PAY
500

V-TOTAL PAY- ALL EMPLOYEES
9000

-16000 -8000 0 8000 16000   -16000 -8000 0 8000 16000

328

CHAPTER 16

KEY INDICATORS AND THE GRAPHIC MANAGEMENT INSTRUMENT PANEL

As mentioned in Chapter 2, managers at all levels tend to use information in a highly predictable way. For each area of responsibility they use a set of key indicators to control those applications.

Within this handbook, we have identified those applications, or key factors, common to most organizations. There is a chapter devoted to each application that identifies those key indicators and supporting chart sequences that can be used to control each application. Managers at all levels now have the ability to receive a regular graphic printout or management instrument panel that provides them with current readings on those key indicators they use to control their applications.

This management instrument panel may range in sophistication from a set of weekly printouts to video monitors with live graphics of the key indicators. The monitors may be positioned on or near their desks and may be used in much the same way we use the gauges and dials on a car to monitor its status.

The installation of the GMIS allows the manager to identify important trends in the indicators more quickly than if presented in tabular printout. Once the trend is spotted, the GMIS then allows the manager to quickly trace through layers of the database to search for the cause of the change or variance in the indicators. Finally, the GMIS allows the manager to understand how each indicator affects other applications, thus new information not previously available to the manager can now be used for effective decision making.

As each manager will be responsible for a different level and area of responsibility, the key indicators will often be different. It is important in the design of the GMIS that the managers receive those key indicators that they can use to make effective decisions for their areas of responsibility. For example, the management instrument panel (or regular printout) of the manager of the purchasing department would contain all of the key indicators as presented in the accounts payable and purchasing chapters, Chapters 10 and 14, respectively. The CEO's management instrument panel, or regular report, would have a completely different set of key indicators. His or her indicators might be the Dun & Bradstreet Key Business Ratios and the set of graphic financial statements (see Chapter 5). One or two of the indicators would relate to accounts payable and purchases. If these indicators were off from budget or prior year, the CEO might have the Purchasing Director investigate, who would then look to his or her detailed set of indicators specific to purchasing.

This chapter and Chapter 5, provide the tools for designing the Management Instrument Panel for the managers at each level of the organization. Exhibit 16.1 lists all of the key indicators by Application as presented in this handbook. Exhibit 16.2 lists the Dun & Bradstreet Key Business Ratios. The right-hand column notes the chapters in this handbook to which the ratio would disaggregate. For example, if it is desired to show the net income to working capital ratio, this ratio would disaggregate into the income statement and funds control applications in Chapter 5. The graphic application systems designed for each of the applications could be used to investigate any trends uncovered by this ratio. Exhibit 16.3 provides the same information for the ratios used by Robert Morris and Associates. Exhibit 16.4 presents the same information for the ratios used by Standard and Poor. Exhibits 16.5 through 16.8 provide an index of Charts, of Exhibits, of Schematics and of Tables, respectively.

EXHIBIT 16.1

	Application System	Chapter	Ratio
1.	Income	5	Operating Expense as a Percentage of Sales
2.	Income	5	Administrative Expense as a Percentage of Sales
3.	Fund Control	5	Source and Use of Funds
4.	Cash	6	Net Cash Position—Rolling 12 Month
5.	Cash	6	Revenue on Cash
6.	Accounts Receivable	7	Accounts Receivable Balance
7.	Accounts Receivable	7	Accounts Receivable Turnover
8.	Accounts Receivable	7	Average Collection Period
9.	Accounts Receivable	7	Days to Billing
10.	Inventory	8	Inventory Balance
11.	Inventory	8	Inventory Turnover
12.	Inventory	8	Average Investment Period
13.	Inventory	8	Inventory to Working Capital Ratio
14.	Fixed Assets	9	Fixed Asset Turnover
15.	Fixed Assets	9	Fixed Assets to Net Worth
16.	Fixed Assets	9	Return on Fixed Assets
17.	Fixed Assets	9	Return on Total Assets
18.	Fixed Assets	9	Annualized Depreciation as a Percentage of Sales
19.	Fixed Assets	9	Annualized Depreciation Over Fixed Assets
20.	Accounts Payable	10	Accounts Payable Balance

EXHIBIT 16.1 (continued)

	Application System	Chapter	Ratio
21.	Accounts Payable	10	Accounts Payable as a Percentage of Purchases
22.	Accounts Payable	10	Average Payment Period
23.	Accounts Payable	10	Accounts Payable as a Percentage of Current Assets
24.	Accounts Payable	10	Discounts Taken Over Discounts Available
25.	Long Term Debt	11	Times Interest Earned
26.	Long Term Debt	11	Long-Term Debt to Net Worth
27.	Long Term Debt	11	Long-Term Debt to Working Capital
28.	Net Worth: Equity	12	Return on Investment
29.	Net Worth: Equity	12	Current Liability to Equity
30.	Net Worth: Equity	12	Fixed Assets to Equity
31.	Net Worth: Equity	12	Total Debt to Equity
32.	Net Worth: Equity	12	Sales to Equity
33.	Sales/Cost of Goods Sold/Gross Margin	13	Sales
34.	Sales/Cost of Goods Sold/Gross Margin	13	Gross Margin Percentage
35.	Sales/Cost of Goods Sold/Gross Margin	13	Cost of Goods Sold Percentage
36.	Sales/Cost of Goods Sold/Gross Margin	13	Gross Margin as a Percentage of Sales
37.	Sales/Cost of Goods Sold/Gross Margin	13	Cost of Goods Sold as a Percentage of Sales
38.	Sales/Cost of Goods Sold/Gross Margin	13	Return on Sales
39.	Purchases	14	Purchases by Month
40.	Purchases	14	Purchase Orders—YTD
41.	Purchases	14	Open Purchase Orders
42.	Purchases	14	Open Purchase Orders as a Percentage of Annualized Purchase Orders
43.	Payroll–A	15	Payroll Expense
44.	Payroll–A	15	Payroll as a Percentage of Revenue
45.	Payroll–A	15	Average Pay per Employee
46.	Payroll–A	15	Revenue per Employee
47.	Payroll–B	15	Overtime Pay as a Percentage of Total Pay
48.	Payroll–B	15	Overtime Hours as a Percentage of Total Hours
49.	Payroll–B	15	Billable/Productive Pay as a Percentage of Total Pay
50.	Payroll–B	15	Nonbillable/Nonproductive

EXHIBIT 16.1 (continued)

Application System	Chapter	Ratio
51. Payroll–B	15	Pay as a Percentage of Total Pay Billable/Productive Hours as a Percentage of Total Hours
52. Payroll–B	15	Nonbilable/Nonproductive Hours as a Percentage of Total Hours

EXHIBIT 16.2. Dun & Bradstreet key business ratios[a]

Ratio Name	Disaggregates To	Chapter
1. Net Income to Working Capital	Income	5
	Funds Control	5
2. Net Income to Sales	Income	5
	Sales	13[b]
3. Net Income to Net Worth	Income	5
	Net Worth: Equity	12[b]
4. Current Liability to Net Worth	Funds Control	5
	Financial Control	5
	Net Worth: Equity	12[b]
5. Total Debt and Net Worth	Long Term Debt	11
	Financial Control	5
	Net Worth: Equity	12[b]
6. Long Term Debt to Working Capital Capital	Long Term Debt	11[b]
	Fund Control	5
7. Sales Over Inventory (Turnover)	Sales	13
	Inventory	8[b]
8. Fixed Assets to Equity	Fixed Assets	9[b]
	Net Worth: Equity	12[b]
9. Sales to Net Worth	Sales	13
	Net Worth: Equity	12[b]
10. Sales to Working Capital	Sales	13
	Fund Control	5
11. Current Ratio	Financial Control	5
	Fund Control	5
12. Inventory to Working Capital	Inventory	8[b]
	Funds Control	5
13. Current Liabilities to Inventory	Financial Control	5
	Fund Control	5
	Inventory	8
14. Quick Ratio	Funds Control	5
	Financial Control	5

[a]Ratio Analysis from Dun & Bradstreet Corp.

[b]Denotes chapter in which ratio is shown in this text.

EXHIBIT 16.3. Robert Morris Ratio Analysis[a]

Ratio Name	Disaggregates To	Chapter
1. Current Ratio	Financial Control	5
2. Quick Ratio	Financial Control	5
3. Sales to Receivables	Sales	13
	Accounts Receivable	7[b]
4. Cost of Sales to Inventory	Cost of Goods Sold	13
	Inventory	8[b]
5. Sales to Working Capital	Sales	13
	Financial Control	5
6. EBIT to Interest	Income	5
	Long-Term Debt	11[b]
7. Cash Flow to Current Maturities	Financial, Funds Control	5
Cash Flow to Long-Term Debt	Cash	6
	Long-Term Debt	11[b]
8. Fixed Assets to Net Worth	Fixed Assets	9[b]
	Net Worth: Equity	11
9. Debt to Net Worth	Corporate Control	5
	Equity: Net Worth	12[b]
10. Percentage Profit Before Taxes to Net Worth	Income	5
	Net Worth: Equity	12
11. Percentage Profit Before Taxes to Total Assets	Income	5
	Corporate Control	5
	Fixed Assets	9[b]
12. Sales to Net Fixed Assets	Sales	13
	Fixed Assets	9[b]
13. Sales to Total Assets	Sales	13
	Corporate Control	5
	Fixed Assets	9[b]
14. Percentage Depreciation, Amortization, Depletion Expenses to Net Sales	Income	5
	Fixed Assets	9[b]
	Sales	13
15. Percentage Lease and Rental Expenses to Sales	Income	5[c]
	Sales	13
16. Percentage Officers' Compensation to Sales	Income	5[c]
	Sales	13

[a]Ratios from: Robert Morris Associates, Annual Statement Studies, 1981 Edition, pp. 7–11.
[b]Denotes chapter in which ratio is shown.
[c]Denotes chapter where ratio is described.

EXHIBIT 16.4. Standard and Poor Ratio Analysis[a]

Ratio Name	Disaggregates To	Chapter
Management Efficiency		
1. Return to Equity	Income	5
	Net Worth: Equity	12[b]
2. Return on Assets	Income	5
	Fixed Assets	9[b]
3. Net Income as a Percentage of Sales	Income	5
	Sales	13[b]
4. Operating Income as a Percentage of Sales	Income	5
	Sales	13[b]
Investment Ratios		
5. Dividend Payout Ratio	Income	5
	Financial Control	5
6. Price-Earnings Ratio	Income	5
7. Yield	Income	5
	Financial Control	5
	Net Worth: Equity	12[b]
Liquidity and Leverage Analysis		
8. Debt to Equity Ratio	Long Term Debt	11[b]
	Net Worth: Equity	12[b]
9. Debt as a Percentage of Net Working Capital	Accounts Payable	10[b]
	Financial Control	5

[a]Ratios from: Standard and Poor's Industry Survey, July 16, 1981, Section Two, "Food Processing Basic Analysis."

[b]Denotes chapter in which Ratio is shown in this text.

EXHIBIT 16.5. Index of Charts

Exhibit No.	Chart No.	Description	Page
		Chapter 3	
3.1		Blank representation of Data	22
3.2		Graphic Representation of a Number	22
3.3	10-998	Element's Components	23
3.4	10-005	Sales by Division	23
3.5	10-008	Sales per Month	24
3.6		Symbol for Time Series Chart	24
3.7	10-350	Return on Sales	25
3.8		Graphic Symbol for Ratio Format	25
3.9	10-315	Addition of Elements	26
3.10	10-109	Sales by Product Type (Without Budget)	26
3.11	10-109	Sales by Product Type (With Budget)	27
3.12	10-109	Sales by Product Type (Product A less than Budget)	28
3.13		Graphic Symbol for Component Format	28
3.14	10-110	Sales by Product Type (Item)	29
3.15	10-013	Accounts Receivable by Age	29
3.16		Graphic Symbol for Item Chart	30

EXHIBIT 16.5. Index of Charts (continued)

EXHIBIT 16.5. Index of Charts (continued)

EXHIBIT 16.5. Index of Charts (continued)

EXHIBIT 16.6. Index of Exhibits (continued)

EXHIBIT 16.7.   Index of Schematics

Description			Page
System	Level	Page	
Chapter 5			
Overall	1 of 1	1 of 1	70
Income	1 of 3	1 of 3	73
Income	2 of 3	2 of 3	78
Income	3 of 3	3 of 3	82
Balance Sheet Corporate Control	1 of 1	1 of 1	91
Financial Control	1 of 1	1 of 1	99
Fund Control	1 of 1	1 of 1	103
Chapter 6			
Cash	1 of 2	1 of 2	108
Cash	2 of 2	2 of 2	112
Chapter 7			
Accounts Receivable	1 of 2	1 of 4	121
Accounts Receivable	2 of 2	2 of 4	126
Accounts Receivable	2 of 2	3 of 4	129
Accounts Receivable	2 of 2	4 of 4	132
Chapter 8			
Inventory	1 of 2	1 of 3	140
Inventory	2 of 2	2 of 3	145
Inventory	2 of 2	3 of 3	147
Chapter 9			
Fixed Assets	1 of 2	1 of 3	156
Fixed Assets	2 of 2	2 of 3	161
Fixed Assets	2 of 2	3 of 3	163
Chapter 10			
Accounts Payable	1 of 2	1 of 4	169
Accounts Payable	2 of 2	2 of 4	174
Accounts Payable	2 of 2	3 of 4	177
Accounts Payable	2 of 2	4 of 4	179
Chapter 11			
Long Term Debt	1 of 1	1 of 1	187
Chapter 12			
Net Worth	1 of 1	1 of 1	194
Chapter 13			
Sales	1 of 2	1 of 4	202
Sales	2 of 2	2 of 4	206
Sales	2 of 2	3 of 4	210
Sales	2 of 2	4 of 4	214
Cost of Goods Sold	1 of 2	1 of 4	219
Cost of Goods Sold	2 of 2	2 of 4	229
Cost of Goods Sold	2 of 2	3 of 4	238
Cost of Goods Sold	2 of 2	4 of 4	247
Chapter 14			
Purchases	1 of 2	1 of 4	264
Purchases	2 of 2	2 of 4	271
Purchases	2 of 2	3 of 4	278
Purchases	2 of 2	4 of 4	284

EXHIBIT 16.7.   Index of Schematics (continued)

Description			Page
System	Level	Page	
Chapter 15			
Payroll-A	1 of 2	1 of 4	296
Payroll-A	2 of 2	2 of 4	301
Payroll-A	2 of 2	3 of 4	306
Payroll-A	2 of 2	4 of 4	310
Payroll-B	1 of 1	1 of 1	319

EXHIBIT 16.8.   Index of Tables

Table No.	Description	Page
3.1	Table of standard charts	49–51
4.1	Disaggregation Pattern for Each Data Level by Type of Indicator	61

CHAPTER 17

PRESENTATION GRAPHICS

The distinction between what is called *Presentation Graphics* and *Information Graphics* has been given a lot of space by the computer graphic industry. The question is: Is there an *inherent* difference between information graphics and presentation graphics? The answer is no! The only difference between them is the medium. If all of the media were fully organized in the industry so that the same quality graphics could be obtained from the CRT and the high-speed output devices, and with the same color and quality, there would be no need to differentiate between information graphics and presentation graphics.

The fact is that there is a substantial difference between the quality of the imagery shown on the CRT and that which can be reproduced in hard copy, and even further, there is a substantial difference between the quality of the hard copy output devices. The dot matrix printers produce one or more levels of graphic output, the thermal devices produce another type of image, the plotter creates a third type, the Xerox-type copiers produce a fourth type, the ink jet printers a fifth, the color ribbon printers a sixth, the laser printers a seventh, and there will be more and different types of hard copy devices coming to the market each year. In addition, there are 35 mm slide makers, movie makers, overhead devices and, soon, direct-to-videodisc imagery. The point is that the quality of the output is not consistent. The colors are not consistent and the resulting transfer of information will not be consistent. The information transferred by a CRT may be different than that transferred on hardcopy, or a large screen with a 35 mm overhead projector. Selecting the appropriate blend of output devices to match the appropriate charts is one of the more critical issues in the design and installation of the GMIS. As you may suspect, the costs of producing the various types of images vary as widely as the quality.

PRESENTATION GRAPHICS. Presentation graphics is the art of describing a point graphically that has already been determined by studying the information. The objective is to make the point with specific or heightened emphasis using the full range of high quality graphic media. A key distinction in practice is that presentation graphics are usually supported verbally by the individual using the chart, or with a written description of the point being made, such as those shown in the annual reports. Graphic highlights are used to point out relationships the preparers want to show, and to play down points that they may not want anyone to see. For example, arrows can be used on the chart to draw attention to a specific point. Differing shades of color can indicate that some data on the graphic should be examined. There are almost endless types of indicators available to the graphic artist. Presentation graphics are normally thought of when speeches are made and the charts displayed on the screen use words as points to be made. The words control the sequence of the presentation and provide emphasis.

INFORMATION GRAPHICS. Information graphics are designed to be the input device for the right brain pattern recognition function. Whereas presentation graphics are designed to get a specific point across about data already analyzed, information graphics are designed to provide a specific pattern created by the relationships of the data. The critical difference is that the data relationships create the pattern and the information is transferred to the viewer through the basic pattern or by a change from the basic pattern, and by the relationships between the patterns. The point is that data drive the pattern and the patterns have to be known to understand the meaning of a change in data relationships. Making sure that the patterns are consistently shown in the most cost effective way will invariably lead to the development of presentation quality graphics as shown in this chapter. Unfortunately, the difference most often alluded to in the literature is that presentation graphics are high quality and information graphics are not, a bad distinction.

Color is probably one of the most controversial areas in the use of business graphics. Research has shown that color is best used to identify. For example, if brown is used as a color to represent inventory, when you see a chart with brown borders and a brown heading, you will know that you are looking at an inventory chart (see Exhibit 17.6). Color is also very good at highlighting specific information on the charts. See how the "big red arrow" points out the inventory turnover in Exhibit 17.10.

As described earlier, if the chart is a ratio chart, you will always know you are seeing a ratio chart of inventory, and if you read the heading you will know it is an inventory turnover picture (see Exhibit 17.8 later on in this chapter). However, if you know a specific chart will always appear in a set position in a known series of information charts, the position in the sequence tells you the chart you are viewing. For example, if you know that the sequence is always (1) a time series of a ratio, (2) the ratio, and (3) a twin component of the ratio, you will know exactly what you will see next because of the consistency of the presentation. Therefore, information about the chart can be transferred by the format, the sequence of the chart in the presentation, and the color.

But *be careful* with color. Color has lots of advantages as we will show in this chapter, but here are some practical problems with using color:

1. Duplication with color is often very expensive and the costs may be prohibitive.
2. Approximately 8–10% of American males are color blind.
3. Certain colors have different meanings to different people. For example, the color red often has a bad connotation to accountants and business people, such as "operating in the red." For this reason, a highly emotional color such as red should be limited for specific purposes as described later in this chapter.

Presentation quality graphics should be the natural result of a well planned, well organized and operated GMIS. The process would clearly define the various roles of the output and the appropriate devices selected. High-speed devices should be used for high volume. To the extent that you can get high quality, such as with the laser printers or high quality dot matrix printers, you can create presentation quality graphics with volume. If the presentation sequence is structured in a consistent manner, then the understanding and the presentation are both enhanced. If the appropriate color can be added to the high-speed output, then three of the major media information transfer constraints have been resolved. The design of the system should cause a natural flow to high quality presentation output. There will be times when it is necessary to take specific examples from a sequence and show them for special presentations to board meetings, to outside investor groups and other special groups. at this point the charts may be taken out of the natural flow of the system and enhanced as described further in the rest of this chapter.

1. EXAMPLES OF DIFFERING PRESENTATION MEDIA

The five critical issues in graphic presentation are as follows:
1. Size of the chart.
2. Graphic quality of the output image.
3. Sequence of the images in the presentation.
4. Color.
5. Media, such as CRT, film, overheads, 35 mm slides, printed copy, and so on.

This section of the chapter describes the implications of these critical issues.

EXHIBIT 17.1

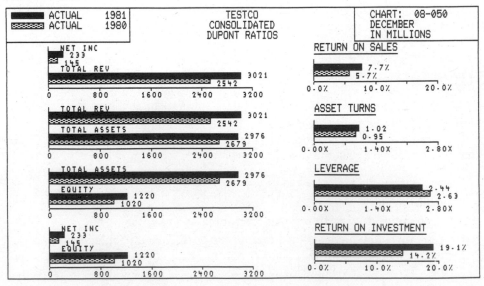

EXHIBIT 17.2

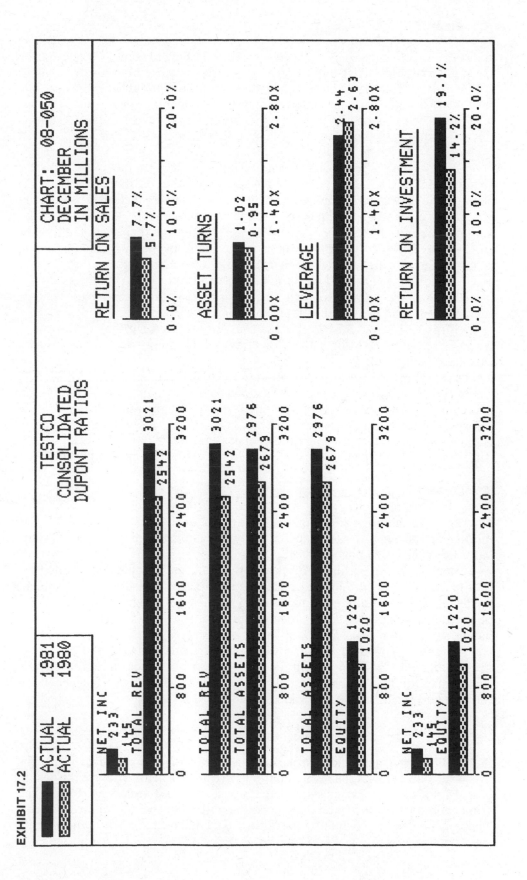

A. Size

Size is one of the more critical issues in deciding how to transfer information through graphics. If the quality of the image reproduction is excellent, reasonably small charts can show a lot of information quickly and can be easily seen by the human eye. On the other hand, that same image enlarged to the size of a large wall using high quality 35 mm slides or overheads, presents a different message than the small chart. A BIG picture carries a BIGGER message.

In one instance, a firm has plotted their management control panel showing 12 key ratios on a single 8-1/2 by 14 piece of paper that easily folds into a coat pocket. The instrument panel is produced weekly and is constantly used at the luncheon table and in other meetings to discuss changes. However, those same 12 charts are also plotted on much larger wall hangings each month and hung on the wall surrounding the "war room." This approach provides both the larger imagery which is easily seen by the executive committee as they meet to discuss problems. The wall hanging builds a context for the meetings. Those same images are reinforced with a pocket-sized replica of the management control panel that is available at all hours of the day and night.

Exhibit 17.1 shows a ratio chart of the Consolidated DuPont Ratios taken from Chapter 3, Exhibit 3.19. This chart is the same size as that shown throughout the book.

That same chart using the same graphic output device is shown in Exhibit 17.2 except it is now a full page chart. The charts are shown opposite each other to give you an idea of the impact of the bigger chart and the amount of information that can be transferred.

A large statement of Income is shown in Exhibit 17.3 on a wall. See the difference of the impact simply because of the size of the presentation.

B. Quality

Now another change is added to this same chart, as shown in Exhibit 17.4. The quality of the image is enhanced simply by using a more refined graphic output device, a pen plotter.

The chart shown in Exhibit 17.5 is exactly the same chart shown in the first four examples except that the quality of the image is now enhanced by using different alpha and numeric fonts and the addition of a logo to the chart. This particular chart is plotted on a pen plotter, but the same type of chart could have been printed on a high quality dot matrix printer or on a high quality laser printer. The difference in the quality would be noticeable but not necessarily critical if the output devices were of high enough quality. These first five exhibits are all shown in black and white, the only difference being the size and the quality of the reproduction medium.

C. Sequence

Sequence is the next most important consideration in understanding the presentation of charts. The other chapters in the book are devoted to the design of a proper disaggregation sequence. If the sequence is used consistently, you will become familiar with the sequence and will expect certain charts to occur. There is no need to spend any more time on this point since it is thoroughly covered elsewhere.

EXHIBIT 17.3

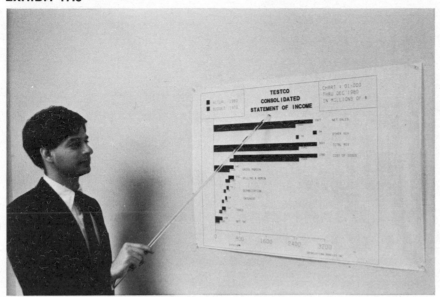

EXHIBIT 17.4

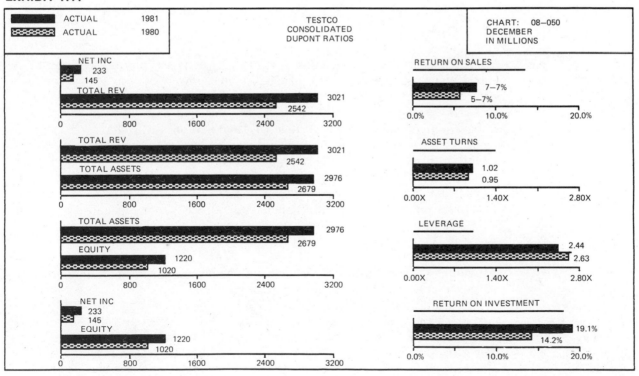

EXHIBIT 17.5

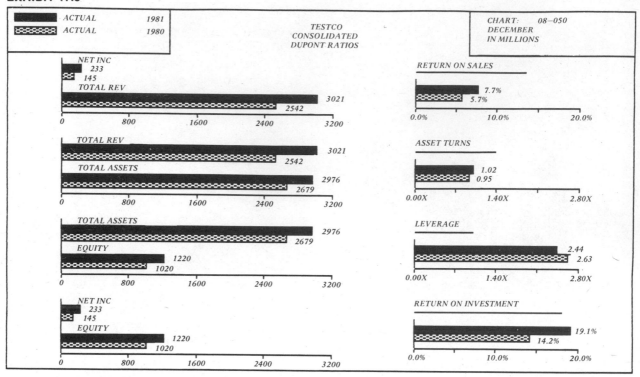

D. Color

The use of color with a high quality image is a different picture. Exhibits 17.6 and 17.7 show how color can be used to index the charts. In this example we have used the color green to indicate that this chart is in a control series. Two charts are shown. The first one shows the Corporate DuPont Ratio Charts, and the second one shows the Northern Division DuPont Ratio charts. In this case both charts use the same green headings and border indicating that they are both in the *control series*. Now that you know green is the control series and that the first chart is always the corporate consolidated chart and the second chart is always the Northern Division, both color and sequence are used to transfer information. Assuming you forget the sequence, you can always read the heading.

For the next example, Exhibit 17.8, we have used the same ratio chart format and we show the inventory turnover for the four divisions. The inventory turnover chart uses a brown border and headings to indicate that this chart is from an inventory control sequence.

Exhibit 17.9 is the same inventory control chart with the same brown borders and headings, except the background and the bars themselves have been colored, showing a considerably different picture than that shown by the original black and white chart. You will have to determine whether the difference in the quality and the additional information transferred are worth the additional costs. The research in the field is not sufficient to provide the basis for a cost/benefit analysis regarding the information and usefulness of the information transferred with color.

EXHIBIT 17.6

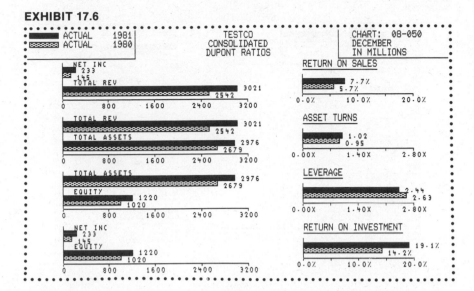

EXHIBIT 17.7

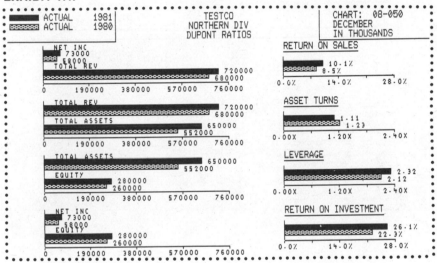

Note: Dotted line represents green.

Color can be used to highlight. Shown here are two examples. Exhibit 17.10 shows what we call "The Big Red Arrow" example. In this example the inventory control charts shown in Exhibits 17.8 and 17.9 show that the Eastern Division turnover is below budget. Assuming that such a difference in turnover has broken the "confidence levels," you see the GMIS has drawn "The Big Red Arrow." Notice how your eyes immediately go to where the big red arrow points. We highly recommend that red be used only for this purpose. If red is consistently used to indicate that attention must be given to where the red is used, its usefulness will grow over time.

In Exhibit 17.11 the same chart is shown where red is used to border the division rather than used as an arrow. You must determine the way to highlight. Remember, a little red ink goes a long way!

EXHIBIT 17.8

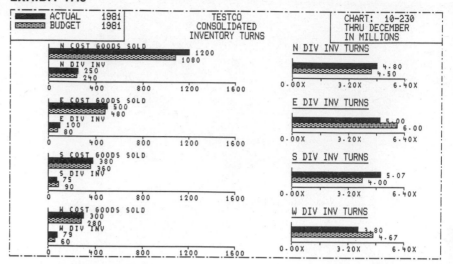

EXHIBIT 17.9

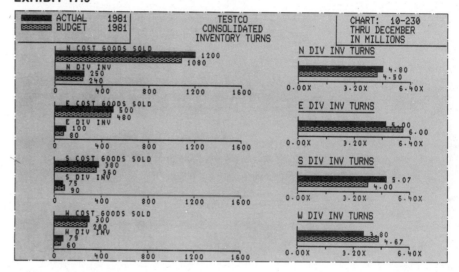

EXHIBIT 17.10

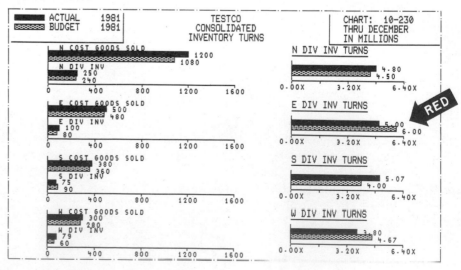

Note: Series of dots and dashes represents brown.

EXHIBIT 17.11

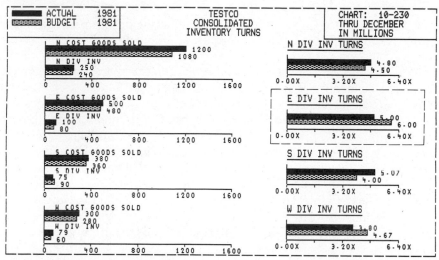

Note: Broken line represents red.

E. Media

Finally, the medium itself is crucial to the proper transfer of information in graphics. As noted earlier, one company uses a 8-1/2 by 14 replica of a management control panel for an instant take-along reference by all of the executive committee. The same charts on the panel are enlarged to wall hangings where they build a context for the war room where the executive committee meet. The information is further enhanced with the use of overhead transparencies for supporting charts to be reviewed. Finally, a large screen CRT is used to show the results of "what if" scenarios. This four-pronged approach to pattern recognition is repeated over and over and the group is becoming sufficiently sophisticated to determine even the slightest change in the patterns being shown. 35 mm slides can be used to display information similar to that shown by the transparencies. There is a debate in the graphic art field whether the 35 mm slide is a more effective presentation than the overhead for simple presentations. We will not attempt to resolve that debate here and simply offer both of them as options from which you will have to choose.

The point is that the medium you use will in itself deliver a message. To repeat, Marshall McLuhan said, "The medium is the message." That famous saying has never been more appropriate than in the development of the computer graphic presentation of your information.

It is possible to go beyond the media described here and develop a full scale film with cartoons, movement, and sound or a multimedia sound and light show with 35 mm slides. We are not proposing these approaches, only suggesting that the range of media is extremely wide and should be given careful consideration by media experts prior to the finalization of the design of the GMIS.

2. IMAGE TRANSFER AND REPRODUCTION PROBLEMS

As noted in the preceding section, one of the major problems in information graphics is the image transfer and reproduction problem. The color seen on a CRT screen is not what is available in the hard copy. For example, some black and white screens have reverse image options and the operator can reverse the images. If you design a system to be shown with black bars and white background, the operator can change that picture by simply reversing the images at the terminal. You can also reverse the images printed using the same technique. A number of CRT screens use green and the printout is in black and white. And finally the color output shown on the CRT screen may be printed on a black and white device, on a plotter with a palette, or limited color that can only show solid colors. The color output range is extremely limited and you may have to select from a limited number of colors to represent what could be an almost infinite range of colors presented on the CRT. The range of shading available on a CRT is different than what is practically available on a plotter.

The reproduction problems are certainly one of the most serious problems in the design and installation of the GMIS. Considerable effort is being expended to correct the problem and it will be corrected, sometime. But in the meantime, careful consideration should be given to this particular aspect of the GMIS.

3. OTHER BASIC CHART FORMATS

We have concentrated on the horizontal and vertical bar charts in this book because these two imageries provide the best basis for transferring the most information in a highly structured sequence of events. However, there are several other chart formats that may be used in certain circumstances and that should be considered when developing a final presentation. A brief explanation of each follows.

A. Pie Charts (Exhibit 17.12)

Pie charts are useful in a limited range of presentations. They are useful when there are no more than five simple components to be shown and where each of the components is 15 degrees or more. If one or more of the components is very small, the pie chart is not an effective device.

Pie charts are good for showing components where words are used rather than numbers. For example, you might want to say that the four phases of management are planning, organizing, directing, and controlling. The four words could be shown on the pie chart in four quadrants with different colors. As each word is explained, the charts following the slides would be color-coded back to the original pie.

Pie charts are also good for showing overlaps in activities where the activity of one division could be shown to overlap the activity of another division. As long as the surface of the overlap is not indicative of any type of volume, this presentation can be a useful way to describe overlap.

Here are some don'ts with pie charts.

1. Don't use them when there are a lot of components and/or the difference between the largest and the smallest component is significant.

EXHIBIT 17.12

Aliens Naturalized: 1960 to 1973

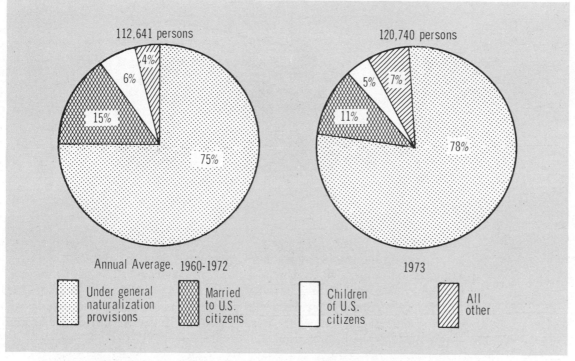

Source: Chart prepared by U.S. Bureau of the Census. Data from U.S. Immigration and Naturalization Service.

2. Don't compare the volume of one pie chart to another. The human eye cannot make an accurate comparison.

3. Don't try to show consistent pie charts over a long period of time with actual numbers. Businesses sometime have negatives and negative components cannot be shown on a pie chart.

4. Dont' explode parts out of the whole, unless you want to highlight only that one piece. It's hard enough to see the component whole without exploding a part out. Exploding a piece of the pie does, in fact, highlight that piece, but it also makes it almost impossible to see the relative size of that piece as compared to the rest of the pieces in the pie.

In conclusion, pie charts are useful, but careful consideration should be given prior to using them.

B. Line Charts (Exhibit 17.13)

Line charts are good for showing continuous data when no more than three or four lines are to be shown. They are the best way to show analogue data. One of the problems with line charts is that if the lines cross a lot or the data run too close together, it is difficult to distinguish between the lines. A great deal of research has occurred showing which is the best type of lines to show which type of information. Because line charts indicate a continuous flow of data, an analogue, there are few situations in business where they are truly appropriate. They could be used to show daily movements over a long period of time where the data points are close enough to be considered continuous. However, showing one year with four (representing quarterlies) data points as a continuous line might be misleading.

EXHIBIT 17.13

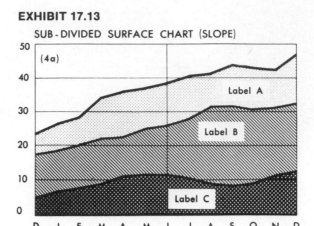

SUB-DIVIDED SURFACE CHART (SLOPE)

If there is a great deal of fluctuation in the range of activities in any given period, for example, the range of hourly productivity, it could be shown in a high-low chart similar to that used by the stock brokers. These high-low charts show the range of productivity for each day and do not connect the points with a line. Such a picture would give you an idea of the range and will also show you the trend over a time period. A trend line with confidence levels can be fit through the information.

C   Step and Surface Charts (Exhibits 17.14 and 17.15)

These two charts present similar kinds of pictures but also show some very important differences from what is normally shown by bar charts or line charts. Step charts indicate that the volumes move in measured steps. Such may not be the case and then the presentation gives a different picture than the way the business behaves. The surface chart is useful when the size of the surface shown on the chart is indicative of some kind of volume. For example, if a line chart is used to show the volume of production or profit over time, filling the surface under the line gives a much more dramatic picture of the results. In this instance the surface would have a direct relationship to the

EXHIBIT 17.14

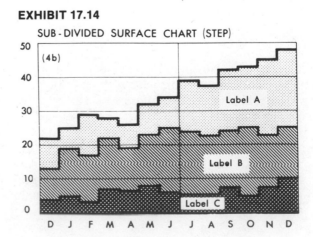

SUB-DIVIDED SURFACE CHART (STEP)

EXHIBIT 17.15

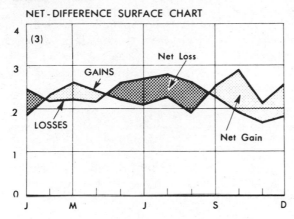

NET-DIFFERENCE SURFACE CHART

actual amount being depicted. Remember, when either of these charts is used there is a limited amount of data that behave the way they are shown and comparisons are difficult, if not impossible, to make. Once again, these are special purpose charts, and we would refer you to Calvin Schmidt's fine book on the use of graphic design.

EXHIBIT 17.16

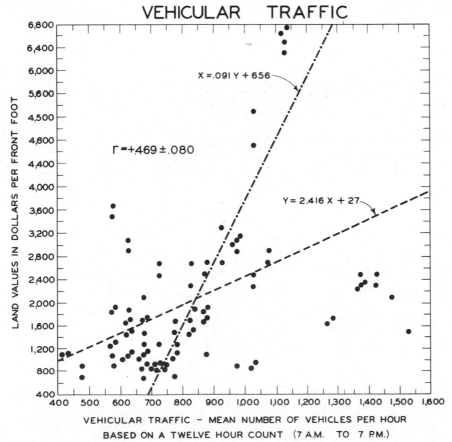

VEHICULAR TRAFFIC

$X = .091\,Y + 656$

$r = +.469 \pm .080$

$Y = 2.416\,X + 27$

LAND VALUES IN DOLLARS PER FRONT FOOT

VEHICULAR TRAFFIC – MEAN NUMBER OF VEHICLES PER HOUR
BASED ON A TWELVE HOUR COUNT (7 A.M. TO 7 P.M.)

D.   Scatter Diagram (Exhibit 17.16)

Finally, the scatter diagram is an appropriate statistical chart and should be used when the viewer is familiar with the data to be shown and when appropriate to the data.

There are a number of special three-dimensional and special effect charts, but they are not discussed.

4.   CONCLUSION

This chapter was designed to show that presentation graphics are the natural and designed output of a good information system. You would not want to spend a great deal of money for daily production charts that are going to be in the plant and thrown away each day However, if the information presented can be critical to the overall profit of the company, it is worth having them done as accurately, as effectively, and with the highest quality the technology will permit. Differing media presentations can be utilized. Even daily production charts can be plotted on big wall hangings and made available to each production line so the workers can get a clear picture of their daily performance. The use of charts and graphs in motivating production has not been fully developed. If the GMIS is to fully utilize the power and potential of the computer-generated graphics, you must carefully design, plan, cost, and control its design, installation, and operation. A good GMIS does not just happen, it is the result of a lot of well planned work!

BIBLIOGRAPHY

Barber, J.L., and Garner, W.R., "The Effect of Scale Numbering on Scale Reading Accuracy and Speed." *Journal of Experimental Psychology* (1951), 298–309.

Bartlett, N.R., Reed, J.D., and Duvoison, G., "Estimations of Distance on Polar Coordinate Plots As a Function of the Scale Used." *Journal of General Psychology* (1949), 47–65.

Chapanis, A., and Leyzorek, M., "Accuracy of Visual Interpretation Between Scale Markers As a Function of the Number Assigned to the Scale Interval." *Journal of Experimental Psychology* (1950), 655–667.

Chernoff, H., "The Use of Faces to Represent Points in N-Dimensional Space Graphically." Technical report No. 71, Department of Statistics, Stanford University, December 1971.

Croxton, F.E. and Stein, H., "Graphic Comparison by Bars, Squares, Circles and Cubes." *Journal of the American Statistical Association* (1932), 54–60.

Cuff, D.J., "Colour on Temperature Maps." *Cartographic Journal* (1973), 17–21.

Culbertson, H.M., and Powers, R.D., "A Study of Graph Comprehension Difficulties." *Audiovisual Communications Review* (1959), 1–19.

Durniak, Anthony, ed., "The Spurt in Computer Graphics," *Business Week*, June 16, 1980, pp. 104–106.

Eells, W.C., "The Relative Merits of Circles and Bars For Representing Component Parts." *Journal of the American Statistical Association* (1926), 119–132.

Friend, David, "The Promise of Information Graphics." Paper Presented at Harvard Computer Graphics Week, Boston, Mass., July 7, 1981.

Huff, D., Mahajar, V., and Black, W. "Facial Representation of Multivariate Data." Working Paper No. 80-022, Wharton, 1980.

Jarett, Irwin, "Computer Graphics: A Reporting Revolution?" *Journal of Accountancy* (May, 1981), p. 461.

Jarett, Irwin, "A Proposed Set of Standards For Computer-Generated Graphics." Presented at Harvard Computer Graphics Week, Boston, Mass., July 7, 1981.

Jenks, C.F., and Knos, D.S., "The Use of Shading Patterns in Graded Series." *Anals of the Association of American Geographers* (1961), 316–334.

MacDonald-Ross, Michael, "How Numbers Are Shown, A Review of Research on the Presentation of Quantitative Data in Tests." *Audiovisual Communication Review* (Winter 1977), 359–409.

Marcus, Aaron, "Computer-Assisted Chart Making From the Graphic Designer's Perspective." Association for Computing Machinery, *SIGGRAPH PROCEEDINGS*, New York, 1980.

McGill, Robert, "Some New Types of Graphics Displays." Paper Presented at Harvard Computer Graphics Week, Boston, Mass., July 7, 1981.

Meihoefer, H.J., "The Utility of the Circle as an Effective Cartographic Symbol." *Canadian Cartographer* (1969), 105–117.

Meifoefer, H.J., "The Visual Perception of the Circle in Thematic Maps: Experimental Results." *Canadian Cartographer* (1973), 63–84.

357

Moriarity, Shane, "Communicating Financial Information Through Multidimensional Graphics." *Journal of Accounting Research*, (Spring 1979), 205-224.

Morse, Alan, "Some Principles for the Effective Display of Data." Association for Computing Machinery, *SIGGRAPH PROCEEDINGS*, New York, 1979.

Peterson, L.V. and Schram, W., "How Accurately Are Different Types of Graphs Read?" *Audiovisual Communication Review* (1954), 179-189.

Schmid, Calvin, and Schmid, Stanton, *Handbook of Graphic Presentation*, New York: John Wiley and Sons, 1979.

Schultz, H.G., "An Evaluation of Formats for Graphic Trend Displays, Experiment II." *Human Factors* (1961), 99-107.

Subcommittee Y15.1 of the Committee of Preferred Practice for the Preparation of Graphs, Charts and Other Technical Illustrations, *American Standard: Illustrations for Publication and Projection*, New York, American Society of Mechanical Engineers, 1959.

Takeuchi, Hirotaka and Schmid, Allen. "New Promise of Computer Graphics." *Harvard Business Review* (January 1980), 122-131.

Townsend, Borris, "The Physiology and Psychology of Color." *The British Journal of Photography* (January 1969), 104ff.

Vernon, M.D., "Scale and Dial Reading." Medical Residence Council Unit in Applied Psychology, Cambridge University, England, June 1946.

Von Huhn, "Further Studies in Graphic Use of Circles and Bars: A Discussion of the Eells Experiment." *Journal of the American Statistical Association* (1927), 31-36.

Washburne, J.N., "An Experimental Study of Various Graphic, Tabular and Textual Methods of Presenting Quantitative Material, Part 1." *Journal of Educational Psychology* (1927), 361-376.

Wright, P., "Understanding Tabular Displays." *In Ergonomics Research and The Society for Visual Presentation of Technical Data*. Great Britain's University of Reading Typography Unit, 1973.

INDEX